Japan's New Party System

Japan's New Party System

Ronald J. Hrebenar

**with contributions by
Peter Berton, Akira Nakamura,
and J.A.A. Stockwin**

Westview Press
A Member of the Perseus Books Group

Copyright © 2000 by Westview Press, A Member of the Perseus Books Group.

Published in 2000 in the United States of America by Westview Press, 5500
Central Avenue, Boulder, Colorado 80301-2877, and in the United Kingdom by
Westview Press, 12 Hid's Copse Road, Cumnor Hill, Oxford OX2 9JJ

Find us on the World Wide Web at www.westviewpress.com

Library of Congress Cataloging-in-Publication Data
Hrebenar, Ronald J., 1945–
    Japan's new party system / Ronald J. Hrebenar.
        p.   cm.
    Includes bibliographical references and index.
    ISBN 0-8133-3056-4 (hc.)—ISBN 0-8133-3057-2 (pbk.)
        1. Political parties—Japan. 2. Jiyå Minshutå. I. Hrebenar, Ronald J., 1945-
Japanese party system. II. Title.

JQ1698.A1 H74 2000
324.252'01—dc21   99–051526

The paper used in this publication meets the requirements of the American
National Standard for Permanence of Paper for Printed Library Materials
Z39.48-1984.

10 9 8 7 6 5 4 3 2 1

Contents

Chapter 4: The Liberal Democratic Party: Still the Most Powerful Party in Japan   85

Chapter 5: The New Parties of the Second Party System   149

Chapter 6: The Komeito Returns: The Party of "Buddhist Democracy"   167

Chapter 7: The Social Democratic Party (Formerly Socialist Party): A Turbulent Odyssey · 209

Chapter 8: Japanese Communist Party: The "Lovable" Party · 253

Chapter 9: The Future of the Second Japanese Party System · 301

Abbreviations

CGP	Clean Government Party, or Komeito
DP	Democratic Party
DSP	Democratic Socialist Party
HC	House of Councillors, or upper house
HR	House of Representatives, or lower house
JCP	Japan Communist Party
JSP	Japan Socialist Party
LDP	Liberal Democratic Party
LP	Liberal Party
NFP	New Frontier Party, or Shinshinto
NLC	New Liberal Club
SDPJ	Social Democratic Party of Japan

Preface

The authors of this book have joined together for a third time to produce a book on Japanese political parties and elections. The first two books under the title of *The Japanese Party System* were also published by Westview Press in 1986 and 1992. This book, *Japan's New Party System*, has a different purpose than the previous volumes. The first two books had as their task the presentation of a vast amount of material on the various parties of the 1955–1993 party system. Since 1955, Japanese politics and parties had been rather uneventful and predictable; consequently, many Japanese political scientists preferred to study other nations. Decade after decade, the Liberal Democratic Party (LDP) ruled Japan while the permanent opposition party, the Japan Socialist Party (JSP) revolved around it but could never even come close to replacing it in power on the national level. All of this changed in 1993 after the LDP split, new parties emerged and formed a non-LDP government, and a new party system began. This book is about the Second Party System and how Japanese politics has changed from the old LDP-dominated First Party System.

This book begins with an introduction to Japanese party history and electoral behavior. The next two chapters address changes in Japanese election law and political finance. Chapter 4 presents the LDP and discusses its fall from and return to power in the 1990s. Japan's new parties are presented in Chapter 5, and the surviving parties from the system of 1955 are described in Chapters 6 through 8. Finally, a brief discussion of the future of the new party system is offered in Chapter 9.

Expert analysis is provided by two of the world's most knowledgeable professors on Japanese political parties. J.A.A. Stockwin of Oxford University and the recently retired Peter Berton of the University of Southern California offer their considerable insight on the Socialist and Communist parties of Japan. Professor Akira Nakamura of Meiji University in Tokyo contributes his enormous knowledge of Japanese politics to the chapter on the LDP. I thank these three political scientists for their significant contributions. Without them, this book would not have come into existence.

As the lead author, I want to express my appreciation to all the academics and journalists who helped with the data collection and reading of these chapters. I acknowledge that any errors remaining are entirely my responsibility, despite the efforts of these experts to teach me about Japanese politics and parties. I sincerely thank them for their efforts on my behalf.

I also want to thank those who helped produce this book. Especially important are Carol Jones and Steve Haenel at Westview Press and Lesley Rock at PageMasters & Company who labored to turn confusion into communication. Amy Rogers of the University of Utah's Department of Political Science also made important contributions in Chapter 2 and in the conversion of the text into a readable form on the computer.

Japanese politics in the late 1990s has stopped being boring and has become fun. We hope the reader will find this book to be a helpful guide to understanding Japan's new party system and politics.

Ronald J. Hrebenar

Note on Personal Names

As is common practice in Japan, all Japanese names are written with the family name first and the given name last. If the Japanese scholar is living in the United States or publishes in English, I have presented his or her name in the American style—for example, Haruhiro Fukui or Akira Nakamura.

one

The Changing Postwar Party System

Ronald J. Hrebenar

The Japanese political system is democratic, has several parties, legislates through a parliament (the Diet), and has a well-educated, supportive, but basically uninvolved, electorate. It has also been defined by the continuous rule for three decades of the conservative Liberal Democratic Party (LDP), which held a majority of seats in the Diet between its formation in 1955 until it lost its majority in the House of Councillors (HC) in 1989 and then its control of the House of Representatives (HR) in 1993. In this introductory chapter these basic characteristics of the Japanese party system will be explored to provide the reader with a foundation for the subsequent detailed examination of the major parties in the current party system. The chapter is based on a variety of types of data, especially public opinion polls of the Japanese electorate.

JAPANESE PARTY POLITICS IN THE LATE 1990s

Prime Minister Hashimoto Ryotaro announced his resignation on Monday, July 13—the day after the LDP "defeat" in the 1998 HC elections. Immediately, the Japanese media began the frequently played game of speculating on who would be the next Japanese prime minister. The names put forward were truly "the usual suspects," including former LDP president Kono Yohei, who had stepped aside three years earlier to give Hashimoto his clear shot at the prime ministership; former LDP president and prime minister Miyazawa Kiichi, who was prime minister when the LDP split in 1993, allowing the opposition to form the first non-LDP government since 1955; Obuchi Keizo, the foreign minister and leader of the most powerful faction within the LDP and boss of Hashimoto's faction; Kajiyama Seiroku, the most crafty deal maker left in the LDP; and Koizumi Junichiro, one of the most unconventional LDP Diet members. Obuchi was the winner of the

LDP's internal decision-making process and became the prime minister several days later when the Diet was called into special session to approve the new government.[1]

These events can tell us much about the nature of party politics in contemporary Japan. The central theme of this book is that Japan has moved into a new style of party politics since the breakup of the LDP in 1993. This new era of politics is called the Second Postwar Party System (SPWPS). The First Postwar Party System (FPWPS) began with the creation of the LDP and the JSP in 1955 and died in the disarray of 1993. One of the interesting aspects of this change in party systems is that some things never seem to change in Japanese politics. First, despite the emergence of new parties and the destruction of old parties, the LDP still rules Japanese national politics. When the LDP lost seats in the 1998 HC elections, it did not have to relinquish control of the government or even resign the prime ministership. Hashimoto resigned because he had so inflated expectations prior to the voting that the winning of 44 of the 126 seats contested (the most seats won by any party) was considered a defeat, since he and other LDP leaders were talking about winning more than 69 seats and, surely, at least 61, the number they were defending in the election. The LDP still had a 13-seat majority in the crucial HR. The second feature is that the LDP continues to recycle one weak prime minister after another as though they were all faceless cogs in a perpetual machine. The question regarding the possible successors to Hashimoto were all focused on whether any of these LDP leaders could actually lead the nation in its troubled times. Japan's economy had been stagnant since 1990, and the various LDP and opposition leaders had no idea how to break the nation free from the pattern. Third, the LDP leaders, and thus the prime ministers, still emerge from the murky depths of the party's internal factional maneuvering despite the official disbanding of the factions in the early 1990s. The fact that Obuchi was seriously considered a potential prime minister had nothing to do with his new ideas, leadership skills, or great public respect and support because, clearly, these did not exist. He was the heir of past prime ministers such as Tanaka and Takeshita who had led his faction in previous decades, and thus he automatically was a contender for the post of prime minister. Kono was one of the few sincere reformers in the party, and Miyazawa was one of the few LDP members who understood economics. Each represented different LDP factions in competition for party and governmental power. Strangely, another candidate emerged, the hard to categorize Koizumi Junichiro, who represented the Mitsuzuka faction and appeared to appeal to younger LDP Diet members who were concerned with their electoral prospects if the party chose a leader such as Obuchi.

The fourth lesson from the 1998 leadership change was the that opposition parties, although more important than they were in the FPWPS,

TABLE 1.1   New Parties Coming from the Breakup of the Shinshinto: January 1998

Parties	Leader	Diet Members
Liberal Party	Ozawa Ichiro	54
New Party Peace (Shinto Heiwa)	Kanzaki Takenori	37
New Party Fraternity (Shinto Yuai)	Nakano Kansei	23
Voice of the People (Kokumin no Koe)	Kano Michihiko	18
Dawn Club (Reimei Club)	Shirahama Kazuyoshi	18
Reform Club (Kaikaku)	Ozawa Tatsuo	12

NOTE: Other Shinshinto members became independents (8) or joined the LDP (2); one joined the From the Five Party.

SOURCE: *Japan Times Weekly International Edition*, January 12, 1998.

still had a very small role to play in the process. The opposition controlled the HC but not the HR, and it was the latter that controlled Japanese politics. By defeating the LDP in an HC election, the opposition could drive an LDP prime minister and his cabinet from office; but it could not drive the LDP from the prime minister's office. By controlling the HC, the opposition parties could give their candidate, former prime Minister Kaifu, a majority of votes in that chamber, but the vote of the HR would be decisive. When the two chambers name different candidates for prime minister, the Constitution states that the winner in the HR will become the prime minister. The opposition continued to be fragmented among several parties and thus presented the voters an unclear alternative to the continued LDP leadership. The opposition did not offer a clear alternative regime to the voters.

An old Chinese wish (or a curse to some) says, "May you live in interesting times." We are lucky. We live in interesting times in terms of Japanese politics. It has not always been that way. For most of the postwar era, Japanese politics has been very predictable. The prime minister was always a LDP member. The opposition was never in the game. It was like watching a baseball season in which the same team wins every game, every year. Very boring! However, it got a lot more exciting in 1993 when the LDP split, and since then Japanese politics has been characterized by great unpredictability. New parties are created and then disbanded shortly afterward (see Table 1.1). Diet members moved from one party to another and then back again. Handbooks on the two house of the Diet are often out of date and inaccurate even before they reach the bookstores.[2] Some of the major leaders of Japanese parties belonged to four different parties during the 1993–1999 period. The middle and late part of the 1990s have certainly not been boring. Confusing, yes, but not boring. The purpose of this book is to break through the confusion and give the reader a grasp on these changes and a useful understanding of the current nature of Japanese party politics. Since Japanese politics now changes from month to month, we will also try to present some ideas on where Japanese party politics may be going in the coming months and years. However, before we can explore the future, we must have a firm foundation on the past, and that requires an understanding of recent Japanese political history, voting behavior, and electoral laws.

THE TWO JAPANESE PARTY SYSTEMS: 1955 AND 1993

There have been two party systems in the post–World War II Japanese national politics: the First Party System of 1955 and the Second Party System of 1993. This book explores the development of these systems, with emphasis on the system that began in 1993 and is still not clearly defined and may not be until after the turn of the new century. The concept of party systems has probably emerged from the study of American political parties over the two hundred years of their history and the changes that have defined that political party system.[3] The Americans have had five historical party systems and an ongoing debate on whether the long-term Fifth Party System has been replaced by a new Sixth Party System or whether the Fifth is merely disappearing as the American political society loses its party identities. A *party system* is defined as a particular pattern of party organizations, voter identities with the various parties, and a set of electoral system outcomes and characteristics that make an era unique. Some of these characteristics of a party system deal with the levels of competition that may exist during a specific time frame on the various levels of politics in a nation. So, in a given nation, there may be one pattern of competition on the national level in terms of total numbers of seats won in a national legislative chamber; another and perhaps very different pattern of political competition on the subnational level (states, prefectures, or departments); and still possibly very different patterns of competition in various regions or individual cities within the subunits.

Individual party systems may also be characterized by particular patterns of voter behavior that are habitual in terms of support of one party or another or even nonsupport of parties.

In the United States and other Western democracies, a great deal of what political scientists do involves the study of various groups in their societies and the careful tracking of their behavior in political events, especially in elections. In the United States, the breakdown of the electorate (and even nonelectorate) into dozens of subgroups through sophisticated polling techniques has become a major part of media coverage of elections and the basis for predictions of electoral outcomes and systems analysis. As groups change over time, they will also change the strength and consistency of their partisan affiliations, and this may affect the success or failure of the various parties with a given party system. One particularly significant group in almost all party systems is composed of the youngest voters, who are beginning to "play the game of politics" and in most cases have not yet formed rigid party identifications. As these party attachments gradually solidify, they provide evidence for the future of a party system, since it is these youthful voters who will be in the electorate for the longest time, and often they will represent a very large part of the electorate.

A party system may also be defined by a "style of politics." Such a systemic style may be a pattern of politics within government as divided government when houses in a national legislature have split control, as has been the case in Japan since 1990, when the opposition parties took control of the HC until the 1999 coalition. Other style aspects of a party system may include the style of election campaigns, with varying degrees of media participation, or "the feeling" of campaigns in terms of civility or acrimonious relations among the parties and their candidates. Some systems may be characterized by highly confrontational politics in the everyday business of government, others by the frequent use of coalitions and even a cooperative style of politics between the government and the opposition. Given that the study of party system has evolved into something much more complex than indicated in the preceding introduction, those who are interested in this framework for evaluating parties within a nation may want to explore some of the research presented in the notes to this chapter. But for the application of this concept to the Japanese party system, I will proceed with a presentation of the First Party System of 1955, a comparison of that system and the pre–World War II party system, and the emergence of the Second Party System of 1993.

FROM A ONE-AND-ONE-HALF PARTY SYSTEM TO A MULTIPARTY SYSTEM

When Japan returned to a democratic, parliamentary system in 1946, a period of great confusion in party politics preceded the first postwar elections, which were held in April. The Diet members of the great prewar parties had mostly been purged by the U.S. Occupation authorities. Of the incumbent Diet members of the Progressive Party, 260 out of 274 were purged; in addition, 30 of the 43 Liberal Party Diet members, 21 of

23 Cooperative Diet members, and even 10 of the 17 Socialist Diet members were prevented from running for public office. Thus, the first postwar election introduced a nearly new set of candidates to the voters. Not only the candidates but also the parties were new. A total of 267 "parties" participated in these elections.

Many of these parties were just the personal organization or label of a given politician; others operated only in a very limited geographic area; still others were the reconstituted organizations of some of the famous pre-1940 parties. Among the successful candidates to the lower house (the HR) at this election, only 19 percent had served in that body previously. However, over the next decade these parties gradually disappeared until, in 1955, a merger of conservative parties on the one hand and Socialist parties on the other produced a de facto two-party system on the national level. In the first HR election (1958) held after the two mergers, the LDP and the JSP captured 453 of the 455 House seats won by political parties. One seat was won by the Japan Communist Party (JCP), a second seat was won by a minor party, and 12 seats were held by independents. This two-party system lasted only two years. In January 1960 the JSP split into two parts, with 40 of its moderate Diet members departing to create the Democratic Socialist Party (DSP). A reorganized JCP went from a single seat in the 1958 elections to 3 seats in 1960, to 14 in 1969, and to 38 in 1972. Meanwhile, the lay organization, Soka Gakkai, of the Nichiren Shoshu Buddhist sect, had formed its own political party in 1964—namely, the Komeito, or Clean Government party (CGP)—and it captured 25 seats in 1961 and 47 seats in 1969. Thus, by the 1960s, what seemed to be a "two-party system" (in the words of many Japanese political commentators) consisting of the LDP and the JSP or, as some called it, a "one-and-one-half-party system" (the LDP plus a splintered and seemingly permanent opposition JSP and a very small DSP), quickly moved to true multiparty status as the DSP demonstrated its staying power and the JCP and CGP proved they could regularly win 20 to 50 HR seats. By the mid-1970s, these five parties seemed to be permanent parts of the Japanese national political system. In the 1972 House elections, the percentage of seats won by the LDP and JSP had dropped to 81.5 percent from the 99.5 percent they had held in 1958. There was defection in the ranks of the LDP in the summer of 1976. Although minor in terms of numbers, the defection was significant in its impact on the proliferation of new parties. Kono Yohei, a young LDP Diet member, led five other Diet members out of the LDP, set up a new Diet-level party, and named it the New Liberal Club (NLC). From this humble start of only a few seats, the NLC exploded to 18 in the December 1976 election and touched off a Kono and NLC boom in the Japanese media. This boom subsequently encouraged the establishment of other new parties in the 1977, 1979, 1980, 1983, and 1986 general elections. The 1983 elections to the upper house (the HC) had on the ballot twelve new small parties (mini-*seito*), which collectively captured over 15 percent of the vote and won 5 seats (10 percent). Japan now has a seemingly established multiparty system operating on the national level of politics.

COMPARING THE PREWAR AND POSTWAR PARTY SYSTEMS

A comparison of the post–World War II party system with the system that existed in prewar Japan is useful. Considerable scholarly effort has produced a very good perspective on the problems of the prewar Japanese party system. The work, for example, of Gordon M. Berger, Peter Duus, Robert A. Scalapino, T. J. Pempel, and others is well done and well known to scholars of Japanese politics.[4]

Because all political institutions are products of their history, it is necessary to present some generalizations about the prewar party system. Pempel has noted that the prewar party system was inflexible in its retention of ties to rural agricultural and urban commercial bases despite the rise of new social groups. Consequently, the parties of the 1930s were "largely irrelevant, either as the vehicles or the reflections of social changes."[5] Pempel suggests that contemporary Japanese parties have the same problem of being "locked into past constituencies,"[6] which would have been the rural sectors for the LDP and the industrial labor unions for the Socialists. In actuality, then, parties did not have a long history of significant influence in Japanese politics. Following a long emergence period beginning in the decade after the Meiji Restoration of the 1860s, it was not until the post–World War I period that cabinets were formed on the basis of electoral results. Yet by the 1930s, parties were effectively excluded from real political power. Sustained party control of Japanese government can be perceived as having begun only in the years since the end of World War II. Another parallel between the prewar and postwar party systems is the dependence of the conservatives on "big business." Just as the Jiyuto and Seiyuhu were the "financial children" of the *zaibatsu* (Japan's prewar industrial conglomerates Mitsui, Mitsubishi, Sumitomo, and others), the postwar LDP, NLC, DSP, Democratic, Liberal, Shinseito, and Shinshinto are the dependents of the Keidanren Federation of Economic Organizations (corporate Japan) and other business organizations of modern Japan.

In the prewar system the incumbent parties always won; in the postwar era the LDP has lost only one election, the largely symbolic 1989 HC elections. Moreover, in both party systems, the incumbent parties almost never lost power as a result of electoral defeat. As Pempel notes, government changed, but it did so usually prior to the elections.[7] The 1993 power shift from the LDP to the Hosokawa coalition was unusual because it came about following a general election. In addition, the conservative parties in both systems were infiltrated by the bureaucracy. Such support forced the parties to deal with the elite on a day-to-day basis, rather than encouraging the development of mass followings or support groups to confront it.

Having observed the similarities between the two party systems, we can now look at their differences. For example, the prewar party system was characterized by the lack of a dominant party. Only 18 percent of the prewar elections produced a majority party, whereas in the post-1955 period, every election (after independents were sorted out) produced an LDP lower house majority until the 1993 LDP split. Moreover, during the prewar period, only 18 percent of the governments were actually party cabinets; since the war, all governments have been put together by party leaders.[8]

When compared with the prewar party system, the postwar system is significantly broader in its ideological range. Despite the existence of leftist parties, the prewar party system was overwhelmingly conservative. Leftist parties were seldom allowed to participate fairly in elections. Whereas the prewar system was in essence a mechanism to legitimize the ruling clique, the postwar system, despite certain significant distortions such as malapportionment, is a much fairer representation of the political attitudes of Japan's electorate.

The postwar Japanese party system is a difficult one to portray on a liberal-conservative continuum. Although most might agree with the placement of the LDP on the conservative end and the JSP and JCP on the leftist end of the continuum, the so-called center parties might be much more difficult to position correctly. Do the DSP, CGP, and Social Democratic Federation (SDF) collectively represent the center, the Left-center, or the Right-center? Or do they really belong in the center at all? Some argue that the DSP and CGP are essentially conservative parties despite their socialist rhetoric. Others ask whether the party farthest to the left in Japan is the JCP or the JSP.

A ONE-PARTY-PREDOMINANT SYSTEM

The Japanese party system has been described in a variety of ways—that is, as a one-party, a one-and-one-half party, a two-party, and a multiparty system. Actually, part of the explanation for this variety of labels lies more in their "snapshot" nature (i.e., their descriptive function at a particular moment in time) than in the fundamentally different interpretations of the system. When Robert Scalapino and Junnosuke Masumi surveyed the Japanese political scene in 1960, they observed the two-party system of the ruling LDP, a strong opposition in the JSP, and two very small parties (i.e., the JCP and the newly formed DSP). Thus, they described the political scene as a "one-and-one-half" party system in its actual operation because the "one" party is always in power and the "half" party is permanently out of power.[9] Nobutaka Ike correctly perceived that, by the early 1970s, the Japanese party system had fundamentally changed. It was now a system with five parties receiving significant portions of the vote, but Ike did not choose to call it a multiparty system because the opposition parties never shared political power with the LDP. He thus decided to label it a "one-party-dominant system." Such a system, Ike observed, was not unique to Japan but could also be found in Mexico and India.[10]

Perhaps the best work in the area of party system classifications is credited to Giovanni Sartori, whose *Parties and Party Systems: A Framework for Analysis* classifies party systems by numbers of parties and the significance of the parties within the system.[11] Sartori argues that a predominant-party system differs significantly from the dominant-party system described by Maurice Duverger and Gabriel Almond.[12] Using their broader definitions, Sartori classifies twenty-one systems—ranging from France (1968) to Uruguay (1966) into the latter category. The dominant-party system is generally conceived as being one in which a single party is significantly stronger than the others. Sartori, however, suggests that a predominant-party system includes both party pluralism (in which other parties are legal and legitimate) and one-party domination (in which the same party manages to win, over time, an absolute majority of seats in Parliament). Japan's First Party System fits this predominant-party-system class very effectively, given that its six-party system was coupled with unbroken LDP lower house majorities since the founding of this system in 1955 until its collapse in 1993. In fact, it can be argued that Japan is the "ultimate predominant-party system" given that of all the industrialized democracies only Japan has had uninterrupted one-party rule on the national level from the 1950s until the 1990s. If one had to come up with a single concept that best characterized the nature of the Japanese First Party System, it would probably be this one-party rule of the LDP in the 1955–1993 period. Hence the crucial question to be asked if one is to understand the Japanese First Party System is the following: Why did the opposition parties fail to displace the LDP as Japan's ruling party on the national level for almost four decades?

THE PERMANENT OPPOSITION

One problem for the opposition in both the First and the Second Party System has been the difficulty of forming the various opposition parties into a coalition capable of taking power away from the LDP. The nature of the alternative coalition government able to replace the single-party rule of the LDP was a major topic of conversation in Japanese political circles throughout the late 1970s and the 1980s. And discussion of just how such a coalition could be constructed has frustrated opposition politicians as they tried somehow to piece together enough seats to displace the LDP. Because such a displacement seems to be virtually impossible, discussion turned in the early 1980s to the question of which opposition parties could join with the LDP and assist the conservatives in ruling Japan. The Japanese public, as well, has been involved in these coalition-making efforts, through both their electoral voting decisions and expression of their opinions on possible coalition patterns through the newspaper polls. In the spring of 1980, just prior to the "double elections" of June, a "coalition boom" occurred in the media and among opposition party leaders. One major poll found that half of the public wanted an end to the single-party rule by the LDP; 30 percent wanted it to continue; and 20 percent had no opinion or refused to answer the question. Less clear were the public's feelings about the nature of the coalition that would replace the LDP. A small plurality supported a coalition of conservative and so-called middle-of-the-road parties—that is, the LDP, NLC, DSP, and CGP (18 percent). The second choice was a "grand coalition" of all parties except the JCP (15 percent). The third preference (15 percent) was for a conservative coalition of the LDP and NLC. A leftist coalition centered on the JSP in combination with CGP received 8 percent support, and the extreme leftist coalition of the JSP and JCP was the choice of 5 percent. Finally, a minority government of the LDP alone was the choice of almost 11 percent of the people polled. Nearly three years later, a coalition between the LDP and the NLC was constructed on a limited basis. When the LDP joined with the NLC in December 1983 to form a coalition government, it opened a new era of Japanese politics that many people had been anticipating since the 1976 election. In this instance, the coalition was one of convenience rather than necessity, given that although the LDP won only 250 seats out of 511 total—a shortfall of 6 seats from a pure majority—it came to control 259 seats when nine conservative independents joined the party immediately following the election. Soon after, the LDP accepted the NLC into the government in an attempt to give the party the additional votes it needed in the HR to effectively manage the Diet.

Prior to 1983, the most realistic hope held by the opposition parties for entering a national government as a coalition partner was that a split in the LDP would occur and that a new government would be formed by several departing LDP factions in combination with the numerous perennial opposition parties. Each time the LDP has suffered an electoral setback (as in 1979 and 1983) or endured another scandal (recent LDP prime ministers who have been severely hurt by scandals include Tanaka Kakuei, Takeshita Noburu, and Uno Sosuke), the media have carried rumors that the factions were about to leave and join with the DSP, CGP, or other parties to change the landscape of Japanese politics; yet, each time, the advantages of staying inside the LDP have apparently outweighed those of splitting and joining with the longtime opposition. That was the situation until 1993 and the decision by the Ozawa-Hata faction to leave the LDP and join with the opposition to form a government.

Clearly, the Japanese public did not demand a one-party LDP government during the 1990s. A *Sankei Shimbun* poll taken just before the February 1990 HR elections (perhaps the last of the normal elections in the First Party System) indicated 19 percent supported an LDP one-party government, whereas 54 percent wished to see some form of LDP opposition parties coalition.[13] After the elections, the *Mainichi* poll showed the governmental combinations the Japanese public was supporting for organizing Japanese national government: one-party LDP government, 12 percent; one-party JSP government, 2 percent; LDP + CGP + DSP coalition, 17 percent; LDP + JSP coalition, 29 percent; part of the LDP + middle-of-the-road parties + part of the JSP, 15 percent; JSP + DSP + CGP coalition, 9 percent; and JSP + JCP coalition, 2 percent.[14]

The best description of the reasons behind the continued rule of the LDP in the First Party System stems from the classic military and political recommendation to "divide and conquer." And as Michael Taylor and V. M. Herman have noted, "The more divided the opposition, the easier it is to rule."[15] In other words, a fragmented opposition tends to be less moderate and thus will probably increase the prospects for systemic instability, but it is also less efficient in its ability to replace the ruling party and thereby contributes to the stability of the ruling party. Perhaps the most difficult concept to implant into a polity is the concept of opposition. Yet, ironically, this idea was apparently so firmly adopted by Japan that it became a permanent characteristic for at least the JSP and JCP, the original opposition parties of the 1955 system. A central aspect of opposition is that it must always be ready to take over the seat of government on a periodic basis. As already noted, however, Japan is unique among developed democracies because it had not experienced such an alteration in power in nearly four decades. Moreover, as the late

Raymond Aron observed in a lecture at the London School of Economics and Political Science on October 27, 1981:

> For the last thirty years, the same party has been in power in Japan; opposition parties, which sometimes win in local elections, do exist; newspapers, which freely criticize those in power, also exist. Because of this continuity, Japan has risen to be one of the foremost nations; it is Japan which has best withstood the shocks of the oil crisis; it is Japan which has been most successful in achieving a close cooperation between the Ministry of Industry and private enterprises; it is Japan which most successfully combines medium-term (even long-term) planning and the free play of the market. None of this would have been possible if, from one day to the next, the plans of the government and its priorities and values were in danger of being upset by the results of the elections. In our countries, proud of alternation in government, the changes in public opinion and in the electorate every two, four, or seven years add to the hazards of the world economic climate. On reflection, I abandoned this somewhat facile argument. Does Japanese prosperity owe a great deal to the lack of alternation, or is it the other way round? The same party wins the elections because the majority of the electors approve of its policy and admit that it is successful. Do not the alternations in Europe and America express the dissatisfaction of the governed? And is not peaceful alternation better than violent revolt? . . . A second consideration dissuades me from drawing conclusion from the Japanese experience. Japan, as we well know, cannot be imitated. It retains the cult of unanimity, symbolized in the sacred person of the emperor, a cult which democratic practices conceal but do not destroy. No other people seems to be so homogeneous; nowhere is social control so effective, omnipresent, gently peremptory. Some observers may remark that the continuity of the party in power is grounded in a disciplined base, on a lifestyle which Western men would consider incompatible with their individualistic philosophy. Democratized Japan has not become individualistic. Let us therefore leave Japan aside, and merely note that there is one country—and perhaps only one—which demonstrates, against the tide of fashionable opinion, that a political party can withstand the wear and tear of government and that a democratic regime without alternation does not always degenerate.[16]

In the category of nations in which parties do not alternate in power, the situation is usually a result of governmental violence against its opponents—a violence that prevents them from communicating to voters, running their slates of candidates, or even having a legal party organization. But this pattern of governmental oppression does not apply to Japan. Elections in Japan are open, and the opposition parties are legal and have many open channels of communication with the Japanese electorate. Several European nations (Sweden, for example) have experienced patterns of one-party domination somewhat similar to that in Japan. Of course, there were many reasons for the continuation in power of the Social Democratic Party of Sweden, but a significant parallel to the Japanese experience is the fact that the opposition parties in Sweden were badly fragmented. These parties lacked the necessary resources to challenge the ruling party and had no alternatives that would identify the opposition with a distinctive character of its own. The opposition was also hindered by weak organization. As Swedish Prime Minister Tage Erlander said in 1951, "This is an opposition that represents almost half of the citizens, but which never has an opportunity of trying its strength as the government and which never has practice in assuming the responsibilities which this involves."[17]

Erlander's description could easily fit the Japanese party system as well. Why have the Japanese voters continued to maintain the LDP in power election after election for nearly four decades? This question can be looked at in a variety of ways, but let us begin with the responses to a 1982 *Yomiuri Shimbun* poll question concerning the reasons a person would support the cabinet of LDP Prime Minister Suzuki Zenko. The most common response was "because it was an LDP cabinet" (44 percent). Other responses pertained to the cabinet's "sense of stability" (16 percent), to trust in the prime minister (9 percent), and to appreciation for the cabinet's actions, both domestic and foreign (15 percent).[18] Following the 1990 lower house victory for the LDP, the *Tokyo Shimbun* poll asked the Japanese public why the opposition parties failed to win the elections. Thirty-four percent answered "because the opposition parties' policies were not attractive," and 33 percent replied "because the people feared political instability."[19] The LDP has clearly established itself as the party responsible both for the great prosperity Japan has experienced and for the set of diplomatic and security policies under which the country has regained a measure of worldwide respect since the dark days after the Pacific War. By contrast, the five opposition parties of the First Party System were not able to establish their image as a responsible alternative to the rule of the LDP. When the *Yomiuri Shimbun* asked its respondents in September 1985 why the LDP had remained in office for so long, the three most frequent responses were as follows: "There is no other political party" (48.4 percent); "They agree with its policies" (38.2 percent); and "The other parties cannot cooperate against the LDP" (34.2 percent).[20] (multiple responses produce a total of more than 100%).

In one of his 1982 speeches, former LDP prime minister Miki Takeo spoke of the problem of failed opposition in Japan:

> Party politics with no change of administration is a divergence from the norm. And if one party holds on to power too long, it becomes corrupt. I would therefore like to propose to the members of the opposition that they form a new party capable of taking upon itself the government of Japan. What Japan needs today is the formation and healthy growth of a new party which will not throw the nation into confusion or cause anxiety to the people.[21]

To some it may seem strange that an LDP factional leader and former LDP prime minister is encouraging the opposition to reform in order to defeat his party. However, Miki had always been a nonmainstream leader in the LDP, characterized by the systematic attack on him and his policies by most of the other factional leaders, especially those of the Tanaka and Fukuda factions. Realistically speaking, there were perhaps only two ways out of the First Party System stalemate of Japanese politics: (1) as Miki suggested, through the construction of a new alternative party and the destruction of the current fragmented opposition; or (2) through the destruction of the LDP, the withdrawal of one or more of the major factions, and the joining of the moderate elements of the existing opposition. This is exactly what happened in 1992–1993 when Hosokawa established the Japan New Party and the Ozawa-Hata faction of the LDP left the party to form the core of a unified group of parties that became the NFP.

Another of the critical problems faced by the Japanese opposition revolves around the concept of "excluded" or "nonlegitimate" parties.[22] For example, despite the fact that the Communist Party of Italy is the second-largest party in the nation in election after election, it was never included in the inevitable coalition cabinet until the ruling Christian Democratic Party fell apart in the 1990s. The Japan Communist Party (JCP) has a somewhat similar problem. It was specifically excluded from all coalition proposals in the First Party System and was never invited to participate in any of the coalition governments of the Second Party System. Because no non-LDP coalition government could be formed during the First Party System without the JCP's 30 or so seats, the only possible coalitions had to be directed by the LDP. The JSP was also an "excluded party," but in a sense slightly different from that of the Italian model. In the famous Katayama government of 1947, the JSP did take the lead in establishing the only leftist-led government in Japanese history. But it also fell apart quickly and was by nearly every account a failure. In all honesty, part of the blame for its failure must be given to some of the conservatives in the government who were not unhappy to see their own government fail. The Socialists were so discredited by this fiasco, by their subsequent splits, and by their ideological wrangling over the next three decades that the JSP has become a "delegitimized party" (delegitimized in that few saw the JSP as a possible participant in a future national-level government of Japan). The Socialists became the "gang that couldn't shoot straight." Granted, they were capable of leading a prefectural government on occasion (as was the JCP), but given Japan's unitary system, there was little danger in permitting such a minor check on nearly uncontrolled LDP hegemony.

One can see indications of the "illegitimacy" of the JSP in its lack of support even among the critics of the continued role of the conservatives. In July 1981 an *Asahi Shinbun* editorial on the Tokyo Metropolitan Assembly elections called for the total overhaul of the JSP—"even if this means dissolving the party." The editorial writer noted: "As the number one opposition party, we should be able to find many of its members qualified to hold important posts, such as that of finance minister or director-general of the Environment Agency, but actually, we cannot name a single one . . . the JSP is not a political party . . . the JSP is a party of government employees. . . ."[23] The public opinion poll carried out by the *Asahi Shimbun* showed that people chose the word *undependable* more than any other when asked to describe the image of the JSP. As long as the leading opposition party cannot be trusted by the general public, the LDP is safe.[24]

Results from the 1989 HC and the 1990 HR elections actually help us understand Japanese voters' lack of confidence in the JSP. In the HC elections, voters could cast a "safe protest vote" against the LDP without worrying about an LDP loss endangering the performance of their national government because the HC has little real political power. However, when the significant elections for the all-powerful HR came up about six months later, many voters thought it was too dangerous to cast such a protest vote, and the LDP went on to a clear victory.

One of the serious problems facing the JSP was that this party of the working class was poorly supported by that class. Only 28 percent of the labor union members in the Kansai area supported the JSP, according to a 1977 poll by the Labor Research Institute. Even if we examine just the party support of Sohyo (the labor confederation supporter of the JSP), we find that only 44 percent were willing to identify themselves as JSP supporters.[25] Thus, when the Labor Ministry reported in December 1983 that the union members had declined in number to 29 percent of the labor force—the lowest point for organized labor in Japan since 1948, when the yearly statistics were initiated—the plight of the JSP was quite clear. In short, this was a party that represented a declining sector of society—and that sector was not supporting the JSP very enthusiastically in the first place. Although 1 million new workers were added to the labor force in 1983, the membership of Sohyo fell 9 percent, to 4.5 million.[26] Hence, assuming that less than a third of the labor vote went to the JSP regularly, one could view the JSP as a party supported by less than a third of a third of the unionized working force.

Even the JSP's own polling efforts have detected the magnitude of the burden under which this party is operating. In a JSP-sponsored poll conducted in late 1982, the support rate for the party was only 9.8 percent, compared with a support rate for the LDP of 36.7 percent. For a series of questions pertaining to images of the parties, the negative responses were greater than the positive ones in every case for the JSP: For the "reliable" category, negative responses exceeded the positive by 18.1 percent; "familiar," by 17.6 percent; "youthful," by 20.4 percent; "future oriented," by 24.4 percent; "clean," by 0.9 percent; and "aggressive," by 15.6 percent. Responses to the same set of images for the LDP were all strongly positive, except in the categories of "cleanliness" and "youthfulness."[27]

Many Japanese thought of the FPWPS opposition parties as being largely incompetent. In a government-sponsored poll conducted in late 1980, the respondents felt that the main reason the LDP has remained in power for so long was that the opposition parties lacked competence to take over the government (27 percent) and that the opposition parties could not conceivably improve government (21 percent). Then, when asked in a *Yomiuri Shimbun* poll in September 1985 why the JSP continues to decline in political power, 38 percent responded that the party cannot lead even the opposition; 36 percent indicated that the JSP's policies were not realistic; and 33 percent said that the JSP was always fighting within itself. The study by Tomita, Baerwald, Hoshino, and Nakamura of the 1977 upper house elections discovered that 13 percent believed the JSP had a negative image.[28] An *Asahi Shimbun* poll discovered that the public saw the JSP as undependable, too radical, inactive, dominated by labor unions, and ridden with factions.[29]

The parity *(hakuchu)* between the LDP and the opposition during the 1980s had brought some prestigious opportunities to the opposition parties. In 1990, opposition party members chaired eight of the sixteen regular committees in the HC as well as half of the eight special committees.

In addition, since the 1970s, the vice speaker of the lower house and the vice president of the upper house have been members of the JSP. It still remained in the public's mind, a collection of unproven and untrustworthy politicians. Even the rise of the SDPJ's leader, Doi Takako, to the speakership of the HR in the mid-1990s did not save the party from its path to oblivion. The behavior patterns of the opposition during the latter part of the FPWPS, which found their extreme as recently as in the early 1970s, have become more moderate. Slowdown demonstrations (also known as "cow walking") ended in the late 1970s, as have useless votes of no confidence against the entire cabinet. After the LDP lost its upper house majority in 1989, the LDP was forced by JSP and JCP opposition to abandon its plan to send Japanese troops to support the Middle East operations against Iraq in 1990. In many of the bills passed by the Diet in the late 1980s, several of the opposition parties joined with the LDP to secure passage. Krauss calls this pattern one of "concurrent majorities."[30]

What could the opposition parties have done to reverse the long-term pattern of LDP domination? Robert Dahl has noted six strategies that might be pursued by an opposition: (1) strict electoral competition, (2) coalition seeking, (3) bargaining with the government, (4) multiple-site conflict and bargaining, (5) organizational survival, and (6) revolution. Each nation has its unique pattern of opposition, and, as Dahl further notes, there is no standard pattern among Western democracies.[31] However, with respect to Japan, the opposition parties fought among themselves to be a suitable partner for the LDP if the latter needed some votes to control the HR.

Other points can be made to explain continued LDP dominance.[32] Krauss and Pierre suggest the LDP adopted a series of parliamentary strategies that successfully dealt with the challenges of the opposition parties during the 1970s and 1980s.[33] More important, as Muramatsu and Krauss have noted, the LDP was flexible enough to change with the times. The LDP adopted as its own the popular demands for increased social expenditures and environmental protection. With these and other policies, the LDP was able to broaden its supporting coalition during the 1980s and remain until 1993 the world's last dominant one-party rule in a true democratic political system.[34]

JAPANESE POLITICAL CULTURE AND VOTING BEHAVIOR

The main characteristics of electoral behavior in Japan have been an interesting case of relatively high levels of voter turnout in elections combined with a disinterest or perhaps even hostility toward politicians

and political parties and, except in the actual act of voting, a very passive, noninvolved citizenry. Japan is an important case for the comparative study of political participation. It is a highly developed
industrialized nation with five decades of real experience with mass par-
ticipatory democracy. Japan is also probably the world's most "social"
society—a society literally composed of many groups—and such groups
can be very important for the structuring of political activities. As Y.
Kuroda has observed, for many Japanese, voting is not so much a political activity as it is a part of general social behavior.[35] Citizens are encouraged to vote as a function of their responsibility to the social unit to
which they belong, whether occupational, geographic, or self-chosen.
Indeed, throughout the postwar period, rural communities have competed among themselves for the honor of having the highest voter
turnout rate in an administrative district. Cash awards have been given
to communities with the highest turnout. When one town could muster
only 86 percent of its voters in the 1975 elections, town leaders declared,
"We must not repeat that dishonorable record." Some towns have given
televisions and sports equipment to communities having the highest
turnouts in elections.[36] Bradley Richardson has noted that the Japanese
feelings of civic obligation are very important motivations for voting in
Japan. The idea of the citizen having distinct obligations and duties is, of
course, a long-term theme in Japanese political culture, dating at least
back to the Tokugawa era.[37]

In recent years, Japan, like the United States, has experienced a
decline in voter turnout that has worried many Japanese. It is interesting
to note that the Japanese pattern of turnout is similar to that found in the
United States—the more rural the district, the higher the turnout rate. In
the 1990 U.S. off-year general elections for Congress and state-level
offices, the highest turnout rates were registered in Maine and Montana.
By comparison, the highest turnouts in Japan in the 1990 HR elections
were in rural Shimane (86.45 percent), Tottori (84.0 percent), Oita (82.18
percent), Fukui (83.79 percent), and Yamagata (83.26 percent), whereas
the lowest turnouts were in the metropolitan prefectures of Osaka (65.06
percent) and Tokyo (65.55 percent).

One reason for the reduced levels of voter turnout in recent elections
was the decline in competition for many of the contests in Japan. In the
multiple-seats HR constituency system, the winners were often known
far in advance of the elections, since the top three, four, or five candidates in the districts won election. On the prefectural gubernatorial
level, a recent trend has been the running of an individual as a joint
candidate of the LDP and three or four other parties. In 1998 the governor of Kagawa was elected easily after he was endorsed by the LDP,

Democratic Party, Liberal Party, Social Democratic Party, and the Komei. The new governor defeated three independent candidates, including one backed by the JCP. The turnout was a low 39 percent.[38] In 1990, 34 of the 46 prefectural governors were coalition candidates. By 1993, the total was 37.

Because the Japanese are often described as group oriented, it should not be surprising that organizations advocate that their memberships vote together for certain parties or candidates. Patterns of social-based voting can be detected in the support patterns of many Japanese organizations. Major labor confederations, for instance, were strongly supportive of the various Socialist parties. And Japan's various religious associations are quite active in urging their members to support candidates of favored political parties beyond the expected Soka Gakkai–Komeito relationship. One of the largest of these organizations is the Rissho Koseikai, a neo-Buddhist group numbering 5 million members and strongly supportive of many LDP candidates. Rissho Koseikai leaders have estimated that between 2 and 3 million votes from members were cast for the endorsed conservative candidates in the 1980 double elections.[39] Among other major "new religions" (those formed since 1945), the Seicho-no Ie supported the LDP in 1980, whereas others such as Kyusei Kyo, Reiyu, Perfect Liberty, and Bussho Gonen-kai made great efforts to elect conservative candidates usually selected from their own membership ranks.[40]

More specifically directed toward the Japanese phenomenon is A. D. Shupe's study of political participation in Japan, which revealed that three measures—voting, political distrust, and political cynicism—stand apart from the other modes of participation. The lack of relationship between the act of voting and participation in politically oriented Japanese organizations is a major difference between the Japanese political system and the expectations of Western political theory. Shupe concluded that voting in Japan is such a passive act that it fits with the traditional Japanese pattern of avoiding overt political actions if at all possible.[41]

Bradley Richardson and Scott Flanagan suggest that the best model for understanding Japanese voting behavior is one based on social networks. Such a model appears to work for Japan, given the persistence of personal ties, the significance of the group in an individual's life, and the ability of the group to enforce conformity among its members.[42] Flanagan argues that Japanese voting behavior can be understood in terms of such traditional attitudes as the recommendation system (*sub-sensi*), feelings of obligation (*giri*), local district consciousness (*jimoto*), and supporters' organizations (*koenkai*).[43] Regarding *subsensei*, rural

Japan is largely organized and given political direction by its deference to community leaders, who traditionally control or influence the votes of many of their fellow citizens. Often entire groups will follow the recommendations of a particular leader. In the urban areas, such a pattern can often follow the wishes of a particular group, union, professional, or religious leader. *Giri* refers to a sense of obligation based on personal relationships, which constitute a significant aspect of Japanese society. One often sees a rather strange geographic pattern in given candidate's voter support. Regarding *jimoto* not only does the "hometown" turn out for the local candidate (and the candidate provides constituent services for the hometown or district), but the personal ties involved even more firmly cement the voting relationship. Finally, almost all LDP and many other party candidates have their own *koenkai*, which function to seal the personal relationship between candidate and voter. A koenkai will cost the politician great amounts of money to maintain, but it translates into votes come election day.

These patterns, described by Flanagan in 1968, are still part of Japanese political life in the 1990s—but they are so to a lesser degree, largely because the Japanese society has become more urbanized. As J. Watanuki suggested in 1967, "cultural politics" still exists in the rural sector of Japan.[44] In this style of politics, "political participation [is] based on the culturally prescribed personal relationships of indebtedness" established between persons and their social superiors, kin, or peers. However, Shupe has correctly noted a breaking down of this pattern inasmuch as traditional relationships frequently have been replaced by more functional or occupational bonds—especially for those who have moved from rural to urban areas.[45] In addition, Curtis has identified a rise in the number of candidate-controlled supporters' organizations, which for the conservatives and many JSP members have "bypassed the rural bosses."[46]

The passive form of citizen participation in Japan is effectively illustrated by the surveys taken by the NHK Public Opinion Research Institute, which focused on the value orientations of Japanese citizens. Among the various interesting questions dealing with preferred lifestyles, roles in marriage, and moral and religious values were questions pertaining to political values. In the 1973 survey, specifically, the question "What is the most desirable form of political behavior for the general public?" yielded the following responses: (a) We should select an excellent politician by election and entrust political affairs to him (63 percent); (b) When a problem occurs, we should make sure that the politician we support reflects our opinions in politics (12 percent); and (c) We should help the growth of the political party or body that we usually support, so that we can realize our views (17 percent). K. Kojima and D. Kazama designated response a as the disassociative orientation toward politics, response b as the intermediate orientation, and response c as the associative orientation. Because 63 percent of the sample supported the disassociative orientation, the NHK researchers concluded that the Japanese people's "concept of participation in politics is largely limited to voting."[47]

A lack of trust for politicians seems to be widespread throughout Japanese society. Among the working class, there is little public support even for reformist politicians. A poll of 5,000 members of six unions in the Tokyo-Yokohama area produced the following results: Of those surveyed, 1 percent trusted conservative politicians; 1 percent trusted fortune-tellers; and 1.8 percent trusted progressive politicians. Negative responses regarding conservative and progressive politicians ("I don't trust them" or "I don't trust them very much") were 79.1 percent and 70.5 percent, respectively. Yet, when asked what profession they considered the most important in Japanese society, these workers gave first place to politicians, followed by production workers, judges, and doctors.[48]

Another indication of the lack of trust in Japanese politicians came from the results of a poll quoted in a *Mainichi Shimbun* editorial in 1980. Respondents were asked to what degree they could trust the following, and these were their responses: weather forecasts (84 percent), newspapers (81 percent), doctors (77 percent), fortune-tellers (21 percent), and politicians (3 percent).[49] These responses fit well with the pattern found in U.S. cities operating under what Daniel Elazar calls an individualistic political culture—certainly a strange term to use as a parallel for the Japanese political culture, which is most decidedly nonindividualistic.[50] The city of Chicago, for instance, is full of professional politicians who prosper in their field and have relatively little interchange with average citizens except in their role as "brokers." These politicians are perhaps looked down upon by the residents of the city, but they are also recognized as very important to the survival of the democracy. As previously noted, the Japanese workers, when asked to name the profession they considered the most important, gave first place to politicians.[51]

The NHK surveys apparently discovered no correlation between the sense of political efficacy and the level of political knowledge. However, when the two dimensions were analyzed together, the NHK researchers discovered that almost half (i.e., 47 percent) of the Japanese population sampled exhibited both low political knowledge and a low sense of political efficacy. At the other end of the scale, only 10 percent of the sample fell into the category of high political knowledge and a high sense of efficacy. These figures were quite stable through the 1970s, but small changes were recorded at the upper and lower ends of the age-group spectrum; that is, better-educated, older respondents revealed high rates in both knowledge and efficacy, whereas even the best-educated youth were found in the low knowledge–low efficacy grouping.[52]

We can see one remnant of the persistence of traditional political values if we look at which level of politics is of the greatest interest to Japanese voters. In sharp contrast with the United States, where local elections often draw less than 20 percent of the eligible electorate, a sizable proportion of Japanese voters (37 percent) in a Prime Minister's Office poll conducted in 1982 cited the election of city, ward, town, and village assembly members as the most important election for them. Approximately 20 percent selected HR elections, and about 17 percent chose the election of the heads of their local governments. Only 4 percent indicated prefectural gubernatorial elections; 3 percent, prefectural assembly elections; and 1 percent, HC elections. The location of the citizen's home is quite important in shaping how he or she viewed elections. People living in smaller towns and villages placed great importance on their local city elections, but Tokyo residents thought the national-level HR elections were most significant.[53]

In general, however, most Japanese seem to have little interest in Japanese politics. The average citizen does not spend much of his or her time talking about politics. Nearly half the Japanese public (46 percent) indicated in a 1982 Prime Minister's Office poll that they "seldom talked about" social and political topics, while 40 percent said they "sometimes talked about" such topics. Those who seldom discussed politics increased by 5 percent over a 1980 poll, and those who sometimes discussed politics declined by 3 percent—a result some felt supported the theory that the trend toward political apathy actually accelerated in the 1980s.[54]

An important characteristic of any party system is the intensity with which voters identify with the component parts. In the Japanese political system, an important characteristic is weak identification with the political parties in the system. S. Verba found that only 16 percent of the Japanese expressed a strong degree of identity with their political parties—the lowest such figure among the nations studied by this author. Conversely, 53 percent exhibited weak identifications—the highest such total in the Verba study. In addition, nearly 30 percent identified themselves as independents. Only India had more independents than Japan at the time of this survey. Finally, it has been estimated that only 4 to 7 percent of Japanese formally belong to political parties, a range that is equivalent to the levels in India and the United States.[55] After studying a number of democracies, Richardson concluded in 1975 that Japanese party attachment levels (70 percent) were comparable to those of Norway, India, and Germany, and far behind the populations of the United States (90 percent) and Great Britain (90 percent).[56] Of greater interest still are the comparatively low intensities of party support found in Japan as compared with the two major Western democracies. The Japanese pattern of low overall support levels and low intensity of support was distinctive among the nations studied. In the United States, the percentage of nonparty supporters (independents) declines as they get older, but in Japan these nonsupporters are found in relatively similar proportions across the various age cohorts. Little difference is found among male respondents by age-groups, but women in general tend to be weaker "party identifiers," and older women are the most apolitical category of all.[57] Richardson also found party loyalties among young Japanese to be less developed than those among U.S. youth.[58]

Richardson has also concluded that the party is often not a very salient institution for many Japanese living within an electoral environment. Often on the national level, but most commonly on the local level, many candidates run and are elected as independents. Although the local levels were largely nonpartisan, the prefectural level was decidedly party oriented—a pattern similar to that in the United States, with its nonpartisan city elections and very partisan county- and state-level contests. One should also keep in mind that even in the Japanese HR's medium-sized constituencies, the real battle (before 1996) was often among various factions of the LDP rather than between the LDP and the opposition parties. The 1990 lower house elections in Aomori First District illustrated well this type of intraparty competition. Six candidates contested four seats, with one being the "symbolic" JCP candidate and another being the JSP and top vote-winning candidate in the district. Four LDP candidates backed by four of the LDP major factions battled among themselves for the three remaining seats. The lack of parties and party symbols especially at the local levels of politics, Richardson has concluded, makes Japanese electoral politics different from those of many comparable nations.[59] Yet, when the politics of the United States is compared with that of Japan, the pattern seems to be very similar with respect to partisan activities by governmental levels (see Tables 1.2 and 1.3).

Because most Japanese are not emotionally tied to a specific party, it seems reasonable that Japanese would know more about the individual parliamentary candidates than citizens in other democracies.[60] In survey after survey, Japanese voters emphasize the "candidate" over either "party." A *Nihon Keizai Shimhun* poll conducted in March 1990 asked Japanese voters what standard had guided their vote for candidates in the 1990 lower house elections. Half responded that they considered the

TABLE 1.2   Partisan Divisions at the Local Level of Politics in Japan, Large
            Cities, 1997

Party	Seats
Liberal Democratic	1,710
Shinshinto (New Frontier)	200
Minshuto (Democratic)	1
Socialist Federation	66
Social Democratic (SDPJ)	1,302
Japan Communist Party	1,706
Sakigake (Pioneer)	32
Komeito (CGP)	1,781
Democratic Socialist	78
Other parties	230
Independents	11,965
Total	19,071

SOURCE: Home Affairs Ministry, Elections Report, 1997, p. 63.

policies of the candidate and the party; 36 percent mentioned the candidate's personality; 15 percent needed a sense of affinity with the candidate; 11 percent relied on how familiar they were with the name of the candidate; and 12 percent followed the recommendations of other persons or mass media coverage of the campaign.[61] As Richardson has indicated, only in HC elections do the voters emphasize party more than candidate in making their voting decisions. Whereas rural voters tend to see Diet members as their envoys to the capital, urban voters place more emphasis on party labels and issue orientations.[62]

By and large, most Japanese do not strongly dislike the two major political parties. Very few Japanese strongly disliked the LDP and JSP in the First Party System, but the two most disliked parties were the JCP and the Komeito.[63] But, just because most Japanese do not strongly identify with their political parties does not mean that the Japanese voters do not think parties are important. Most Japanese appear to think the political parties and financial circles *(zaikai)* are the powers that move Japan. Five percent of the respondents believed election results to be most significant; 9 percent indicated the bureaucracy; 2 percent, mass movements, 4 percent, interest groups; 6 percent, other nations; 9 percent, the idea of public opinion; 28 percent, financial circles; and 27 percent, political parties.[64]

TABLE 1.3   Partisan Divisions, Prefectural Assembly Members, by Party, 1997

Party	Seats
Liberal Democratic Party	1,373
Shinshinto (New Frontier Party)	144
Minshuto (Democratic Party)	0
Social Democratic Federation	5
Social Democratic Party of Japan	293
Japan Communist Party	116
Sakigake (Pioneer Party)	9
Komeito (CGP)	189
Democratic Socialist Party	2
Other parties	106
Independents	639
Total prefectural assembly seats	2,911

SOURCE: Home Affairs Ministry, 1997 Elections Report, p. 63.

One reason the LDP remained in power for so many years is that the Japanese electorate is essentially conservative and resistant to change. It is conservative not in a true ideological sense, but in the sense that it resists fundamental changes. Moreover, as Yasusuke Murakami has suggested, the LDP is largely based on consummatory values, in that it emphasizes stability and order but not a return to traditional values.[65] Responses to public opinion polls in Japan tend to support the existence of a conservative Japanese public. In a Ministry of Health and Welfare poll in October 1979, the respondents to the question "Do you think your way of thinking and acting is rather conservative or rather reformist?" replied with conservative answers. Seventy-three percent described themselves as conservative, whereas 22 percent answered "reformist." The pattern varied little among the various age cohorts.[66]

Although the LDP has traditionally based its voting strength on the foundation of rural interests and small-business people, in recent years it moved to add the urban middle class to its coalition. The conventional wisdom had been to assume that this latter group was more likely to support opposition party candidates, but, as Gerald Curtis has argued, the "LDP has been transformed from a party dependent on farmer and small businessmen support to one whose main base of support lies in the new urban middle class."[67] Polls in the 1980s showed strong support for the LDP among young urban voters. Curtis saw this new urban middle class as essentially conservative in the sense of favoring stability and being reluctant to endorse radical changes in existing governmental policies.

The poll data and election results indicate that the LDP is not only the leading party of rural Japan but also the most powerful party in urban Japan. In the 1986 and 1990 lower house elections, the LDP won its highest percentage of votes in the rural and semirural districts, but it is also the strongest urban and metropolitan party. In fact, its vote-drawing power in the cities continued to grow into the 1990s.

In many democracies young voters are often the force behind liberal or leftist parties. Japanese youth, however, appear to be uncommonly conservative in their political orientation. A survey of 60,000 male students in their third year in universities and colleges throughout Japan revealed that 54 percent supported no political party, and another 7 percent responded to the question with "don't know." Of the 40 percent who named a party they supported, the LDP was the party with the greatest support: 17.3 percent. The leftist parties received a total of only 9 percent. A poll of 2,470 incoming freshmen at the elite Tokyo University produced a very similar conservative pattern of party support. Freshmen at the university were largely nonpolitical, with 60 percent not supporting any political party; but of the 40 percent who did, almost 60 percent supported the LDP. It is interesting to note that support for the JCP, which had been running at a 20 percent rate among those students supporting parties, fell to only 3 percent in the late 1970s.[68]

Japanese youths appear to be dissatisfied with their society and yet reluctant to engage in serious reforms. When the NRC survey asked its sample of male college juniors if they were satisfied with the nature of government in Japan, only 1.3 percent replied that they were satisfied, and 18.8 percent were "more or less satisfied." On the other hand, 33.8 percent were "dissatisfied," and 45.8 percent were "more or less dissatisfied." Yet this majority of dissatisfied students were not eager to change the governmental system. Forty-six percent felt "insecure about a major change in society," and only 22 percent wanted "basically to alter the political and economic system."[69] Many of these dissatisfied but conservative students will eventually end up as the businessmen of Japan. In a poll conducted by the Japan Junior Chamber of Commerce of business executives under forty years of age in 1980, 62 percent supported the Japan-U.S. Security Treaty; 54 percent supported a nuclear-armed Japan "some day in the future," and 71.3 percent supported the LDP.[70] In their study of the 1980 "double elections," Oyama Shigeo and

Michisada Hirose, using *Asahi Shimbun* poll data from a sample of more than 100,000 people, concluded that although young Japanese (ages twenty to twenty-four years) were the most nonpartisan (47 percent), their support rate for the LDP (28 percent) was greater than their combined support for all six of the opposition parties (25 percent). In addition, since the 1979 HR elections, the young voters have evidenced increasing support for the LDP. Among those voters in the twenty- to twenty-four-year-old age group, support for the LDP increased from 39 percent in 1976 to 49 percent in 1980.[71] Similarly, among the voters in their late twenties, LDP support rose by 9 percent between 1976 and 1980. The large jumps in LDP support among these younger voters occurred in and around the major regional cities and contributed to the fine showing of the party in the 1980 elections. One interesting question that remains to be answered is how the long recession of the 1990s will impact the long-term voting patterns of many of the youths who have and will have difficulty finding employment following their college years.

With respect to the age cohorts in Japan, interest in politics and voting turnout has been observed to be lowest among those in their twenties, especially the youngest group, aged twenty to twenty-four. This group makes up a disproportional percentage of the nonparty supporters in Japan (the so-called floating vote). Of this uncommitted vote, which makes up roughly 40 percent of the electorate, only 16 percent of the voters are over seventy; but the category also includes 45.6 percent of those in their twenties. In their analysis of the 1979 HR elections, Okamoto Hiroshi and Oyama Shigeo discovered that 44.7 percent of the nonpartisans voted for the LDP, compared with 20.8 percent for the JSP. Consequently, of the total LDP vote in 1979, 69 percent was derived from its own partisans, 21 percent from nonpartisans, and the remaining 10 percent from partisans of other parties.[72]

The floating vote is usually categorized into three major types of citizens: (1) those concerned about society and politics but irritated by contemporary politics and parties, (2) those whose life activities are centered on the home and who show little interest in politics, and (3) those whose lives are centered on pastimes and who have little political interest. Most of the people in this floating-vote category are twenty to forty years old. The *Asahi Shimbun* poll just prior to the 1979 general election reported that 53 percent of the public had "an interest in politics in normal times," whereas 42 percent did not, and 5 percent refused to answer the questions.[73]

Given the restrictive nature of Japanese electoral law (see Chapter 2) and the resultant passive nature of many Japanese voters, it should not be surprising that some Japanese journalists refer to the Japanese system as a "spectator democracy."[74] Tominomori Eiji has suggested that this term refers to the Japanese pattern of high interest in and high dissatisfaction with government and politics, but he has also noted the great separation between the citizen and the Japanese party system.[75] In an *Asahi Shimbun* poll only 18 percent of the respondents felt they could consult party members or political parties. Only 16 percent either had personal ties with parties or had participated in the activities of parties. A majority (57 percent), on the other hand, responded that they did not support a party, did not trust parties, had no interest in parties, or felt that parties had no connection with their daily life.[76] Richardson and Flanagan perceived two different groups of spectators in contemporary Japan: the older, less-educated, rural, deferential, and politically disinterested (i.e., traditional) group, and the newer group of younger, better-educated, urban, issue-oriented, and cynical citizens.[77] The election campaign laws deliberately seek to keep citizens from participating in the election process; thus it is not surprising that the vast majority of Japanese appear to be mere spectators.

One of Japan's most interesting characteristics is the lack of traditional cleavages that are common in European societies. In terms of party support, Japan exhibits no significant religious, racial, or ethnic splits. Yet this is not surprising, given that Japan is perhaps one of the most homogeneous nations (with respect to population characteristics) and also one of the least religious. As Flanagan and Richardson have argued, Japanese electoral cleavages during the FPWPS tended to be based on political issues such as support for the 1947 constitution and the Japan-U.S. Security Treaty, relations with the Communist bloc, and the continuing debate over capitalism and socialism as principles for societal organization.[78]

Bradley Richardson is also the author of one of the major new studies of Japanese party politics and voting entitled *Japanese Democracy*.[79] He notes that social class theory is not very useful in understanding Japanese voting behavior and suggests that the values cleavage model of Scott Flanagan has more utility. The split seems to be between those holding traditional Japanese values and those with more modern value sets. But even values data seem to be somewhat unclear as an explanation for Japanese voting behavior. Richardson and others such as Susan Pharr seem to be moving toward a voter alienation explanation for understanding voting behavior in the late 1990s.[80] Alienation based on news reports of corruption and policy failures would seem to help us understand the surprise results of the 1998 HC elections, which forced a confident LDP and Prime Minister Hashimoto to try to explain why the electorate gave the LDP such a relative defeat after the early polls of the campaign seemed to promise a good result for the party.

The data presented in the preceding discussion make clear the reasons for long-term LDP rule—at least in terms of voting behavior patterns. Not only was the LDP rural stronghold still intact and, thanks to the continuing malapportionment of the Diet, still powerful, but the conservatives had expanded their support in the cities as well and became a powerful national party—the only one fielding sufficient candidates to run the national government by itself. All of this suggested the LDP would continue to single-handedly rule Japan on the national level—if it could keep its large number of Diet members together in the same party. It seems as though the only way the LDP would lose its grip on the Diet was by organizational suicide. That is exactly what happened in 1993.

THE STRUCTURE OF JAPANESE PARTIES

One of the primary methods of comparative analysis of party systems involves careful examination of the structural aspects of the component parties. The Japanese political parties described in the remaining chapters of this book are usually portrayed as being elite cadre parties. Because modern Japanese parties began on the parliamentary level and only later extended their organizations to the subnational levels, it is not surprising that they today retain almost all of their organizational strength on the national level.[81] The inability of the national parties to construct effective grassroots operations is at least partly a function of the important tendency of the Japanese electorate to view politics as a necessary but distasteful activity—one that should be avoided as much as possible by the average citizen. Moreover, Japanese electoral law tries to keep the citizens and the parties as separate as possible. On various occasions, the party leaders have attempted to build grassroots organizations, but each time they failed. That is, the JSP (in its drive for 100,000 members), the LDP (in its expansion to 2.4 million members for LDP presidential primaries, discovered for the most part to be paper members only), and the NLC (in its offer of "political participation for the price of a cup of coffee," although an insufficient number of supporters responded to finance the party) have all failed in recent years. The parties relied either on their Diet members' fund-raising efforts (as in the SDF) or on their supporting organizations: Soka Gakkai in the case of CGP, Domei in the case of DSP, Sohyo in the case of JSP, and corporate Japan in the case of LDP and NLC. Of the six major Japanese parties, only the JCP has a reasonable mass-party organization, as well as its own independent fund-raising and campaign support activities.

Thus, Japanese parties tend to be highly centralized, exclusive in their membership patterns, and often lacking in even the essential organizational strengths necessary to perform the traditional functions of political parties.[82] Because it is often difficult to compare data on party organizations, the Japanese model cannot easily be placed among its counterparts abroad. Certainly the FPWPS socialist parties (the JSP, DSP, and SDF) lacked the mass membership base of the socialist parties of Western Europe. Moreover, although the conservative parties of Japan, Western Europe, and the United States share a common reliance on corporate support, the Japanese parties appear to have by far the weakest organizational ties to the average citizen.

With respect to informal organization, however, Japanese parties have factional patterns similar to those of the parties of Italy. The Socialist Party of Italy (PSI) and the JSP of Japan each had four or five major factions and a pattern of secession of several splinter parties (the Socialist Proletarians and the Social Democrats in Italy, and the DSP and SDF in Japan). Like the Japanese factions, those in Italy tended to be well organized and cohesive. According to Raphael Zariski, "Factions have their own newspapers or journals, their own parliamentary subgroups, their own sources of income, and their own share of party patronage."[83] Factionalism also played a key role in the nomination of party officials and parliamentary candidates in Italy.

Part of the reason behind the existence of factions can be traced to individual political ambitions and the creation of organizations to further these ambitions. When the Second Party System produced several new parties, they were also characterized by extreme factionalism, often based on previous party loyalties or links to specific party leaders. The NFP (Shinshinto) broke up over the leadership style of Ozawa and the loyalty of a major segment of the party to the Soka Gakkai's political agenda.

Factions may also be based on ideological orientations. It would be an accurate generalization to note that the LDP and the Italian Christian Democratic Party (CDP) share a pattern of factions largely based on personal ties, ambition, patronage, and fund-raising, whereas the JSP and PSI tend to have more ideologically based factions. In both the LDP and CDP, cabinet and subcabinet positions are awarded largely on the basis of factional shares and legislator seniority.

Thus, one of the most distinctive features of the Japanese party system—factions—mirrors the pattern exhibited by a number of Western European parties. As noted, the foreign party system most similar to the Japanese system seemed to be the Italian system, which incidentally has suffered a collapse in the 1990s similar to that in Japan. In both Japan and Italy, the informal organizations (factions) are at least as important as the formal party structure. Italy, by Sartori's count, had five to seven "relevant parties" (as does Japan) and as many as twenty-five "sub-party currents" in the ruling Christian-Democratic and Socialist Parties.[84] Although the Japanese LDP featured five or six major factions in the 1970s, the CDP of Italy displayed eight or nine "currents" of significance during that period. Both the LDP and CDP factions are largely "semi-sovereign" in that members owed their primary allegiance to the factions rather than to the parties.[85] As Sartori concluded, "With respect to factional politics the similarity between Italy and Japan seems impressive: It is a similarity verging on twinship."[86]

Among the dissimilarities is the Italian tendency to conduct electoral campaigns on the basis of parties, whereas the Japanese used factions and personal campaign support organizations in LDP and JSP campaigns, but the CGP, JCP, and DSP ran their campaigns largely by party. As Sartori has further noted, the Italian system requires coalition governments with factional alliances crossing party lines, whereas the Japanese system avoided coalitions in the First Party System (except for the very unusual case in 1983–1986 involving LDP-NLC coalitions, as unnecessary as those were) and had factions operating within their respective parties.[87] Finally, as Sartori has indicated, the Japanese factions came into being through the "fusions" of 1955, but the Italian factions were generated by "fissions" (i.e., by the gradual development of factions from an original party).[88] The important point to remember in this comparison of Japanese and Italian party factions is simply that the Japanese system is not unique (as many Japanese think it is!); it shares important characteristics with other parliamentary systems.

In summary, then, the Japanese political system is multiparty in nature, with a predominant party that has controlled national politics since 1955, with the exception of the 1993–1995 period. The reason for the LDP's long-term rule can be found in part in Japan's essentially conservative and passive electorate and in part in the ineptitude of the opposition parties (especially the JSP, the main opposition party) in both the First Party System and fragmentation of the opposition in the Second Party System. In the next two chapters, the rules of the electoral game will be presented in terms of their impact on the party system; then, in the remainder of the book, each of the major and minor parties will be discussed.

NOTES

1. Now that the Internet is available to students for research, several sites provided by Japanese English-language newspapers are particularly useful to the following of Japanese politics. Particularly useful is Japan's largest circulation

newspaper's English version, the *Daily Yomiuri* and the *Japan Times,* which maintains an archive of past editions at its Web site as well as the current news. This account of the events of the summer of 1998 through early 1999 was downloaded from these sites. For these Web sites, see the bibliography.

2. Several political handbooks regularly published in Japan provide the reader with a wealth of data on recent Japanese elections, the Diet, parties, and the government. Two of these are *Seikan* [Politics-Bureaucracy] *Handbook* (Tokyo: Jijitsushinsha) and *Seiji* [Political] *Handbook* (Tokyo: Seiji Koho Center).

3. There has been a great deal of research published in the United States on the subject of party systems in American political history. The origins of the concept came from the writings of V. O. Key, who constructed a theory of critical elections that was elaborated upon by others such as Walter Dean Burnham and James Sundquist. See V. O. Key, "A Theory of Critical Elections," *Journal of Politics* 17 (February 1955): 3–18; James Sundquist, *Dynamics of the Party System* (Washington, D.C.: Brookings, 1973); and Walter Dean Burnham, *Critical Elections and the Mainspring of American Politics* (New York: Norton, 1970).

4. Gordon Berger, *Parties Out of Power in Japan, 1931–1941* (Princeton: Princeton University Press, 1977); Robert A. Scalapino, *Democracy and the Party Movement in Pre-war Japan* (Berkeley: University of California Press, 1953); Peter Duus, *Party Rivalry and Political Change in Taisho Japan* (Cambridge, Mass.: Harvard University Press).

5. T. J. Pempel, "Political Parties and Social Change: The Japanese Experience," in *Political Parties: Development and Decay,* ed. L. Maisel and J. Cooper (Beverly Hills, Calif.: Sage, 1978), p. 312.

6. Ibid., pp. 311–312.

7. Ibid., p. 313.

8. Ibid., p. 319.

9. Robert A. Scalapino and Junnosuke Masumi, *Parties and Politics in Contemporary Japan* (Berkeley: University of California Press, 1962).

10. Nobutaka Ike, *Japanese Politics: Patron-Client Democracy* (New York: Knopf, 1972), p. 76.

11. G. Sartori, *Parties and Party Systems: A Framework for Analysis* (Cambridge: Cambridge University Press, 1976), chap. 5.

12. Maurice Duverger, "La Sociologie des Partis Politiques," in *Traitt de Sociologie,* ed. G. Gurvitch (Paris: Presses Universitaires, 1960), p. 44; G. Almond, in *The Politics of the Developing Areas,* ed. G. Almond and J. Cokman (Princeton: Princeton University Press, 1960), pp. 40–42.

13. *Sankei Shimbun,* February 10, 1990.

14. *Mainichi Shimbun,* April 13, 1990.

15. Michael Taylor and V. M. Herman, "Party Systems and Governmental Stability," *American Political Science Review* 65 (March 1971): 32.

16. Raymond Aron, "Alternation in Government in the Industrialized Countries" (speech given at the London School of Economics, October 27, 1981).

17. Quoted in Robert Dahl, ed., *Political Opposition in Western Democracies* (New Haven: Yale University Press, 1966).

18. *Yomiuri Shimbun,* February 6, 1982.

19. *Tokyo Shimbun,* April 3, 1990.

20. *Yomiuri Shimbun,* September 21, 1985.

21. *Japan Times,* July 29, 1982.

22. See Ariel Levite and Sidney Tarrow, "The Legitimization of Excluded Parties in Dominant Party Systems: A Comparison of Israel and Italy," *Comparative Politics* 15, no. 3, 295–324.

23. *Asahi Shimbun,* July 8, 1981.

24. "Vox Populi Vox Dei," *Asahi Shimbun,* July 7, 1981.

25. *Sankei Shimbun,* June 26, 1977.

26. *Japan Times,* December 26, 1983.

27. *Mainichi Daily News,* December 12, 1982.

28. *Japan Times,* January 9, 1981.

29. See Nobuo Tomita, H. Baerwald, K. Hoshino, and Akira Nakamura, "Japanese Politics at a Crossroads: The 11th House of Councilors Election," *Bulletin of the Institute of Social Sciences* (Meiji University) 1, no. 3 (1978). See also *Yomiuri Shimbun,* September 21, 1985.

30. Ellis Krauss, *Conflict in Japan* (Honolulu: University of Hawaii Press, 1984).

31. Dahl, *Political Opposition in Western Democracies,* p. 344.

32. T. J. Pempel, ed., *Uncommon Democracies: The One-Party Dominant Regimes* (Ithaca: Cornell University Press, 1990).

33. Ellis S. Krauss and Jon Pierre, "The Decline of Dominant Parties: Parliamentary Parties in Sweden and Japan in the 1970s," in Pempel, *Uncommon Democracies,* pp. 225–259.

34. Michio Muramatsu and Ellis S. Krauss, "The Dominant Party and Social Conditions in Japan," in Pempel, *Uncommon Democracies,* pp. 282–305.

35. Y. Kuroda, *Reed Town, Japan: A Study in Community Power Structure and Political Change* (Honolulu: University of Hawaii Press, 1974), p. 194.

36. *Mainichi Daily News,* April 8, 1979.

37. Bradley M. Richardson, *The Political Culture of Japan* (Berkeley: University of California Press, 1974), pp. 85–90. See also Bradley M. Richardson, "Japan's Habitual Voters: Partisanship on the Emotional Periphery," *Comparative Political Studies* 19 (October 1986): 356–384; and Bradley Richardson, "Constituency Candidates Versus Parties in Japanese Voting Behavior," *American Political Science Review* 82 (1988): 695–718.

38. *Daily Yomiuri,* August 1998.

39. *Mainichi Daily News,* June 12, 1980.

40. *Mainichi Daily News,* June 2, 1980.

41. A. D. Shupe, "Social Participation and Voting Turnout: The Case of Japan," *Comparative Political Studies* 12 (July 1979): 238.

42. Bradley M. Richardson and Scott C. Flanagan, *Politics in Japan* (Boston: Little, Brown, 1984).

43. See Scott C. Flanagan, "Voting Behavior in Japan," *Comparative Political Studies,* vol. I, no. 3 (October 1968): 396–411. See also James W. White, "Civic Attitudes, Political Participation, and System Stability in Japan," *Comparative Political Studies* 14, no. 3 (October 1981): 372; Flanagan and Richardson, "Political

Disaffection and Political Stability," in *Comparative Social Research,* ed. R. T. Jannuzzi (Greenwich, Conn.: AI Press, 1980), pp. 19–27; and O. Feldman and Kasohisa Kawakami, "Leaders and Leadership in Japanese Politics," *Comparative Political Studies* 22 (1989): 280.

44. J. Watanuki, "Patterns of Politics in Present-Day Japan," in *Party Systems and Voter Alignments,* ed. S. M. Lipset and S. Rokban (New York: Free Press, 1967).

45. Shupe, "Social Participation and Voting Turnout," p. 232.

46. G. Curtis, *Election Campaigning: Japanese Style* (New York: Columbia University Press, 1971), p. 209.

47. See Daiji Kazama and Toyoko Akiyarna, "Japanese Value Orientation: Permanence and Change," *Studies of Broadcasting,* no. 16 (1980). See also K. Kojima and D. Kazama, "Japanese Value Orientations," *Studies in Broadcasting,* no. 1 (1975); Scott C. Flanagan, "Changing Values in Advanced Industrial Societies," *Comparative Political Studies* 14 (January 1982): 403; Ronald Inglehart, "Changing Values in Japan and the West," *Comparative Political Studies* 14 (January 1982): 445–479; and M. Maruyama, "Patterns of Individualism and the Case of Japan: A Conceptual Scheme" in *Changing Japanese Attitudes Toward Modernization,* ed. M. B. Jansen (Princeton: Princeton University Press, 1965); and Ikuo Kabashima and Jeffery Broadbent, "Referent Pluralism: Mass Media and Politics in Japan," *Journal of Japanese Studies* 12 (1986): 329–359.

48. Reported in *Asahi Evening News,* December 14, 1979.

49. *Mainichi Daily News,* January 3, 1980.

50. Daniel Elazar, *American Federalism: A View from the States* (New York: Harper and Row, 1972), chaps. 2 and 3.

51. *Asahi Evening News,* December 14, 1979.

52. Kojima and Kazama, "Japanese Value Orientations."

53. *Japan Times,* April 13, 1982.

54. Ibid.

55. S. Verba and J. King, *Participation and Political Equality* (Cambridge: Cambridge University Press, 1978), p. 96.

56. Bradley M. Richardson, "Party Loyalties and Party Saliency in Japan," *Comparative Political Studies* 8 (April 1975): 42.

57. Ibid.

58. Ibid., p. 43

59. Ibid., p. 47.

60. Ibid., p. 49.

61. *Nihon Keizai Shimbun,* March 26, 1990.

62. Richardson, "Party Loyalties," p. 49.

63. *Asahi Shimbun,* September 10, 1979.

64. Ibid.

65. Yususuke Murakami, "The Age of New Middle Mass Politics: The Case of Japan," *Journal of Japanese Studies* 8 (Winter 1982): 171. The original work by Murakami on this subject appeared in *Chuo Koron.* (December 1980).

66. See the Ministry of Health and Welfare poll conducted in October 1979, reported in *Japan Times,* January 9, 1981.

67. Gerald Curtis, *Look Japan*, August 10, 1980.

68. *Mainichi Daily News*, May 5, 1979.

69. *Asahi Evening News*, August 14, 1978, and July 18, 1978; *Japan Times*, June 15, 1979.

70. *Mainichi Daily News*, March 30, 1980.

71. Oyama Shigeo and Michisada Hirose, "Nonpartisans and Youths Turn to the LDP," *Japan Echo* 7, no. 4 (1980): 18–37.

72. Okamoto Hiroshi and Oyama Shigeo, "Teiryu de henka shita senkyo no Yoso" [Election forecast faces unexpected turn of events], *Asahi Janaru*, October 19, 1979.

73. *Asahi Shimbun*, September 10, 1979.

74. *Asahi Evening News*, April 5, 1976.

75. Ibid.

76. Ibid.

77. Richardson and Flanagan, *Politics in Japan*, p. 225.

78. Scott C. Flanagan and Bradley M. Richardson, *Japanese Electoral Behavior: Social Cleavages, Social Networks and Partisanship* (Beverly Hills, Calif.: Sage, 1973), p. 108.

79. Bradley Richardson, *Japanese Democracy* (New Haven: Yale University Press, 1997).

80. At the 1998 annual meeting of the American Political Science Association in Boston, Susan Pharr presented a paper that used alienation as the primary explanation for recent Japanese political behavior. Bradley Richardson also noted the changes that have occurred in the 1990s in Japanese voting behavior and the changing roles of party identification and personal relationships.

81. Ibid., p. 88.

82. Ibid., p. 99.

83. Raphael Zariski, *Italy: The Politics of Uneven Development* (Hinsdale, Ill.: Dryden, 1972), p. 147.

84. Sartori, *Politics and Party Systems*, p. 88.

85. Alan S. Zuckerman, *The Politics of Faction: Christian Democratic Rule in Italy* (New Haven: Yale University Press, 1979).

86. Sartori, *Parties and Party Systems*, p. 20.

87. Ibid., p. 92.

88. Ibid.

two

Rules of the Game:
The Impact of the Electoral System
on Political Parties

Ronald J. Hrebenar

Japan is one of several nations (along with Italy and New Zealand) that have recently changed their electoral systems for electing their most important house of their national legislatures. The new dual electoral system for the Japanese House of Representatives (HR) has 300 single-seat districts and 200 more seats elected in large regional districts by proportional representation (PR). This new system was used for the first time in the 1996 HR elections, and some say it has the potential to fundamentally change the nature of the Japanese party system and, thus, Japanese politics.

Political scientists have long suggested that there is a strong relationship between the nature of a nation's electoral laws and its political party system. Rae and others have argued that two-party systems are based not only on cultural and historical factors but also on an election system that is conducive to the evolution of a two-party system.[1] The First Party System was strongly associated with the Medium District Constituency system, which was used for all the HR elections during the 1955–1993 period. The first HR's election (1996) of the Second Party System was conducted under a new reformed election system, and some political observers see a two-party system emerging from the results of the late 1990s. Actually, the new electoral system appears to be moving in two directions: toward a two-party system and toward the continuation of a medium-magnitude (six to eight parties) multiple-party system.

THE FIRST PARTY SYSTEM
AND THE DOMINATION OF THE LDP

The First Party System was characterized by an election law based on multimember parliamentary districts, chronic malapportionment, and a straitjacket campaign activities restrictions law. The net effect of these laws operated to keep Japan a one-party-dominant nation. The Liberal Democratic Party (LDP) ruled the nation uninterruptedly, without ever needing to resort to coalition, since its inception in 1955 until its loss of power in the summer of 1993. Of the many political, economic, and social influences that have assisted the LDP during this period of dominance, one of the most significant has been the favorable impact of the electoral system on the LDP's parliamentary fortunes.

The First Party System began a nearly perfect two-party system. The early elections resulted in an almost complete domination of the HR seats by just two parties: the LDP and the Japan Socialist Party (JSP). First, the JCP gradually emerged as a viable opposition party after early returns, which seemed to indicate the party would never survive with a presence in the Diet. Beginning in 1960, the system began to fragment, first with the DSP's splintering from the JSP, followed by the establishment of the Clean Government Party (CGP, or Komeito) in 1964. Later, the New Liberal Club left the LDP in 1976, and the Social Democratic Federation splintered from the JSP. What had been a two-party system had developed into a seven-party system by the early 1980s. The fragmentation of the 1955 Japanese political party system can be viewed only against the background of the election system that facilitates such developments. Two fundamental electoral laws—the Public Offices Elections Law and the Political Funds Control Law—have formed the riverbank that has channeled the parties of modern Japan. The former has set the basic rules of representation for both chambers of the Diet, while the latter, which was extensively revised in 1975, deals with the significant problem of attempting to regulate the flow of *seiji kenkin* (political contributions) within Japan politics.

THE IMPACT OF THE PUBLIC
OFFICES ELECTIONS LAW

The stated purpose of the Public Offices Elections Law as found in Article 1 is "to establish an electoral system . . . based on the spirit of the Japanese Constitution, to ensure that these elections are conducted fairly and properly according to the freely expressed will of the electors, and thus aim at the healthy growth of democratic politics."[2] This law established the unique Japanese multimember/single-vote election districts and the national PR district for the House of Councillors (HC). The law has two serious weaknesses: an unworkable reapportionment provision and the establishment of a comprehensive set of stringent campaign restrictions, both of which operated to preserve LDP majorities in the Diet.

The apportionment of legislators into constituencies can best be understood in terms of district magnitude—namely, the number of seats assigned by electoral law to any election district. Two major categories of district magnitudes are found throughout the world: the single-seat, or small-constituency, system; and the multimember constituency system, which can be subdivided into medium and large multimember districts. Single-seat districts are used in the United States for congressional elections, and in the Canadian, British, and Australian national lower house elections. The political outcomes of the single-member, single-ballot system have been well researched, and the normal tendency to reward dominant parties with many seats in excess of their vote percentages is well known. However, the multimember districts of the largest magnitudes are usually found in electoral systems using some form of PR; the more extreme form of this system is found in the Netherlands and in Israel, where the election district is the entire nation.

Japan's First Party System's medium-magnitude districts for national HR elections were unique among democratic nations. Japanese HR district magnitudes ranged from 2 to 5 seats, except for one single-seat district and one 6 seat district. Following a revision of Japanese election HR districts prior to the 1986 elections, the 512 seats were divided among 130 constituencies, for a mean magnitude of 3.94 seats per district. Four of the districts were 2-seat constituencies; 42 were 3-seat constituencies; 39 districts had 4 seats each; and 43 districts elected 5 Diet members. The Anami Islands had the single-seat constituency, and Hokkaido's first district had 6 seats. What makes the Japanese system unique is the combination of multimember districts and a single nontransferable vote. This combination produced a de facto PR result without being a formal PR election system.

The Japanese have experimented with each of the major types of constituencies over the past century. Before the current medium-sized constituency was introduced in 1925, the single-seat constituency was part of Japan's first election law of 1889 and was readopted in 1919 following the use of a large multimember system in the first two decades of this century. The 1946 election was held in association with a large multimember system, but all of the other postwar elections until 1996 were held under the medium-sized multimember constituency system.

One explanation for the adoption of a medium-sized constituency system in 1925 is that it protected the three parties that were joined in governmental coalition at that time: Seiyukai, Kenseikai, and Kokuminto. The Seiyukai wanted a small district system, whereas the other parties wanted a large district system based on prefectures. The compromise decision was the adoption of the medium-sized district system.[3]

TABLE 2.1   Total Party Vote and Seat Percentages: Election System Bias
in the 1990 General Election (HR)

Party	Party Vote	Percentage of Total Vote	Seats	Percentage of Seats	1990 Bias
LDP	30,315,417	46.1	275	53.7	+7.6
JSP	16,025,472	24.4	136	26.6	+2.2
CGP	5,242,675	8.0	45	8.8	+.8
JCP	5,226,987	8.0	16	3.1	−4.9
DSP	3,178,949	4.8	14	2.7	−2.1
SDF	566,957	.8	4	.8	−.1
Independent	5,147,854	7.9	22	4.3	−3.6
Totals	65,704,311	100.0	512	100.0	

NOTE: The one-seat district was captured by the LDP.

In actual operation, the Japanese 2- to 6-seat constituency system produced a nonformal but de facto pattern of party seat divisions that was roughly proportional to the parties' percentage of the total national vote. The two major parties tended to win seats in approximately the same proportion in districts of all three magnitudes, but the middle-sized parties tended to win most of their seats in the larger districts. The seat-winning power of the LDP and JSP was impressive. Frequently, the LDP and JSP together won all 3 seats in the smallest districts, and 3 out of 4 or 5 in the larger districts.[4]

The degree of proportionality between party votes and seat percentages for the 1990 House elections was quite clear (see Table 2.1). The 1990 election was the final "normal" election of the First Party System, since by the 1993 election the LDP had splintered, and several other new parties such as Hosokawa's New Japan Party had emerged. The major parties, the LDP and JSP, both crossed the important barrier of 20 percent of the total vote and consequently received additional seats above their vote proportions. The LDP won 46 percent of the vote and nearly 54 percent of the seats; the JSP secured 24.4 percent of the vote and 26.6 percent of the seats. The party that appears to suffer the greatest discrimination under the medium-sized constituency system was the JCP, which won only 3 percent of the seats but 8 percent of the total vote. In fact, this was quite a common fate for the JCP in the First Party System. In 1976, for example, both the JCP and Komeito won about 10 percent of the vote, but the Komeito Party won 38 more seats than its Communist rival. The explanation for this discrepancy can be found in the different strategies of the two parties in the selection of constituencies in which to run their candidates. The JCP generally tried to run a candidate in each of the nation's 130 districts, whereas the Komeito ran candidates in selected constituencies and in 1990 endorsed only 58 candidates. Consequently, although the JCP collects votes from every part of Japan, the separate totals are frequently insufficient to elect Communist Diet members. The JCP was willing to accept this situation, given the educational nature of its campaigns in many districts. The good news for the JCP is that this strategy will be much more successful in terms of seat payoffs in the Second Party System's new PR constituencies.

The relationship between constituency magnitude and LDP success was also clear in the 1990 HR elections. The fewer seats elected in a district, the better success rate the LDP achieved. The LDP won the seat in the single-seat district; 62.5 percent of the seats in the 2-seat districts; 57.9 percent in the 3-seat districts; 53.3 percent in the 4-seat districts; 52.6 percent in the 5-seat districts; and 33.3 percent in the 6-seat district.

The burden of calculating the correct number of candidates each party should endorse in specific districts was another important outcome of the medium-sized constituency system. If, for example, in a 5-member district a party miscalculated its electoral power and endorsed two candidates, the party vote in that district divided among its candidates may have placed both out of the top five vote winners. This strategic element was a problem only for the LDP and JSP, which run multiple candidates in some districts.[5] In 1969 the JSP failed to calculate the relationship between its vote-drawing power and the number of party candidates, and thus suffered the consequences. The Socialists decided to increase sharply the number of party candidates; then, when the voters' support declined, the party's seat total declined by 50 seats (see Table 2.2).

In 1972, given a more realistic endorsement policy in which the vote percentage was nearly identical to that in the previous election, 28 seats were added to the previous JSP total.

The concern of the smaller parties was more one of deciding whether they had a chance to win one seat in a district and, if that prospect was not likely, whether to join in a "joint struggle" coalition in that district. Toward the end of the First Party System (late 1980s) joint struggles, JSP-JCP and DSP-Komeito coalitions were the most frequent.

An example of how the LDP could miscalculate the correct number of candidates, with disastrous results, can be found in the Osaka fifth constituency in the 1983 HR elections. In this 4-seat district, the winners were the Komeito (143,532 votes), the JCP (122,200), the DSP (109,497), and the JSP (100,734), whereas all four defeated candidates were from the LDP, representing three different factions with a combined total of over 197,000 votes.

TABLE 2.2   Number of Party Candidates in Recent House of Representatives
             Elections

Party	1990	1993	1996SS	1996PR	Both
LDP	338	285	288	328	261
SDPJ	149	142	75	75	43
JCP	131	129	299	53	31
CGP	58	54	—	—	
DSP	44	28	—	—	
Sakigake	—	16	13	11	9
SDF	6	4	—	—	
NFP	—	—	235	133	7
New Japan	—	57	—		—
Democratic	—	—	143	159	141
Minor	71	62	240	77	75
Independent	156	109	—	—	
Totals	953	955	1,261	809	567

NOTE: In the 1996 elections, parties ran candidates in the 300 single-seat districts and
        sometimes different candidates in the PR bloc districts. Minor and independent
        candidates are calculated together for the 1996 elections.

SOURCE: *Nihon Keizai Shimbun,* October 14, 1996.

   Four additional points regarding the political effects of the medium-
sized constituency system should be made. First, it tended to result in
low levels of party competition because parties (except the JCP) tended
to run candidates only in those districts where there was a reasonable
chance to win an HR seat. The 1986 HR elections were the second-least
competitive of the postwar elections in terms of the number of candidates seeking Diet seats. Including minor parties and independents, only
838 candidates competed for 512 seats—a ratio of 1.64 candidates per
seat.[6] The extreme case has been represented by a number of districts in
which three Diet members were elected among only three serious candidates plus a symbolic JCP candidate. Usually 80 percent of the seats
were considered safe, and meaningful competition often has occurred
only for the last seat in a district.
   At least partly as a result of the effects of the medium-sized constituency system, competition rates in elections have plummeted to postwar levels. The number of candidates seeking seats in the upper house
also represented a postwar low. Even on the prefectural and local levels,
competition was dying out as the parties reduced their candidate totals
to contest only sure and possible seats. On the prefectural legislature

level, about 20 percent of the seats were uncontested; about one-third of mayoral elections and often half of such positions on the city and the village levels were uncontested.

Second, the multimember, single-vote districts resulted in serious intraparty conflict among the parties that ran multiple candidates. The LDP, which nearly always ran two or more candidates in a district, experienced serious intraparty conflict because each candidate sought to build his or her share of the conservative vote and usually accomplished this by subtracting votes from his party running mates. This conflict had been one of the supporting forces behind the LDP's factional system, inasmuch as the financial and political support to establish a separate candidate campaign organization had been provided by such LDP factional leaders as Takeshita (now Obuchi), Mitsuzuka, and Watanabe. Often the real opponents of an LDP candidate in his district were the other LDP candidates sponsored by rival factional leaders eager to add one more follower to their Diet organizations. Moreover, although in the spring of 1977 the LDP's factions were formally dissolved in an effort to refurbish the tarnished image of the party, other LDP members (such as the former chairman of the party's Policy Affairs Research Council, Matsuno Raizo) argued correctly the previous summer that the party factions would never disappear as long as the present medium-sized constituency system is in operation. The LDP factions did not disappear after their official dissolution in 1977 or after they were again dissolved in the early 1990s. With the election system reforms starting in the 1996 HR elections, many political commentators have suggested that factions were in the decline in the LDP. The results of the 1998 LDP presidential selection process indicated the factions were still important within the LDP, but also suggested that their characteristics were also significantly changing as well.

Third, the medium-sized constituency system operating as a de facto PR system has encouraged the birth of new political parties that can compete with reasonable expectations of success with as little as 5 percent of the vote. Whereas, it seemed in 1955 that the "two-party era" had arrived in Japanese politics, the success of subsequent spin-off parties such as the DSP, as well as the creation of the Komeito, would never have been possible under a small-seat system.

Finally, the proliferation of political parties under the medium-sized system has resulted in the fragmentation of the opposition into small parties seemingly incapable of forming an alternative government. Ever since the 1976 elections raised the hopes of the opposition, a great deal of speculation had been generated regarding potential coalitions of opposition parties in the future. The primary speculation centered on the JSP's desire for an all-opposition party coalition (including the JCP) and on the rejection of that idea by the middle-of-the-road parties, especially the Komeito and the DSP. Thus, the fragmentation of the opposition into relatively impotent, small organizations had facilitated the LDP's continuance in power during the First Party System. The opposition parties never came together until a short time in the mid-1990s, a splinter from the LDP under the leadership of former LDP members Ozawa and Hata managed to glue together a large non-LDP new party under the name of the Shinshinto or New Frontier Party. That party rather quickly collapsed, and the Second Party System moved from an early two-party system to a multiparty system.

The two chambers of the Diet have moved toward each other in terms of the nature of their electoral systems. The 252 members of the HC are elected from two types of constituencies: local (152) and national (100). The local districts were based on prefectural boundaries, with each prefecture electing one to four councillors every three years. The LDP controlled the HC quite easily until the 1989 elections. The LDP monopolized the 26 single-seat districts, winning 96 percent of the seats in 1983 and 88 percent in 1986. However, in the "protest 1989 HC elections," the LDP managed to win only 3 of the contested 26 seats. Usually the fifteen 2-seat districts were dominated by the LDP and the JSP. In the 1986 HC elections, these two parties won 27 of the 30 seats, and even in 1989 the two powerful parties lost only 5 seats to other candidates. The smaller parties of the First Party System (CGP, JCP, DSP, SDF) won most of their local constituency seats in the 3- and 4-seat districts. In the two 4-seat districts, the minor parties held the LDP and JSP to 5 seats in 1986 and to only 3 seats in 1989. The LDP was able to win only slightly more than half the seats in the four 3-seat constituencies, where the CGP managed to win 3 of the 12 seats in 1989. Overall, the LDP won 45 percent of the local constituency vote in 1986 while winning 66 percent of the seats, but its share fell in 1989—to 30.7 of the vote and to 28 percent of seats.

In the national constituency, however, the LDP was at a serious disadvantage. Prior to 1983, 100 councillors were elected in a nationwide constituency in which each voter cast only a single, nontransferable vote. Every three years, half of these seats are up for election. In 1989, the LDP captured only 30 percent of these seats. In the 1998 HC election, the LDP was able to win only 14 PR seats out of 50 on only about 25 percent of the vote. The LDP did fairly well on the local level, but it obtained 3 million fewer votes on the PR level compared with the local level.

The reasons for the LDP weakness in the national PR contests could be found in the party's lack of grassroots organization and its inability to organize its supporters to vote in an efficient manner. The JCP, for example, divided the country among its disciplined local organizations and assigned each specific candidate to a certain region, thus concentrating the votes for individual candidates in certain parts of the nation. The Komeito followed a similar strategy, as did the JSP in some elections. However, the LDP had to rely on its general vote-gathering power, with the result that a large number of votes were wasted for a handful of very popular candidates.[7] Each of the smaller parties won seat proportions in excess of their vote proportions in the 1974 upper house national constituency. In 1977 the success of the smaller parties in this favorable environment encouraged new political parties to field candidates in the national constituency. They included the NLC for the first time, the Socialist Citizens League (formed by the late former JSP vice chairman Eda Saburo), the United Progressive Liberals, and the Japan Women's Party. In later elections, even the Sports Party was able to win a seat in the HC for a pro wrestler! Hence, the nature of Japan's multimember districts in both chambers of the national Diet and in almost every level of prefectural and local politics encouraged a proliferation of political parties much as a formal PR system would have done. The year 1977 finally confirmed the beginning of the end of the "one-and-one-half" or "1955 party system"; certainly, the conducive environment of the multimember districts was the most important structural support for Japan's multiparty era.

THE CONTINUING MALAPORTIONMENT PROBLEM

On April 14, 1976, the Japanese Supreme Court issued a decision that initially appeared to have the potential to radically alter the postwar patterns of the nation's politics. The court's 8 to 7 decision ruled that the allocation of lower house seats was unconstitutional because of malapportionment, which denied equal rights to urban voters as guaranteed by the Japanese constitution. The case was brought to the courts by a group of voters from the Tokyo "bedroom" prefecture of Chiba and was the first challenge to the malapportionment problem, found in both houses of the Diet, to reach the Supreme Court. Normally the Japanese judicial system, especially the Supreme Court, has been extremely reluctant to become involved in any case affecting the political party system. However, the combination of powerful postwar migratory patterns from rural to urban sectors of the nation and the reluctance of the ruling LDP to adjust the resulting imbalances forced the court to consider such a case.[8]

Since World War II, the Japanese population has shifted from 25 million urban people and 50 million rural people to 85 million urban people and 40 million rural people, with over 40 percent of the population jammed into a metropolitan band consisting of just three cities: Tokyo, Osaka, and Nagoya. The total population of Japan as of 1998 was 125.5 million.

As stipulated in the Public Offices Election Law, the Diet must adjust the number of Diet members in each electoral district so that they are proportionate to the population size after each five-year census. But the law is not equipped to deal with such regular reapportionments; moreover, for reasons of political advantage, during the First Party System the LDP repeatedly refused to reapportion the Diet completely. Instead, the party relied on partial adjustments, such as the addition of new seats to urban constituencies, when forced by occasional public and political pressures. Nineteen seats were added in 1964, and an additional 20 brought the total to 511 HR seats in the 1976 election. Prior to the 1986 HR elections, seats in 8 constituencies were increased and in 7 decreased, for a net gain of 1 seat and a new total of 512. Under these adjustments, the first 6-member HR district was created in Hokkaido, and four 2-seat districts were newly established.

Despite these changes, a serious problem remained. The problem continued and can be seen when the results from the 1990 HR elections are considered. Thirteen candidates failed to win a seat, although their vote totals exceeded 100,000, whereas a JCP candidate in Tokyo's eighth district won a seat with only 44,154 votes. The surprise is that it was an urban district, not the usual rural district, that had the winner with the fewest votes. Despite the curious 1990 result, the metropolitan prefectures and their adjacent "bedroom" prefectures have been the primary victims of the failure of LDP politicians to carry out their legal responsibilities to reapportion the Diet fairly. Kanagawa prefecture, adjacent to Tokyo, had the dubious honor of containing the most underrepresented constituency in Japan during the late First Party System. In 1990 its fourth district contained 336,061 persons per Diet member, whereas the most overrepresented district, Miyazaki's second, had only 105,682 persons per Diet member—a ratio of 3.18:1.

The major losers of this lower house malapportionment were the citizens of urban and metropolitan areas, as well as the smaller political parties that gather most of their support in the large cities. The *Asahi Shimbun,* in its analysis of lower house malapportionment, concluded in 1976 that a fair reapportionment would add 67 seats to urban constituencies and subtract an equal number from the rural areas.[9] Urban voters are discriminated against as a result of the rural bias of the Diet. This bias can be seen in LDP public policies, which were geared to benefit the agricultural sectors in such basic areas as rice production subsidies and special arrangements to protect domestic beef producers—all at the expense of the urban consumer. Some members of the LDP went as far as to argue that the rural areas needed the extra seats in the Diet because they had so few other advantages in Japanese society. The smaller opposition parties were disadvantaged by malapportionment in that they have fewer seats to compete for in urban areas, where most of their strength could be found. Komeito, DSP, JCP, and JSP all scored their highest percentages in the twenty-three metropolitan constituencies.

Ironically, the JSP, until its collapse in 1996, appeared to be a truly national party, winning about 20 percent of the total votes in urban constituencies but scoring slightly better than that in the rural part of the nation. Meanwhile, in the 1980 election, for example, the LDP won a respectable 32.9 percent of the metropolitan votes but obtained more than 70.4 percent of the votes in the rural constituencies.[10] In summary, the major political parties most victimized by malapportionment were the two urban-based ones, the JCP and the Komeito.[11]

However, it should be noted that one reason that reapportionment was not implemented until 1993 was the lack of public support for such changes. A *Mainichi Shimbun* poll published in February 1990 indicated that 29 percent of the public was content with the current 3:1 imbalance in HR districts; about half (46 percent) wanted the imbalance reduced to 2:1; and only 15 percent wanted it reduced to 1. The public was also uncertain about the proposed reforms in the size of election districts.[12] Another *Mainichi Shimbun* poll published in February 1990 indicated that 40 percent thought the existing medium-sized constituencies were the best type; 10 percent wanted a system of all small constituencies; and 23 percent supported the proposed small districts plus PR system—the reform that was finally adopted for the 1996 HR elections. The remaining 27 percent supported other ideas or had no opinion.[13]

The new 1996 election apportionment of 300 single-seat districts was the product of years of discussion and planning, and it still has the nagging problem of malapportionment. By 1998 the most populated single-seat district had 2.4 times the population of the least populated district (Kanagawa's 14 had 580,000 people and Tottori's 3rd had 240,000 people). The ratio was 2.13:1 when the districts were designed in 1994.[14] The problems now stem from the desire of the map drawers not to split cities or towns between districts unless absolutely necessary, as well as the rule that each prefecture, regardless of population, requires at least one member of the HR. A fairer apportionment still giving each prefecture at least one district would give five prefectures (Saitama, Chiba, Kanagawa, Shiga, and Okinawa) one more district; and five prefectures (Hokkaido, Tokyo, Yamagata, Osaka, and Oita) would lose one district.

The fairest arrangement, which apportions seats without the require-ment to give each prefecture one seat, would add three more districts to Tokyo, and Saitama, Chiba, and Osaka would get two more districts. However, it seems unlikely that such reapportionments will occur in the near future.

Even more serious in terms of the degree of malapportionment con-tinues to be the problem of the imbalance of local constituency seats in the HC. When the election system was first implemented in 1947, the councillors were apportioned among the prefectures in proportion to the population distribution recorded in the 1946 census. Since the initial allocations, only one change has been made—namely, the addition of a pair of seats for Okinawa prefecture in 1970, when Japan regained politi-cal control of the islands. As in the lower house, the massive shift of pop-ulation to the cities has created a serious imbalance that greatly favored the rural prefectures.

On August 19, 1982, the LDP succeeded in passing a major electoral reform bill through the Diet—a bill that, in fact, could be considered the first major electoral reform under the 1947 postwar constitution. Beginning with the 1983 elections, the 100 national constituency seats of the HC were—and continue to be—elected under a PR system. This sys-tem uses the d'Hondt method, which requires voters to cast their national constituency votes for a party, not for individual candidates as in previous elections. Because all votes must be cast for parties, the inde-pendents in the upper house are forced to join together in party slates in order to have a place on the ballot. If a party is to earn a ballot spot, it must have one of the following: (1) 5 Diet members, (2) 4 percent or more of the total popular vote in the last national election, or (3) more than 10 candidates (local and national constituencies) in an upper house election. Each participating party will be required to form a list of candi-dates who will be elected to councillor seats based on the percentage of the total vote cast for each party.[15]

The adoption of the PR system in the upper house was largely sup-ported by the Japanese media as a means of reducing the skyrocketing costs of election campaigning in the national constituency.[16] The *Mainichi Shimbun* described the PR system as "epoch making" and sug-gested that it would have "a revolutionary effect on the traditional Japanese election system."[17] This reform was strongly supported by the LDP and JSP—both of which saw it as a golden opportunity to reduce campaign costs. The LDP has estimated that it spent 7 billion yen on its 1980 national constituency campaigns, whereas the JSP's main support organization, Sohyo, has estimated that it spent 300 mil-lion yen per candidate in 1980. The PR reform was strongly opposed by the Komeito and the JCP—the best-organized parties in such election campaigns.[18]

When the first PR national constituency elections were held in 1983, the results did not follow some of the predictions that suggested the reforms would aid the LDP. The LDP captured only 35.33 percent of the vote and won 19 seats of the 50 contested. These totals represented declines of over 7 percent (2 seats) as compared with its 1980 non-PR results. All in all, none of the major parties (except the JCP) were happy with the results.

THE 1994 ELECTORAL SYSTEM REFORMS

After the LDP lost power in 1993, the new Hosokawa-led government introduced reforms to change the election system for the HR and make changes in the Political Funds Control Law. Prime Minister Hosokawa and the new LDP president Kono Yohei agreed in January 1994 to pass a reform bill after it was clear that the government could not pass reforms without LDP cooperation. The core of the reforms would be the first overhaul of lower house electoral system since 1947. The number of single-seat constituencies was set at 300, and number of PR seats at 200. PR votes will be counted on a regional basis by dividing the nation into eleven blocs. Under the original version of the legislation, the votes would have been counted on a nationwide basis.[19]

The Japanese have tried all the major types of election systems at one time or another, with the exception of PR. It had long been discussed in LDP closed meetings that the best way to preserve conservative control of government when the party's vote is no longer sufficient to produce absolute seat majorities is through adoption of a single-seat district system. This method was first proposed in the postwar era by the Hatoyama coalition cabinet, which introduced just such a small-constituency plan into the Diet in the 1950s; but the plan was tabled after significant opposition threatened to halt more important legislation in the Diet. Revived during the 1960s and again tabled, it was proposed by the Tanaka government in 1973 in a somewhat different form. The Tanaka scheme, which called for a combination of single-seat districts and PR seats, was similar to the proposals that had emerged from a series of governmental Electoral System Councils during the 1960s and early 1970s.

All of the opposition parties were strongly opposed to the single-seat constituency reform. The JSP and JCP party organs, in particular, called for the "complete crushing of the minor constituency system," terming it a threat to democracy and saying that the "LDP plan aimed at one-party despotism."[20] At that time a new political phrase referring to Tanaka Kakuei's reapportionment plan, Kaku-mandering, appeared in Japan. The conservatives have played an interesting game with regard to their support of significant reform in the election system. When the opposition parties demanded that the government reapportion the Diet seats fairly, the LDP had replied that it would also change to a single-seat system, which all understood will eliminate many members of the opposition.

One aspect of the reforms that most journalists and the vast majority of the Japanese public do not understand or like is the "second chance" provision for the PR constituencies. The parties put together their PR list of candidates for each of the PR bloc districts. Each party's list may contain names of candidates unique to the PR list, such as former prime minister Nakasone, who was asked by the LDP to run in the PR constituency to allow a younger candidate from a powerful political family (Fukuda Yasuo, son of the former prime minister) to run in the single-seat districts in Gumma prefecture. The parties can also place the names of candidates who are running in the single-seat districts. If these double candidates lose in the single-seat districts, they can win in the PR district if they are placed high enough on the party list. The media in 1996 called these lucky Diet members "second-chance winners." In 1996 there were 83 such Diet members elected to the HR. Of the LDP 288 single-district candidates, 261 were also listed on the PR lists. For the Democratic Party 141 of its 143 candidates were dual candidates, as were 43 of 48 SDPJ candidates, 9 of Sakigake's 13, and only 31 of the JCP's 299 candidates.[21]

THE POLITICS OF CAMPAIGN REGULATION

Japanese election campaigns are conducted under a set of comprehensive laws deemed to be the most restrictive in the democratic world.[22] When the Home Ministry promulgated campaign rules in 1924, it acted under the assumption that the nation's voters were not sufficiently sophisticated to evaluate effectively the appeals of politicians and thus might be easy targets for the rising Socialist movement that so worried Japanese leaders in the early part of the century.[23] Almost every type of campaign activity that would involve the voter in any but the most superficial way was prohibited. In particular, door-to-door campaigning, signature drives, polling, providing food or drink, mass meetings, parades, unscheduled speeches, multiple campaign vehicles, and canddate-produced literature are illegal in contemporary Japanese campaigns. Instead, a candidate's contacts with his or her potential voters must, by law, be channeled through a limited number of government-produced postcards, posters placed on official signboards, a maximum of five government paid newspaper ads of a specific size and content, several television and radio announcements, a number of joint speech meetings, and government-financed handbills and brochures.

Many of these restrictions have been commonly flouted by the candidates, especially those regarding the official campaigning period and the provision of food and drink to potential voters.[24] For instance, prior to either HC or HR elections, illegal posters and other district activities are a normal part of the Japanese politics. Candidates have also been known to demonstrate tremendous ingenuity in evading the intent of the campaign restrictions. Some potential candidates have increased their contacts with voters by holding political study meetings with increasing frequency as an election draws near. Others have sent telegrams to constituents announcing the end of a Diet session, communicating winter or summer greetings, or expressing congratulations for almost any kind of event.

Among the Western-style democracies, only Japan and South Korea have such a ban on canvassing. In 1950 the Hiroshima High Court ruled the Public Office Election Law ban on door-to-door canvassing unconstitutional because it ostensibly violated Article 21, which guarantees freedom of expression. Such a ban has been declared unconstitutional by lower district courts on several occasions since the mid-1960s. However, the Supreme Court declared the ban constitutional in a decision on a Tokyo case in June 1980. One poll conducted prior to the 1979 general elections indicated that 90 percent of the candidates supported the removal of the ban on canvassing.[25] However, when the 1994 reforms were enacted, a proposal to end the ban on canvassing was deleted. One interesting aspect of the restrictive campaign rules was the governmental decision to make illegal Internet Web pages put together by candidates for the Diet. The government, in essence, ruled that since there was no mention of the World Wide Web in the law, its use must be illegal in Japanese campaigns.[26]

It should be noted that the 1994 reforms did result in some liberalization of the restrictive laws. Still, the most prevalent form of campaigning seems to be the repeated litany over the loudspeaker: "This is Tanaka. This is Tanaka. This is Tanaka." Over and over again, from early morning to early evening as the campaign van moves through one neighborhood after another. The law allows only one such van at a time and limits the amount it can be used to "just" twelve hours a day. The book that lists the various restrictions on modern Japanese campaigns is 478 pages long![27] In the 1996 HR elections, some individual candidate TV spot ads were allowed. Some candidates produced a spot ad and ran it several times on commercial television in addition to the free short campaign speech on public television with all the other candidates in the district. The public TV spots have been part of Japanese Diet campaigns since 1970. The adoption of commercial TV spots in 1996 was very stressful to many Japanese politicians, much as it was to American politicians in the early 1950s. As one noted: "It is like you open the door to Hell."[28] The new TV ads were difficult, since it is considered improper to attack one's opponent directly and even by name. Still, modesty and politeness are highly valued, even in politics in Japan. It was estimated that the LDP and the NFP spent about $10 million each in commercial television in the 1996 campaign: a drop in the bucket when compared with the amounts spent in American campaigns, but a large initial amount for Japan. Two types of party television broadcasts occurred in 1996: fifteen- to thirty-second party spots, and what is called the party "public policy broadcast," which were a series of short messages from individual candidates broadcast in a nine-minute block. The latter used to be the talking head speeches sitting in a chair in a studio. These now may take place in any setting desired by the candidates. Nine minutes are allocated to each district, and the number of candidates may vary greatly, with urban districts tending to have more candidates than rural districts. Consequently, in such crowded urban districts, a given candidate may get only twenty or thirty seconds to make an impression on the viewers. One additional media change has been the growth of the Sunday morning political discussion television programs. In previous years these usually were very boring nonevents, but as the participants have become more comfortable with the format, these programs have actually become newsworthy in their own way, just as *Meet the Press* and similar programs have been politically important forums in the United States. Newspapers allowed pictures of the candidates only if all the candidates' photos were shown. In a typical HR district a candidate in 1996 was allowed to distribute 1,000 posters to communicate with over 300,000 voters, plus the 500 posters that are posted on the official poster boards on main streets and public sites.

The campaign restrictions have done little to reduce the costs of election campaigning but have had other serious outcomes. The combined effect of the restricted nature of a typical campaign has been to prevent Japanese voters from becoming involved to any significant degree in a politician's campaign. The voters are expected to be passive and noninvolved—mere spectators watching the election as though it were a Noh play, without excitement. As survey after survey has produced evidence of such low voter involvement and interest in Japanese elections, there is general agreement among Japanese political scientists that the unreasonable campaign restrictions should be liberalized to facilitate greater participation.

The current system also operates to protect the incumbents from successful challenges. Because most candidate-voter contacts must be channeled through official media routes, new names have little chance to gain the name recognition or issue familiarity necessary to defeat an incumbent. And since most Diet members are also members of the LDP, the restrictions obviously work to protect this party. Moreover, the laws have been adjusted to establish environments conducive to the success of the major parties. Changes enacted in 1975 focused on the question of distributing campaign literature or party newspaper "extra" editions primarily at train stations or department stores. An alliance developed between the LDP and JSP, which favored the restriction of these types of campaigning frequently used by the JCP and the Komeito. The reasons behind this split of opinion were quite clear: Whereas the JCP and the Komeito had sufficient staff to utilize this technique effectively, the LDP and JSP did not have enough volunteers to compete with the Communists and the Buddhists. In another proposed reform, the LDP has indicated a desire to restrict or abolish the joint speech meetings requirements—one of the three pillars of Japanese-style election campaigns. (The others are the official elections bulletins and the candidates' radio and television broadcasts.) In particular, the LDP members seem to object to the time required and to the catcalls and angry shouts that often invade such events. Both the JSP and the JCP were opposed to any such limiting of joint speech meetings.

One consequence of the government's attempts to regulate campaign behavior has been the reduction of public respect for politicians, who are constantly observed to be breaking and evading the election laws. All in all, then, the campaign restrictions have not been effective. The costs of elections have not been reduced to reasonable levels, and the restriction of the use of media in campaigns has forced politicians to revert to even more expensive, and often illegal, means of communication.[29] Essentially, the experience of these laws has demonstrated the futility of attempting to prevent the necessary communication between candidates and voters.

THE EXPANSION OF THE JAPANESE ELECTORATE

When the first HR elections were held on July 1, 1890, suffrage was restricted to male citizens twenty-five years of age and older who had paid 15 yen or more in taxes for at least a year. With these restrictions, only about 450,000 men were qualified to vote—a mere 1.1 percent of the

TABLE 2.3   Expansion of Suffrage in Japan

Year	Qualification			Eligible Voters as % of Population	No. of Eligible Voters
	Tax Payment	*Minimum Age*	*Sex*		
1889	¥15	25	M	1.1%	450,000
1900	¥10	25	M	2.1%	980,000
1919	¥3	25	M	5.4%	3,060,000
1925	—	25	M	20.0%	12,400,000
1945	—	20	—	—	36,870,000
1983	—	20	—	—	84,252,608
1990	—	20	—	—	90,322,908
1998	—	20	—	—	99,000,000

SOURCE: *Facts and Figures on Japan* (Tokyo: Foreign Press Center of Japan, 1980). Updated by author.

total population of 44.5 million. Among the electorate, 93.9 percent voted in that first election. An amendment in 1900 enfranchised all male citizens paying annual taxes of 10 yen or more and thus increased the electorate to 2.2 percent of the population. Following another small increase in 1919, a major change occurred in 1925 when the tax requirement was eliminated, thus enlarging the eligible electorate by 400 percent to a total of 20 percent of the population. Female suffrage came after World War II, and the current minimum voter age of twenty years was established in 1945 (see Table 2.3).

Because the Japanese government assumes the responsibility of ensuring that voters are properly registered, nearly all eligible citizens are registered to vote. As of the summer of 1998, approximately 99 million Japanese were on the voting rolls, out of a total population of about 125 million persons. Voter turnout in national elections has usually been in the 65 to 80 percent range, but in prefectural and local elections it is considerably lower.

Voting in Japanese elections had always been made difficult by the rules established by the government. In HR elections, for example, voters had to write the name of the candidate they wanted to vote for on the paper ballot. Japanese elections do not use voting machines or any of the modern types of punch-out ballots used in many other nations. The revised Public Office Election Law, which went into effect in 1998, eased the procedures for absentee voting. In prior elections, only voters who had work-related or other compelling reasons for missing an election day vote were permitted to submit absentee ballots.[30] Under the new law, even voters who plan to spend election day shopping or playing golf will be able to cast absentee ballots. The revised law has also extended the voting day by three hours until 8:00 P.M.

The second component of the election laws that attempts to control the nature of Japanese political parties and campaigns is the Political Funds Control Law. This law has been much discussed in Japan during the 1990s as scandal after scandal has highlighted its inability to control the corruption that seems to pervade Japanese campaigns. The next chapter will examine the major weaknesses of this law and its effects on the Japanese party system.

NOTES

1. There has been much written about the relationships between electoral law and a given party system. One of the most important of the early works in this area is Douglas W. Rae, *The Political Consequences of Electoral Law* (New Haven: Yale University Press, 1971). See also Gary W. Cox and Francis Rosenbluth, "The Electoral Fortunes of Legislative Factions in Japan," *American Political Science Review* 87 (1993): 577–89; and Gary Cox and Emerson Niou, "Seat Bonuses Under the Single Nontransferable Vote System: Evidence from Japan and Taiwan," *American Political Science Review* 92 (1998). The impact of the electoral system is also an important discussion in Masaru Kohno, *Japan's Postwar Party Politics* (Princeton: Princeton University Press, 1997), chap. 3. "Politics of Electoral Reform."

2. See Law No. 100 of April 15, 1950, revised in 1975. For a summary of this law in English, see *Election System in Japan* (Tokyo: Ministry of Home Affairs, 1985). The author wishes to acknowledge the invaluable assistance given to him in this project by Japanese scholars in the field of electoral law. Both Professor Nishihira Sigeki of Sophia University and Professor Sakagami Nobuo of Tokyo shared with me their recent research findings and special insights into Japanese election laws and devices. The helpful assistance of Professor Kyogoku Junichi of Tokyo University during my 1975 research trip was also much appreciated. The most useful Japanese-language studies on this subject are Sakagami Nabuo's *Nihon Senkyo Seidoron* (Tokyo: Seiji Koho, 1972); and Nishihira Sigeki's *Nihon No Senkyo* (Tokyo: Shiseido, 1969). My research was supported by a grant from the Research Committee of the University of Utah.

3. Kiyoaki Murata, "An Election Reform," *Japan Times*, May 14, 1982.

4. In the years from 1963 to 1972, the LDP was remarkably consistent in capturing lower house seats in all three district magnitudes. The party captured 61 percent of the seats in three-member districts, 59 percent of the seats in four-member districts, and 56 percent of the seats in five-member districts. The main rival, the JSP, won about 26 percent of the seats in each type of district over that period. See Nishihira Shigeki, *Nihon No Senkyo*.

5. In the 1980 elections the LDP officially endorsed 310 candidates, whereas the SP ran only 149. The JSP supported 129 candidates; Komeito, DSP, NLC, and the SDF ran 64, 50, 25, and 5 candidates, respectively, in carefully selected districts. Thus the LDP is seen by the voters as the only party that offers a sufficient number of candidates that it can govern without resort to coalition. The DSP's case is interesting in that its total vote percentage decreased in 1976 but its seat total increased. The explanation is simply that the party cut back on the number of official candidates, thus reducing its national total vote but also concentrating its resources in fewer districts. It was also during the 1976 election that all six parties were represented in only 10 of the 130 districts, and the "old five parties" were in competition in only 45 constituencies.

6. Changes in the Political Offices Control Law enacted in 1975 tripled the deposit money that a candidate must forfeit if he does not receive a certain percentage of the total votes cast in his district. The deposits are now 1 million yen (US$5,880) for house candidates and local district candidates for the upper house, whereas national constituency candidates must poll at least as many votes to equal one-fifth of the total obtained by dividing the total vote by the number of seats in the district. In 1980, 146 candidates lost their deposits, including 60 CP candidates. This deposit system is another method designed to limit the degree of competition in the Japanese elections.

7. The difficulties faced by the LDP in the national constituency can be demonstrated by the case of Miyata Teru, who won a seat with 2.59 million votes in 1974, although 7 LDP candidates with over 500,000 votes apiece failed to secure seats. The LDP is unable to regionally apportion its votes (as the JCP has done so successfully), but the JSP and DSP can use their affiliated labor unions or religious organizations (e.g., Komeito) to allocate their votes effectively.

8. For a study of the postwar small-district system and malapportionment in Japan, see Shimizu Keihachiro, *Sengo Nihon no Senkyo no Jittai* [The real picture of elections in postwar Japan] (Tokyo: Kokin Shoin, 1958).

9. *Asahi Shimbun,* December 8, 1976.

10. In 1980 the LDP won 33 percent of the vote in twenty-three metropolitan constituencies, followed by Komeito's 19 percent. The LDP's vote percentage in city, semiurban, semirural, and rural constituencies increased to 61 percent, 50 percent, 66 percent, and 70 percent, respectively. See *Mainichi Shimbun,* June 24, 1980.

11. According to the *Asahi Shimbun,* if the results of the 1980 HR general elections had been reapportioned on the basis of a plan suggested by the Kanagawa citizens' group, the estimated seat totals would have been as follows: LDP, 265; JSP, 102; CGP, 41; DSP, 32; CP, 36; NLC, 17; and SDF, 2. See *Asahi Shimbun,* January 16–18, 1981.

12. *Mainichi Shimbun,* February 2, 1990.

13. *Mainichi Shimbun,* February 10, 1990.

14. *Daily Yomiuri,* August 10, 1998.

15. *Yomiuri Shimbun,* August 19, 1982. The continuing malaportionment problems of the HC are discussed in *Asahi Shimbun,* July 14, 1998.

16. See the LDP's *Liberal Star* of September 10, 1980; the *Asahi Shimbun* editorial of July 31, 1980; and the *Daily Yomiuri* editorial of May 31, 1980.

17. See the *Mainichi Shimbun* editorial of July 4, 1982.

18. *Asahi Evening News,* July 15, 1982.

19. See Kohno, *Japan's Postwar Party Politics,* chap. 2. Also Raymond Christensen, "Electoral Reform in Japan," *Asian Survey* 34 (July 1994): 589–605. See also John Hickman, "The New Electoral System in the Japanese Lower House" (paper presented at the 1995 annual meeting of the American Political Science Association, Chicago, September 1995). For a discussion of the effects of the electoral reforms, see Sato Seizaburo, "LDP: The Failure of Electoral Reform," *Japan Echo* 24 (Spring 1997): 60–70.

20. Kawamura Toshi, "Intrigue and Background of Tanaka Cabinet," Toriyama Sadao, "LDP Plan Aimed at One Party Despotism," and "Parliamentary Democracy and Small Constituency System," *Zenei* (June 1973); Ito Shigeru, "For the Complete Crushing of the Minor Constituency System," *Shakaito* (July 1973).

21. Lucky winners are discussed in the various Japanese newspapers (*Asahi, Mainichi,* and *Yomiuri*) following the October 1996 HR elections.

22. The evolution of the campaign restrictions has been well reported by Gerald Curtis. The initial law after World War II allowed a party to engage in political activities during campaigns as long as those actions were not aimed at securing votes for the party's candidate. Revised in 1952 and 1954, the law prohibited all political party activities during the campaign period. Parties could legally participate in campaigns only as third parties, similar to voters. Another revision in 1962 made it possible for parties to participate in election campaigns to secure votes for candidates in general but not for a particular candidate. For example, a party could display posters announcing a speech by one of its candidates, but it could not mention the candidate on the poster. A more recent revision in 1975 significantly expanded the range of permissible party activities during the campaign period. If a party met certain minimum size requirements, it could display posters asking for support in an election. Restrictions on handbills were also liberalized. Party leaders may mention their candidates' names at speech meetings and endorse them. Parties can also advertise in newspapers and on TV and radio, but the names of specific candidates may not be mentioned. Gerald L. Curtis, *The Japanese Way of Politics* (New York: Columbia University Press, 1988), 161–166. The decisions regarding which days will be election days and how the voters will indicate their candidate preferences are uniquely Japanese. Election days fall on Sundays in Japan. Because Sunday is a holiday, primary and junior high schools can be used as voting sites; moreover, it is assumed that more citizens will be able to vote on a Sunday. But the choice of which Sunday is usually left up to the politicians. Frequently, the old Japanese lunar calendar is consulted to ascertain which Sundays are *taian* (lucky) days. Ironically, of the four Sundays considered for the 1980 elections, the LDP leaders reportedly favored July 13 over the actual election day of June 22, but they were forced to change the date after the vote of no confidence carried. See *Daily Yomiuri* (March 14, 1980). According to the pre-1994 election law, vacancies in the

HC were filled by a special election called within forty days after the prefectural Elections Administration Commission received notice of a vacancy resulting from death or resignation. Vacancies in the HR were not filled by special elections but are left vacant until the next HR general elections. Consequently, the HC by-elections were considered referenda on government performance and politics; for example, the Aichi prefecture HC special election in fall 1990 was considered a gauge of public opinion on the proposed sending of Japanese Self-Defense Forces to Saudi Arabia during the Kuwait crisis. When the LDP candidate failed to win a big victory over the JSP candidate who made the sending of troops her primary issue, this outcome and other political signs forced the government to abandon its plans. However, when the new single-seat constituency system went into effect for the 1996 HR elections, the use of by-elections also went into operation. The 300 districts now have only a single Diet member, if a vacancy occurs, a new Diet member must be appointed or else the district would not have any representation until the next general election. During the first two years following the 1996 elections, eight by-elections have been held, for an average of one every three months. Both the LDP and the Democratic Party have complained about the frequency and cost of such elections. Even though the LDP won all six of the by-elections held in late 1997 and 1998 (up to October), the party was ready to offer a bill to revise the elections law and allow such elections on a regular schedule. *Daily Yomiuri,* September 24, 1998.

23. Elections during the early Meiji period were often violent. Especially noteworthy were the elections of March 1894, in which 1 person was killed, 252 persons were wounded, and 1,015 cases of bribery were reported. See *Japan Times,* February 28, 1898.

24. Curtis notes that many of the campaign restrictions, such as the prohibition on canvassing, are ignored by a growing number of campaigners. There is no strong constituency for reform—among the parties or in the Home Ministry—because of the practice of widespread evasions. Curtis, *The Japanese Way of Politics,* 111.

25. See *Japan Times,* June 11, 1980; and *Asahi Evening News,* October 6, 1979.

26. *Asahi Shimbun,* June 17, 1998.

27. "Japan Tries Aggressive Campaigns," *New York Times,* October 17, 1996.

28. "The Attack of the Japanese Politicians," *Washington Post National Weekly Edition,* October 7, 1996.

29. Throughout the four years preceding the 1976 general elections, the police issued 24,400 warnings of illegal campaign activities. During the actual campaign period, 991 persons were arrested and 18 others were placed on a nationwide wanted list for election law violations. The police questioned 4,511 persons on suspicion of vote buying (the average cost per vote being between 2,000 and 3,000 yen, thus reflecting the recession occurring at the time), 281 for house-to-house visits, and 256 for illegal distribution of campaign literature.

30. *Mainichi Shimbun,* July 3, 1998.

three

The Money Base of Japanese Politics

Ronald J. Hrebenar

Ozaki Yukio, a Japanese writer in the early Showa era, once noted that "the leader of a party in our country must have five qualifications: one to four are money, and the fifth one is political ability."[1] More than fifty years later, it appears that very little has changed in the nature of Japanese politics. Money is still the crucial ingredient in political success. A great portion of the political activities of the major leaders of the various parties and factions is devoted to the raising of political funds. This activity became a very controversial issue in Japan as a result of what seems to be a constant series of political money scandals in which a large number of conservative politicians, including several prime ministers, were implicated. This chapter will examine the nature of political money *(seiji kenkin)* in Japan within the context of the law that purports to regulate this crucial activity—namely, the Political Funds Control Law (PFCL). It will also look at various fund-raising techniques in some detail and focus on the last major overhaul of the PFCL in an effort to understand the problems of political financing facing the party system.

THE POLITICAL FUNDS CONTROL LAW

As noted in previous chapters, the law that requires the reporting of various political funding activities is the Political Funds Control Law. The PFCL has been revised several times in recent decades, with the 1976 revision being the most extensive. The revisions of 1976, part of the larger election reform, were passed by the Diet after a bitter political battle that raged throughout the summer of 1975. The requirements for disclosure of the sources of political money were tightened by the revisions, and some of the major loopholes present in the old law were at least narrowed. Under the old law, for example, less than 20 percent of the funds collected by the five parties of the First Party System were identified by source in the 1975 midyear disclosures. Even this small percentage is misleading, for 78 percent of the Liberal Democratic Party (LDP) funds were obtained from a collection organization, Kokumin Seiji Kyokai (National Political Association), which serves merely as a funnel for collecting money from corporations for the LDP. Only 0.8 percent of the JCP funds, 0.3 percent of the JSP funds, and none of the Clean Government Party (CGP, or Komeito) funds were identified by sources.[2] The failure of disclosure becomes even more obvious when the LDP factional funding is examined. The major LDP factions led by Ohira Masayoshi, Miki Takeo, and Fukuda Takeo provided no reports on their sources of funds. In addition, whereas the old law allowed parties and factions to cover up sources of funds by listing them as party fees, subscriptions to party organs, or "on-the-street" contributions, the 1976 revisions required that all income and expenditures over 10,000 yen be reported. However, despite these reforms, the PFCL was still a law designed to hide much more than it revealed.

Each fall, the annual report on the nature of political fund-raising is released to the nation's media. Although this is the *official* report of the PFCL, in many respects it has borne, until the mid-1990s, little relationship to reality. At the same time as the major parties' incomes are reported, the official statements of political funding are released for several thousand other political organizations. These include the various LDP factional organizations, as well as the large "funnel" organizations that collect funds for the LDP and some of the other conservative parties. Overall, the various organizations reported the collection of the equivalent of almost $1.4 billion in political contributions in 1996 (1997 Report).[3] The huge amounts of money spent on Japanese politics must be put into perspective, however. Japanese business, for example, reported in the early 1990s that it spent $32 billion per year for entertainment and gifts (*kosaihi*) for employees and customers.

DISCLOSURES OF THE PFCL POLITICAL FUNDS REPORTS

The Japan Communist Party (JCP) ranked first in 1997 in fund-raising, as it has in almost every year's reports, followed by the LDP, Komeito, and the now defunct New Frontier Party (NFP).[4] Table 3.1 also provides the totals for the major "funnel" (fund-collecting) organizations of the LDP and the other new conservative parties. The funds from these organizations, which were donated to the parent parties, are included in the party totals in the upper half of the table.

TABLE 3.1   Party Revenue, 1997

Party	*Revenue (billions of yen)*
JCP	30.87
LDP	24.56
Komeito	13.33
New Frontier	10.88
Democratic	5.59
Social Democratic	4.55
Sakigake	.56
Rengo	.50
Liberal	.49

Party political fund-raising organizations, 1997 (millions of yen)

Kokumin Seiji Kyokai (LDP)	7023
(Shinshinto)	357
(Liberal)	84
(Democratic)	65
(Sakigake)	24

SOURCE: Home Affairs Ministry, Political Funds Control Law, 1998 Report (*Asahi Shimbun*, September 11, 1998).

Although many political critics contend that political fund reports are inaccurate in many significant ways, they can be useful in discerning general trends or patterns. Each of the major parties, for example, has a characteristic fund-raising pattern that tells us something about the nature of that party. The JCP's leading totals for the last dozen years certainly do not accurately reflect its fund-raising capabilities vis-à-vis the LDP. The JCP's totals (and those of the CGP as well) reflect income derived from party businesses. Because production costs are usually about 80 percent of declared income, one can estimate the JCP's real income at about 6 billion yen.[5] The LDP, whose reported income is just a headquarters income, vastly underreports its real income. In addition to 24 billion yen in party funds, the big five factions of the LDP reported funds collected at a total of 16 billion yen, and seven individual senior LDP politicians reported combined donations received of well over 2.8 billion yen. Yet however large these sums may seem, most political observers believe the real total income of the LDP could be as great as 500 percent more than reported.

Japan's major opposition party during the First Party System, the Social Democratic Party of Japan (SDPJ), reported receiving 4.5 billion yen. In constant financial trouble, the SDPJ is the one party that relies

TABLE 3.2   General Sources of Party Revenues, 1995 (in percent)

Party	Corporate Contributions	Party Dues	Business Income	Other	Subsidies
LDP	26.2	13.2	2.9	1.0	56.7
NFP	6.9	0.8	24.2	24.2	68.1
SDPJ	—	14.3	23.6	7.3	54.8
Sakigake	13.2	—	16.4	14.1	56.2

SOURCE: Home Affairs Ministry, Political Funds Control Law, 1996 Report.

most heavily on membership dues and also derives much of its income from the sale of party publications (see Table 3.2). For the most part Komeito's income is derived from party publications; almost all the remainder is accounted for by party member dues. The NFP's financial plight was so serious that it had to float loans for about one-quarter of its income in 1997.

Table 3.3 lists the LDP sources of revenue in 1995 by industries. Nearly one-quarter of the LDP's revenue came from the banking industry, longtime financial supporters of LDP. This represents a decline from the 33 percent levels the banks delivered to the LDP at the beginning of the 1990s. As a result of the continuing Japanese recession and the crisis of the Japanese banking community, it would have looked very bad for the banks to continue their heavy contributions to the LDP while begging the LDP-led government for trillions of yen to help them out of their insolvency.[6] In most years the construction and real estate indus-

TABLE 3.3   LDP Finance Sources, 1995

Industry	Total	Percent of LDP Funds
Banks	996	22.4
Automobiles	404	9.1
Electric/communications	290	6.5
Construction/real estate	255	5.7
Heavy industry/metals	130	2.9
Oil	123	2.8
Transport/railroads	116	2.6
Pharmaceutical	101	2.3
Stock/brokers	101	2.2
Others	1,930	43.4
Totals	4,446	—

SOURCE: Home Affairs Ministry, Political Funds Control Law, 1996 Report.

tries are represented in the top ranks of LDP contributors. Both are "well wired" with the LDP and the recipients of huge portions of the government's budget spending each year. It is interesting to note that major export industries such as automobiles and electronics are heavy LDP contributors in an era in which the United States is placing constant pressure on the Japanese government on the subject of imports and exports. Curtis noted that the pattern of corporate giving changed after 1975. Previous major supporters such as the steel industry declined as contributors, and new growth industries such as consumer electronics, securities and life insurance, and local banks grew in importance as fund sources.[7]

Fund-raising totals reported by the LDP factions during the First Party System must be viewed with some care. In the early 1980s, both the Fukuda Takeo and Nakasone Yasuhiro factions were reporting billion-yen incomes in an effort to impress LDP Diet members with their fund-raising powers and to win the prime ministership. The Komoto Toshio faction, one of the party's weaker factions, had been collecting large amounts of money for the party presidency race since 1978. The Tanaka faction, the LDP's most powerful and richest in the early 1980s, was reporting low levels of fund-raising as it sought to keep a low profile while Tanaka's legal problems continued. The Tanaka faction's senior Diet members were collecting large amounts of money, but they reported the amounts not by faction but by individual politicians.

Table 3.4 indicates the reported incomes of the five LDP factions for the 1997 period. The Obuchi faction, which emerged from former prime minister Takeshita's faction and is the financial successor of the former Tanaka faction, was rocked in the late 1980s by serious political funds scandals. After the Recruit Cosmos scandal toppled the Takeshita prime ministership in 1988, the Takeshita faction reported relatively small amounts of funds raised. However, by 1997, the Obuchi faction had regained the title as the LDP's strongest political funds collector. One

TABLE 3.4   **LDP Factional Fund-Raising, 1997 (in millions of yen)**

Rank	*Faction*	*Donations received*
1	Obuchi	5,450
2	Mitsuzuka	4,211
3	Watanabe	3,769
4	Miyazawa	1,666
5	Komoto	1,387

SOURCE: Political Funds Control Law, 1998 Report (*Yomiuri Shimbun*, September 11, 1998).

can see the Obuchi faction is far ahead of the nearly tied Mitsuzuka and Watanabe factions, and all three are significantly ahead of the financially weak Miyazawa and Komoto factions.

As the previous discussion indicates, large sums of political funds are raised by individual senior leaders in the various factions. Table 3.5 displays the top ten individual politician fund-raisers in 1997. Seven of the ten are LDP members, and the other three are former LDP members who have defected from the party and become leaders of new conservative parties in the mid-1990s. The list also identifies those LDP Diet members who are considered by many as potential prime ministers or party presidents. Heading the list in 1989 was the future prime minister Hashimoto Ryutaro, who was the LDP secretary-general in 1989. The LDP secretary-general is in the perfect position for fund-raising and is considered a "crown prince" for selection to the prime ministership. One sure way of being mentioned as having the qualities needed for party leadership is to have clearly demonstrated the skills of a very successful money raiser. A similar list from 1984 contained the names of all the current faction leaders.[8]

Finally, Table 3.6 presents the reported political contributions of Japanese corporations in 1997. Listed are those businesses ranking among the top ten in terms of total political donations. When the list is compared with the 1984 political funds report, banks replaced Japan's heavy industries as the financial godfathers of LDP fund-raising efforts by 1990 but disappeared by the 1997 report. In 1984 Nippon Steel and Mitsubishi Heavy Industries were the second- and fourth-ranked con-

TABLE 3.5   Political Funds Collected by Individual Politicians, 1997 (in millions of yen)

Rank	*Politician*	*Party/Faction*	*Donations Received*
1	Kato Koichi	Miyazawa	473.78
2	Ozawa Ichiro	NFP	415.86
3	Yamazaki Taku	Watanabe	413.37
4	Mori Yoshiro	Mitsuzuka	407.65
5	Kamei Shizuka	Mitsuzuka	329.49
6	Obuchi Keizo	Obuchi	308.07
7	Hata Tsutomu	NFP	213.18
8	Hashimoto Ryutaro	Obuchi	198.26
9	Hatoyama Ikuo	Democratic	166.39
10	Miyazawa Kiichi	Miyazawa	158.30

SOURCE: Political Funds Control Law, 1998 Report (*Yomiuri Shimbun*, September 11, 1998).

TABLE 3.6   Major Corporate Political Funds Contributors to Parties, 1997
(in millions of yen)

Rank	Corporation	Total Contributions	To Parties Funded
1	Toyota (2)	6,900	L,S,M,J,SG
2	NEC (4)	4,800	L,S
3	Nissan (4)	3,910	L,S,M,J,SG
4	Mitsubishi Automobile (13)	3,780	L,S,M,J,SG
5	Toshiba (6)	3,762	L
6	Hitachi (6)	3,762	L
7	Matsushita Electric (9)	3,550	L
8	Japan Steel (17)	3,300	L,S
9	Honda (17)	3,290	L,S,M,J,SG
10	Isuzu (23)	3,110	L,S,M,J,SG

NOTE: L = Liberal Democratic Party (Jiminto); S = New Frontier Party (Shinshinto); M = Democatic Party (Minshuto); J = Liberal Party (Jiyuto); SG = New Pioneer Party (Sakigake).

SOURCE: Home Affairs Ministry, Political Funds Control Law, 1998 Report (*Asahi Shimbun,* September 11, 1998).

tributors. Five years later, in 1990, all of the top twelve and nineteen of the top thirty-five corporate contributors to the LDP were banks. Of the top thirty-five corporations and banks in 1990, all but three gave money to both the LDP and the DSP. It was significant that during the First Party System corporate contributions were overwhelmingly in favor of the LDP; only small contributions, largely symbolic, were made to the DSP, which was considered a "safety value" party by corporate Japan. In 1997 the major export industries represented nearly every spot on the corporate donor list. Five of the ten gave money to each of the five major conservative political parties, while the other five made contributions to only the LDP or the LDP and the small Sakigake splinter party, which had been part of the governmental coalition in 1997.

One hundred and fifty billion yen represents a huge amount of money—more than $1 billion at the 130 yen to $1 exchange rate of 1997. Even if the PFCL report contains an accurate portrayal of Japanese political financing, the implications would be disturbing—but according to many informed observers, these figures still represent only one-third to one-fourth of the real totals. Just what was there about Japanese party politics during the First Party System that required such enormous amounts of money? I will turn to that question in the next section.

AN EXPENSIVE STYLE OF POLITICS

The financial restrictions incorporated into the Japanese election laws described in the previous chapter might lead one to anticipate that elections would be very inexpensive in Japan. But the reality of the situation is just the reverse. The government has attempted to reduce the costs of elections both by subsidizing the cost of campaigns and by prohibiting certain types of campaign activities.[9] In the 1975 election law revision package, the government increased its direct subsidy to Japanese parties and candidates by paying every candidate the costs of using an election campaign automobile, printing posters, and placing five advertisements in newspapers, in addition to the free franking privileges for two campaign leaflets per candidate. Yet, upon examining the total picture of a Japanese campaign, we find that these campaign subsidies and restrictions have not controlled the problem of extraordinarily expensive elections. What has been accomplished is the designation of most campaign expenses as illegal.

Although all parties must raise funds to compete in elections and to maintain their party organizations, the problem was especially acute for the Liberal Democratic Party during the First Party System. The Socialist parties, the JSP and DSP, relied on their labor union supporting organizations to carry their efforts, and the JCP and Komeito have their efficient grassroots organizations. Clearly, the conservative party has the greatest need to resort to money politics. Consequently, in the discussions of money politics prior to 1996 in the remainder of this chapter, the references (unless otherwise noted) are to the LDP or conservative independent candidates and their financial practices.

Candidates for the Japanese Diet are, by law, limited to a certain maximum level of campaign expenditures. This limit is usually computed on the basis of a flat sum plus so many additional yen per voter in the constituency. But the limit was almost universally ignored by candidates, and the disclosure reports to the Home Affairs Ministry were usually carefully falsified. Particularly among LDP and JSP candidates, it was a tradition to send in a disclosure report listing expenditures slightly under the legal limits while actually spending many times the reported amount. Yet no member of the Diet has ever been prosecuted or denied a seat because of these practices. The 1977 House of Councillors (HC) election imposed a 21-million-yen limit on expenditures, but incumbent JSP member Sasaki Shizuko from Osaka announced that she would not seek reelection because she could not raise the 100 million yen needed to finance a "bare-bones" campaign. In the national constituency, 500 million yen ($1.7 million) was considered a necessity for a successful 1974 campaign; by the 1980 election, that figure had risen to 700 million yen. These extremely costly campaigns were a direct result both of the use of the medium-sized constituency system in HC prefectural district elections and of the severe burden placed on national constituency candidates to build a successful campaign in a nationwide election district prior to 1983. After 1983, the introduction of the proportional representation (PR) national constituency did sharply reduce the cost of these PR list campaigns.

With respect to the lower house races, insiders have estimated that any incumbent needed at least 40 million yen to retain his or her seat prior to 1996 but that most spend at least 100 million yen, whereas a newcomer needed at least twice that figure.[10] As a former LDP construction minister once noted, "You cannot win an election unless you spend about 100 million [yen] during the six months just before the election is called, and more than 100 million [yen] during the official campaign period."[11] A candidate can incur significant expenses during these precampaign periods. Many politicians held periodic preelection speech meetings, which cost 3 to 5 million yen each. Five to ten of these meetings were held in an election year, for a total cost of 30 to 50 million yen.[12]

Being a Diet member can be a very expensive occupation. In 1989 the *Asahi Shimbun* ran a series of articles on the expenses associated with such a career in politics. A survey discovered that the average LDP Diet member or his or her representative attended over thirty ceremonies, receptions, or funerals each month. One Tokyo member claimed to have "attended" over three hundred such events on the average each month. In addition, politicians are expected to attend seasonal parties, and about one in every six reported attending over two hundred such parties a year. Each of these events requires a "gift" or contribution from the politician: funerals 10,000 yen ($76), weddings 30,000 yen. The average LDP Diet member claimed to spend about 1 million yen per year on parties. When class reunions and store openings in a member's district are added, the *Asahi Shimbun* noted that for the average Diet member, such political costs were a little less than 100 million yen per year.[13] Diet members received slightly over 18 million yen per year in salary and bonuses ($140,000). The government pays for only two secretaries, but most members hire more than two.

With a significant gap between government-provided money and the political expenditures of the office, the typical LDP Diet member must find money from other sources. The *Asahi Shimbun*'s survey noted that about 39 percent of these funds came from corporate contributions, 17 percent from fund-raising parties, 15 percent from individual contributions,

12 percent from the government salary or subsidies, 9 percent from the member's factional leader, and 8 percent from loans.[14]

Elections were most expensive when the LDP or conservative independent candidates were in conflict within the same constituency. In such cases, which occurred in all 130 constituencies during the pre-1996 HR elections, the real battle was among the conservatives, not between the conservatives and opposition parties.[15] In the most extreme cases, these conflicts resulted in an ever-escalating pattern of money politics and even vote-buying. In the 1979 HR elections, for instance, the race in Chiba's second constituency drew the media's attention because of widespread charges of vote-buying by the conservative candidates. As described by the press, the political culture of the second district was one in which all candidates are expected to buy votes. LDP Diet member Toru Uno was subsequently charged with spending 260 million yen to buy approximately 110,000 votes at 2,000 yen per vote. Some reports indicate that all three conservatives paid for many of their votes. On the HC level, another conservative candidate's regional campaign manager was convicted of vote-buying during the 1974 elections, when he paid 21 million yen to local campaigners in fifteen western prefectures.

The LDP gave to each of its 311 official candidates in the 1986 lower house elections a maximum of 30 million yen. All of its candidates received 5 million yen each, and those who had previously served in a cabinet received another 5 million. "Backbenchers" (those without cabinet service) received a maximum of 5 million yen from the party. In a special grant, members from a constituency in which the number of seats had been reduced for the 1986 elections received a maximum of 30 million yen.[16] The LDP in 1990 collected enough money that it allocated 25 million yen for each of the endorsed incumbents through the factional bosses.

Various sources estimate that the LDP and its candidates spent more than 200 billion yen ($1.3 billion) in campaigning for the 1990 lower house elections.[17] The LDP was much better prepared financially for these elections because it was able to instill a sense of crisis into its fundraising that was based largely on the JSP victories in the 1989 HC elections. The business world responded—for example, Keidanren chairman Saito declared total support for the LDP in terms of fund-raising and voter mobilization. In order to evade the limits on corporate donations, a system of bank loans was secured in 1990 based on the expected contributions from individual corporations over a three-year period. The LDP asked its business allies for 20 billion yen in loans; the nine leading city banks provided 12 billion yen of that total by themselves. It was reported that the LDP used its Tokyo headquarters building as collateral.[18] Finally, one must remember that the LDP holds periodic internal campaigns for the post of party president, who, of course, also serves as prime minister of Japan. This internal conflict among the major factional leaders requires the organizational and financial support of hundreds of thousands of potential voters among the paying members, but for many the dues are paid by one of the factional leaders. All in all, conservative politics during the First Party System has been expensive politics.

FUND-RAISING IN JAPAN

Each of the six political parties in the First Party System had its own special fund-raising methods. By and large the two Socialist parties (SDPJ and the DSP) relied on their supporting labor union federations for the bulk of their funds. Both the SDPJ and the DSP counted on former Sohyo and Domei labor confederations for about 400 to 500 million yen, respectively, during an HR campaign. The DSP also received a substantial portion of its funding from corporations and other organizations that also gave larger amounts to the LDP. Komeito and the JCP raise less money but have the best grassroots organizations in the nation. The JCP claims that nearly 90 percent of its funds are raised by selling party publications, including *Akahata*, its daily newspaper.

My primary focus in this context, given the sheer magnitude involved, must necessarily be directed to the LDP's fund-raising techniques. The primary source of LDP funds during the First Party System was "corporate Japan." During the late 1970s, Japanese business gave an officially reported total of about 9 billion yen per year to the LDP. Again, this is the official figure derived from the PFCL reports, but it is also only "the tip of the iceberg."[19] In addition, an estimated three to four times that total is transferred from the business community to factional leaders and politicians during a given year. The LDP established a special organization, Kokumin Seiji Kyokai, to facilitate the collection of corporate money for the LDP.

Politicians, mostly conservatives, have developed ingenious methods to raise funds—often by evading the spirit, if not the intent, of the PFCL. One technique adopted from the United States in the mid-1970s is the fund-raising party, which is a technique used most frequently by the conservatives. During a time prior to an anticipated election, such fund-raisers are scheduled nearly every day. Even as small a party as the NLC managed to raise 295 million yen by holding nine such parties. Contributions to fund-raising parties are often provided by corporations. In December 1980 Prime Minister Suzuki gave a speech at a party in Osaka where 2,000 businessmen gave 50,000 yen each, for a total of

100 million yen. On the average, a successful fund-raising party can bring 20 million yen to a politician's coffers, and an especially influential politician can expect to raise 50 million yen. And on June 20, 1985, a fund-raising party was held for LDP Vice President Nikaido Susumu at the Hotel New Otani. An estimated 8,000 supporters attended the affair, which was sponsored by the Mokuyo Club of the Tanaka faction, and over 30,000 tickets priced at 30,000 yen each were sold to raise an estimated 900 million yen—a record at the time for the most money raised at a single Diet member's fund-raiser. These fund-raising parties have become so important for the LDP that during the 1980s, often one-third to one-half of some of the LDP factions' political funds were raised at them.

As rumors of a pending House of Representatives (HR) election begin to circulate, the major Tokyo hotels are booked up by politicians reserving space for fund-raising parties. Prices for a single ticket to such a party honoring or encouraging a politician are often in the 50,000-yen range. Even on the prefectural level, parties are significant fund-raisers. Sometimes, major corporations will buy up to 1,000 tickets at a price of 10,000 yen per ticket.

An understanding of the political accounting of these fund-raising parties is instructive. According to the PFCL, in the pre-1995 period, politicians were not required to report "party earnings," although the Home Affairs Ministry urged them to do so.

If the fund-raising party is sponsored by a political organization (*seiji dantai*), the organization must report the funds raised. The LDP tends to report only about half of these parties and the fund-raising.[20] Among the opposition parties, the JCP and CGP do not hold fund-raising parties. The SDPJ's parties are almost always held in the election districts and are almost never reported to the Home Ministry. Many DSP parties are held, but the accounting for these parties is seldom reported.[21]

Under the PFCL, moreover, contributions to individual politicians are either retained under the politicians' personal control, donated to a designated political organization, or channeled automatically into support groups. If the last course is followed, the money need not be reported. Of the 887 reporting politicians in 1981, 604 did just this; another 191 used the designated organizations method; and only 92 retained control of the money.[22]

Scandals in recent decades have exposed some of the "kickback" practices in which needed money is delivered to conservative politicians. Matsuno Raizo, a former director general of the Defense Agency, admitted he had received 500 million yen from Nissho-Iwai Company between 1967 and 1971. Much money seemed to flow to LDP politicians as "gifts" for services they have performed. Japan is a society in which gift-giving and money-giving are commonplace upon introductions or requests for assistance from other more senior or prestigious people. This custom is especially prevalent in politics. One former cabinet minister from the Tanaka faction noted, "Whether or not you are able to persuade a government department to do something you want is directly related to your ability to raise political funds." Another Tanaka HR member told the *Asahi Shimbun* that "politicians now say 'I will arrange for you to get your contract and you will give me 1 million [yen].'" When Ito Hiroshi, former managing director of the great Marubeni trading company, decided to give Prime Minister Tanaka some money when he asked for Tanaka's assistance on airplane sales to All-Nippon Airlines, the decision made was that 500 million yen seemed appropriate.[23]

Although construction industries are legally prohibited from contributing to governmental officials, many make substantial regular contributions based on a percentage of the contracts they are awarded.[24] Other associations, such as the Japanese Federation of Tax Accountants Association, made substantial contributions to both LDP and opposition Diet members while a revision to a tax accountant law was in the Diet. Some politicians were paid up to 500,000 yen in the way of "transportation fees" prior to the 1979 general elections.[25]

One of the interesting coincidences in the Japanese economy is the sharp rise that occurs in the Tokyo stock market prior to nearly every election. A traditional method of fund-raising involves providing politicians with inside information on stock market transactions and then permitting the market to be manipulated by brokers to provide "quick-in-quick-out" transactions guaranteeing quick profits for the politicians. One such stock doubled in value within ten days in the year prior to the 1979 elections, only to return to its original price twenty days later.[26] Some politicians are offered land at extremely low prices and through low-cost loans; then, when quick funding is needed for an election, the land will be purchased by corporations at extremely inflated prices. The result in such cases is a large, unofficial campaign contribution.

The Kokusai Denshin Denwa (KDD) scandal provided some insight into two of the more bizarre methods of transferring corporate money to campaigns. KDD apparently persuaded art dealers to buy back art items sold to KDD for far in excess of the purchase price, whereupon the politicians converted the "gifts" to cash, and KDD paid the difference. Most of these gifts were made to Diet members connected with the Posts and Telecommunications Ministry, the supervising ministry of KDD. The

KDD was charged with compensating art dealers who purchased the name cards of politicians at prices of up to 1 million yen per card. The name cards were addressed to top KDD officials, who later purchased inexpensive paintings priced at several million yen apiece. The difference was an unreported contribution to the politician.[27]

REFORMING THE PFCL: 1975 AND 1994

On November 3, 1975, representatives of Japan's conservative LDP and the nation's largest corporations and banks announced an agreement to collect political money totaling 5.2 billion yen ($17 million) from the business community and donate it to the conservative party of Prime Minister Miki Takeo before January 1, 1976. As in the past, the total amount was to be divided among various business organizations, such as the Iron and Steel Federation and the Federation of Bankers Association in Japan. Then individual corporations were assessed their portion according to such criteria as capitalization and recent earnings. Subsequently, the quota of the Automobile Manufacturers Association was reported to have been set at 500 million and that for the less prosperous Shipbuilders Association of Japan at 150 million, whereas the Bankers and the Iron and Steel federations were assigned to collect 500 million yen each. The real significance of the announcement was to signal to all concerned that the Liberal Democrats and big business had done their penance following the 1974 election scandals, and that they were returning to "business as usual" in *seiji kenkin*—that is, money politics.[28] It was also a valuable piece of evidence for understanding the financial relationship between the LDP and corporate Japan. The former desperately needs the money from the latter, which desperately needs access to the party, which has ruled Japan since 1955 and makes the policies that can mean huge financial windfalls to the various businesses of Japan.

The setting for the reforms in the PFCL in 1975 were the 1974 HC elections. The national constituency (before the PR reforms in the 1980s) of the HC was a very expensive election site for the LDP, and the party was compelled to turn to business for additional assistance in what it viewed to be a critical election in 1974. The corporations were also asked to adopt specific candidates and to sponsor their campaigns, and some corporations ultimately functioned as political organizations, providing money, organization, meetings, contacts, and votes for their candidates. Direct corporate sponsorship was a logical extension of the role played by business as the financial godfather of the LDP. For instance, the huge Mitsubishi company was asked to sponsor a little-known former

bureaucrat named Saka Ken for an anticipated easy victory. A Saka supporters' organization *(koenkai)* was formed and staffed entirely by
Mitsubishi personnel, and Saka was packaged and marketed to the public much like hundreds of other Mitsubishi products. In addition,
Hitachi, the electronics giant, sponsored a female television model
named Santo Akiko; the *Asahi Shimbun* reported that Hitachi management had pressured retail store outlets, employees, and subcontractors
to support the Santo candidacy.

Tremendous amounts of money were spent both by the LDP and by
corporate supporters of the sponsored candidates. However, the strategy
backfired when the Japanese media began to explore the unique role
played by the corporate "parties." The adverse public reaction ultimately spelled the failure of several of these corporate candidates,
including the "unbeatable" Saka, to win seats.[29]

The LDP had successfully weathered other electoral storms during
the 1967–1974 era without being forced beyond vague promises to
reform its methods of political financing. Each time, a reform bill was
allowed to die in the Diet when the LDP sensed that the public's attention had drifted to other subjects. However, the 1974 scandals proved to
require more than the usual conservative reaction to demands for
reform. The hue and cry of the opposition parties, mass media, and certain articulate sectors of the general public forced the LDP and its business allies into a masterful performance of symbolic politics.

Correctly evaluating the initial intensity of demand for positive steps
toward reform, the LDP and the business community offered the first
gesture of response. The president of the most powerful business organization, Keidanren, announced that it would no longer assess its member
corporations for political donations to the National Association
(Kokumin Kyokai), an organization whose sole purpose was to funnel
business money into the coffers of the LDP. Other corporate giants followed the Keidanren lead, and the electric companies, the iron and steel
industry, and the banks all announced that they would suspend pay-
ments to the LDP until effective reforms were implemented.

The National Association, the recipient of so many billions of yen in
donations to the LDP over the years, was now tainted. It was reorganized out of existence and replaced by a "new image" organization
called the National Political Association (Kokumin Seiji Kyokai). The
crowning touch was the selection of the respected former head of NHK
(the national public broadcasting corporation), Maeda Yoshinori, as
chairman of the new organization. Maeda came to the chairmanship
with many interesting ideas on how to reform the processes by which
political funds were collected by the parties. For example, he proposed

that the new organization funnel money not only to the LDP but also to other Japanese political parties. Maeda, who saw the new organization as the possible model for a system of funding to the nation's parties based primarily on contributions from individuals, proposed that the new National Political Association establish its financial base on the small donations from 600,000 individuals rather than on the concentrated wealth of the corporate giants.

Eventually the LDP settled on a plan for political money reform and introduced it into the HR. The new plan included a series of graduated steps that allowed a large corporation to give up to 100 million yen per year—500 percent higher than the figure specified in an earlier plan. In addition, the limit on donations to a faction or an individual candidate not requiring specific reporting was raised from 600,000 to 1 million yen.

The LDP "reform revision" essentially made legal and legitimate various practices that had received heavy criticism during the previous year. Financial conduits such as the National Association, created to collect and donate billions of yen to the LDP, were now legalized, and each political party was allowed to designate one such organization to handle its fund-raising activities. Corporate contributions were completely legalized and thus legitimized; even de facto quotas were established, thus probably making it more difficult for corporations to avoid giving financial support to the LDP. The annual ceiling for political contributions by companies whose capitalization exceeds 5,000 million yen was 30 million yen; for those between 1,000 million and 5,000 million yen, it was 15 million yen; and for those capitalized under 1,000 million yen, it was 7.5 million yen. But for the growing number of giant corporations, the ceiling rose 5 million yen for each 5,000 million yen in capitalization over 10,000 million yen, to a maximum of 100 million yen. Labor unions were given ceilings based on total membership; unions claiming over 100,000 members are allowed to contribute a total of 30 million yen; then the limits gradually fall, ending in those smaller unions of fewer than 50,000 members, which cannot give more than 1.5 million in a single year.

These so-called restrictions are a very light burden for the LDP business alliance to bear. Nippon Steel, with capital funds of over 230,000 million yen, is limited to a total contribution of 100 million yen to parties and another 50 million yen to factions and other organizations. When Nippon Steel Corporation complained to the *Mainichi Shimbun* that it used to give between 2 billion and 2.5 billion yen per year in political donations and now was limited to only 150 million yen per year because of the PFCL, Takeuchi Kiyoshi, an LDP HC member, said, "Money collection means went underground."[30] Mitsubishi and Fuji Bank contributions to parties are "restricted" to only 78 million yen per year. Given that in 1974 the National Association received 400 million yen each from the Tokyo Bankers Association and the Japan Steel Association, the restriction that the LDP imposed on itself did not seem to be the cause of much discomfort for the conservatives. As President Nagano Shigeo of the Japan Chamber of Commerce and Industry reflected on December 8, 1975, "This [revision law] means that the LDP will have to collect relatively small amounts from a larger number of companies."[31] In order to effectively broaden its financial base, the LDP announced in December 1975 the creation of the Jiyu Seiji Renmei (Free Politics League), whose purpose is to serve as a fund-raising body among medium-sized and small businesses. For some time, the LDP has been concerned about the JCP inroad into the smaller Japanese businesses and, hence, the amount of political funds being collected by the Communist Party organ, Minsho.[32]

For the 1974 elections, the LDP borrowed money from banks in exchange for promissory notes usually signed by the party secretary-general and later repaid by the nation's corporations, each of which was allotted a share of the total cost. However, following the 1974 elections, the flow of business contributions ceased almost completely, and the party was not able to pay off its loans. The conservatives had to clear past debts before they could begin to prepare for the next election. And, because the revision of the PFCL would not go into effect until January 1976, there was still time to appeal to their old business allies for sufficient funds to pay off the old debt. One-half of the debt was allocated to the large business associations. But the problem of the second 5 billion yen proved more difficult. At first, the suggestion was made that the banks could merely write off the sum as a bad debt or, perhaps more politically, as a contribution. On December 13, 1974, however, Prime Minister Miki announced that the several party factions would be asked to pay off the 5 billion yen.[33] Of course, the LDP factions receive their funds from exactly the same source as their party—the business community.

The LDP tried a series of *seikei bunka paatii* (political, economic, and cultural parties—the Japanese version of the $100-a-plate political dinner) in major cities during that year, and it grossed several hundred million yen. A young Tokyo LDP Diet member attempted a fund-raiser with many television personalities and managed to attract over 10,000 citizens, who paid 700 yen each to attend the event. But after all the expenses were deducted, only 1 million yen were left.[34]

The LDP strategy of symbolic response to the demands for reform was completely successful. The tactic of suspending corporate contributions, the creation of a "reformed" new funding channel with a "reform" image figurehead leader, the selection of a "clean" prime minister, and the highly publicized revision of the political funds law, in combination with a series of announcements of new fund-raising ideas, had "poured oil on troubled waters" and allowed the LDP to ride out the storm with little long-term damage.

The 1974 revisions to the PFCL have significantly reduced the pressure to solve the continuing problems of political finance in Japan. Many of the problems have been legitimized by the revisions, and the public appears to be satisfied with the reforms, at least for the moment.

The LDP has adapted well to the 1975 restrictions. Keidanren officials estimated that it gave the LDP 15 billion yen for the 1980 elections and noted that "there are a lot of corporate and industry associations that have not yet reached the donation ceiling set by the PFCL."[35] Member corporations could make an aggregate donation of 25 billion yen every year if each member corporation was willing to make its maximum donation. Leading corporate contributors to the LDP during the 1980s continued to be the banking, construction, steel, and electric power industries.

Among "corporate Japan's" political contributions of 49 billion yen during 1984, almost 300 million yen were donated to the opposition parties. Nevertheless, the LDP received more than 90 percent of the business world's monetary gifts to parties. The Japanese Medical and Dental Associations gave a combined 1 billion yen. And the political contributions from other economic sectors included 1.22 billion yen from the commercial banks (36 percent of the total political money raised in 1984); 450 million yen from the steel and machine industries (13 percent); and 380 million yen from the electrical machinery/telecommunications industries (11 percent).

By 1985 the LDP was still able to fund its lower house campaigns by floating large bank loans and then paying them off over a three-year period—ironically, with the help of large contributions from the banking community. Corporate Japan still feels restricted by the limits on how much a corporation may give in political contributions in a reporting year, and both the LDP and the business sector would like to liberalize that part of the law. The business sector would also like to do away with the heavy schedule of fund-raising parties that has resulted from the limitations on corporate contributions. Because the opposition parties are strongly opposed to any such revisions, significant change in the near future is unlikely.

As the required 1981 review of the PFCL approached, money critics of the law noted that major loopholes still existed. No one was required to report donations of less than 1 million yen per year. Many politicians have established multiple supporting organizations to collect as many of these smaller donations as possible. Conservative politicians, in particular, use multiple fund-raising organizations to conceal the sources of their funds. For instance, Kato Mutsuki, of the Tanaka faction, used an organization named Jozankai to raise 147 million yen in 1980. No names of the companies giving money were reported by this group. However, other fund-raising organizations used by Kato reported the following: (1) Seikei Kondankai (Political and Economic Discussion Council): 500,000 yen from the head of the Tokyo Metropolitan Truck and Bus Association; (2) Sogo Seikei Konwakai (Overall Political and Economic Discussion Club): 1.4 million yen from Nippon Express Co.; and (3) Kindai Kotsu Seisaku Kenkyukai (Modern Transportation Policy Research Council): 1 million yen each from the Aichi and Osaka Truck and Bus Political Leagues.

Politicians seem to love these lofty names for their fund-raising organizations. Nikaido Susumu, one of the leaders of the former Tanaka faction and LDP secretary-general under both Suzuki and Nakasone, included the following among his fund-raising groups: Group 21, New Century Planning Research Council, Japan National Land Planning Council, and the New Foreign Policy Research Council. These and other such groups collected a total of 120 million yen in 1980, but no corporate names were disclosed.[36] More significantly, individual politicians are not required to make public the means by which they acquired a political donation or expended it.

The bill requiring all political organizations to report collections and expenditures died in the 1980 Diet session. Indeed, it was unclear how money raised by political fund-raising parties was accounted for under the current law. Finally, under the PFCL, only those politicians actually receiving illicit donations are punishable, and the politicians' aides are the only ones prosecuted, as in the Fujima Hospital scandal in 1980. By early 1981 the LDP, feeling confident following its victory in the 1980 double elections, figured it was time to consider rolling back some of the restrictions placed in the 1975 revisions. The LDP's Election System Study Committee recommended raising the ceilings for corporate contributions to parties, increasing individual contribution limits, and lowering ceilings for contributions in election years.

THE RECRUIT COSMOS SCANDAL

An earthshaking scandal involving Recruit Cosmos, a property holding company, exploded in 1988–1989 and demonstrated the magnitude of funds that could be collected by politicians with influence. The president of Recruit, Ezoe Hiromasa, sought to buy political access for his relatively new set of companies through massive political funds contributions and sweetheart stock deals to key governmental personnel. Recruit also bought many tickets for key politicians' fund-raising parties, in one such case contributing 14 million yen to the "reform" prime minister, Kaifu Toshiki. Finally, the Recruit company loaned its employees to politicians to use during election campaigns.

Prime Minister Takeshita admitted that in the months prior to assuming office he received 151 million yen ($1.6 million) from Recruit in preissue stock shares in Recruit Cosmos, which was about to be traded on the Tokyo Stock Market, and in the purchase of tickets to his fund-raising parties. Takeshita later admitted that he received another 50 million yen ($381,000) from Recruit that he had forgotten to report. Over 1.3 billion yen ($10 million) in total was donated to a variety of politicians by the Recruit company.

Takeshita and four LDP cabinet ministers were forced to leave the government. More than a dozen people were arrested, including two former vice ministers and the former chairman of Nippon Telegraph and Telephone. All of the major LDP faction leaders except Komoto were involved in the scandal in one way or another. Additionally, this scandal was unique because major opposition party politicians were also the recipients of Recruit money; both DSP leader Tsukamoto Saburo and CGP chairman Yano Jun'ya had to resign their party chairmanships. The personal secretaries of Abe and Miyazawa resigned, and Takeshita's secretary took his own life when the scandal began to envelop his boss.

Kuroda and Miyagawa suggest that the Recruit scandal was the most important of the many political funds scandals of the postwar era. Among its direct outcomes were the 1989 upper house defeat of the LDP; the rising sense of ethical standards that toppled not only Takeshita but also his successor, Uno Sosuke, in 1990; and the perception that the LDP was vulnerable for the first time to losing control of the reins of government on the national level. The scandal also showed many how "lobbying" in Japan was accomplished when special interests lacked normal access to the decision-making networks of the LDP, bureaucracy, and favored interest groups.[37]

Along with the proposed reforms of the national HR election system, the Election System Council in 1990 also recommended a series of reforms to the political finance laws. One proposal was that each Diet member be limited to only one fund-raising committee in his or her home district and one in Tokyo, and that all donations under 1 million yen would not have to be reported, a measure specifically addressing the pattern of Diet members having several fund-raising committees and using them to collect many small contributions from the same person or corporation, thus evading the requirement that all donations over 1 million yen be reported to the government. The council also recommended that Diet members be required to list all donors by name for contributions over 10,000 yen to committees other than the two proposed. A ban on the giving of money by corporations and unions to any organizations other than political parties seeking seats in the Diet was also suggested. Finally, the committee urged that when a secretary of a Diet member is found guilty of violating the PFCL, the member would lose his or her Diet seat and be banned from running for the Diet for a period of five years.[38] As of early 1991, these proposals were still being debated, and it was quite uncertain whether these or and reforms would be implemented.

THE 1994 REFORMS

Throughout most of the 1980s and early 1990s, there has been nearly constant discussion regarding the need to reform the PFCL. The changes, which were made in the wake of the Recruit Cosmos scandal of 1988, included providing for greater transparency of the political fundraising process, including the new requirement that each politician had to use a single fund-raising organization. The reformed PFCL went into effect in January 1995. One part of the reform package was the passage of the Law of Public Finance of Political Parties, which provided for governmental subsidies for the major parties.

In terms of sources of political money collected by Japan's parties in 1997, the role of government subsidies must be emphasized. In the case of the LDP, the government subsidy represented more than half the money collected by the party. The LDP's other sources of funds were business income (1 billion yen), dues (2.5 billion yen), individual contributions (300 million yen), and corporate contributions from the party's fund-raising organization (5 billion yen).[39] The other major parties must rely heavily on the governmental subsidies for much of their incomes. The now defunct Shinshinto Party led by Ozawa and Hata generated nearly 90 percent of its income from governmental funding in 1997. The Democratic Party's governmental subsidy accounted for a lower percentage of its total income (50 percent), but it also had to borrow about 40 percent of its funds. The SDPJ obtained half its income from the subsidies and another quarter from sales of its party newspaper. The governmental subsidies for the two largest political parties for 1998 were LDP, 15.2 billion yen; Democratic Party, 6.38 billion yen.[40] The amount of the subsidy depends on the number of Diet seats held by a party and the number of votes it received in the most recent election in either house. Parties must have at least five members of the Diet as party members, or they must have secured at least 2 percent of the popular votes in the most recent election. The first year of the governmental subsidies for political parties resulted in more than the equivalent of $272 million dollars in party aid. This amount divided by the total Japanese population means that each citizen effectively contributed about $227 to their parties.[41]

The post-1994 reforms in the laws governing political finance changed several of the reporting requirements. Donations of more than 50,000 yen have to be reported and disclosed. The old law had a 1-million-yen threshold for reporting. The change resulted in the disclosure of over 80 percent of donations, compared with only 4 percent in 1994. The change went into effect for the 1995 year, and the first disclosures were made in the 1996 annual report. Another change required that each politician establish a single fund-collecting organization instead of the many such organizations used by politicians in past years.

Nineteen ninety-five was also the first year of the new governmental subsidies for political parties. The idea behind the adoption of subsidies was that governmental money could be an effective substitute for corporate contributions. Corporate donations are now limited to 500,000 yen to a given politician through a political fund management organization or to a party. There is also a new limit to the total amount of money a corporation can donate in a given year. Private companies are now permitted to give a total of 50 million yen to these management organizations. In addition, corporations can give no more than 100 million yen to various political parties. The goal is to completely eliminate corporate contributions to parties by shortly after 2000. It remains to be seen if that goal will be realized or just become another ignored part of the most recent reform package.

Tickets for fund-raising "parti" events still offer politicians a loophole that allows them to hide the donors of some of their funds. Buyers of tickets for fund-raising parties of less than 200,000 yen do not have to be reported. Individual ticket purchasers must be identified if their expenditures are more than 50,000 yen. The 1998 PFCL report noted the significance of "parti" money generated for individual politicians. The biggest fund-raising "parti" of 1997 was held by the Mitsuzuka faction and produced nearly 3 billion yen for the faction. Other prominent LDP leaders also did well with such "parti" events, with nineteen of the top twenty-two such events generating money for either LDP factions or senior LDP politicians. The Democratic Party generated more than 2.6 billion yen;

Ozawa, leader of the Liberal Party, produced 1.6 billion yen; and the Sakigake got a little over 1 billion yen.[42]

The reformed PFCL is scheduled to be reviewed in 1999. One of the most significant aspects to be considered focuses on the promise to end corporate funding of candidates and parties after the year 2000. The LDP is very reluctant to keep this promise, since it has been almost completely unable to develop any type of foundation of fund-raising from individual contributors. In 1997, only 13 percent of the LDP fund-raising came from individual contributors. Consequently, when the Hashimoto government indicated its lack of enthusiasm for such an ending of corporate funding, it probably was a harbinger of an expected policy shift as the year 2000 approached.[43]

THE CONTINUING PROBLEM OF POLITICAL FINANCE IN JAPAN

One can find in these chronicles of the money problems of the LDP many clues that point to serious illnesses infecting the Japanese body politic. The conservatives rely on corporate generosity because they have no real base in the Japanese public. The LDP local infrastructure is quite weak, and most citizens feel that their stake in the Japanese political game is not important enough to warrant contributions to a preferred political party. In addition, the Japanese electoral law, that complex and tremendously restrictive set of rules, does everything possible to prevent the average Japanese citizen from becoming involved in the political process. Japanese voters are spectators rather than participants; they are less involved than democratic voters anywhere else in the world.

Most democratic nations have discovered that financial support of parties is closely tied to direct, active citizen participation in the nation's political process and to a sense of a stake, psychological or otherwise, in the outcome of elections. Because the LDP has dominated without a break since its creation in 1955 until 1993, and because the electoral laws inhibit active citizen involvement in elections, the average voter is usually bored by the elections. Public opinion surveys, as well, continually discover that most Japanese do not have a deep interest in politics and elections. Therefore, why should they give money to support a party, especially a business-oriented and business-financed party?

Those who, like Maeda, have dreamed of shifting the burden of LDP finances from the shoulders of big business to the average citizen are doomed to disappointment for the foreseeable future. As one Tokyo newspaper lamented following the resumption of the LDP–business financial ties, "Nothing has changed."[44] Kono Yohei's NLC also hoped to build on a base of individual contributions, but it failed to provide enough money for political activities. Reform in *seiji kenkin* can be undertaken only as part of a sweeping reform—a reform that alters the very foundations of Japanese politics. Anything short of such a "revolution" is likely to produce only variations on the present theme. One such opportunity was the 1993–1994 era, when the LDP lost control of the Diet and non-LDP politicians emerged to become prime ministers. However, the reforms proved to be much more fundamental in terms of the electoral system. The reforms that occurred in the political finance sector, while important, still failed to deal decisively with the problem of corporate financing of the conservative political parties.

NOTES

1. "Vox Populi, Vox Dei," *Asahi Shimbun,* June 22, 1980.

2. See Ronald J. Hrebenar, "The Politics of Electoral Reform in Japan," *Asian Survey* 18 (October 1977): 978–996. The original source is *Mainichi Daily News* (December 28, 1975).

3. Home Affairs Ministry, *1998 PFCL Report.* (Tokyo: Home Affairs Ministry, 1999).

4. Ibid.

5. *Asahi Evening News,* September 2, 1982.

6. *Kyodo News,* October 5, 1997; and *Japan Times,* September 19, 1997.

7. Gerald L. Curtis, *The Japanese Way of Politics* (New York: Columbia University Press, 1988), p. 189.

8. How do ambitious faction members use money to gain supporters for a future run at the LDP presidency? Gerald Curtis notes how Takeshita used the huge amount of political funds he collected in 1984. Takeshita saved 550 million yen for future political activities. He then gave the rest in units of 5 million to 10 million yen to members of the Tanaka faction and units of 100,000 to 1 million yen to members of other factions. Finally, he gave 92 million yen to his faction and 2 million yen to Nikaido, the senior member of his faction. Ibid., pp. 182–183.

9. The amount of public money expended in the 1990 lower house elections in subsidies to parties and candidates and direct election management costs totaled approximately 35.3 billion yen. (PFCL 1990 Report.)

10. *Japan Times,* April 5, 1979. Curtis concludes that a well-established LDP incumbent probably spends about the equivalent of $1 million in his reelection campaign to the HR. A new LDP candidate will spend much more than that to have a chance to win a seat. Curtis, *The Japanese Way,* p. 176.

11. *Mainichi Daily News,* January 19, 1980.

12. *Japan Times,* September 20, 1979.

13. *Asahi Shimbun,* April 5–11, 1989. Curtis estimates that the typical LDP Diet member needs an extra 5 to 10 million yen per month to cover extrapolitical

costs, and that in an election year those totals would have to be 200 to 300 percent higher. Curtis, *The Japanese Way*, p. 177.

14. *Asahi Shimbun*, April 5–11, 1989.

15. See Gerald Curtis, *Election Campaigning Japanese Style* (New York: Columbia University Press, 1971); and J.A. A. Stockwin, *Japan: Divided Politics in a Growth Economy* (London: Weidenfeld and Nicolson, 1982).

16. *Asahi Evening News*, June 10, 1986.

17. *The Economist*, May 5, 1990.

18. *Mainichi Shimbun*, April 10, 1990; and *Asahi Shimbun*, December 10, 1989.

19. *Japan Times*, September 20, 1979.

20. *Asahi Shimbun*, September 9, 1982.

21. Ibid.

22. *Japan Times*, September 19, 1982.

23. *Asahi Evening News*, June 17, 1982.

24. *Mainichi Daily News*, June 14, 1980, and January 15, 1980.

25. *Mainichi Daily News*, February 3, 1980.

26. *New York Times*, August 4, 1979.

27. *Mainichi Daily News*, January 21, 1980; and *Asahi Evening News*, January 7, 1980.

28. Much of this section was originally taken from Ronald J. Hrebenar, "Political Money, the LDP and the Symbolic Politics of Reform," *Japan Interpreter* 10, no. 3 (September 1976): 66–73. See also Frank Baldwin, "The Kokumin Kyokai," *Japan Interpreter* 10, no. 1 (September 1976).

29. See Michael K. Blaker, *Japan at the Polls: The House of Councillors Election of 1974* (Washington, D.C.: American Enterprise Institute, 1976).

30. *Mainichi Daily News*, January 21, 1980.

31. *Asahi Shimbun*, November 7, 1975.

32. Ibid.

33. *Japan Times*, November 7, 1975.

34. Ibid.

35. *Mainichi Daily News*, January 21, 1980.

36. *Asahi Evening News*, June 15, 1980.

37. Yasumasa Kuroda and Takayoshi Miyagawa, "The Recruit Scandal in the Japanese Diet: Its Nature and Structure" (paper presented at the 1989 meeting of the American Political Science Association, August 31, 1989, Atlanta, Georgia).

38. *Tokyo Report*, May 2, 1990.

39. *Asahi Shimbun*, September 11, 1998. For a good summary of the 1994 PFCL reforms, see *Rippo to Chosa* [Legislation and research] 181 (April 1994); *Juristo* (Jurists) 1045 (June 1994); and *Yomiuri Shimbun*, August 12, 1994.

40. *Daily Yomiuri*, August 12, 1998.

41. *Asahi Shimbun*, September 11, 1998.

42. Ibid.

43. *Japan Times*, October 14, 1996.

44. Shimizu Minoru, "Revival of the LDP-Business Collusion," *Japan Times* (October 16, 1975). In a *Mainichi Shimbun* editorial on July 27, 1975, the comment was made that the LDP reform effort "was after all a farce."

four

The Liberal Democratic Party: Still the Most Powerful Party in Japan

Ronald J. Hrebenar and Akira Nakamura

The Liberal Democratic Party (LDP) was the national-level ruling party of Japan throughout the entire First Party System (1955–1993). Among the political systems of non-Socialist developed nations, Japan is unique in that except for a short period after World War II, when a Socialist-centered coalition government ruled Japan in 1947–1948, conservative forces have continuously held power on the national level. In 1955, when two conservative parties merged to form the LDP, conservative rule was concentrated within that single organization and maintained its reign as the governing party for thirty-eight years. It lost its majority in the weak House of Councillors (HC) in the 1989 elections and then lost its control of the crucial House of Representatives (HR) in 1993. However, it returned to the cabinet in January 1996 and gained a majority of HR seats in September 1997. Since the fall of 1997, the LDP has returned to its long-term position as the sole ruling party on the Japanese national level of politics. However shaky the LDP's current hold, its record is certainly unprecedented among the ruling democratic parties in the world. All of its competition for the "years in power" record have fallen by the sidelines over the decades. The Socialist Party of Sweden and the Christian Democratic Party of Italy have both fallen on hard times in recent years, and whereas the Socialists have managed to regain power in Sweden in a coalition, the CDP of Italy has self-destructed while the leftists have run Italy since 1996.

The LDP prime minister in office when his party regained a majority in the HR, Hashimoto Ryutaro, seemed to have a good future to continue on as the prime minister until the new century, but it all collapsed in July 1998 when the LDP was hammered in the HC elections. Hashimoto was forced to resign, and the apparently secure LDP had to contemplate new elections for the HR less than two years after the

BOX 4.1   Coalition Governments in Postwar Japan

The LDP-Liberal Party coalition government established in January 1999 was the tenth such coalition government in the postwar era. Five of these coalition governments have been formed during the Second Party System (1993–).

Several of the early coalitions were formed by various parties from both the left and right wings of Japanese politics in the years of the later 1940s. The first coalition was formed in 1946 by Prime Minister Yoshida Shigeru between the Liberal and Progressive Parties. Perhaps the most famous of these pre-1955 coalitions was the 1947 Katayama coalition government, which was the first and last Socialist government until the 1994 Murayama coalition. Beginning in 1955 with the formation of the LDP, there were no coalitions of any type until the LDP invited Kono Yohei's New Liberal Club, a conservative splinter group from the LDP, to join the Nakasone cabinet in 1983. The LDP had won only 250 HR seats in the 1983 elections, and after adding 9 independents to the party it had a pure majority but not a comfortable "working majority." The eight HR seats held by the NLC provided that margin sought by the LDP. The NLC filled the home affairs minister portfolio in two Nakasone cabinets and received a total of three ministries and three parliamentary vice ministers positions during the three years of the coalition (1983–1986).

The beginning of the Second Party System in 1993 has been marked by a coalition-government style of politics. Hosokawa's cabinet was a combination of ministers representing almost all the HR parties except the LDP and JCP. The Hata government, which lasted only a few weeks in 1994, represented all the HR parties except the LDP, JCP, and Socialists.

The most interesting, and certainly the most unexpected, coalitions were the two Murayama "grand coalitions" of the LDP-SDP-Sakigake Parties. The LDP had the numbers—both in the HR and in the cabinets—while the SDP got the prime minister and a few minor cabinet ministries and the Sakigake received the finance ministry at a time of unremitting financial troubles in Japan. These "grand coalitions" continued until after the October 1996 HR elections in which the LDP did well enough to form a minority government cabinet with Sakigake and SDP support in the Diet. These noncabinet "coalitions" fell apart after the LDP secured enough seats in the HR in September 1997 to have a pure majority by itself.

However, the LDP was unable to regain a majority in the HC in the 1990s. After losing more seats in the 1998 HC elections, the LDP approached the Liberal Party with an offer to join the Obuchi government in an effort to gain more seats in the HC. When the totals of the LDP and the Liberals are combined, they total 304 seats (of 500) in the HR, but still fall 10 seats short of a majority in the HC.

SOURCES: Various including the *Yomiuri Shimbun,* January 15, 1999.

TABLE 4.1   Japanese Prime Ministers in the First and Second Party Systems

Prime Minister	Party	Period
First Party System		
Hatoyama	LDP	12/10/54~
Ishibashi	LDP	12/23/56~
Kishi	LDP	2/5/57~
Ikeda	LDP	7/19/60~
Sato	LDP	11/9/64~
Tanaka	LDP	7/7/72~
Miki	LDP	12/9/74~
Fukuda	LDP	12/24/76~
Ohira	LDP	12/7/78~
Suzuki	LDP	7/17/80~
Nakasone	LDP	11/27/82~
Takeshita	LDP	11/6/87~
Uno	LDP	6/3/89~
Kaifu	LDP	8/10/89~
Miyazawa	LDP	11/5/91~
Second Party System		
Hosokawa	NJP	8/9/93~
Hata	Shinseito	4/28/94~
Murayama	JSP	6/30/94~
Hashimoto	LDP	1/5/96~
Obuchi	LDP	8/30/98~

SOURCE: *Asahi Shimbun, Japan Almanac,* 1996, p. 58.

previous contest. The LDP still governs Japan, but its grip on power is shaky (see Table 4.1).

Four elections illustrate the tenuousness of LDP rule in Japan: the HC elections of 1989 and 1998 and the HR elections of 1993 and 1996. The following section will examine these elections to try to understand why the LDP's hold on the Diet has become so tenuous in the 1990s.

The LDP loss in the July 1989 HC election was a contest held against the background of four "negatives" impacting the LDP's political fortunes. First, there was a series of political scandals generally referred to as the "Rikuruto" (Recruit) affairs. The Recruit Cosmos Company distributed large amounts of its stock to a list of Diet members, including such conservative leaders as Nakasone and Takeshita. By cashing them in later, these politicians made handsome, tax-free capital gains. Second, the insider trading by the Diet members naturally outraged the Japanese electorate, particularly because the conservatives instituted a new indirect tax despite strong opposition from many sectors of the society. From April 1, 1989, the Japanese began to pay a 3 percent consumer tax for all items across the board, even for daily food, childbearing, and funeral expenses. Third, as if these would not be enough, the Liberal Democrats drove their traditional supporters into a fury in yet another way. Prime Minister Uno Sosuke, who ascended to the post after Takeshita stepped down in the wake of the Recruit scandal, was publicly exposed as having a mistress. Although womanizing had not been unusual among Japanese politicians, and historically such personal behavior had been considered irrelevant to political affairs even among Japanese mass media, clearly the rules had changed in 1989. Uno's sex scandal was followed by similar exposés of other LDP members. These affairs gradually became a significant political liability for the conservative party. Finally, the eroding relationship with the United States over trade issues tended to place many in the LDP in a precarious position. To alleviate the imbalance, the Japanese government needed to accede to U.S. demands and pledge to open its market for major agricultural commodities by April 1992. Rural voters, the bedrock of the conservative governance, were naturally unhappy with this decision and did not hesitate to show their discontent.[1]

In the HC election, 50 seats were at stake in the proportional representation constituency. Both the LDP and the Socialists listed 25 candidates. In these lists, the conservatives were mindful of the fact that the Socialists were led by a woman, Doi Takako, and that women voters appeared unhappy about the consumer tax and the scandals. As a way to appease this electorate, the LDP thus ranked a female at the top of its candidate list. However, the political ploy was not successful. A number of past surveys have demonstrated that the Japanese electorate is not only rather passive but also indifferent to national problems. Generally, Japanese voters are so concerned about local issues that they often show loyalty to Diet members from their own district. Many claim that this is one of the main reasons that so many Diet members who have been involved in scandals are often left unpunished in the general election and remain active and powerful in the national legislature. To be sure, such trends continue especially in rural districts; however, the 1989 elections appeared different from past contests. National issues seemed to become the key determinant of voting behavior for large numbers of the Japanese electorate. When the results came in, the conservatives won only 37 seats, whereas the Socialists overtook the conservatives by winning a total of 52. When these numbers were added to the seats not up for election, the new totals for the LDP were 110 seats, down by 32 from the previous share of 142. Socialist seats were increased from the old strength of 43 to a stunning 74 members.[2] Other than the Socialists, the newly formed Japan Trade Union Confederation (Nihon Rodo Kumiai Sorengokai, or Rengo) also performed extremely well. The group won 11 seats, mostly in single-member districts, and advanced its strength to a total of 12 seats. Interestingly, except for the Socialists and Rengo, other parties did not do well. The Komeito, Japan Communist Party (JCP), and Democratic Socialists reduced their share by 2 or 3 seats in the upper house.

The 1989 HC election thus brought a new political landscape to Japan. The contest left the Liberal Democrats 17 seats short of the majority in the HC. If the Japan Socialist Party (JSP) cooperated with other groups, these forces could become a serious stumbling block to the conservative domination of Diet politics. The chairwoman of the JSP, Doi Takako, observed that "the mountain has moved," indicating that Japanese politics had entered a new era.

However, one should not underestimate the political resilience of the conservative party. The conservatives have been highly sensitive to the public mood and quick to adopt aspects of it in their political agenda. When, for instance, the public outcry for welfare programs became rampant, as in 1972, the LDP (then headed by Tanaka) took up the issue and announced its intention to increase expenditures for the handicapped and the elderly. Again, during the Miki administration, as the Lockheed scandal (former LDP Prime Minister Tanaka was convicted of taking huge bribes for influencing the decision to buy Lockheed planes for Japan Airlines) caught the attention of the public, the conservatives responded by announcing their determination to entrench political ethics in the party and its policies.

In the February 1990 election for the HR, the first contest after the electoral debacle of summer 1989, the LDP once again took a highly pragmatic approach to ease the growing discontent among its regular supporters. In this campaign, the LDP was not reluctant to use openly whatever leverages it could command. The 1989 supplementary budget, which was compiled by the government approximately a month prior to the 1990 election, was one of the best examples of this LDP effort. For two consecutive years, the size of the supplementary budget grew, reaching nearly 6 trillion yen. The inflationary trend of this budget was clearly the result of the conservatives becoming highly sensitive to political attitudes of a large number of annoyed voters. By parceling out the public fund to different groups, the governing party tried to buy favors of these disgruntled electorates. When the LDP encountered trouble with rural voters during the 1990 HR elections, a special extra grant of

50 billion yen was provided for traditional supporters of the LDP in the rural constituencies. Likewise, another 50-billion-yen subsidy was also prepared for those urban voters who owned small- and medium-sized industries. The endowment was made available for these proprietors to improve operation of their firms and factories.[3]

In addition, by the end of 1989, the Liberal Democrats once again had to recognize the need to placate Japan's farming interests. They decided to put off enactment of a measure to reduce arable land for rice growing, despite the recommendations of a nonpartisan advisory commission. Similarly, elderly voters also were targeted by the conservative campaign. In December 1989 the LDP called off a plan to increase a number of medical charges of the national health program for the aged. Taking the coming election into account, the governing party felt the need to keep the elderly voters in check and kept such individual expenses under this program, at least for the time being.[4] Not until December 1990 were individual medical charges in the national health program for the aged finally increased to 1,000 yen per month for outpatient services and 500 yen a day for inpatient services.

The conservatives' efforts apparently worked to their advantage. In the lower house election on February 18, 1990, the Liberal Democrats succeeded in halting further erosion of their electoral fortune. In spite of a large number of preelection projections pointing to another serious defeat of the LDP, the governing party gained a total of 286 seats, including 11 members who were elected as independents but later joined the LDP. The LDP not only mustered a majority of the 512 lower house seats but also surmounted one of the major political crises in its party history.

Interestingly, the JSP also advanced its share of seats in the lower chamber, increasing to 141 from its previous 83 seats. However, other opposition parties declined: The Clean Government Party (CGP, or Komeito), for example, lost 9 seats for a total of 46, the Communists reduced their share by 11 to a total of 16 seats, and the Democratic Socialists declined to a mere 14 seats from the preelection total of 26.[5]

The next three years saw the LDP trying to deflect the impact of additional political money scandals, which eventually claimed Prime Minister Miyazawa in May 1993. Former LDP member Hosokawa established the New Japan Party in 1992 as a protest to the scandal-ridden LDP style of politics, and it provided a site for LDP voters to support and still vote for a conservative party. Internal LDP factional politics also set the stage for the LDP fall from power. After Takeshita was forced from the prime minister's post and his faction's power broker, Kanemaru, was jailed in 1992, the faction suffered through a successor battle that resulted in a split of the LDP's largest faction into two factions. The mainstream of the Takeshita faction stayed under the leadership of Obuchi; the losers first formed a new LDP faction under Ozawa-Hata leadership and then, in May 1993, left the LDP to form a new conservative party, the Shinseito.

The significance of the departure of the Ozawa-Hata group was enormous. As noted earlier in this book, the only way the LDP could lose control of the Japanese national government appeared to be by the party's self-destruction or splitting into smaller parts. The walkout of the Ozawa-Hata group reduced the LDP HR seats to fewer than a majority, and a vote of nonconfidence against the Miyazawa government forced an HR general election in July 1993. The LDP slumped to 226 seats; the new Ozawa-Hata party Shinseito won 56 seats; Hosokawa's New Japan Party won 37 seats; another LDP splinter party, the Harbinger Party, led by Takemura Mayoshi, won 13 seats; whereas the JSP collapsed from 136 seats in 1990 to only 69 in 1993; and the CGP, DSP, and JCP won 52, 15, and 15 seats respectively. The LDP's 226 seats represented only 44 percent of the HR total seats and thus opened the door for Ozawa and other leaders to try to put together a non-LDP government for the first time since 1955. The new eight-party coalition government was led by NJP's Hosokawa—a compromise choice made by the more powerful rivals for the post (see Box 4.1).

The LDP, now in opposition with the JCP, regrouped under the new party president Kono Yohei. The new government, a somewhat unusual collection of eight parties—some conservative (Harbinger, NJP, Shinseito) and some leftist (JSP, SDF, and DSP) and the always ambiguous CGP, seemed to agree on only the need to reform the electoral system for future HR elections. Despite a general agreement on the goal, the parties disagreed on the details, and reform could not be achieved until Kono and the LDP forced Hosokawa to compromise and agree to a variant of a reform plan.[6]

Hosokawa was forced to resign in 1994 following the disclosure of a personal financial scandal, and the coalition broke up in the subsequent successor battle. Hata claimed the prime ministership but could only put together a minority coalition government when the JSP joined the LDP and JCP in opposition. That government lasted just a couple of months before it collapsed in June 1994.

Its replacement was incredible! No one could believe that Japanese politics had become so unpredictable as to produce a LDP-JSP "grand coalition."[7] Takemura, the leader of the small Harbinger party, brokered the new three-party government when he reminded the LDP of its need to participate in a new government after almost two years in the very unfamiliar role of an opposition party and the JSP of its desperate need

TABLE 4.2   Party Representation in the Second Murayama Coalition
            Government, August 8, 1995

Party	Number	Cabinet Posts
SDPJ	(6)	Prime Minister
		Health and Welfare
		Post and Telecommunications
		Labor
		Chief Cabinet Secretary
		National Land Agency
LDP	(13)	Deputy Prime Minister/Foreign Minister
		Justice
		Education
		Agriculture, Forestry and Fisheries
		MITI
		Transportation
		Construction
		Home Affairs
		Management and Coordination
		Hokkaido and Okinawa Development
		Defense Agency
		Science and Technology
		Environment
Sakigake	(1)	Finance
Nonparty	(1)	Economic Planning Agency

to play a leading role in the depressing new political environment of its declining numbers and political power. Kono gave the prime ministership to the JSP (now called the SDP) leader Murayama, and the LDP occupied almost all the key ministries in the new government. Kono retained the deputy prime minister and foreign minister portfolios. Japan's media and public were stunned by this most improbable combination. Still, just like the Hosokawa coalition, the "grand coalition" could agree on only a few issues. Most seriously, the main crisis of the coalition's time in office, the Kobe earthquake, indicated the new government was incapable of making effective decisions in such situations. Even more serious (in the long run), the government was incapable of responding to the continuing economic crisis facing Japan since 1990.

Torn between conservative and socialist economic policy choices, the government did little or nothing.

In the fall of 1995, Hashimoto, representing the Obuchi group, the LDP's most powerful faction, announced his intention to challenge Kono in the LDP's presidential election. Kono counted his votes and decided not to contest the election. Hashimoto won easily and took over the number two position in the Murayama cabinet. When Murayama unexpectedly decided to resign in January 1996, Hashimoto assumed the post of prime minister, and the LDP formally led the coalition government it had informally controlled (Table 4.2).

The October 1996 HR elections were called by Hashimoto to restore the LDP to power. The LDP won 239 seats out of the new 500-seat HR—just 12 seats short of a pure majority. The SDP collapsed to only 15 seats, and the JCP rose to 26. The new opposition party organized by Ozawa, the New Frontier Party (Shinshinto), won 156 seats; another new party, the Democratic Party, or Minshuto, won 52 seats; and the Harbinger Party was reduced to a pair of seats. The old coalition partners, the SDP and Harbinger, had been reduced to only 17 seats, but when combined with some of the nine independents who were conservatives, agreed to support the Hashimoto government on specific issues but not to be represented in the new cabinet. This nonparticipating coalition was perfect for the LDP, since it could continue to control the HR and fill every post in the cabinet with deserving LDP members.[8]

Gradually, the number of LDP members in the HR rose during 1997 with a series of defectors from the opposition parties willing to return or join the LDP. Finally, in September 1997, the LDP secured a pure majority in the HR.[9] By the July 1998 HC elections, the LDP held 263 of the 500 HR seats. It still was a minority in the HC, but it expected to reverse that pattern in the scheduled HC elections in July 1998. The preelection polls predicted an LDP victory of over 69 seats of the 126 to be contested. As election day drew closer, Hashimoto and his supporters reduced their expected seats to 61—the number they were defending in the election. The number won was only 44, and even though the LDP continued to hold a majority in the HR, Prime Minister Hashimoto was forced to resign.

The Japanese electorate apparently used the relatively insignificant HC elections to send a message of nonconfidence in the Hashimoto government. It was the sixth-longest prime ministership in the postwar era, but it had the "bad luck" to be in office during an era of no growth. It seemed frozen in its inability to take action in such an environment, and the voters, although not supporting a non-LDP government, indicated their displeasure with the Hashimoto cabinet and a desire for someone else in the

TABLE 4.3   Parties and LDP Factions as of January 1999

Party	Faction	HR	HC	Total	History
LDP		265	104	369	
	Obuchi			93	Former Takeshita
	Kato			70	Former Miyazawa
	Mori			61	Former Mitsuzuka
	Murakami-Kamei			60	Former Watanabe/ Nakasone
					Former Mitsuzuka
	Yamazaki			30	(Former Watanabe)
	Kono			17	(Former Miyazawa)
	Independents			15	
	Others			2	
Liberal		38	12	50	Mostly LDP Ozawa
Democratic		94	55	149	LDP+DSP+JSP
Komei		52	24	76	Komeito
Social Democratic		13	14	27	Old JSP
Communist		26	23	49	JCP
Independent/others		12	20	32	
Totals		500	252	752	

party to try to solve the nation's economic problems. Once the Obuchi government was formed, the next question of the political agenda was how long it could last in office before being forced to call new elections for the HR. The LDP had outlasted each of the new party challenges to it during the 1990s. The Shinseito and Shinshinto parties of Ozawa had been defeated and disbanded. Ozawa had been reduced to the leadership of the small Liberal Party. Hata and other rivals had moved to the Democratic Party (Minshuto), which proved to be a worthy rival in the 1998 HC elections. Will this coalition party last long enough to be a rival in the next HR elections? Another alternative could be the breakup of the Liberal Party and a merger of parts of it with the LDP. Whether the Second Party System will evolve into a real two-party system is yet to be determined. The current party system is summarized in Table 4.3

LDP HISTORY

Any discussion of postwar Japanese politics must start off with an explanation of the particular importance of the year 1955. It was in November of that year that the two major conservative political parties, the Liberals and the Democrats, joined to create the Liberal Democratic Party. See Figure 4.1 for the subsequent development of factions within the LDP.

FIGURE 4.1 Lineage of the Factional Development of the LDP, 1956–1991

April 1956	March 1957	July 1962	October 1970	June 1980	January 1986	March 1991
ex-Ogata	Ishi	Ishi	Ishi			
ex-Yoshida	Ikeda Sato	Ikeda Sato	Maeo Sato	Ohira Tanaka Hori	Suzuki Tanaka	Miyazawa Takeshita
Kishi	Kishi	Kawashima Fukuda Fujiyama	Kawashima Fukuda	Shina Fukuda	Fukuda	Abe
Ono	Ono	Ono	Funada Murakami	Funada Mizuta		
Hatoyama	Ishibashi					
Kono	Kono	Kono	Mori Nakasone	Sonoda Nakasone	Nakasone	
Miki	Miki Matsumura	Miki	Miki	Komoto	Komoto	Komoto

SOURCE: Watanabe Tsuneo, ed., *Shin Seiji no Jyoshiki* [New common knowledge of politics] (Tokyo: Kodansha, 1977) p. 92. Updated by authors.

Furthermore, in October 1955, just shortly before the birth of the LDP, the formerly divided Right and Left factions of the Socialist Party merged to form a regenerated JSP. Thus, by late 1955, the plethora of parties that had appeared during the period of confusion following World War II had essentially consolidated, at least for a time, into a two-party system.

In view of these significant developments, the Japanese mass media, as well as many academics, tended to become sanguine about the political future of Japan. They not only regarded Japanese politics as having finally emerged from the disorderly postwar period but also were inclined to consider the appearance of the two-party system as a favorable step toward constructing a mature democracy. These enthusiastic responses were attested by the fact that the situation was labeled by academics and journalists alike as "the political system of 1955" (*gojugonen taisei*).[10]

The decision of the conservatives to merge was expedited by two external forces: pressures from "corporate Japan"—what is called the financial world, or *zaikai*—and the reunification of the progressive or Socialist parties and their strengthened challenge to the conservatives. Historically, there have been extremely close ties between conservative parties and corporate Japan. This tight relationship has led some to refer cynically to the cooperative efforts of the government and the *zaikai* as "Japan Incorporated." It is also attested by the fact that the primary income of the LDP has been and still is drawn almost completely from the contributions of the giant corporations. At the end of every August, the contributions reported to the Ministry of Home Affairs are made public. In 1989 the record showed that the LDP generated over 24.6 billion yen as political funds. Of this amazing total, 54.1 percent came as political contributions, mainly from major businesses or industries. In 1997 (the most recent year for which the political funds reports are available), the LDP's total was still 24 billion yen—despite a series of scandals and major defections from the LDP's ranks in the post-1993 period. In addition to these moneys, political contributions would usually go directly to leading party members or major factions of the LDP. The leading factions still manage to collect large sums of contributions. In 1989, for example, the huge Takeshita group alone collected a total of 1,053 million yen. The Abe faction and the Nakasone faction each also collected more than a billion yen. When these figures were added to the funds amassed by two other groups, Miyazawa and Komoto, the five main factions in the LDP together acquired the staggering sum of 5,492 million yen from various sources in the 1989 reporting period. Of the different types of businesses, banking and financial institutions were the top contributors. The contri-

TABLE 4.4 Obuchi Cabinet, Formed July 30, 1998

Ministry	Minister	Age	House	District	Times Elected	Faction
Prime Minister	Obuchi Keizo	60	HR	Gunma 5	12	Obuchi
Finance	Miyazawa Kiichi	78	HR	Hiroshima 7	11	Miyazawa
Justice	Nakamura Shozaburo	64	HR	PR Mi Kyoto	7	Mitsuzuka
Foreign	Komura Mashiko	56	HR	Yamaguchi 1	6	Komoto
Education	Arima Akito	67	HC	PR	1	None
Health	Miyashita Sohei	70	HR	Nagano 5	7	Mitsuzuka
Agriculture/Forest	Nakagawa Shoichi	45	HR	Hokkaido 11	5	Mitsuzuka
MITI	Yosano Kaoru	59	HR	Tokyo 1	7	Watanabe
Transport	Kawasaki Jiro	50	HR	PR Tokai	5	Miyazawa
Post & Telecommunications	Noda Seiko	37	HR	Gifu 1	2	Komoto
Labor	Amari Akira	48	HR	PR Mi Kanto	5	Watanabe
Construction	Sekiya Katsutsugu	60	HR	Ehime 1	8	Watanabe
Home	Nishida Mamoru	70	HR	PR Shikoku	7	Obuchi
Cabient Secretary	Nonaka Hiromu	72	HR	Kyoto 4	6	Obuchi
Management	Ota Seiichi	52	HR	Fukuoka 3	6	Miyazawa
Hokkaido	Inoue Kichio	75	HC	Kagoshima	5	Obuchi
Defense	Nukaga Fukushiro	54	HR	Ibaraki 2	5	Obuchi
Economic Planning	Sakaiya Taichi	63	—	—	—	—
Science/						
Technology	Takeyama Yutaka	64	HC	Shizuoka	3	Obuchi
Environment	Manabe Kenji	63	HC	Kagawa	3	Miyazawa
Land Management	Yanagisawa Hakuo	62	HR	Shizuoka 3	5	Miyazawa

Factional summary: Obuchi 6; Miyazawa 5; Mitsuzuka 3; Watanabe 3; Komoto 2; none 2.

NOTE: Sakaiya Taichi is a famous writer and former Finance Ministry bureaucrat; Arima Akito is the former president of Tokyo University.
SOURCE: *Japan Times Web Page*, 1998.

butions by banking and financial organizations accounted for more than 29.1 percent of the total political donations in 1989. Aside from them, real estate and construction industries were the second-largest donors of political funds. A number of academ-ics argued that these large contributions had been one of the main reasons that the conservative government, responsive to the interests of these land-related firms, had eased land price controls and allowed the value of land to spiral out of sight, contributing to the bubble economy and the subsequent crash in 1989. Others argue that the LDP has been particularly slow in reforming the Japanese banking system because of its fear of hurting some of its important financial contributors. In 1997 the LDP's major sources were corporate contributions (26 percent) and government subsidies (57 percent). Banks were still the single largest source of the party's finances in 1997. Among the LDP's factions in 1997, the Obuchi faction (the former Takeshita faction) was the top fund-raiser at over 5 billion yen, followed by the Mitsuzuka and Watanabe factions, with the Miyazawa and Komoto factions trailing far behind. The totals of the Obuchi faction should not be surprising, since the then prime minister, Hashimoto Ryutaro, was a member of that faction and Obuchi went on to replace Hashimoto as the LDP president and prime minister in 1998 following the HC elections in July. The Obuchi cabinet is listed in Table 4.4.

A third category of LDP funding is related to the fund-raising abilities of its individual Diet members. The most successful fund-raiser in the 1998 Report was Kato Koichi, then the top lieutenant of the Miyazawa faction and a candidate to replace Obuchi as party president in 1999. All of the other top LDP individual fund-raisers were either current or former prime ministers (Obuchi, Hashimoto, and Miyazawa) or "wannabe" prime ministers (Yamazaki, Mori, Kamei, and Kato). Money flows to those in the LDP who have power or seem likely to have power in the foreseeable future. For Japanese corporations, such contributions seem to be very safe investments that produce high returns over the years.

The reason the business world, especially the banking community, has supported the LDP more than the other parties lies in the fact that the conservatives have helped provide the most favorable environment for rapid economic expansion. Japanese economic development has been marked by heavy investments in plants, facilities, and equipment on the part of the various levels of government and especially by the private sector. To invest in modern equipment and factories, corporations had to borrow money from banks and other financial institutions. With these financial means available, Japanese industries have been able to scrap archaic facilities and build new and sophisticated plants, often equipped with the most modern robots. By means of such heavy borrowing, Japanese companies have been able to produce reliable products that have been very competitive in the international market. However, this pattern of heavy borrowing has naturally put almost all Japanese firms into perennial debt; indeed, the debts owed to the various banks by the average major Japanese enterprise account for roughly 80 percent of its entire capital. If this situation occurred in the United States, the company in question would have declared bankruptcy. But this is not the case in Japan for several reasons. First, the major stockholders of the big businesses are, with few exceptions, banks and lending institutions, which prefer to keep lending money to the corporations and to generate profits on the loans. Second, as long as the company is a leading one, the government would be likely to rescue it if for any reason it is in danger of bankruptcy—particularly if the government fears serious repercussions for other sectors of the economy. It follows that the banking institutions are by and large failure-proof, thanks to the government policy of promoting the economy by means of capital investment. It is therefore not surprising that the leading banks are one of the major contributors to the LDP's treasury.

The political influence of the zaikai was perhaps even more pronounced during the 1950s than it is today. The Japanese economy was still in a period of recovery, and business leaders were strongly united in their objective of attaining high economic growth. In implementing this goal, business first sought to establish political stability as an essential condition for maintaining economic growth. Such stability was of particular concern given that the conservative politicians were divided into two rival parties and had engaged in a pattern of serious power rifts. From the viewpoint of corporate Japan, that political situation was detrimental to the achievement of economic goals and had to be rectified by nearly any means. Fortunately for Japanese business interests, they had sufficient leverage to correct the situation and were not reluctant to utilize their power.[12]

Even though the conservatives had separated into the Liberal and Democratic Parties before the unification of 1955, the two parties were similar in that both had depended heavily on the zaikai for their political funding. The zaikai was then, and still is today, the only reliable source of political funds for the conservatives. Business, wanting its needs in Japanese politics to be articulated by a single powerful political party, forced the conservatives to resolve their differences.

Four major business organizations constitute what is commonly referred to as the zaikai: the Federation of Economic Organizations (Keizai Dantai Rengokai), the Japan Federation of Employers' Association (Nihon Keieisha Dantai Renmei), the Committee for Economic Development

(Keizai Doyukai), and the Japanese Chamber of Commerce and Industry (Nihon Shoko Kaigisho). These four groups had called for the merging of the conservatives as early as 1952. As a result of their pressure, two conservative groups were forced to reconcile, and from January 1955 the zaikai began to channel the flow of their political contributions through a single organization, thereby establishing the Economic Reconstruction Forum (ERF, or Keizai Saiken Kondankai). The purpose of this organization was to administer political contributions from the business world, which had previously flowed directly from each company to its preferred party or parties. The conservative politicians eventually knuckled under to the zaikai's financial pressures and moved to form the LDP in November 1955. Responding to this positive act by the politicians, the ERF made periodic political contributions of 20 million yen to the LDP between 1955 and 1961, when the ERF was dissolved—for a total of approximately 3.8 billion yen.[13]

The second factor promoting the merger of the conservatives was the advance of the progressive political forces within Japan. The peace treaty that brought Japan back into the international society of nations was signed by forty-eight nations, including the United States, in September 1951. This brought an end to the Occupation of Japan by the Allied Powers and officially ended World War II for the Japanese. Consequently, Japan regained its status as an independent nation, and a new era of domestic politics began to emerge. Concomitant with the signing of the peace treaty, Japan signed a security treaty with the United States that encouraged Japan to play an increasingly vital role in the U.S. world strategic plan against the Soviet Union. The conservative and progressive camps clashed head-on over these treaties, but the progressives were sharply divided among themselves as well. A deep division within the Socialist movement made the split between the Left and the Right even more serious. The Left opposed both treaties, whereas the Right approved of the peace treaty but opposed the security treaty with the United States. The difference of opinion was so intense that it could not be easily reconciled by either faction. The two Socialist factions eventually recognized that they could not resolve the conflict at the time, and thus the party was split into two parts in 1951.[14]

Despite the split, the strength of both the Left and the Right Socialist parties continued to grow. In the lower house election of 1952, the first such election after the party split, the Left captured 54 seats and the Right won 57 seats. This brought the total number of seats held by Socialists to 111, or 23.8 percent, of the 466 seats in the chamber. Although both the Right and the Left made gains in the next lower house elections, the Left began to increase its seat totals from 54 to 72, and the Right increased its share by 9 to a total of 66. The total number of seats held by Socialists, both Right and Left, thus increased to 138 (29.6 percent of the total) in 1953.[15] Adding the seats held by other small minor opposition parties to the Socialists' totals, we find that the anti-conservative forces held nearly one-third of the house seats. In the February 1955 HR elections, the opposition, composed of the Right and Left Socialists, the Farmer Labor Party, and the Communist Party, made still more gains. The Left Socialist Party alone surged to 89 seats, and the progressives as a whole took 162 seats, or over 34 percent of the total seats.[16] Partly because of this series of electoral triumphs, the Socialists believed that control of the national government would soon be theirs. Under the leadership of the Left, the Socialists moved to suspend their factional differences and reunited the party in October 1955. In the eyes of both the conservatives and the Japanese business community, this reunification of the Socialist party undoubtedly posed an alarming threat to the future stability of Japan. Grave concern was voiced for the new Socialist party, and its string of electoral victories appeared to represent the first realistic step toward the realization of a Socialist Japan. Conservative politicians began to discuss methods to combat the threat. Miki Bukichi, in particular, a conservative leader who had participated in conservative politics since prewar times, was a leader in these discussions. Miki and other Old Guard leaders were highly dissatisfied with the division within the conservative camp—a division they felt was largely based around personal conflicts, to the detriment of conservative policies. From their point of view, if such a state of affairs continued, the Socialists would sooner or later overwhelm the conservative forces. As a means to prevent such a disaster, Miki Bukichi proposed that the conservatives be unified. In this manner, only one month after the unification of the Socialist party, the Liberals and the Democrats merged on November 15, 1955. Japan had a two-party system for the first time in the postwar period, and a new era had begun.[17]

THE DEVELOPMENT OF THE FIRST PARTY SYSTEM

The promising appearance of a party system dominated by two large parties did not endure. In retrospect, it seems that the "system of 1955" (1955–1960) did not have a solid enough substance to be accurately termed a party system. A deviant pattern (1960–1993) from the original two-party system of 1955 has instead evolved, with the continuation of the LDP in a status of permanent power as its central characteristic. The primary change in the "system of 1955" was the fragmentation of the opposition into a number of parties from the single-party opposition of the Socialists (plus the nearly invisible JCP) in 1955. The explosion of opposition parties began in 1960 with the splintering of the DSP from the JSP and then accelerated in 1964 with the formation of the Komeito. Many reasons accounted for the rise of the opposition parties, but a major one has been the existence of an election law that is supportive of minor parties. For a more detailed examination of this Japanese electoral system, consult Chapter 2; for the purposes of our present examination of the LDP, however, we make the following observations.

THE IMPACT OF ELECTORAL LAW ON THE LDP

The medium-sized constituency system used for the HR had a profound impact on the nature of the LDP. The distinctive feature of this election system was that each voter casts but a single vote for one candidate, yet in each district multiple members of the HR were elected. Of the total of 130 election districts, one constituency, that of the Anami Islands, elected a single member, whereas four districts returned two. And only one, the first district of Hokkaido, had six winners. These districts were the exceptions, however. The most popular patterns were the constituencies returning from 3 to 5 members for the HR; there were 42 districts with 3 members, 39 constituencies with 4 members, and 43 districts with 5 members. Under this pre-1996 system, a strong party could run multiple candidates in the same district. The LDP often does this, usually electing two or three party members in its strong constituencies. A good example of this pattern can be seen in the third constituency of Chiba Prefecture, which has a total of five seats, four of which were held by the LDP in the 1993 election; the other seat was won by the JSP. It is important to understand that the political situation in such multimember constituencies differed significantly from that found in single-seat districts in many Euro-American-style democracies. In particular, as evidenced in the case of the third Chiba district, a situation may develop in which the bitterest competition often occurs between members of the same political party rather than between rival parties. The five big LDP factions often recruit a factional candidate to run in a given district and then give him significant support in his race to defeat candidates supported by rival LDP factions in the same district. The real contest in a district was between a Takeshita candidate and a Miyazawa candidate but not between the LDP and the JCP or JSP.

In the final analysis, the year 1955 is important for a number of reasons. Beginning in that year, the LDP took on its role as Japan's seemingly permanent governing party (on the national level) and eventually proved that it could work with those interested in maintaining a policy of high economic growth—a growth that would enable Japan to become an economic giant by the 1970s. The year 1955 also marks the beginning of the collapse of the expectation of those who believed Japan was about to embark upon a path of a stable two-party system such as that of the United States. Eventually, however, there developed a party system characterized by the LDP at its center and surrounded by a host of opposition parties unable to gather enough strength to seriously challenge the LDP's political supremacy. This system lasted until the LDP split in 1993.

LDP ELECTORAL SUPPORT: A TREND ANALYSIS FROM A HISTORICAL PERSPECTIVE

The fact that the LDP has ruled Japan since 1955 does not necessarily suggest that the base of conservative support has remained unchanged. As we have already indicated, significant changes have occurred in the LDP's base of support during the last nearly four decades. The first election following the formation of the LDP was held in 1958. In this election, the LDP and the JSP together shared 90.7 percent of the total vote and also took 97.0 percent of the seats. This outcome proved to be the beginning of—and the peak for—the LDP-JSP system of 1955, as both parties experienced a decline in vote percentages. In terms of the number of seats, the Socialists have never been able to surpass the conservative share, leaving Japan's party system as a one-and-a-half rather than a genuine two-party system. It also ought to be pointed out that the 1955 system soon began to disintegrate as several moderate parties gradually came to play a significant role in Japanese politics in the 1960s and 1970s. First, two moderate factions in the JSP left the party and formed the Democratic Socialist Party (DSP) in 1960. This was followed by the formation of the Komeito (CGP) as a political arm of the religious organization Soka Gakkai in 1964. As an open expression of protest against money politics, Kono Yohei split away from the LDP and formed the New Liberal Club in June 1974. Ever since the beginning of 1960, these moderate parties in general and the Komeito in particular increased their political strength and developed into forces to be reckoned with in the Japanese political environment. It is primarily because of this rise in the power of the moderate parties that the LDP's vote-getting ability declined below the 50 percent mark for the first time in 1967 (to 48.8 percent), while its share of the seats also fell to under 50 percent (to 48.7 percent) in 1976. In view of the continuing erosion of its base of conservative support, the LDP tried to lure independent Diet members to its camp and barely remained in power by adding them as new members to its ranks. Particularly from 1976 to 1983, the competition and rivalry between the conservative party and these moderate forces became so fierce that it literally put an end to the nascent two-party system in Japan.

Historically, the LDP has been said to be strong in rural communities and weak in urban constituencies. Those who live in rural Japan tend to reside in the communities of their birth and also remain in the same districts. At the same time, chances are good that these rural voters own houses in their respective areas of residence. These variables were also positively associated with high voter turnout because the rural voters living in the place of their birth for a long time in their own homes were generally inclined to have a strong sense of "community consciousness" and strong concern for their home districts. A large number of the LDP candidates also shared the same characteristics and concerns with the rural electorates, and they had a better chance of establishing a rapport with these rural voters than did other party candidates. In the eyes of a large number of the rural Japanese, the conservatives appeared to be highly conscious of and eager to look after the well-being of their communities. In contrast, our investigation demonstrated that urban communities with large populations living in densely populated districts and with large numbers of the labor force in tertiary industries reflected an inverse relationship with respect to voter support of the conservatives. These seemed to be the major reasons for the general decline of the LDP's popularity in the late 1960s and beyond.[18]

This downward trend in the LDP's fortunes was clearly foreseen by some even within the conservative camp. The decline in the LDP vote share did not necessarily mean a reduction in its number of seats in the HR, since the electoral system, until its reform in the 1996 elections, rewarded the LDP with seats far in excess of its voting percentage. In the elections of the 1960s, the LDP won 296 seats in 1960, 283 in 1963, 277 in 1967, and 288 in 1969. In terms of percentages of seats captured, the LDP ranged from 57 percent in 1967 to 63 percent in 1960 and finished the decade with almost 60 percent in the 1969 elections. In the LDP's case, the percentage of seats it captured was always higher than its voting percentage—a fact that helps to explain how it has managed to hold on to power for so long at the national level of Japanese politics. It also must be noted that the bias in the LDP's favor is a most important result of one aspect of Japanese electoral law—namely, the malapportionment of the electoral districts. The apportionment of the lower house was originally based on the census of 1946. A very large rural population existed at that time as a result of the marked population decline of the great urban centers such as Tokyo, which in turn resulted from such war-related factors as persons leaving for military service, civilian evacuations, and the Allied bombings. However, the reindustrialization of the urban areas in the years immediately after the war led to a mass migration to the cities.[19] Despite the enormous increase in urban population, the apportionment of HR seats has not been adjusted, except for minor changes, including small additions in 1964, 1975, and 1986, when seats were added to some urban constituencies.[20]

The decline of the conservative support tapered off somewhat by the mid-1970s despite a number of significant demographic changes that were inimical to the LDP's political fortunes. The reason for this reduced decline ought to be found in the fact that the LDP has been strong in Japan's rural sector, and rural Japan benefited most from the rapid economic growth of the 1970s. Certainly, urban residents benefited from economic expansion, but they also had to cope with many of the side effects of that growth (e.g., pollution and urban congestion). Urban residents have often expressed their doubts about the LDP's high economic growth policies by supporting opposition parties in national and local elections. In marked contrast, rural residents tend to be largely untouched by the ill effects of economic development. They can enjoy the fruits of the expanding economy to the extent that the traditional image of rural Japan has become obsolete.

As the 1980s opened, the LDP appeared to begin to restore its popularity among voters. Except for the election of 1983, the conservatives won more than 50 percent of the vote in the elections from 1980 through 1990. This growth of the LDP's support is generally attributed to a rise of neoconservatism among the Japanese electorate. As Japanese economic expansion has progressed since the 1960s, a large number of people have come to identify themselves as a part of the middle class. In fact, every public poll indicates that more than 90 percent of Japanese usually believe that they belong to the middle-class social stratum. By the 1980s, the majority of Japanese voters thus came to possess something important in the form of either property, savings, or durable expensive goods. Becoming members of the "have" group, these voters naturally tended to act and think more conservatively than was previously the case.

In addition, once many Japanese became materially satisfied, they also tended to seek nonmaterial values. One example of this change is a growing public concern over "amenities," even though the Japanese language does not have an equivalent concept or expression. In this regard, the fact that the LDP has no solid ideologies seems to have worked to the conservatives' advantage. Without ideological restraints, the LDP can be highly attentive to the public's demands and can formulate various programs to cater to popular needs.

LDP FACTIONALISM

It is impossible to discuss the LDP and its dynamics without a thorough examination of its factional nature. Essentially, the LDP is an alliance of factions in which the greater part of the party's affairs is conducted by the factions. Most important, the factions play a crucial role in the resolution of party personnel matters: the selection of the party president (who also usually serves as the nation's prime minister), the appointment of cabinet ministers, and the naming of important party officials. Opportunities to acquire important governmental and party posts differ greatly depending on the party faction in which a given Diet member may hold membership. In the face of the factional nature of the LDP, the abilities of individuals, no matter how capable, have little if any influence over whether they will receive key political positions. To this degree, the factions of the LDP form a "system" and become inextricable from LDP politics. Each faction maintains its own offices and holds meetings at regular intervals.

These factions are, in essence, parties within a party, and hence the LDP must be viewed as composed of several parties..[21] Currently, there are five major factions within the LDP. The largest and most powerful is the Obuchi faction, officially led by former foreign minister and at the time of this writing Prime Minister Obuchi Keizo. The previous leader

BOX 4.2	Chronology of Japan's Political Events and New Parties: 1992–1999
1992	Takeshita faction, the largest in the LDP, splits into two factions led by Obuchi and Hata.
May 1992	Hosokawa forms *New Japan Party* and wins 4 seats in HC elections.
May 1993	Hata faction decides to vote for motion of nonconfidence against LDP prime minister Miyazawa's government. LDP loses vote on motion, and new HR elections are called for July 1993. Groups of LDP Diet members leave the party and form new parties. Hata and Ozawa faction forms *Shinseito*, and Takemura and followers form *Sakigake*.
July 1993	New parties do well in HR elections and form first non-LDP government under Prime Minister Hosokawa.
Jan. 1994	Hosokawa and LDP president Kono agree to compromise after SDPJ HC members kill original reform package on political reforms and adopt new HR election system and weakened political finance reforms.

Apr. 1994	Hosokawa resigns from prime ministership following scandal disclosure. Hata forms minority cabinet without support of SDPJ.
June 1994	Hata government resigns prior to nonconfidence vote.
June 1994	LDP, SDPJ, and Sakigake form new coalition government with SDPJ chair Maruyama as prime minister, LDP's president Kono as foreign minister, and Sakigake's chair Takemura as finance minister.
Dec. 1994	Shinseito, Komeito, New Japan Party, and DSP plus several other groups form *Shinshinto*. Former LDP prime minister Kaifu elected president and Ozawa selected as secretary-general.
Sept. 1995	Kono decides not to run for reelection as LDP president. Hashimoto wins the post.
Dec. 1995	Ozawa defeats Hata for Shinshinto president.
Jan. 1996	Maruyama resigns as prime minister, and LDP's Hashimoto becomes prime minister. Three-party cabinet coalition continues.
Sept. 1996	*Democratic Party* formed by Hatoyama and Kan just prior to October 1996 elections.
Oct. 1996	HR elections held, and LDP emerges as the winner but does not win a majority of HR seats. Noncabinet coalition with Sakigake and SDPJ is established on issue-by-issue basis. Democratic Party, Shinshinto, and JCP survive elections in new election system, but SDPJ nearly disappears.
Dec. 1996	Hata leaves Shinshinto and forms *Taiyo Party*. Later joins DP.
Jan. 1998	Shinshinto collapses following bitter presidential election where Ozawa rises to top post in party. Six small parties formed by former NFP Diet members. Most join Democratic Party, but former Komeito members form several groups, and Ozawa forms *Liberal Party*.
July 1998	LDP performs poorly in HC elections, and Prime Minister Hashimoto resigns. LDP holds internal elections for president. Obuchi wins and becomes prime minister, but LDP factions fragment into several new groups. Sakigake and SDPJ end LDP cabinet support.
Nov. 1998	*New Komeito* is established, bringing together several former Komeito Diet members' groups into a new Komeito organization. Sakigake dissolved.
Jan. 1999	LDP forms new government with Ozawa's Liberal Party in coalition. The opposition is Democratic Party, New Komeito, and JCP.
Oct. 1999	LDP forms Obuchi's third cabinet with New Komeito and Liberal Party.

SOURCE: Compiled by author from Japanese news sources.

was former prime minister Takeshita Noboru. This group was originally led by Tanaka Kakuei, who was arrested in 1976 on suspicion of having accepted bribes from the Lockheed Corporation. A district court in Tokyo issued a guilty verdict in October 1983, which forced him to retire from the main stage of conservative politics. After Tanaka suffered a stroke, a mutiny occurred within his huge faction. One of Tanaka's closest confidants, Takeshita Noboru, planned to organize his own faction, the Future Creative Society (Sosei-kai), within the Tanaka faction. By so doing, Takeshita was taking the first step toward his objective of gaining the LDP presidency and the prime ministership after Nakasone. Takeshita's challenge to the faction boss angered Tanaka, who ordered several measures to torpedo Takeshita's plans. Tanaka was obviously worried that Takeshita's plan to form his own faction within the larger Tanaka factions would force the elder leader into political oblivion. It was about this time that Tanaka suffered his stroke. Takeshita subsequently took over the Tanaka faction and later became the prime minister of the country after Nakasone (Figure 4.1).

Another important group within the LDP is the Kato, or former Miyazawa, faction. This group, led by Miyazawa Kiichi for much of the past several decades, is an heir to the faction spearheaded by Ikeda Hayato, who directed Japan's period of high growth during the 1960s. After Ikeda's death, the faction was temporarily taken over by Maeo Shigesaburo and then by Ohira Masayoshi. Prime Minister Ohira died suddenly during the campaign of the double elections of 1980 (so named because the elections for both houses were held simultaneously). Suzuki Zenko, Ohira's loyal assistant, then took over the faction and became LDP president and prime minister with the strong support of the Tanaka faction. However, he decided to step down from the premiership in 1982 and relinquished his government to Nakasone. Subsequently he also transferred his factional leadership to Miyazawa. Miyazawa passed the leadership on to Kato Koichi in late 1998.

While he was the prime minister from 1982 to 1987, Nakasone Yasuhiro led his own faction, which had about 67 members. With a small faction such as this, Nakasone was unable to run either the party or the affairs of government by himself. He simply never could have become party president or head of the government without the support of the Tanaka and Suzuki factions. Indeed, the very existence of the Nakasone government depended on its leader's ability to sustain its cooperation with these two powerful factions. In effect, the two supporting factions had a near-veto power over policies advanced by Nakasone. The Nakasone cabinet's lack of independence regarding policy matters was strongly criticized by some who called the government the "Tanaka-

Sone Government." However, once Nakasone scored substantial victories in the 1986 double elections, he began to assume a much more independent political posture vis-à-vis his rival factions. This was testified by the fact that he initiated a number of critical measures, including administrative reforms and an introduction of consumption tax, regardless of the desires of the Takeshita and other factions. Yet, as it turned out, Nakasone's reign could not last long. When he was implicated in the Recruit scandal, Nakasone was forced to leave the conservative party and reluctantly transfer his factional leadership to Watanabe Michio. Watanabe led the faction until his death in 1998, and Nakasone took over leadership in the interim until a younger factional leader could be selected. In early 1999 the leadership of the faction was assumed by Murakami Masakuni, and the group then merged with another faction led by Nakayama Taro and Kamei Shizuka to form the Murakami-Kamei faction, with a total of 60 members, in April 1999.

To use the parlance of Japanese politics, these factions sustain the incumbent government, dominate the LDP, and are called the "mainstream factions" *(shuryu-ha)*. Factions that are actively opposed to the mainstream factions are termed antimainstream *(han-shuryu-ha)* or nonmainstream *(hishuryu-ha)*. The mainstream and nonmainstream factions fluctuate somewhat. In the past, the Mitsuzuka (formerly the Abe faction and its predecessor, the Fukuda group) as often as not played an antimainstream role, even though both factions also collaborated from time to time with other leading cliques in order to stabilize the conservative party government. The Abe faction traced its lineage to the group led by two former prime ministers, Kishi Nobusuke and Fukuda Takeo. It had nearly 90 members in the early 1990s, and many assumed that Abe would be the successor to Kaifu as prime minister in 1991. However, with Abe's death, the faction was thrown into disarray, and its leader, Mitsuzuka, was bypassed in the races for prime minister. In late 1998 the Mitsuzuka faction was taken over by Mori.

The last remaining and smallest faction within the LDP is the Komoto faction, led by Komoto Toshio. Among the LDP factions, it enjoyed a "liberal" image and, more often than not, gave an impression of being relatively free from money politics. It is for this reason that, although Komoto himself has never assumed the prime ministership, his favorite son, Kaifu Toshiki, could take control of the government in the summer of 1989 amid the Recruit political scandals. It was also in the middle of the Lockheed affair that Kaifu's mentor, Miki Takeo, was chosen as a "clean" prime minister despite the fact that Miki, Komoto's predecessor, commanded the fewest followers among the rival LDP factions. When Miki was selected, he thus remarked that it was the unlikeliest and least expected event in his life. To that degree, Miki's power was tenuous within the context of conservative politics. Miki was eventually deposed, however, when he ordered the minister of justice to arrest Tanaka. From the viewpoint of other powerful factions, this was an outrageous act, and they decided to withdraw their support of the Miki government. The faction's next prime minister, Kaifu, also had a shaky term in office, since his cabinet was dependent on the Takeshita faction's support for its very existence. He served in office until Takeshita decided it was no longer in the latter's interest to maintain that particular government. The Komoto faction largely disappeared in the chaos of the factional realignments of the late 1998 to early 1999 period.

LDP FACTIONAL FRAGMENTATION IN 1998

The once-powerful LDP factions suffered a sharp decline in power in 1998. Signs of the decline initially surfaced during the battle to choose a successor to Prime Minister Hashimoto following the party's defeat in the July HC elections. The Obuchi faction, the successor of the previous Tanaka and Takeshita factions, was determined to make its leader the second straight LDP president and prime minister from the faction. Normally, when the party's dominant faction makes its desires known, several other factions rush to its side to confirm the new party leader. This time the process was quite different. Factions with their own candidates for party president/prime minister offered their own candidates; even more surprising, other candidates emerged whose supporters crossed traditional factional boundaries. Several of the "rebel candidates" attracted large numbers of younger factional members in the HR who feared an Obuchi victory would anger Japanese voters and endanger their reelection chances in a subsequent general election. As a result, the 1998 LDP presidential election was one of the messiest in decades, leaving the party factional pattern weaker than it has ever been (see Figure 4.2).

The second factor that tended to weaken factions in 1998 was the need to replace an unusually large number of factional leaders during the same year. Former prime minister Miyazawa announced in November that he was giving up the factional leadership position and that Kato Koichi, the former LDP secretary-general, would succeed him as the party's boss and logical candidate for LDP president. If Kato was to become the party president, the Miyazawa faction would have to have the support of the Obuchi faction. Some of the Miyazawa faction members reacted negatively to this and began to form their own group around the faction's other senior leaders such as former chief cabinet secretary Kajiyama Seiroku or former party president Kono Yohei. Kono's policy group, however, contained many who are at least luke-

FIGURE 4.2   LDP Factions, 1998–1999 Changes

Obuchi	Obuchi (93)
	Yamazaki
Watanabe	Former Watanabe (Nakasone) — Murakami—**Murakami/Kamei (60)**
Miyazawa	**Kato (70)**
	Kono
	Kajiyama
Mitsuzuka	**Mori (61)**
	Koizumi
Komoto	Former Komoto

NOTE: By early 1999, the Komoto faction still existed on paper. Major factions are in bold.

SOURCE: *Yomiuri Shimbun*, March 19, 1999.

warm Kato supporters. In late December 1998 the Miyazawa faction began to collapse. Miyazawa (age seventy-nine), the former prime minister and then current minister of finance in the Obuchi cabinet, called a meeting to hand over the faction's leadership to former LDP secretary-general Kato Koichi at a factional meeting on December 22. But about fifteen members of the faction who were loyal to former faction member and former LDP president Kono Yohei (age sixty-one) left the faction and decided to follow Kono, who had been an independent member of the LDP since he left the Miyazawa faction in 1994. The reason given for the splintering by the Kono group was their opposition to Kato's negative position on the proposed new coalition government of the LDP with Ozawa Ichiro's Liberal Party. Kono and his supporters have been advocates of the coalition idea. Kato noted after the split that it would not be good for the faction to have kept the Kono supporters against their will. The now Kato-kai was left with a total of 70 members. Most observers assumed that Kono would be forming his own faction, with about 12 members of the HR joining the new faction.[22]

Several of the LDP factions had been drifting under weak leadership during 1998. The Watanabe faction has been led by former prime minister Nakasone Yasuhiro following the death of Watanabe, even though Nakasone is not a realistic candidate for a return to the prime ministership. A major second-tier leader in the Watanabe faction split with the group in late 1998. Frustrated in his inability to rise to the top of the faction, Yamasaki Taku (age sixty-one) quit the Watanabe faction in December 1998 and launched his own faction with about 35 former

Watanabe faction members. Yamasaki's group had disagreed with the Watanabe faction's de facto leader, former prime minister Nakasone Yasuhiro, and his support for a possible coalition between the LDP and former LDP factional leader Ozawa Ichiro. The Mitsuzuka faction has also experienced splits with former construction minister Kamei Shizuka supporters joining with members of other factions to form a new faction. Until recently, the Komoto faction, the party's smallest, has been led by the ailing Komoto Toshio and has also been drifting for several years, since no new leader has emerged to replace Komoto.

One of the LDP presidential candidates in 1998 also has formed his own supporters' group to enhance his chances of winning the post in 1999. Former chief cabinet secretary Kajiyama Seiroku was a member of the Miyazawa faction, but as it became apparent that Miyazawa would turn the faction over to Kato, he resolved to try to form his own group to pursue the party presidency. Kajiyama's supporter group was formed with members who came from a number of factions and were united to support Kajiyama's losing efforts in 1998. Kono Yohei had supported Kajiyama in the 1998 presidential elections, and it is not clear if the two emerging groups will end up as separate groups.

In 1993 there were six factions in the LDP: Obuchi, Watanabe, Miyazawa, Mitsuzuka, Komoto, and Hata; by late 1998 there were eight factions: Obuchi (93), Kato (70), Mori (62), former Watanabe-Nakasone (40), Yamazaki (30), Kamei (23), Komoto (17), and Kono (17). Within a few months these had sorted themselves out to the Big Four factions: Obuchi (93), Kato (70), Mori (61), and Murakami-Kamei (60). One prediction is easy to make regarding LDP factions—by the time this book reaches print, there will be more changes.[23] A chronology of events and parties is given in Box 4.2.

Why Are There Factions in the LDP?

As can be seen from the preceding discussion, the LDP factions are not usually divided by differences in ideology or policies. Rather, they are exclusively the instruments by which struggles for political power are carried out, and the main reasons for their existence are the need to form personal ties to advance the careers of both leadership and followers, the need to raise large amounts of money for political activities, and the need to provide organizational support for Japan's frequent election campaigns. In any faction, individuals of ability who have been prime ministers or have held important posts in the government or the party tend to assume leadership positions in the factions as well. These people usually possess some charismatic qualities that assist them in their rise to power. But frequently, hardworking individuals such as Obuchi, a man without any of the so-called charismatic qualities, may rise to factional leadership and even the prime ministership under special circumstances. Underlying the rise of factions is the role played by presidential elections. But why do they play such a significant role within Japanese conservative politics? Why have they become semi-institutionalized and resistant to all efforts to eliminate them over the years?

Some analysts have linked the factions to broader patterns within Japanese political culture, especially the tendency toward groupism. Within almost any group of Japanese there is a value placed on hierarchical order and the identity of the group. It is thus possible to argue that the existence of factions within the LDP is nothing more than the political manifestation of a cultural pattern prevalent throughout Japanese society. Although this may be true, there are more important reasons behind the emergence and maintenance of factions. One of the most important is the fact that they arise chiefly in connection with the struggle to attain control both of party leadership positions and of the Japanese government. More precisely, they have come about primarily because of the regular battles held to select an LDP president. Indeed, according to many analysts, the presidential battles are the source of many detrimental forces operating against the conservatives. It is conventional wisdom that each time the LDP selects a new president, several billion yen are spent to accumulate sufficient votes to win the office.

The multiseat HR electoral system used prior to the 1996 elections was also one of the major supporting institutions behind the persistence of factions in the LDP. As discussed earlier, the LDP ran up to four candidates in some of the 4- and 5-seat districts, and the factions supported factional members or potential factional members in these district-level HR battles. One should not forget that these political activities were very expensive; as a result, the factions had to establish a close relationship with corporate Japan, and "money politics" became a central characteristic of the LDP.

Money politics can be explained in great part by the nature of LDP presidential elections and the enormous amounts of money required for these contests. For these and other reasons, it is not inaccurate to state that the presidential elections are a root cause of the various negative aspects of conservative politics.[24]

It was in 1956 that the LDP first began to elect its party presidents, who had always served as prime minister as well. Based on the bylaws of the party, an election was held in that year to select a successor to the party's first president, Hatoyama Ichiro. According to the bylaws, those eligible to cast ballots in this election were all the Diet members belonging to the LDP and the representatives of the local prefectural chapters of

FIGURE 4.3   Formal Organization of the Liberal Democratic Party

Executive Bodies	*Decision Makers*	*Policy Research*
President	Party Convention	Deliberation Committee
Vice President	Joint Meetings of	of the PARC
Secretariat	Diet members	Divisions of the
Secretary-General	Executive Council	PARC
Deputy Secretary		Special Committee
Secretaries		of the PARC
General Management		Research Committee
Party Finance Committee		of the PARC
Committee on National		
Party Organization		
Conference of Executive		
Officers		
National Office of		
Political Campaigns		
Diet Committee		
Public Relations		

Elections	*Party Discipline*	*Audit Committee*
Committee for Election Campaigns		

the party. In general, the candidate who captured a majority of votes from this electorate was declared the winner and party president. If no candidate was able to muster a majority on the first ballot, a runoff election was held between the top two vote-getters. These methods were in use until 1978, when a reform set of rules were enacted. However, it is not at all unusual for the LDP to ignore its own rules and to fill the office by some other procedure that better fits the circumstances of the particular situation. In 1987, for instance, three contenders sought to succeed Nakasone: Takeshita, Miyazawa, and Abe. Because none of them seemed to command a decisive majority, they held a series of marathon bilateral conferences in hotel suites and teahouses in downtown Tokyo. However, because each insisted that he should be named president, the discussions merely confirmed the deadlock. To break the impasse, the three candidates agreed to ask Nakasone to pick one of them as his successor. Consequently, he sought the seclusion of his resort villa to ponder his choice and in late October called on Takeshita to assume the leadership of the party and the country. Once this decision was made, Miyazawa and Abe openly promised to support the new Takeshita administration.[25]

As LDP politicians prepared for the 1956 presidential election, some became active in the establishment of formal factions to support candidates for that office. These activities revolved around two factors. One found its origin in the government of Yoshida Shigeru, the man who led Japanese politics during the confused postwar era. The other is related to the fact that the LDP was originally formed by the amalgamation of two separate parties—the Liberal Party and the Democratic Party. From the outset, therefore, the party had a significant potential for factionalism. Let us note how this potential was realized. Hatoyama Ichiro took part in the reconstruction of political parties in the aftermath of World War II and became the founding father and first president of the Liberal Party in 1945. In the following year, the Liberal Party won the general election, and Hatoyama was expected to become the new prime minister. Before he could assume the office, however, he was purged by the Occupation forces, and Yoshida Shigeru assumed the prime ministership. Yoshida's government commenced in May 1946 and, aside from two brief periods during which a Socialist alliance controlled the government, lasted until late 1954. This period, known as the "Yoshida era," was also characterized by Yoshida's encouragement of many young bureaucrats to enter the political arena under the banner of the LDP. Yoshida himself was known as a man with a strong sense of elitism and a knack for conducting affairs in secret, and as a former bureaucrat in the Foreign Ministry. However, his favoritism for politician-bureaucrats was not merely a result of personal idiosyncrasy. These former bureaucrats were, in effect, the only group not drastically affected by the postwar purges. Other significant groups such as the Zaibatsu (huge pre-war Japanese corporate conglomerates) and military cliques were dissolved, and most of the prewar conservative politicians were purged and barred from political offices. Among those purged beginning in January 1946 were such prominent politicians as Hatoyama Ichiro (a prewar cabinet minister and the first president of the LDP) and Kono Ichiro (a politician who would recover from the purge to become an important figure in the LDP).[26]

These young bureaucrats, encouraged by Yoshida, entered the political world and stepped in to fill the void left by the purge of the majority of the prewar conservative leaders. It should be noted that future prime ministers Ikeda Hayato and Sato Eisaku made their first appearances on the party scene as Yoshida's subordinates at the time of the 1949 lower house elections. Because Yoshida immediately placed such men of obvious talent in important governmental positions, the Yoshida era is often remembered as a period during which freshman Diet members were appointed to cabinet posts upon their election. Of the twelve such cases, seven were former bureaucrats with no previous political experience.[27]

In the summer of 1951, the purge was ended and a wave of prewar politicians returned to the political scene, thus causing an additional strain in the conservative political world. Although the center of conservative politics had shifted to Yoshida and his former bureaucrats, the returning politicians found no room for them to reenter into such an alignment.

When they attempted to make their reentry during the period prior to the founding of the LDP, the conflict between these new and old politicians developed into the factional conflict between the Yoshida and Hatoyama factions. As the two antagonists engaged in a number of heated struggles, the Hatoyama faction eventually broke off from the Liberal Party and formed the Democratic Party. The latter was established through an integration of such anti-Yoshida forces as the group led by the depurged Kishi Nobusuke and the group composed of former members of the old Progressive Party. In time, the Democratic Party, under the leadership of its president, Hatoyama Ichiro, triumphed in its rivalry with the Liberal Party and took control of the national-level government.

The conflict between the Yoshida and Hatoyama groups subsequently reemerged in a somewhat different form—namely, as the LDP presidential election of 1956. By this time eight factions had formed in the LDP, and their lineages were very complex. Four had derived from the Liberal Party: the Ikeda, Sato, Ono, and Ishii factions; the other four can be traced back to the Democratic Party: the Kishi, Kono, Matsumura-Miki, and Ishibashi factions. Another grouping is also possible, however: the Kishi, Sato, and Ikeda factions are "bureaucratic factions" in that they once held large numbers of former public officials within their ranks.[28] The remaining factions, which were largely dominated by traditional party politicians, are called *tojin-ha*.

The most important factors in determining the course of conservative politics, up until at least 1965, were the LDP factions formed prior to the LDP presidential elections of 1956. Eventually, the eight factions were reorganized into five main factions, which have endured to the present time. Thus the party election of 1956 can be seen as having given birth to the LDP pattern of factions. The three main candidates during this party contest were Kishi Nobusuke, Ishibashi Tanzan, and Ishii Mitsujiro. Supporting Kishi were the Kono and Sato factions; the Matsumura-Miki and Ono factions stood behind the Ishibashi candidacy; and the Ikeda faction supported Ishii. When the ballots of the initial round of voting were tabulated, Kishi led with 223 votes, Ishibashi followed with 151 votes, and Ishii captured 137 votes. Because no candidate had a majority, a runoff between the top two candidates was in order, but some of the factions had already come to agreements on what they would do in a second round of voting. For instance, Ishii had agreed to support Ishibashi on the second round—and, indeed, Ishibashi won 258 votes, beating Kishi by only 7 votes in the runoff.[29] Ishibashi held the prime ministership for only about two months because he fell ill and was forced to relinquish the position to Kishi.

This election of 1956 was more than just the prototype for future LDP elections. It set the pattern for the flow of immense amounts of money in presidential contests. It has been estimated that the Kishi faction spent 300 million yen for his election bid, that the Ishibashi faction spent 150 million yen, and that the Ishii faction spent 80 million yen. These totals, representing huge sums for that time, were passed from the candidates to the heads of factions. Not surprisingly, then, the LDP presidential elections became known as "money politics."[30]

The factional pattern of LDP politics became firmly implanted by the transfer of power from Ishibashi to Kishi. The factions became even more firmly established during the Ikeda era. The mainstream factions during the Kishi period were the Kishi, Sato, Kono, and Ono factions, whereas the nonmainstream factions consisted of the Ikeda, Ishii, Matsumura-Miki, and Ishibashi factions. Then, near the end of the Kishi cabinet's term, the Kono and Ono factions broke from the mainstream over Kishi's high-handedness and lack of tact in his manner of dealing with the revision of the Japan-U.S. Security Treaty. This split resulted in the collapse of the Kishi government in 1960.[31]

The Ikeda era, following that of Kishi, was characterized by the start of an economic burst that grew at a phenomenal rate during this period. Throughout the Ikeda era and the Sato period that followed it, the LDP enjoyed what could be considered a golden age. However, the factional conflict not only continued but intensified as the initial Ikeda government was formed by an alliance of the Ikeda, Sato, and Kishi factions. Because the nonmainstream factions were not well coordinated, Ikeda continued to serve as party president for a second term. As he began to move toward a third term, however, differences began to weaken the Ikeda camp. The party politicians of the Kono, Ono, Miki, and Kawashima factions supported Ikeda's bid for a third term. In opposition were the Sato faction and a newly rising bureaucratic group led by Fukuda Takeo, who had inherited the Kishi faction. This election of July 1964 became famous not so much for the third Ikeda victory as for the substantial amounts of money spent in the campaign. Some LDP Diet members took money from both supporters and opponents of Ikeda.

Many felt that the campaign had exhibited an appalling pattern of bribes and expensive entertaining.

Ikeda overcame Sato's challenge and won his third term with just four votes more than a majority.[32] But Ikeda was tragically stricken by cancer at this time and offered his resignation in October 1964. The elders of the party met, agreed to avoid another costly presidential election, and chose Sato Eisaku as Ikeda's successor.

The Sato government was launched in November 1964 and lasted until July 1972—the longest-running government in the postwar history of Japan. The ability of the Sato government to survive for nearly seven years was closely tied to factional affairs. The period immediately before and after the birth of the Sato administration was marked by a chain of deaths of rival faction leaders. Ono Banboku, an archenemy of Sato, died in May 1964; then, in July 1965, Kono Ichiro passed away. Only a month later, Ikeda died as well. The net result of these deaths was that there were no longer any serious rivals to Sato's power. Some of the leaderless factions even began to subdivide, and some members moved into the Sato faction. During this period Fukuda and Tanaka emerged as prominent potential successors to Sato, but Sato was so skillful in his manipulation of party members that he successfully played them off against each other and thus reduced their threat to his continuation in power.[33]

New Regulations for LDP Presidential Elections and the Intensification of Factional Politics

Sato eventually stepped down from the prime ministership in 1972, by which time the reorganization of the factions had been completed. As noted earlier, the eight former factions were replaced by the five factions led by Tanaka (then Takeshita and now Obuchi); Fukuda (later Abe and now Mitsuzuka); Ohira (later Suzuku, then Miyazawa, and now Kato); Nakasone (then Watanabe and now Nakasone again); and Miki (Komoto). Factional politics, which had somewhat abated during the Sato period, reentered a period of intense activity during the 1970s. Supporting evidence for this position was the pattern of rapid changes of government throughout the decade following the end of Sato's administration. The reins of power passed from Tanaka to Miki, from Miki to Fukuda, then to Ohira, Suzuki, and finally to Nakasone.

These changes in LDP leadership could be attributed to the conduct of Tanaka and his faction, and to his style of money politics. Tanaka Kakuei became president of the party after defeating Fukuda in a runoff election in July 1972. It is common knowledge that the force behind Tanaka's victory was the overwhelming use of political money to bribe the neutral factions to support his candidacy. The intense rivalry between Tanaka and Fukuda had been brewing since at least 1966. The two rivals had often collided head-on over such events as cabinet reshuffles and appointments to key LDP posts. As each tried to establish his respective political base in an attempt to succeed Sato as prime minister, the number and intensity of their fights increased. In the name-calling that ensued, Fukuda was labeled as Sato's offshoot who was trying to perpetuate political rule by former high-ranking bureaucrats. Abhorrence of such bureaucrats and of their predominance in the postwar political scene was high even among LDP Diet members. But Tanaka held great appeal for the younger LDP Diet members, and he spent much money courting them. In fact, there were other recent Japanese national-level elections conducted during Tanaka's term as prime minister that earned a reputation as big-money Tanaka-style elections. This was especially true of the July 1974 lower house elections. The financial excesses in this contest were such that even those within the party criticized the flagrant use of business support organizations and the vast amounts of money spent. Tanaka has long had a reputation for being very generous with his supporters; but this pattern, of course, is not too dissimilar from that found in the United States, where machine politics and powerful political organizations (such as that in New York's Tammany Hall) were active in the late 1800s.[34]

After the Tanaka faction had been in office for several years, various aspects of its corruption were exposed in a popular journal, *Bungei Shunju*. The criticism that was generated catalyzed an explosion of additional complaints against Tanaka, from both inside and outside the party. Approximately a year and a half later, during the administration of Miki, the Lockheed scandal came to light, and events led rapidly to Tanaka's arrest. Since then, the factional struggles have remained intense—particularly those being fought over which faction controls the presidency and such key party positions as the post of secretary-general.

In this connection, we should note that a new method for the election of the party president was initiated in 1978. The voting electorate for this post was expanded from LDP Diet members and representatives to include all party members and "party friends" *(toyu)*—a scheme that largely corresponded to the theme of party modernization that had been urged by Miki Takeo for some time. The new election plan actually materialized during the Fukuda administration as a result of factional maneuvering, which led to the downfall of the Miki government. Fukuda's reason for putting the new plan into effect was to respond to the criticism that had arisen following the Tanaka Lockheed scandal. Such a radical reform as a mass-participation primary election would be the first step toward the modernization of the party. Fukuda, however, did not foresee that the reform would lead to the termination of his tenure as prime minister, or that it would cause the expansion of the factional struggle to the levels of the local districts, as each faction built its cadre of primary voters in anticipation of the next primary election.

These unforeseen repercussions sparked factional conflicts to unprecedented levels of intensity. Under the new rules, the election of party president is carried out in two stages. First, general party members and "party friends" participate in a primary election. Prior to this primary, points are allotted to each of the 47 Japanese prefectures at the ratio of 1 point for every 1,000 eligible voters (a total of 1,525 points in 1978). The top two vote-getters in each prefecture share the number of points granted to that prefecture based on the proportion of votes they each managed to obtain. The top two vote-getters nationwide then advance to the second stage, in which the LDP Diet members elect the president by a majority vote. In the 1978 presidential selection process, there were four candidates: Fukuda, Ohira, Nakasone, and Komoto, the new head of the Miki faction. It was crucial for the candidates to survive the primary, finish in the top two categories nationwide, and then go on to the Diet members' vote. Therefore, all four candidates worked hard to increase the general party membership by adding their own supporters to the ranks of the party. Their efforts centered on the electoral districts of the Diet members of the various factions. Membership in the LDP grew dramatically from 500,000 to 1.5 million members (including 170,000 "party friends").

This tripling of the party membership had a number of important side effects, however. First, because most of the new members were brought into the party by factional representatives, these new members often viewed themselves as factional members on the local level. Thus, the problem of factions, once largely confined to the national level of politics, spread across the nation. Second, in many cases the party membership fees of the alleged new members were paid by the factions. Despite the fact that a million new members joined the party, it is very difficult to estimate how many of these are members in the true sense of the word. This type of campaign expenditure also contributed to the high costs of a presidential campaign. A third effect was the enrichment of the local party chapters of the LDP and the relative satisfaction of the general membership's demands to be included in the leadership selection process. Both of these latter two effects have perhaps contributed to the performance of the LDP in recent elections.

The results of the presidential election of 1978, on the other hand, were a shock to the supporters of Prime Minister Fukuda. Ohira, the challenger, gained 748 points, while Fukuda secured only 638 points.

Nakasone and Komoto followed with 93 and 46 points, respectively. Thus, according to the party bylaws, Ohira and Fukuda should have been involved in the second-stage voting by LDP Diet members. However, Fukuda acknowledged his defeat after the primary, and Ohira became party president without a second-stage vote. Fukuda's defeat was a result of his overconfidence as the incumbent and a lack of information stemming from his failure to secure a list of party members. Fukuda had also grown complacent as a result of the mass media's polls and estimates, which had placed him far ahead of Ohira. Ohira, by contrast, had vigorously campaigned for votes on the local level and, more important, had established an alliance with the Tanaka faction. To be sure, the victory of the Ohira-Tanaka factions over the Fukuda faction left the LDP with an unpleasant feeling. Ohira's government was constantly defending itself against attacks from the Fukuda faction. Obviously, this continued conflict caused Ohira many anxieties, which may ultimately have contributed to his death in May 1980. In that month, the Socialist Party presented in the HR a no-confidence motion against the Ohira cabinet. Such motions are fairly routine and ritualistic but rarely successful. Strangely, it was at this time that the Fukuda and Komoto factions, along with a majority of the small Nakagawa faction (all of whom had for some time been unhappy with Ohira's strong connections with the Tanaka faction and various tax policies of the government), left the chamber and did not participate in the vote of no confidence. Much to the surprise of the Socialists, the motion carried. Ohira quickly decided to dissolve the HR and hold an election. It was during this campaign that Ohira died.[35]

In subsequent years, the LDP used a variety of methods to select its presidents. By the count of the authors, six presidents were selected by convention vote (Tanaka in 1972, Kaifu in 1989, Kono in 1993, Hashimoto in 1994, and Obuchi in 1998 and 1999); two were selected in the primaries (Ohira in 1978, Nakasone in 1982); and six in "behind-the-scenes talks or consultations" (Miki in 1974, Fukuda in 1978, Suzuki in 1980, Takeshita in 1987, Uno in 1989, and Miyazawa in 1991). The only rule that seems to be in effect is that the procedure used to select LDP leaders is chosen to be appropriate to the special circumstances of each decision. The next leader could be chosen by any of these methods. It is truly a case-by-case decision-making process.

Although the factional conflicts intensify from time to time, it is also true that the separate factions generally share the common aim of avoiding a splintering of the LDP. The party has been nearly fragmented several times during its existence, and, of course, the Ozawa, Takemura, and other groups left the LDP in 1993 and the years that followed. That the party has avoided self-destruction can be attributed to its fear that if the conservatives should break up, they would not be a match for the opposition. It has also learned an important lesson through past experience—that there has never been a case in which a faction has broken off from a main conservative party and succeeded in becoming a large independent organization. The history of such breaks or attempted breaks has largely involved the Kono family: Kono Ichiro, who abandoned his plan to break off from the party after he decided it could not succeed; and Kono Yohei, his son, who led his followers out of the party in 1976 to form the New Liberal Club, ultimately to return to the LDP after finding that his mini-party would not increase beyond 18 members of the Diet seats at any given time. The jury is still out on the 1993 defectors who started several new parties, including the now-defunct Shinshinto and the still existing Democratic and Liberal Parties.

Therefore, after Ohira's death, Fukuda, sharing the party mood of calling for the closing of the LDP's ranks in times of trouble, shifted to the side of those who supported the selection of Suzuki Zenko, Ohira's successor as leader of the Ohira faction, for the party presidency. In other words, there is a limit to the extent of factional rivalry. This limit can be seen from a different perspective as well. It is customary for the LDP, when forming a new cabinet, to select several cabinet members from the rival factions. This practice has remained true to this date, even though factional politics has been abated somewhat since the beginning of the 1980s. For example, in the case of the second Kaifu administration, which was formed in February 1990, six of the twenty cabinet posts were allotted to the Takeshita faction and four each to the Miyazawa, Abe, and Watanabe factions, respectively, whereas only two were reserved for the Komoto faction, to which Kaifu belonged. The fact that the important cabinet posts were allocated to such factions as Takeshita and Watanabe was an expression of gratitude for the factions' invaluable support of the Kaifu administration. By appointing members of the rival factions to government posts, Prime Minister Kaifu hoped that discontent or open antagonism on the part of the other principal LDP factions against his governance would be mitigated. Cabinet appointments are thus an important leverage for an incumbent leader by which to seek party harmony and unity.

THE FUNCTIONS AND LIMITATIONS OF LDP FACTIONS

As should now be evident, the LDP factions serve as instruments in the struggle for political power, which has as its ultimate prize the acquisition of the post of party president and thus, usually, the prime ministership as well. In this struggle, the unity and relative size of the factions are of great importance.[36] The nickname of the Tanaka faction—the "Tanaka Corps"—once attested to its great strength, which was derived partly from its huge numbers and partly from its history (at least until 1985) of cohesion. Other factions have different resources, however. The range of such resources will be considered in the following discussion.

Japanese elections require immense sums of money. This is especially true for new conservative candidates, who must spend enormous amounts of money for advertisements and personal organization. Such campaigns may cost as much as 200 million yen (roughly $800,000). For that matter, the average cost of election campaigns for experienced LDP Diet members is about 150 million yen ($600,000). Because few candidates can supply such sums on their own, some establish personal support organizations *(koenkai)*, which collect funds from businesses and individuals. Prime Minister Kaifu, for instance, has three separate support organizations: the Kaifu Toshiki Seisaku Kenkyukai, the Seiyukai, and the Shin Seiji Keizai Kenkyukai. Through these organizations, Kaifu collected a total of 333 million yen in 1988 and 229 million yen in 1989, while his rival, Finance Minister Hashimoto, gathered a sum of 420 million yen from his network of organizations in the 1989 reporting period. As these examples indicate, the support organizations function as a money-generating machine, and with these finances, they also work as a vote-getting institution. The Koenkai frequently use up large amounts of money on theater and outings to which supporters are invited.[37]

It is in this problem area of political funding that belonging to a faction has both advantages and disadvantages. Although the details are never clear, at the time of every election campaign the faction leader assists his members with a considerable amount of money. Some experts suggest that approximately 10 percent of conservative campaign funds comes from the purses of leaders. With the tightening of political campaign finance laws in recent years, many "dinner-plate parties" (similar to those in the United States) are held to raise money. In Japan, however, success in collecting funds by this method is contingent upon membership in a faction, given that only a faction would have the big-business connections sufficient to draw crowds to such a dinner. The faction's connections with big business are extremely valuable, and the attendance of factional bosses at these parties is of utmost importance. Tanaka Kakuei, for instance, was used in much the same way that a panda bear attracts children in Japan: His mere appearance at a party for a Diet member of his faction ensured the success of the gathering.

A faction dispenses funds to its Diet members in order to increase their loyalty and their sense of identification with the group. The various factions normally set up dummy organizations to collect these moneys. These dummy organizations usually carry names indicating that they are political research or policy research institutes, but, in actuality, their primary function is simply to collect as much political money as possible from corporate Japan. Despite the fact that laws regulating the collection of political funds have been tightened in recent years, the actual patterns are difficult to decipher because they have been manipulated by extremely complicated accounting methods. The Nakasone (now Watanabe) faction, for example, maintained the Modern Political Research Association (Kindai Seiji Kenkyukai), the New Political Survey Association (Shin Seiji Chosakai), and the Policy Study Research Institute (Seisaku Kagaku Kenkyujo). In 1980 these three institutions together collected nearly 1 billion yen. The New Political Survey Association in particular raised 655 million yen, but the greater portion of this total was recorded as donations from a variety of other political research groups—a procedure that makes it difficult to ascertain the names of the actual contributing corporations or individuals. Those factions without such "political research institutes" have other organizations for collecting funds. Yet in these cases, too, the identities of the actual contributors are extremely unclear.[38]

It is well known that the separate factions in Japan have their own sponsoring corporations. Ties between corporations and factions often begin as personal links between the factional leaders and the corporation presidents. In Japan, connections that have nothing to do with politics, such as those among alumni of the same college or among people from the same region, are often of great significance. Regular meetings between factional leaders and business leaders are commonplace, but those with groups of labor leaders or women's groups are not reported.

LDP factions are deeply involved in a wide array of governmental and party personnel matters. They use the personnel matters in particular as a lever for the expansion of their power and to strengthen factional unity. One such opportunity revolves around the endorsement of LDP candidates. In order for an LDP member to become a candidate for the Diet, he or she must belong to a faction. Under the old HR electoral system, new candidates chose a faction that did not have prior candidates in their particular election district. It was a general rule that a faction would not endorse more than one candidate in a given district—specifically to avoid intrafactional conflicts. Whether or not a candidate can secure the endorsement of the party had crucial implications for his or her chances in the election. Especially in the case of new candidates, the party endorsement was a sine qua non; only rarely was a candidate successful without having received the support of the party. Such an endorsement was made by the party's central committee; moreover, the process tended to be an additional support for the existence of factions given that, in recent years, the factions became more deeply enmeshed than ever in the party's endorsements.[39]

Another form of leverage held by the LDP factions bears more on personnel matters. The awarding of key posts within the LDP is determined by the political balance among the factions. Powerful factions have a much greater opportunity to capture the most important posts of the party. Yet as a function of the Japanese political tradition, the rival factions also received party and governmental posts—not in the same proportion or importance as those awarded the most powerful factions, of course, but they are not ignored either. LDP Diet members who aspire to become cabinet ministers or party executives must therefore attach themselves to powerful factions, continue to work hard, and remain loyal party members in order to gain the same recognition.

Within each faction, the question of who will become a cabinet minister is settled by an established unwritten code. To obtain an important cabinet post it is necessary, in addition to having an affiliation with a faction, to be a multiple-time winner in Diet elections. For the HR, one is expected to be a six-time winner or more, on the average. Without such "experience," one does not have the credentials for becoming a cabinet minister. Some exceptional cases have occurred in which Diet members with less experience were selected for the cabinet, but these involved politicians with unique personal histories or special political circumstances. In the 1980s, even the attainment of nine election victories did not ensure a cabinet position because there were more senior-level Diet members than cabinet positions. Two or three positions in the cabinet are usually reserved for LDP members of the HC. These are usually less prestigious posts; in addition, because the term of office in the upper chamber is six years, a councillor with two election victories usually has a good chance to secure a cabinet position. For members from both chambers, there is an informal rule that they should have served a term as a parliamentary vice minister *(seimu jikan)* or as a minor LDP official before becoming a cabinet member.[40]

In this fashion, LDP cabinet members are selected by "illogical" criteria that have no direct relation to the individual abilities of the politicians themselves. As a result, individuals selected for cabinet positions represent very dubious choices. One candidate within recent memory, the director of the Science and Technology Agency, admitted publicly and without reluctance that she had no scientific knowledge whatsoever. From the perspective of the bureaucrats, however, the best sort of minister is one who says and does very little while securing a large budget for the agency.

One other problem must be noted. The ability to be elected to the Diet in six or more elections increases when a candidate's district is stable and the base of support is firm. Candidates from the metropolitan areas such as Tokyo and Osaka find it very difficult to protect their seats for a decade or longer, whereas candidates from rural constituencies, which are basically stable and conservative, represent the safest seats in Japan. Thus, the LDP Diet members with the best chance to be appointed to the cabinet are those representing rural districts.[41]

APPRAISALS OF THE LDP'S FACTIONAL POLITICS

When scholars and journalists study the LDP's pattern of factional politics, they tend to view it from three main perspectives. First, many in the mass media and academia hold that it is factional politics above all that indicates the backwardness of Japanese politics and constitutes the root cause for the high degree of corruption in conservative politics. As the vital organizations of LDP life, the factions engage in a nearly constant struggle for power in order to control both party and governmental positions. Such a permanent state of conflict requires a great amount of resources, and thus the factions need a constant source of money. In Japan, big business becomes involved in factional politics because it is a primary source of money. The roots of the unprecedented corruption in the Lockheed scandal and the Recruit affair can be found in the institutionalized nature of factional politics. LDP leaders have reputations for collecting money from numerous corporations and then disbursing the funds to Diet members of their respective factions. Because the Takeshita faction was the largest in the late 1980s conservative political scene, the money needed to support such a group must have been enormous. Such a constant demand on the factional leader creates a situation that is ripe for political corruption. For these reasons the Japanese mass media and scholars are nearly unanimous in opposing the factions as obstructions to the health of Japanese politics.[42]

Second, many Japanese believe that the factions prevent the modernization of the party. For all practical purposes, the real organizational strength of the LDP is found in its factions, which gather together under the banner of the LDP only because of political expediency. If a modern party is one that has definite policies and organizations and is also supported by a mass base, then the LDP is clearly not a modern party. It is, however, a party largely found on the national level in the Diet, with only a weak foothold among the people of the nation. Even though its membership base has tripled to 2.1 million members, the level of party identification felt by these alleged party members is not high.

Although it is not yet clear whether the new HR electoral system of single-seat parties will increase voter loyalty, the data from 1998 seem to indicate the election system had little such impact. This new system may also work against the strengthening of the LDP's local-level organizations. The candidates in the 1996 elections relied on their own personal organizations, the *koenkai*, for their campaign support organizations. These supporter associations developed extremely personal ties between the candidate and the members of the association. But the loyalty does not automatically transfer to the LDP. When the LDP seeks to expand its membership rolls, these support associations often play a very important part. LDP Diet members take the list of members of the support association and enroll them as members of the LDP, thus creating the superficial illusion that the party has significantly increased its membership base and, hence, its power. However, the attitudes of those who have become members are unchanged, and their attachments are strong only in their relationship to particular Diet members. As the various faction members try to increase the number of party members who identify with their faction, they frequently find themselves in conflict with membership recruiters from other factions. This tendency conflicts with the original objective of presidential election reform and modernization of the party. And the sense of failure that has resulted is one reason that many are now calling for another reform of the presidential primary system. The last two presidential contests, held in July 1998 and September 1999, chose not to use the primary system but instead used votes from Diet members and prefectural party representatives. A further criticism of the LDP factions is that all key decisions, including policy and personnel decisions, are made by the factional leaders in secret. Consequently, many feel that the opinions of the general public are not well represented in the LDP, but in fact are seriously distorted.[43]

A third appraisal of the factions is one often voiced by U.S. Japanologists and Japanese scholars who have examined the LDP factions in terms of the functions they perform for the party and the political system. These scholars see the rivalries among the factions as creating a situation similar to that found in countries with multiparty systems. They see the LDP as traditionally being made up of five parties, which serve as mutually restraining forces as their constant alliances help to advance Japanese politics. Through this pluralistic process, they argue, the factions give Japanese politics its dynamic quality. Although the factions compete fiercely for power, they do so ostensibly through policy discussions. For this reason, each faction holds repeated research sessions and also tries to secure the services of exceptionally able persons to act as advisers in various policy areas. According to some, the diligence of the LDP Diet members in their studies surpasses even that of the Socialists. In the opinion of the aforementioned U.S. and Japanese scholars, the existence of the factions makes the LDP internally pluralistic and stimulates the basic activities of Japanese politics. Moreover, the factions prevent the LDP from becoming autocratic and thus save the country from falling into a dictatorial regime.

In any case, it is certain that the LDP's factions have both negative and positive aspects. Although all three perceptions of conservative factions may be legitimate, it may be misleading to view the intraparty rivalries as being fought without any relevance to public sentiment and demands. There appears to be a linkage between the LDP presidential elections and these general public feelings, as evidenced, perhaps, by the types of prime ministers the LDP has given the nation. There is a surprising degree of correlation between the main issue of the day and the person selected by the LDP to lead the nation. When the LDP launched its policy of economic expansion, for instance, such former high-ranking officials as Ikeda and Sato, both having a keen sense for economic affairs, took command of politics. However, as the Japanese public gradually came to have some reservations about politics run by ex-bureaucrats, the LDP was quick to sense the change in the public's mood and elected Tanaka, a man with no previous bureaucratic background. When Tanaka's "money politics" gained notoriety, the conservatives selected Miki, who was viewed as a "clean politician" by the media and the general public. This pattern was later repeated with the selection of Nakasone, whose strong sense of nationalism seemed to fit the mood of the nation in the early 1980s. More recently, Hashimoto's selection to prime minister also coincided with a growing sense of resistance to American demands for Japanese reforms. These examples make it clear that the selection of the LDP president involves more than money and group force. The process often echoes the concerns and problems considered important by the public. This fact has often been neglected by both Japanese and U.S. scholars interested in LDP politics. It is a basic rule of politics that politicians must be attentive to the public's mood; if they are not, their prospects for electoral success would indeed be slim.

Finally, U.S. Japanologists also tend to hold the view that the LDP is made up of parties such as the "Obuchi LDP" and the "Miyazawa LDP," and that these parties, by serving as mutually restraining forces and because of their constantly changing alliances, help to advance Japanese politics. Through this pluralistic process, it has been argued, the factions contribute significantly to the dynamism of Japanese politics. It is certainly true that, in most cases, while the LDP factions compete fiercely for political power, they do so ostensibly around matters of policy.

However, the recent political situation—or, more specifically, the rise in influence of money politics—has involved various factors not previously associated with factional politics. Many aspects of LDP politics that seem inseparable from money politics are highly problematic and may necessitate the revision of previously positive evaluations of the usefulness of factions.

THE FORMAL ORGANIZATION OF THE LDP

The formal organization of the LDP has been adequately presented in previous studies by Haruhiro Fukui.[44] The formal organization of the party is presented in Figure 4.3. Nearly every important Japanese party has roughly the same organizational structure. They are all headed by a party president or chairman who, in the case of the LDP, is always one of the party's major factional leaders (or top lieutenants). In this regard, former prime minister Kaifu is an interesting case. He was neither a leader nor a member of a major faction. Usually, the LDP will select such people as party presidents when the party is in deep political trouble. The former defector, Kono Yohei, was tapped to be LDP president in 1993 when the Ozawa group left the party and pushed it from the government. Later, when the political situation had improved, the Obuchi faction member Hashimoto Ryutaro grabbed back the party presidency.

The LDP has provisions for a party vice president, but the post was vacant in recent years until Nakasone appointed Nikaido Susumu, a senior-level aide of Tanaka, in 1984. Vice presidents are usually senior-level LDP Diet members with independent power. Lately, the post has been vacant.

The secretary-general *(kanjicho)* is the second-most important party post. The secretary-general and the chairmen of the two major party committees, the Executive Council and the Public Affairs Research Committee (PARC), are viewed as the three top-level party appointments beyond that of the party president. These posts are usually announced when a cabinet is formed and are considered in the factional balancing that occurs at that time. The secretary-general runs the everyday administration of the party and controls such activities as fund-raising and candidate selection. Because of these significant activities, the post is considered a stepping-stone to the party presidency.

The chairman of the Executive Council, who is on roughly the same level as the secretary-general, not only guides the council in formulating the party's basic policies but also guides the party program through the Diet. Most prime ministers in the 1950–1980 era served as chairman of either the PARC or the Executive Council.[45]

FIGURE 4.4   Overview of the decision-making process of the Liberal
                   Democratic Party

I.	Policy Initiation	Diet members ↓
II.	Policy Formulation	Ministries/Agencies
		Adjustments at Section Level ↓
	Vertical/ Horizontal Coordination	Adjustments at Bureau Level ↓
		Interministerial Adjustments ↓
III.	Policy Deliberation	Divisional Deliberation in the PARC

A.   Division in the PARC

(In the policy deliberation
at one of the Divisions, all
members attend meetings
and receive briefing and
explanations from senior
public officials)

Cabinet (Division)
Local Government
Defense
Legal Affairs
Foreign Affairs
Finance
Education
Social Welfare
Labor
Agriculture
Fisheries
Commerce and Industry
Transportation
Post and Telecommunications
Construction
Science and Technology
Environment

B.   Research Committees
      in the PARC (Total = 39)

Constitution
Foreign Affairs
Public Administration and Finance
Economy and Consumer Affairs

C.   Special Committees
      in the PARC (Total = 46)

Public Safety
Foreign Aid
Regional Development
Narita Airport Development
↓

IV. Policy Confirmation	Policy Affairs Research Council
	The Deliberation Committee of the
(The chairmen of the divisions	Chairman
attend the meetings of the	Deputy Chairman
Deliberation Committee of the	Vice Chairmen 7 (HR 5, HC 2)
PARC. They will explain the	Councillors 20 (HR 15, HC 5)
purpose and intent of various	
policies that are examined by the	
divisions. Senior public officials	
accompany the chairmen of	
divisions.)	
	↓
V. Policy Approval	The Executive Council (30 members)
(The Executive Council is the	Chairman
highest decisionmaking body in	Deputy Chairman
the LDP. Without its approval,	Vice Chairmen 5 (HR 4, HC 1)
no program or policy will	Members 23 (HR 16, HC 7)
move forward to the Diet. Heads	
of the divisions of the PARC attend	
and explain the policy intents to	
the 30 members of the council.	
Bureau chiefs are also present.)	
	↓
VI. Policy Authentication	Diet Deliberation
(Opposition parties become active	
to participate in policy examination.)	

Among the other major divisions of the national-level LDP are the National Organizing Committee, which is in charge of youth, women's, and local politics development activities; the Central Institute of Politics, which operates the LDP's internal education program; and the LDP Convention, which approves decisions made by the party leadership and focuses media attention on the speeches of the party leaders. The party also has the usual array of finance, discipline, Diet policy, and audit committees. The LDP is structured much like the modern mass parties found in some Western European nations.

On the local level it has branch offices in approximately 80 percent of the urban centers of the nation.[46] But almost all meaningful political activities are conducted by the personal support or campaign organizations of the major LDP politicians in each area. Because the *koenkai* (supporters' association) is the real subunit of the LDP, there is little incentive for the party to develop meaningful party organizations separate from their candidates' personal organizations.

CHANGING THE FUNDAMENTALS
OF POLICYMAKING IN JAPAN AND THE LDP?

The study of policymaking in postwar Japan has been the subject of considerable controversy among scholars and the media. The LDP was the ruling party of Japan from its inception in 1955 until its loss of power in 1993. Because the LDP has been in power for such a long time, important policy decisions have inevitably revolved around the conservative party and its internal political process. In this decisionmaking system, the bureaucrats as well as various interest groups, large and small, played important parts. The labyrinth of relationships among these groups of actors occasionally becomes open to the public's scrutiny, but usually it tends to be covert. The real question was the relative power of the various actors in the Japanese policymaking process.

Although for the most part the Japanese public assumed that the LDP acted in coordination and cooperation with the bureaucrats and organized interests to shape Japan's public policies, the question of how these actors really help each other formulate governmental decisions has been left largely unanswered.

Only a few studies have tried to uncover the modus operandi of the Japanese policymaking process. In this area of research and writing, Japanologists in the United States have done much of the work. The collection of studies put together by T. J. Pempel in *Policy Making in Contemporary Japan*, for instance, is one of the pioneering works on this topic. There are many reasons for the lack of serious studies in Japan on policymaking. For one, Japanese academics seem to have been less than well received by politicians because of the fear of the latter that their comments or remarks about the political process may be used against them at a later time. Nor have the political scientists been welcomed by the bureaucrats or interest groups, both of which are also highly cautious. In all fairness, however, one should note the upsurge in interest in policymaking that has occurred among Japanese scholars during the last several years. Still, as noted, a serious shortage of empirical studies remains; for this reason, Japanese policymaking is often described in a highly simplified fashion.[47]

One of the most popular models for the Japanese policymaking process is the "elitist model."[48] According to this model, various policies in Japan are made exclusively by the LDP, the bureaucrats, and big business. As suggested earlier, there appears to be some degree of truth in this description, which therefore becomes useful to the study of Japanese policymaking. Two political patterns that seem to support this model are the large number of bureaucrats who become LDP candidates for Diet seats and the large amounts of political money going from big business to the LDP and its various factions. Elitist theory sees these three groups as holding compatible interests and values and as acting in concert to produce policies that benefit all three and thus entrench their power position.

Its popularity notwithstanding, the elitist theory may be too simplistic to explain the subtlety of Japanese politics. As Fukui argues, the elitist perspective totally ignores factionalism and treats the LDP as a cohesive unit. It also fails to account for rivalries among and within the various ministries. Because Japanese bureaucracies are characterized by sectionalism and competition, it is difficult for them to achieve harmony and cooperation toward a common objective. The same argument applies to the business community. As a result of the continuing economic slowdown, a large rift has become evident among major corporations. Those whose businesses are still on the rise, such as the exporting industries, which include the automobile manufacturing and electronics firms, are often pitted against those who have been seriously hurt by the economic slump, such as agriculture and the steel industry. Because these different groups do not seek the same policy objectives, the chances are good that while one industry may seek the curtailment of governmental spending, another industry may favor the growth of public expenditures.[49]

Because the elitist model is too simplistic and fails to describe the fragmented picture of Japan's key policymakers, Fukui has submitted his own version under the label of "limited pluralism." From Fukui's point of view, the major participants in Japanese policymaking are quite limited. They are essentially the same actors as those postulated by the elitist model, but Fukui takes into account their fragmented nature. Thus Fukui sees policymaking to be a result of the interactions among the various factions of the LDP, the various groups of bureaucrats, and diversified business interests.

Although it is somewhat closer to reality than the elitist model, Fukui's concept seems to regard the major actors as being on a rather equal footing. That is, they are treated as being on a par with each other in terms of political resources and influence. However, the common perception is that these power wielders are not equal in power. Certain groups, owing to their superior position or access to special resources, seem to acquire more political power and thus tend to be more powerful in the political process.

The idea that the bureaucrats predominate in the Japanese policymaking process appears to fit well in this argument and may serve to supplement Fukui's model. The theory of bureaucratic dominance has been argued for some time by Japanese experts and especially by specialists in public administration and local government. Japanese political history tends to support this point. In Japan, high-ranking public officials began to take an active part in national politics in 1918, when a commoner, Hara Takashi, was selected to the prime ministership for the first time in the nation's history. By this time the main architects of the Meiji Restoration had disappeared from the active political scene and had been replaced by graduates from Tokyo University, which had been established in 1877 as a training ground for bureaucrats. The rise of bureaucrats in this century is evidenced by the fact that, of the 21 prime ministers holding office between 1918 and 1945, 20 had former civil or military bureaucratic careers. During the same period, 129 of the 188 cabinet ministers had also served as public officials. Among this latter group, 84 came from such ministries as Home Affairs (23), Finance (14), Foreign Affairs (14), and Justice (11).[50] These data indicate that the bureaucrats had acquired an important position as early as the prewar political period. Up to 1937, the bureaucrats constituted only one group within the power elite, but they were forced to share power with other influential groups, including party politicians, the giant conglomerates called *zaibatsu*, and the military establishment. Then, beginning around 1937, the power landscape started to change in the direction of bureaucratic supremacy. It was in this year that Japan entered into a period of war economy and placed the entire economic sector under governmental supervision. The controlled economy, to be successful, required the abilities of expert public officials. The increase in the bureaucrats' power status in national politics was accentuated in 1940, when all political parties were forced to dissolve and the politicians lost their access to the political arena.[51]

The growth of the power of the Japanese bureaucrats became entrenched as a result of the postwar reforms initiated by the U.S. Occupation. As a consequence of the purges of prewar politicians, the dissolution of the zaibatsu, and demilitarization, the bureaucrats found themselves the only major power group untouched by the postwar reforms. In fact, the Occupation forces, in carrying out their mission in Japan, had to depend on the Japanese civil servants and could not, therefore, make any significant changes in the bureaucracy. The bureaucrats were thus eventually able to step onto the center stage of national politics. Their immunity from the sweeping reforms of the Occupation was directly behind the ascendancy of Ikeda and Sato in the early postwar period.[52]

Yet another account often put forward to explain bureaucratic power in Japan is characterized by its focus on the decline of the Diet. In Japan it is commonly believed that the Diet members leave much to be desired in terms of their policy-planning and oversight functions. Especially in the area of policy formation, the legislators seem to fall far short in their performances, appearing content to follow, instead, the initiatives of the various ministries. Not only is the number of bills sponsored by Diet members substantially lower than that of the bills sponsored by the ministries, but the chances for passage of the legislators' bills are also much less. During the thirty-sixth Diet session (July 1980 to November 1983), a total of 446 such bills were presented to the Diet; of that total, 269 were sponsored by the cabinet, whereas 177 were originated by Diet members. Of the cabinet-sponsored bills, 240, or 89.2 percent, were approved by the Diet, whereas only 47, or 26.6 percent, of the Diet members' bills passed.[53] The reason for the lack of success in the case of the Diet members' bills is that they are likely to be products of the opposition parties intended to harass the government. Even so, the generalization that the bills that pass the Japanese Diet are initiated by the bureaucracy appears to be an accurate one.

In Japanese political and administrative milieus, the word *kanryo* (bureaucrats) carries a special meaning. It refers to a limited number of high-level civil servants in the national bureaucracy. There are several good reasons why these elite public officials are regarded as leaders in Japanese politics. For one, Japanese national bureaucrats command a great deal of discretionary power. When a new law or program is initiated, it is usually the case that a central agency in charge of the problem issues a number of administrative guidelines in the form of cabinet orders, agency circulars, or official notices. One of the rationales for these discretionary policy guidelines lies in the assertion by the *kanryo* that, by these means, the central government has been able to see to it that the original intent of the law or the program is faithfully carried out by both subnational governments and private enterprises. The frequent and prevalent use of administrative guidelines has not been well received in Japan. In fact, it is labeled as "a kanryo practice of making public policy without delegation of power" (i-nin naki rit'tpou). Many argue that the discretionary leverage the kanryo command is tantamount to making the central bureaucracy "the third house" of the Japanese Diet. This is because, in the name of administrative discretion, the bureaucrats are in effect legislating various public policies of national significance. In addition, Japanese central bureaucrats command various licensing and approval powers over thousands of regulations, ranging from an approval power of the Ministry of Finance over interest rates charged by private banks to the licensing authority of the Ministry of Health and Welfare on the marketing of a new medicine. These regulations are so extensive in Japan that even to open a small cleaning store, chances are that the Ministry of Health and Welfare will require hundreds of documents and many prolonged interviews before the agency will validate the license. An increasing number of Japanese have begun to express doubts about the wisdom of bestowing such legal authority upon the central bureaucracy. Whenever these governmental powers are involved, it seems to many Japanese that the market mechanism fails to function and prices of various products begin to rise. Consequently, the Japanese have been forced to pay extremely high prices for beef and rice, as well as for airline and movie tickets, among other items. It was not an accident that controversy was raised over the licensing and approval powers of the central bureaucracy when administrative reform became the national issue in the early 1980s. The question was how best to eliminate various regulations in order to cut the fat out of central administration. Of the more than 10,000 licensing and approval powers, 258 items were eventually singled out as unnecessary authority to be deleted at once. Subsequently, more than 476 regulations were also eradicated by the end of 1987. However, despite the attempts to deregulate in the 1990s, a large number of administrative powers remains in the hands of the kanryo, making Japan's central administration the leading branch of national politics. In fact, as the Japanese financial sector continued in its crisis in 1999, several Ministry of Finance bureaucrats actually claimed the banks' problems were caused by too few regulations and too few regulators.

The third reason bureaucrats are believed to be predominant in public policymaking lies in Japan's unique form of intergovernmental relationships. In these national-local political interactions, the Japanese national government has developed strong centripetal forces with which the kanryo have been able to assume a commanding position vis-à-vis contending groups such as big business in the policy process. Although local autonomy is one of the major hallmarks of the postwar constitution, the national government in Japan has kept overwhelming legal and financial power over prefectural and municipal policies. To describe the state of affairs regarding Japanese local autonomy, the mass media have coined the expression "30 percent autonomy" to illustrate the lack of a self-government tradition in Japan.[54]

There are some who question the assumed power of the bureaucrats. Muramatsu Michio, for instance, argues against the supremacy of these public officials on the basis of an idea he calls "anticipated reaction." Muramatsu claims that the bureaucrats appear to dominate the policymaking process, but that this appearance is misleading inasmuch as the bureaucrats have designed their bills to avoid antagonizing the key members of the Diet. In other words, the civil servants, in anticipation of certain reactions by the Diet members, adjust their bills to ensure their passage. In Muramatsu's opinion, then, the thesis of bureaucratic supremacy must take into account the veto power of the politicians.[55]

Bradley Richardson, in his 1997 book on policymaking, supported a fragmented, nonbureaucratic model.[56] He argued for a horizontal-fragmented model in which power is fragmented, conflict is frequent, and both the LDP and the bureaucracy compete for power in a multipolar system of decision-making and policymaking. Richardson concludes that Japan is a Bargained Distributive Democracy and that this is the style of politics not only of the 1990s but also of the First Party System as well.

Lately, a new perspective on Japan's policy process has gained recognition. This view emphasizes the growing role of the LDP in general and the rise of *zoku* politics in particular. In the daily press, this new phenomenon is described as a shift in the power epicenter from the bureaucrats to the conservative Diet members. A significant cause of this change, its supporters argue, was the oil crisis of 1973 and the economic slump that followed. As a result of the oil slump, the prime theme of Japanese politics has been drastically altered. It is no longer "Who gets what, when, and how?" (as it would be in a period of economic growth) but "Who loses what and how?" Prior to 1973, the gross national product of the country grew an average of 8.1 percent per year. By contrast, during the five years after the oil crisis, the average growth rate was only 3.8 percent. By the time the 1990s began, Japanese growth had largely disappeared, and even negative rates had become common by the late 1990s. A similar trend can be seen in the general expenditures of the national government. From the five-year average of 20.1 percent in the pre–oil crisis period, the average fell to 18.4 percent during the next five years. Especially noteworthy was the year 1975, when the growth rate of public spending was radically cut by the Diet (it had expanded only 9.2 percent from the preceding year). Owing to the shrinkage in governmental income, the central government began to issue debt bonds after the oil crisis. In 1975 the rate of debt bonds issued increased by 50.3 percent compared with the previous year. Although this rate has lessened somewhat since then, the growth rate of the accumulated debt continues to be higher than that of the pre–oil crisis years. By the end of the 1990s, the Japanese government had an annual debt larger than any other nation in the G-5 group of developed nations.

As we will note later, this development has had an important political outcome. This brief economic outline of the pre– and post–oil crisis periods in Japan points to the fact that the Japanese national government no longer had ample resources to continue to fund all existing programs at a constant rate. Because it was likely that the national economic pie would grow only slowly or even shrink, the political results were significant. Public spending for agricultural and forestry programs, for instance, was cut by 9.7 percent in 1975.

Previously, the LDP had acted as representatives for these sectors; but because agriculture and forestry had given the conservatives so much political support over the years, such cuts were impossible in earlier years. In the yearly negotiations, the LDP Diet members represented farmers and other primary economic sectors in their discussions with the bureaucrats, and the bureaucrats seemed to hold the upper hand in this process because they held final control over the budgets. As long as fair shares kept coming to the constituencies and the clientele groups, the conservatives seemed to be content with the fact that bureaucrats were making the allocational decisions. However, when the economy slowed down, the political bargaining process changed. Because the "pie" is smaller, the crucial decisions are not allocational, but the protection of existing subsidies and grants against cuts concerns politicians and bureaucrats alike. Under these new rules, the bureaucrats are not well equipped to deal with the situation. In the politics of "who loses what," any decisions made by the bureaucrats will easily become politicized and expose them to the danger of losing the respect and credibility they had gained over the years. In this new environment, the bureaucrats tend to follow a cautious path by avoiding controversial political decisions. They also appear to consider it the responsibility of the LDP to resolve these various tough questions, and thus the weight of policy-making power has shifted from the bureaucrats to the LDP.

With the rise of the LDP in the policymaking process, the various deliberative components of the party have also become more significant (see Figure 4.4). One of the most important is the Policy Research Affairs Council (PARC), which is where the various interest groups and public officials converge to make demands and negotiate with the leaders of the LDP. According to the party bylaws, all matters relevant to policy affairs must first be examined by the PARC. The policies approved by the PARC are then sent to the Executive Council for final approval prior to being brought to the Diet for legislative deliberation. Despite the fact that the PARC is part of a private organization, it has become the most critical point of Japanese politics with respect to the negotiation of all types of bargains. In normal situations, policy matters initiated by the bureaucrats are referred to one of the seventeen divisions *(bukai)* of the PARC. Because these divisions are organized to parallel the standing committees of the Diet, the problem bearing on a construction issue, say, would be assigned to the Construction Division. The various divisions have spun off well over one hundred subcommittees in recent years, and they tend to function as mini–pressure groups operating within the organizational structure of the LDP. One such subcommittee functions as the voice of the Japan Medical Association. The bureaucrats are not legally required to bring the matter to the appropriate division, but they appear to be well aware that it is unwise to skip a divisional deliberation because a bill would face stiff opposition on the floor of the Diet if it did not have the formal blessing of the PARC. It has become customary for the bureaucrats to participate in such divisional discussions and to make their appeals to the LDP.

In these PARC divisions there are LDP Diet members who are known for their policy expertise. Once a Diet member joins a division, he or she tends to remain with it as long as he or she has a seat in the Diet. By virtue of their long tenure, some LDP Diet members are able to accumulate impressive knowledge on specific policy topics. It is not uncommon to find a group of former division chairpersons who have decided to maintain their membership in a specific division. In fact, the division members are often involved with an issue for longer periods than their counterparts in the various ministries. In this way, a close personal relationship can be built by a conservative politician with both bureaucrats and interest groups. This pattern has become so familiar in recent years that the media have labeled it "zoku politics." *Zoku* literally means tribe—in this context, a tribe of powerful LDP members with years of experience in a particular division, working for the best interests of their clientele groups (including the interest groups and the appropriate groups of bureaucrats).[57] Thus the zoku is the spearhead of pressure group politics within the LDP. Several zoku politicians can be easily identified (Table 4.5).

The LDP ruled Japan singlehandedly between 1955 and 1993, and, as the preceding discussion indicates, its influence appears to be increasing as the power of the bureaucrats has declined in the current period of relatively slow economic growth. In the Second Party System and the "age of coalitions," the LDP is still the most powerful actor in the policymaking process.

The rise of the LDP in the policymaking system is largely related to the clear decline of the bureaucracy in the 1990s. The glory years of the kanryo are clearly over. For decades it seemed as though the bureaucrats could not make a wrong decision, or at least one that did not turn out right in the long run. The run of economic growth covered a lot of weaknesses in the Japanese society, government, and economy. By the late 1980s, the luck ran out, and so did the fortunes of the national-level bureaucrats. The Japanese miracle ended when the land, property, and stock market bubble broke. Suddenly, nothing the bureaucracy did was

TABLE 4.5   Leading Zoku Members of the LDP

Policy Areas	Leading Experts (Zoku Diet members)	Faction
Commerce and Industry	Kajiyama Seiroku Noda Takeshi	Obuchi ex-Watanabe
Transportation	Okonogi Hikosaburo Mitsuzuka Hiroshi	ex-Watanabe Mitsuzuka
Construction	Murata Keijiro	Mitsuzuka
Social welfare	Hashimoto Ryutaro	Obuchi
Education	Mori Yoshiro	Mitsuzuka

correct. The greatest weakness has been its complete cluelessness on how to deal with the continuing Japanese financial crisis and its dragging the Japanese economy down into negative figures. The crisis has continued throughout the 1990s, and the bureaucracy does not have any new plan with a reasonable chance for success. It continues to recycle the solutions used in previous economic crises despite the evidence that such solutions will not solve this much more fundamental problem. The Japanese banks, insurance companies, real estate, construction companies, and bureaucracy all require significant and fundamental reforms, and all have successfully resisted adequate change.

But the downward spiral of the kanryo is caused by more than just a collapse of the economic policies it has advocated in the 1990s. It suffered a major blow when the Kobe earthquake demonstrated that the government, and especially the bureaucracy, was unable to quickly respond to the catastrophe. The Japanese media did not cover up the fact that the *yakuza*, or organized crime, provided quicker disaster relief than the government. Perhaps as serious were the series of bureaucrats, mostly from the elite Finance Ministry, who were charged with bribery and other forms of corruption. As one after another of these members of Japan's "best and brightest" are convicted and punished by the courts, the status and respect for the kanryo declines further.

Japan, Inc. was a cooperative decision-making process of the bureaucracy, the LDP, and the giant corporations of the business world. The bigger problem associated with the decline of the kanryo is the simultaneous decline of the business world. The great Japanese conglomerates, the *keiretsu* have also run out of successful policies. The 1990s have been a disaster for many Japanese corporations.

If the business world and the bureaucracy have both run out of ideas, what does that leave Japan? The LDP? Since the new parties (Shinseito, New Japan Party, Shinshinto, Democratic, and Liberal) have either disappeared or not proven themselves capable of successfully leading Japan out of the 1990s, only the LDP is left. The LDP and professional politicians have tried to move into the void. But, the irony is that the LDP leadership, when faced with the challenge of selecting a leader in the summer of 1998 to lead the party into the next century, chose a politician (Obuchi) with no new ideas and no apparent leadership skills. The LDP has been given an opportunity to grasp the policy leadership of Japan as the twenty-first century begins. So far, it has been reluctant to grab that chance. If it does so and it is successful, the nature of the Second Party System will be easy to predict: a new era of LDP dominance. If the LDP continues to perform as it has in the late 1990s, the Second Party System will continue to muddle on without the political leadership and significant reforms the nation requires. As a 1999 book on the Japanese financial crisis concluded: "A tragedy appears in the making"—an avoidable tragedy if Japanese politicians and especially the LDP can get their act together.[58] A possibility, but don't bet on it in the foreseeable future. That is the nature of party politics in the Second Party System.

THE LDP AND THE FUTURE OF JAPANESE POLITICS

The LDP almost completely dominated the First Party System; survived the transition to the Second Party System (1993–1996); and returned to dominate the initial years of the new system. By late 1997 the LDP ruled Japan with an LDP prime minister and an all-LDP cabinet. The party's numbers in the HR continued to grow until the LDP once again had a pure majority of seats. Admittedly, the party lacked a majority in the HC, but that usually is no more than a relatively minor inconvenience in the broader picture of the problems of governing Japan in the 1990s—the era of slow economic growth. The LDP survived and even prospered during the past decade. It managed to do so without engaging in any significant reforms of party organization, philosophy, or behavior. On the positive side, it managed to rid itself of its long-term rival, the JSP, which finally crashed on the rocks of the 1996 HR elections after it had reached power in the Hosokawa and Murayama cabinets. Also on the positive side, the LDP has emerged from the 1990s with at least the nominal support of the Japanese electorate. New rival parties raised their standards of challenge one after another to the LDP, and the LDP brushed each aside. The current challengers, the Democratic and Liberal Parties, seemingly have peaked in popularity and seem to pose less of a threat to the LDP than did their defunct predecessor, the Shinshinto, or the New Frontier Party. It appears the Second Party System, at least in its early version, is also an LDP-dominated party system.

LDP president and prime minister Obuchi retained both positions by winning the LDP presidential contest in September 1999. He defeated two of his LDP rivals, Kato Koichi and Yamasaki Taku, by putting together a winning coalition that had the endorsements of 5 of the 7 LDP factions. In early October, Obuchi announced his third cabinet, which contained one minister from each of the two other parties that support his administration, the Komeito and the Liberal Party. The new Obuchi cabinet was balanced in terms of LDP factional representation with 3 from the largest Obuchi faction; 3 from the second largest Kato faction; and 3, 3, 1, and 1 from the Kamei, Mori, Yamasaki, and Kono factions, respectively. Obuchi's third cabinet was characterized by the selection of some very senior LDP leaders such as Miyazawa Kiichi and Kono Yohei as Finance and Foreign Ministers, respectively, and the leadership Obuchi displayed by selecting the ministers he wanted in defiance of faction leaders who recommended others from their factions. This cabinet is likely to continue until the next scheduled HR elections, which must be held by October 2000.

Obuchi's third cabinet was also the return to the three-party coalitional politics where the Liberal and New Komeito gave their votes in both the HR and the HC in exchange for a single minister each in the cabinet. The LDP had once again secured pure majorities in both houses of the Diet and it was once again in the driver's seat of national level politics.

NOTES

1. Michael W. Donnelly and Akira Nakamura, "LDP Bashing: The Day Japan's Ruling Party Was Defeated," *Pacific Review* 3, no. 2 (1990): 163–170.

2. *Asahi Shimbun,* July 4, 1989, p. 1.

3. *Asahi Shimbun,* December 1, 1989, p. 3.

4. *Asahi Shimbun,* December 14, 1989, p. 1.

5. Michael W. Donnelly, "No Great Reversal in Japan: Elections for the House of Representatives in 1990," *Pacific Affairs* 63 (Fall 1990): 303–320.

6. Iritani Toshio, "The Emergence of the Hosokawa Coalition: A Significant Break in the Continuity of Japanese Politics?" *Japan Forum* 6, no. 1 (April 1994).

7. Tomabechi Shigemichi, "Live by the Numbers; Die by the Numbers," *By the Way,* September-October 1994, 30–42. For a discussion of the Murayama coalition governments, see *Japan Echo* 21, no. 4 (Winter 1994).

8. Kataoka Masaaki and Yamada Masahiro, "Anatomy of the 1996 Lower House Election," in *How Electoral Reform Boomeranged: Continuity in Japanese Campaigning Style,* ed. Hideo Otake (New York: Japan Center for International Exchange, 1998). The best English-language collection of articles on the 1996 HR elections is found in the journal *Japan Echo,* which is also found on the Internet at www.japanecho.com. The issues devoted to the 1996 elections were vol. 23, no. 1 (Winter 1996) and vol. 24, no. 1 (Spring 1997). Especially good articles on the latter election in the 1997 *Japan Echo* were Kitaoka Shinichi, "The Changing Dynamics of Party Politics," 13–18; and Sato Seizaburo, "LDP Redivivus: The Failure of Electoral Reform," 19–25.

9. *Japan Times,* September 15, 1997.

10. A highly interesting work consisting of discussions by leading journalists on the question of postwar politics is very useful. In fact, it serves as a concise summary of the history of the postwar conservative party. See Goto Moto, Uchita Kenzo, and Ishikawa Masumi, *Sengo Hoshu Seiji no Kiseki* [The development of postwar conservative politics] (Tokyo: Iwanami Shoten, 1982), hereafter referred to as *Sengo.*

11. *Political Funds Control Law, 1998 Report.*

12. Strangely enough, there are not many secondary sources dealing with the postwar development of the major Japanese parties. One reliable source is Tominornori Yoji's *Sengo Hoshuto Shi* [The history of the conservative parties in postwar Japan], hereafter referred to as *Hoshuto.*

13. Haruhiro Fukui, *Party in Power: The Japanese Liberal-Democrats and Policymaking* (Berkeley and Los Angeles: University of California Press, 1970), 146.

14. Tomita Nobuo, et al., *Nihon Seiji no Hensen* [Transitions in Japanese politics] (Tokyo: Hokuju Shupan, 1983), pp. 202–203.

15. See Jichi-sho Senkyo-bu, *Kakkai Shugiin Giin Sosenkyo Kekka Shirabe oyobi Kakkai Sangiin Tsujyo Senkyo Kekka Shrabe I* [The official records of past elections for the House of Representatives and the House of Councillors] (Tokyo: Jichi-o, 1983).

16. Tominornori, *Hoshuto,* pp. 67–72. With respect to the role of Miki Bukichi in the formation of the LDP, see Uchita Kenzo, "Miki Bukichi," in *Nihon Seiji no Jitsuryokusha Tachi III* (Tokyo: Yohikaku, 1981).

17. Robert E. Ward's *Japan's Political System,* 2d ed. (Englewood Cliffs, N.J.: Prentice-Hall, 1978), pp. 87–112, includes a brief summary of the rise of the DSP and the Korneito. See also Nishijima Hisashi, *Komeito* (Tokyo: Sekkasha, 1968).

18. Nobuo Tomita, Hans Baerwald, and Akira Nakamura, "Japanese Politics at the Crossroads: The 11th House of Councillors Election," *Bulletin of the Institute of Social Sciences* (Meiji University) 2, no. 3 (1978).

19. Nakamura Akio, "Teisu Fukinko" [Malapportionment], in *Senkyo to Demokurashi,* ed. Tomita Nobuo and Horie Fukashi (Tokyo: Gakuyo Shobo, 1982), pp. 79–96.

20. By the beginning of 1986, the Diet was deliberating the so called "6–6" reform proposal to subtract one seat from 6 rural districts and to add one seat to 6 urban districts. After the census of 1985, it became apparent that a "10–10" reform was needed, and that became the issue for discussion as 1986 began.

21. Much of what follows in this section with regard to the factional alignments within the LDP was drawn from Uchita Kenzo, *Habatsu* [Factions] (Tokyo: Chuko Shinsho, 1983).

22. *Japan Times*, December 22, 1998.

23. Kato Junko, "Exit, Voice and the Loyalty of Legislative Party Members: The Impact of Intraparty Conflict on the Japanese Party System" (paper presented at the 1994 annual meeting of the American Political Science Association, New York, N.Y., September 1994). For information on the splits and the new factions, see *Yomiuri Shimbun*, November 16, 1998; *Yomiuri Shimbun*, September 7, 1998; *Yomiuri Shimbun*, April 15, 1999; *Yomiuri Shimbun* "Miyazawa Faction Crumbles as Kono Supporters Defect," *Japan Times* (February 1, 1999) "Ex-Minister Kamei to Form New LDP Faction," and *Yomiuri Shimbun* (January 14, 1999) "New Obuchi Cabinet."

24. Regarding these transformations of politics, see Uchita, *Habatsu*, pp. 108, 132; and Goto, Uchida, and Ishikawa, *Sengo*, pp. 140–156.

25. Akira Nakamura, "Factions and Fragmentation: Party Politics in Japan," *Brookings Review* 6, no. 2 (Spring 1988): 30–34.

26. Goto, Uchida, and Ishikawa, *Sengo*, pp. 138–160; Uchida, *Habatsu*, pp. 26–60; Tomiwrnori, *Hoshuto*, pp. 45–56.

27. Nobuo Tomita, Hans Baerwald, and Akira Nakamura, "Prerequisites to Ministerial Careers in Japan: 1885–1980," *International Political Science Review* 2 (April 1981): 235–256.

28. Goto, Uchida, and Ishikawa, *Sengo*, pp. 68–101; Tominornori, *Hoshuto*, pp. 45–56.

29. Goto, Uchida, and Ishikawa, *Sengo*, pp. 104–136.

30. Tominornori, *Hoshuto*, p. 81.

31. Robert A. Scalapino and Junnosuke Masumi, in *Parties and Politics in Contemporary Japan* (Berkeley: University of California Press, 1962), delineate Japanese politics at that time, with special reference to the revision of the security treaty with the United States.

32. Horie Fukashi, "Iketa Hayato Naikaku" [The Iketa Hayato cabinet], in *Nihon no Naikaku III*, ed. Shiratori Rei (Tokyo: Shin Hyoron, 1981), pp. 11–50. See also Goto, Uchida, and Ishikawa, *Sengo*, pp. 198–227; Tomhomori, *Hoshuto*, pp. 109–135; and Itoh Taichi's article on the Iketa administration in Tsuji Seimei, et. al, *Nihon Naikaku Shiroku* (Tokyo: Daiichi Hoki, 1981).

33. Nobuo Tomita, "Sato Eisaku Naikaku" [The Sato Eisaku cabinet], in Shiratori, *Nihon no Naikaku III*, pp. 96–128.

34. Iizuka Shigetaro, "Tanaka Kakuei Naikaku" [The Tanaka Kakuei cabinet] in Shiratori, *Nihon no Naikaku III*, pp. 96–128.

35. See Iwami Takeo, "Ohira Masayoshi Naikaku" [The Ohira Masayoshi cabinet], in Shiratori, *Nihon no Naikaku III*, pp. 211–236. See also Itoh's *Jitsuroku* for more about the Ohira administration.

36. Eric C. Browne and Sunwoong Kim, "Electoral Dimensions of Factional Competition in Japan's Liberal Democratic Party" (paper presented at the annual meeting of the American Political Science Association, Boston, September, 1998).

37. *Asahi Shimbun*, September 14, 1990, p. 11.

38. Nakano Minoru, "Senkyo no Keizaigaku" [The economics of elections], in *Senkyo no Keizaigaku*, ed. Shiratori Rei (Tokyo: Daiamontosha, 1982), pp. 16–66. See also Jichi Sho, "Showa Goju Gonen Do Seiji Shikin Shushi Hokokusho no Yoshi no Koho ni tomonau Setsumei Shiryo" [Explanatory materials on the announcement of the record of political contributions during fiscal year 1980], mimeo (Tokyo: Ministry of Home Affairs, 1980).

39. For information regarding the party nomination process, see Gerald L. Curtis, *Election Campaigning Japanese Style* (New York: Columbia University Press, 1971), pp. 1–32.

40. *Yomiuri Shimbun*, June 4, 1983, p. 9.

41. Tomita, Baerwald, and Nakamura, "Prerequisites to Ministerial Careers," pp. 235–256.

42. Goto, Uchida, and Ishikawa, *Sengo*, pp. 294–320.

43. Uchida, *Habatsu*, pp. 174–181; Hans H. Baerwald, *Japan's Parliament: An Introduction* (London: Cambridge University Press, 1974); and George Totten and Tamio Kawakami, "The Functions of Factionalism in Japanese Politics," *Pacific Affairs* 38 (Summer 1965): 109–122.

44. We strongly urge all readers to consult an excellent article by Haruhiro Fukui, "The Liberal Democratic Party Revisited: Continuity and Change in the Party's Structure and Performance," *Journal of Japanese Studies* 10, no. 2 (Summer 1984): 385–435. Of course, Fukui's work on the LDP is one of the two basic books on the party: Haruhiro Fukui, *Party in Power: The Japanese Liberal-Democrats and Policymaking* (Berkeley and Los Angeles: University of California Press, 1970).

45. Keio University Law School Seminar on the New LDP Leaders; *Bungei Shunju* (January 1984).

46. Hiroshi Imazu, "The Opposition Parties: Organization and Policies," *Japan Quarterly* 24, no. 2 (April–June 1977).

47. An excellent summary of studies on Japanese policymaking has recently become available. See Igarashi Hitoshi, "Gentai Nihon no Seisaku Katei to Jiminto" [The policymaking process and the LDP], in *Kenkyu Shiryo Geppo*, no. 319 (June 1985); Doi Mitsuo et al., "Gentai Nihon ni okeru Seiji Katei eno Apurochi" [An approach to the study of the political process in contemporary Japan], in *Handai Hogaku*, no. 136 (September 1985); T. J. Pempel, *Policy Making in Contemporary Japan* (Ithaca: Cornell University Press, 1977); and Pempel, *Policy and Politics in Japan* (Philadelphia: Temple University Press, 1982).

48. Haruhiro Fukui, "Studies in Policy Making: A Review of the Literature," in Pempel, *Policy Making*, pp. 22–59.

49. Gerald Curtis made a similar argument in "Big Business and Political Influence," in *Modern Japanese Organization and Decision Making*, ed. Ezra F. Vogel (Berkeley: University of California Press, 1975), pp. 33–70. See also Akira

Nakamura, "The Transformation of the Japanese Policy-Making Process: The LDP Governance at the Crossroads," *Governance* 3 (April 1990): 219–233. In Japanese, see Nakamura Akira and Takeishita Yuzuru, eds., *Nihon no Seisaku Katei* [Policymaking process in Japan] (Chiba: Azusa Shuppan, 1984).

50. Tomita, Baerwald, and Nakamura, "Prerequisites to Ministerial Careers," pp. 235–256.

51. Chalmers Johnson, "Japan: Who Governs? An Essay on Official Bureaucracy," *Journal of Japanese Studies* 2 (1975): 13–15. See also Lam Peng-er, "The Liberal Democratic Party's Quest for Local Policy-making Party Organization: The Case of the Kanagawa Forum 21," *Japan Forum* 7, no. 2 (Autumn 1995); and Steven C. Clemons, "Structural Reform in Japan Should Include Innovations in Policymaking," *Daily Yomiuri*, January 14, 1999.

52. Tsuji Kiyoaki, "Kanryo Kiko no Onzon to Kyoka" [The sustenance of the bureaucracy and its consolidation], in *Gendai Nihon no Seiji Katei*, ed. Oka Yoshitake (Tokyo: Iwanami Shoten, 1968), pp. 109–125.

53. Tajima Nobuitsu, "Giin Rippo no Jittai to Kino" [The problems and significance of bills sponsored by legislators], *Jurisuto*, no. 805 (January 1984): 149.

54. For details, see Akira Nakamura, "Different Faces with a Familiar Style: From Bureaucratic Dominance to Conservative Party Governance in Japanese Public Policymaking," *Journal of Management Science and Policy Analysis* 7, no. 3 (Spring 1990): 191–210.

55. Muramatsu Michio, *Sengo Nihon no Kanryosei* [The bureaucracy in postwar Japan] (Tokyo: Toyo Keizai Shimpo Sha, 1981). Haruhiro Fukui, *Party in Power: The Liberal Democrats and Policymaking* (Berkeley and Los Angeles: University of California Press, 1970). One can also consult Fukui's entry on the LDP in the *Kodansha Encyclopedia of Japan* (New York: Kodansha International, 1983), vol. 4, pp. 384–386. The other basic book written in English on the LDP organization is that by Nathaniel B. Thayer, *How the Conservatives Rule Japan* (Princeton, N.J.: Princeton University Press, 1969).

Among some of the more interesting recent articles and books on Japanese policymaking, see Hans Baerwald, *Party Politics in Japan* (Boston: Allen and Unwin, 1986); Kent E. Calder, *Crisis and Competition: Public Policy and Political Stability in Japan: 1949–1986* (Princeton: Princeton University Press, 1988); Peter F. Cowley and Mathew D. McCubbins, eds., *Structure and Policy in Japan and the United States* (New York: Cambridge University Press, 1995); Michio Muramatsu and Ellis Krauss, "Bureaucrats and Politicians in Policymaking: The Case of Japan," *American Political Science Review* 78 (1984): 126–46; and, in Japanese, Yakushiji Taizo, *Seijika vs Kanryo* [Politicians vs. bureaucrats] (Tokyo: Keizai Shimpo-sha, 1987).

56. Bradley Richardson, *Japanese Democracy: Power, Coordination and Performance* (New Haven: Yale University Press, 1997). For some of the newest books written by several of the best scholars on Japanese politics, see Gerald L. Curtis, *The Logic of Japanese Politics* (New York: Columbia University Press, forthcoming); and T. J. Pemple, *Regime Shift: Comparative Dynamics of the Japanese Political Economy* (Ithaca: Cornell University Press, 1999); and Masaru Kohno, *Japan's Postwar Party Politics* (Princeton: Princeton University Press, 1997). This

book has helpful chapters on LDP factions and the impact of scandals on the LDP. To keep up with the various events of Japanese politics, each year the journal *Asian Survey* publishes surveys on each of the Asian nations. Japan was covered in Haruhiro Fukui and Shigeko N. Fukai, "Japan in 1997: More Uncertain, Less Hopeful," *Asian Survey* 38, no. 1 (January 1998): 24–33.

57. Leonard J. Schoppa, "Zoku Power and LDP Power: A Case Study of the Zoku Role in Education Policy," *Journal of Japanese Studies* 17 (1991), 79–106.

58. Karl D. Jackson, *Asian Contagion* (Boulder: Westview Press, 1999), p. 54.

five

The New Parties
of the Second Party System

Ronald J. Hrebenar

From the wreckage of the First Party System emerged a number of new political parties that have changed the nature of Japanese politics and the competitiveness of Japanese national elections. Whereas a large number of minor parties existed in the 1993–1999 period, six new parties led by former Liberal Democratic Party (LDP) members were established. Two still existed at the beginning of 1999, both of which played important roles in the Second Party System. These parties, in order of their establishment, are Japan New Party (JNP), Shinseito, Sakigake or Harbinger Party, Shinshinto or New Frontier Party (NFP), the Democratic Party, and the Liberal Party. A number of other parties have formed and disappeared rather quickly and have functioned as transition sites for major party defectors on their way to one of another of the new parties just noted. Some of these may be mentioned briefly in an effort to include as many of the pieces of the party puzzle as necessary for those readers who may be interested in such minutiae (see Table 5.1).

Several political parties such as the Democratic Socialist Party (DSP) and the Social Democratic Federation (SDF), both splinters from the old Japan Socialist Party (JSP), have completely disappeared, and the JSP or Social Democratic Party of Japan (SDPJ), once the main opposition party of the First Party System, is on the very edge of extinction. The DSP has been merged into the Democratic Party, and the SDF, never more than a handful of members, had its members drift off into other independent groups in the Diet in the middle to late 1990s. The fate of the DSP and Japanese labor unions in general is discussed at the end of this chapter.

Of the new parties noted here, only two survive to play important roles in the Second Party System. The JNP merged into the Shinshinto, as did Ozawa and Hata's Shinseito; the Sakigake dissolved in late 1998; and the Shinshinto collapsed in early 1998. Most of the members of the Shinshinto moved to the Democratic Party, joined several Komeito organizations, or

TABLE 5.1   The New Parties of the Second Party System

Party	Leader(s)	Dates	Fate
Japan New Party	Hosokawa	1992–1994	Merged with Shinshinto
Shinseito	Hata/Ozawa	1993–1994	Core of Shinshinto
Sakigake (Harbinger)	Takemura	1993–1998	Defections/ disappeared
Shinshinto (New Frontier)	Hata/Ozawa Ichikawa	1994–1998	Collapsed/ splintered
Minshuto (Democratic)	Hatoyama/Kan Hata	1996–	Major opposition party
Jiyuto (Liberal)	Ozawa	1998–	Coalition with LDP (1999)

went with Ozawa to form the Liberal Party. The Democratic Party rose to be the major alternative party to LDP rule, while the Liberal Party joined the LDP in a coalition government in early 1999.

Consequently, in 1999 the Second Party System is composed of the LDP, once again the dominant party in the new system, the Democratic Party as the alternative to LDP rule, the Komeito and Japan Communist Party (JCP) as other members of the opposition, and Ozawa's Liberal Party, which seemed to be seeking a way to return to the LDP. If the Liberals do find a way back home to the LDP, the Second Party System will become a slimmed-down version of the First Party System in terms of party organizations (LDP, Komeito, and JCP) with the demise of the socialist splinters (JSP-SDPJ, DSP, and SDF) and the rise of another largely conservative alternative ruling party (Democratic Party) made up largely of old LDP members. How the Second Party System emerged in the mid-1990s is the story of the rest of this chapter on Japan's new parties.

HOSOKAWA'S JAPAN NEW PARTY AND THE VISION OF ALTERNATIVE CONSERVATIVE PARTIES

In May 1992 the Hosokawa Morihiro, a former Kumamoto prefectural governor and former LDP Diet member, organized a new conservative political party dedicated to pursuing political reform. He bolted from the LDP and immediately became a celebrity, receiving extensive coverage in Japan's many weekly news magazines and broadcast media. Hosokawa came from one of Japan's elite political families, and his defection from the LDP served as an indicator that the political earth-quake was about to shake apart the LDP's monopoly on national politi-cal power in the following year.

The JNP performed well in the July 1992 House of Councillors (HC) elections despite the fact that it had little time to recruit candidates and make an impression on the electorate. The JNP's candidates won a total of 3.6 million votes, 8 percent of the total vote, and secured the party's first four seats in the Diet.

After the LDP split and prime minister Miyazawa was forced to call for a House of Representatives (HR) election in the summer of 1993, the new Hosokawa party was the alternative conservative and politically untainted party to capture the votes from those who wished to protest the corruption of the LDP. It won 8.1 percent of the HR vote, for a total of over 5 million votes. Thirty-five NJP candidates won seats, and all of the winners were first-time members of the HR.

When Hata and Ozawa's group left the LDP just prior to the July 1993 elections, it was Hosokawa's JNP that was perfectly positioned to ride the wave of popular support for the new alternatives to the LDP's rule. Now, for the first time since the 1970s and the New Liberal Club (NLC) challenge of Kono Yohei, the voters in an HR election campaign were offered conservative alternatives to the continuing corrupt rule of the LDP. Hosokawa was viewed by the media and the electorate as not part of the LDP corrupt system but also as sufficiently conservative to not rock the boat of economic stability.[1]

Riding the wave of Hosokawa popularity, the non-LDP parties dis-covered that the once-powerful ruling party had lost its majority in the HR and a non-LDP government could be constructed for the first time since the LDP was founded in 1955. The choice to be prime minister in this nine-party coalition was Hosokawa, whose cabinet was formed in the summer of 1993 and lasted for eight months. The Hosokawa gov-ernment had a cabinet made up of members who left the LDP, a num-ber of Komeito ministers, several Socialists, and, of course, Hosokawa as its prime minister and symbol of reform. This cabinet began its term in office with a 71.9 percent approval rating by the Japanese public—the highest such approval for a new cabinet in recent Japanese political history.[2]

An eight party coalition such as that led by Prime Minister Hosokawa was very difficult to manage. The main item on the coalition's policy agenda was political reform—especially of the electoral system for the HR—but also political finance reform, if it could be agreed to by the var-ious interests represented. The question of reform proved too difficult for the coalition to pass through the Diet without the cooperation of the

LDP. In early 1994 the LDP president Kono Yohei offered to help Hosokawa put together a compromise reform bill that would produce a new election system for the HR while leaving political finance essentially intact. This proved to be the only significant piece of legislation (and reform) passed by the Hosokawa coalition. Several months later, stories of personal financial scandal involving Hosokawa emerged in the media, and he was forced to give up the prime ministership in April 1994.

Hosokawa and the NJP merged into the Shinshinto with the other parties that formed the party under the leadership of Ozawa and Hata. When the Shinshinto collapsed in early 1998, the NJP members mostly went to the Democratic Party led by Hatoyama and Kan. Hosokawa left the Shinshinto in June 1997 and subsequently refused to join any of the parties that emerged from the Shinshinto wreckage. Hosokawa finished his Diet career as an independent member of the HR. By 1998, at the age of only sixty, Hosokawa had left the Diet.

HARBINGER PARTY (SAKIGAKE): ANOTHER LDP SPLINTER

The Harbinger Party (Sakigake) was formed by ten LDP defectors led out of the party by Takemura Masayoshi in May 1993. It has been an important player in the Second Party System for three main reasons. First, it was the first home for several former LDP members who have become significant politicians in the other new parties that have emerged since 1996. These politicians include Kan Naoto and Hatoyama, who left the Sakigake to found the Democratic Party, which is now the largest opposition party and the alternative to the LDP for ruling Japan on the national level. Second, the Sakigake did well in the initial elections following the fragmenting of the LDP. By 1996, after one election in each house of the Diet, the Sakigake had over 20 members. This number peaked at 13 HR members, which represented an addition of 3 new Diet members to the original group of 10 who bolted the LDP. Sakigake then played an important part in the Hosokawa and Hata cabinets. Two members held the health and welfare minister position, with one of them, Kan Naoto, later using it to build a popular base for launching his own party.

Sakigake also became the bridge that supported the most unlikely government in modern Japanese politics. Takemura, the Sakigake president, was the link in putting together the LDP-SDPJ-Sakigake coalition in June 1994, following the collapse of the Hata minority coalition government. This coalition was "unthinkable" in terms of normal politics because historically the parties were enemies and stood for two very different views of politics and political values. The only factor that made the LDP more willing to accept such a coalition with the SDPJ was the shock of the long-term ruling party being out of power since the summer of 1993. They were desperate to return to having cabinet positions to distribute to worthy faction members. The former LDP member, Takemura, was able to bring together these two unlikely partners and to have himself named to the second-most prestigious cabinet portfolio, the Ministry of Finance. Takemura and the Sakigake managed to hold this coalition together until the October 1996 HR elections. The LDP did so well in those elections that it decided not to ask the Sakigake and SDPJ to be in the new cabinet. Both parties continued to support the LDP government on a case-by-case basis for the next two years until the July 1998 HC elections were to be held and then dropped their support. By that time the LDP did not need their votes to control the HR, since a sufficient number of Diet members had joined or rejoined the LDP to give it a pure majority by September 1997.

Sakigake was badly hurt by defections of high-profile members such as Hatoyama and Kan to the new Democratic Party. So many of its core members had defected by the fall of 1998 that only the central leadership of Takemura and his executive group was left to disband the party in late 1998.

OZAWA'S AND HATA'S SHINSHINTO: THE LONG-AWAITED UMBRELLA OPPOSITION PARTY

The merger of the Japanese opposition parties occurred in December 1994 when the Shinshinto, or NFP, was formed. Nine separate parties, including the Shinseito, Komeito, DSP, and NJP, merged to form the NFP. In April 1994 Ozawa and his supporters formed a group called Kaishin (Renovation), which sought to join together the various parties of the Hosokawa cabinet without the SDPJ. One reason for this strategy was a frustration with the behavior of the Socialists during the Hosokawa government. The Socialists were more of a problem than the opposition LDP and JCP. Ozawa's plan was to exclude them from the Hata cabinet and find a way to reorganize the political party world without the SDPJ. Ozawa, correctly guessing the SDPJ was moving toward extinction, sought to help them along in this direction. However, the effort was seen by almost all as too heavy-handed, and it cost the Hata government a great deal of media and public support. The Socialists came to understand that their future in the Ozawa-led world of the non-LDP parties was a bleak one, and they then moved to join with the Sakigake to support the LDP after the Hata government collapsed (it was supported by less than one-third of the HR members) in June 1994. The next logical step for Ozawa was to merge all the other parties in a new party that could confront the LDP without the burden of the left-wing Socialists. That party was the Shinshinto.

The Hata government's cabinet was dominated by Shinseito politicians, with the remainder of positions awarded to the Komeito members. This pattern of alliance between the Shinseito and Komeito came to dominate the Shinshinto after it was formed later in the year.

The leaders of this new party were many. It had within its ranks several former prime ministers, including Kaifu of the LDP, Hata of the Shinseito, and Hosokawa of the NJP. It also had an impressive number of politicians deemed to be future leaders and even potential prime ministers. Even though the masterminds for the new consolidated party were Ozawa and Hata, neither one was able to emerge as the first president of the NFP. Former LDP prime minister Kaifu Toshio, backed by Ozawa, was selected as the party's first president by a vote of 131 to 52 over Hata, and Ozawa was made the first secretary-general. Shinseito's Hata Tsutomu, DSP chairman Yonezawa Takashi, and Komeito's chairman Ichida Koshiro were selected as party vice presidents. The other significant party leaders were Komeito's secretary-general as the NFP's new head of political affairs and the DSP's secretary-general as the policy affairs chairman. Whether Hata ever had a firm grip on the leadership of the new party is debatable. Many suggested that he was a figurehead for the more powerful Ozawa, who ran the party from the secretary-general position behind the president's throne but could not emerge to take the top leadership position because he had such low support in public opinion polls.[3]

At the party's formation, it claimed the support of 214 members in the Diet, against 295 for the LDP. In the HR the NFP had 178 members plus another 36 in the HC. For the first time, the LDP could look at the opposition side in the House and see a single, large party offering itself to the Japanese electorate as a viable moderate alternative to LDP rule. At the NFP's initial meeting held in Yokohama on December 10, 1994, the assembled members sang the "Ode to Joy" from Beethoven's Ninth Symphony.[4] Such were the expectations for this first consolidated opposition party in the new post-LDP era.

However, for a party claiming 35 percent of the HR members, it won very low support figures from the Japanese public. In the first polls conducted after the NFP's founding, the party received 14.8 percent support, compared with nearly twice that level of support for the LDP (28.6

percent).[5] By the summer of 1995, the polls indicated popular support had fallen to about one-quarter of the LDP's support level. The primary reason for this plunge seemed to be a combination of the Shinshinto's unpopular tactics in the 1995 Diet session, which included sit-in demonstrations for the first time in decades since the JSP used them against the one-party rule of the LDP and the autocratic leadership style of Ozawa.[6]

The NFP decided to open up voting for the party's president in 1995 to the party's general membership. Over 1.7 million votes were counted, including 1.5 million votes from non–party members. Ozawa Ichiro received 1.1 million votes to 566,000 for Hata. The divisions that occurred within the Shinshinto in this election did not seem to be along old party lines but around individual politicians' preferences between Ozawa and Hata.

Former Komeito NFP members apparently had broken into several groups by the time of the party's 1995 presidential election between Ozawa and Hata. Sixty-eight former Komeito Diet members represented almost one-third of the NFP's Diet members. The *Yomiuri Shimbun* reported that even this once fairly monolithic group was divided into three groups: those favoring Hata, those supporting Ozawa, and a neutral group.[7] The old Shinshinto and Komeito members were somewhat evenly divided between the two candidates. Apparently, more of the old DSP members favored Ozawa, but Hosokawa and the members of the NJP supported Hata. After Ozawa was selected as NFP president, he selected former LDP member Nishioka Takeo as the party's secretary-general. Nishioka came to the NFP from the LDP, which he had also left in the 1970s as part of the Kono Yohei group that formed the NLC. Nishioka was generally viewed as supportive of Ozawa in the NFP's internal conflicts, but he was not a formal part of Ozawa's following. Komeito's Kanzaki Takenori was selected as chair of the party's General Council, and Noda Takeshi was chosen as chair of the Policy Research Committee. The Hata group and the former DSP group were shut out completely in the highest NFP appointments.[8]

With the establishment of the NFP, the nature of the Second Party System as a largely two-party system seemed assured. However, the NFP lasted only three years and fought only a single HR election campaign in October 1996. The Shinshinto began to collapse in late 1997 and fell completely apart by January 1998. One of the reason's for the NFP's lack of longevity can be detected in the factionalism that plagued the party from the very beginning. It was said the NFP had three strong factions: one centered around the leadership of Ozawa, another around his party rival of former prime minister Hata, and the third made up of the many Komeito members who had joined the party when it was formed in 1994. When the party broke up in early 1998, these three groups went their separate ways: Ozawa formed the Liberal Party; Hata and his followers eventually joined the Democratic Party; and the Komeito members went into temporary Komeito groups pending the reestablishment of the new Komeito.

From the start, the NFP had a serious problem trying to establish its own identity as something other than a group of politicians seeking to replace the LDP in power. Policy issues were deliberately left vague, since consensus was hard to reach with a collection of politicians representing nine different parties and spanning the ideological continuum from very conservative to quite liberal. The powerful position of the Komeito members in the party leadership and the foundation of much of the party's strength in the electorate made such policy or platform making very difficult. The initial party platform issued on early December 1994 called for "economic development and world peace . . . abolishing nuclear weapons, . . . protecting the environment, . . . a healthy welfare society and . . . social equality.[9] Among the serious policy differences within the party was a huge gap between the policy preferences of Ozawa and the former Komeito members on security issues, such as whether Japanese self-defense forces should participate in peacekeeping operations under United Nations' administration. Ozawa strongly argued that they could and should, whereas the ex-Komeito members strongly opposed this position. Various polls of Shinshinto Diet members indicated that a large majority opposed the preferences of their leader Ozawa on this important issue.[10]

Another weakness of the NFP was its inability to complete the merger of constituent party organizations into the new party. Komeito allowed only some of its Diet members (HC members up for election in 1995 and HR members) to merge into the NFP. The rest remained in separate Komeito organizations as well as the approximately 3,000 local-level elected Komeito office holders. This lack of organizational mergers with the constituent parties also had an important financial impact on the NFP. The various parties refused to transfer their funds and assets to the NFP. Instead, each of the separate groups held on to their own funds. In order to fund its own activities, the Shinshinto had to obtain a loan of 90 million yen ($900,000 at that time) made in the names of the party's leaders. It also sought to increase its funding from corporate Japan but never really was able to access this source of funding like its rival, the LDP.[11]

By late 1997, some of the Japanese media were describing the NFP as the new JSP of the 1990s. As the *Japan Times* editorialized: "In short, the role of the hapless parliamentary opposition played by the Socialists before 1993 has now been assumed by Shinshinto."[12] By November 1997, challenges to Ozawa's presidential leadership of the NFP were emerging. Kano Michihiko, the party's public relations chair, announced his intention to run against Ozawa in the following month's presidential election. Kano attacked Ozawa for seeking an alliance with the LDP in the Diet. Kano stated, "Shinshinto has not played its role as the largest opposition party." The ex-Komeito members of the party also challenged Ozawa's leadership in December when they announced plans to run their own slate of candidates in the 1998 HC elections. Added to the 40 members of the NFP who had left the party in the 1996–1997 period, Ozawa faced a party-ending set of challenges in December 1998. Former prime minister Hata had left with 13 Diet members in December 1996, and former prime minister Hosokawa had left in June 1997.[13] Consequently, when the Shinshinto finally collapsed in late December 1997 to early January 1998, it seemed to fall from the defectors leaving the party to protest the heavy-handed rule of Ozawa and the increasingly powerful role played by ex-Komeito members. On the other hand, Ozawa himself seemed eager to form his own party, where he could rule without all the infighting that had come to characterize the ill-fated Shinshinto.

DEMOCRATIC PARTY (MINSHUTO) OF KAN AND HATOYAMA

In the First Party System, Japan's largest opposition party was always the JSP, which later was called the SDPJ. From its founding in 1955 to the 1993 election, it functioned as the "alternative party" to LDP rule. However, it was replaced by the Shinseito, then the Shinshinto, and finally, after the collapse of the Shinshinto in early 1998, by the Democratic Party, or Minshuto.

The Democratic Party was the brainchild of Hatoyama Yukio, the grandson of one of the power figures of the LDP (Prime Minister Hatoyama) in the early postwar era. Hatoyama founded the Democratic Party in the summer of 1996, and for a time the Japanese media called it the "Hatoyama new party."[14] Hatoyama had been the secretary-general of the Sakigake Party just prior to his leaving that party and the founding on his new party. He held lengthy negotiations with Sakigake leader Takemura about the Sakigake membership coming en masse into Hatoyama's new party, but that idea was rejected by Hatoyama, since many of the politicians he was recruiting for the new party did not feel comfortable with Takemura, the architect of the LDP-SDPJ coalition government. The Democratic Party started small—largely with Hatoyama and his brother Kunio, who came to the party from his previous party, the Shinshinto. It was Kunio who particularly objected to allowing Takemura to join the new party. The early membership also included several others from the Sakigake and a couple of Diet members from the SDPJ plus 5 members from a minor party, the Citizens Action League. Just prior to the 1996 election, Japan's most popular politician, Kan Naoto, the former health and welfare minister, joined the Democratic Party. Kan had gained popular attention and subsequent support during his tenure as the health minister amid a tainted blood supply scandal in which he demanded honesty and full disclosure by the government of its mistakes and their costs. This behavior, most uncommon for a Japanese politician, made Kan into something of a Japanese folk hero. Another prospective member, Funada Hajime, of the Shinshinto Party, declined to join when the Democratic Party was formed because of his concern over the overly liberal nature of those who joined.

Hatoyama has some unique qualifications for party leadership in addition to his famous political name. He holds a doctorate in engineering and was a student at Tokyo University and Stanford University. Hatoyama and Kan are frequently mentioned as probable prime ministers in the twenty-first century by members of the Japanese media and other politicians. For a time in 1997, the Democratic Party had what amounted to co-leaders, with both Kan and Hatoyama sharing the media spotlight. However, in September 1997, the party membership selected Kan as the party's top leader and Hatoyama Yukio as the party secretary-general, the number two post.

The Democratic Party gradually merged other small groups into its ranks and had a total of 57 HR seats just prior to the October 1996 HR elections. A reconstituted Democratic Party of Japan was declared in April 1998 when it formally merged with four smaller parties. By late 1998, its ranks had increased to a total of 92 HR and 54 HC members and the status of the number one opposition party in the Diet. However, such new parties that have contested only a single HR election (and just held their own in terms of seats in 1996) are much more fragile than the powerful LDP. Kan Naoto, the Democratic Party leader, had risen in the polls in terms of his personal popularity that, in February 1998, he was the public's first choice to be Japan's next prime minister. He was also the top choice in the October 1997 Jiji News Service poll.[15] In the fall of 1998, Kan was attacked in the newsmagazines for his involvement in a sexual affair, and his status as the party's leader was clearly damaged. Just a few months earlier, the Minshuto had risen in the polls to a 16 percent support level compared with just 22 percent for the LDP.[16] That marked the first time the new party had risen above the 10 percent mark in the *Asahi Shimbun* polls. By later in 1998, the Democratic Party had risen to a 22 percent support level in the Kyodo News polls, but that fell back to the 16 percent level after the scandal had reached the media.[17] Clearly, much was expected of the Kan-Hatoyama party, and the next HR elections will indicate whether the new "umbrella party" will survive long enough to be viewed by the voters as a realistic alternative to the government offered by the LDP.

As the conflict within the Shinshinto intensified in 1996 and 1997, various politicians left and started their own parties. One of the most prominent politicians to do so was former prime minister Hata Tsutomu, who bolted and started the Taiyo Party in December 1996 with a handful of supporters. The Taiyo party was disbanded in 1998 after Hata joined the Democratic Party with some of the other groups that emerged from the wreckage of the Shinshinto.

Hatoyama Yukio defeated Kan Naoto in the Democratic Party's leadership selection process conducted in September 1999. The voters consisted of the party's 146 Diet members, 94 local chapter representatives and 166 non-incumbent candidates already slated for the next Diet elections. Hatoyama, the party's then deputy secretary-general, beat Kan in a two-man runoff and later appointed Kan as the party's new policy affairs chairman. Former prime minister Hata Tsutomu was selected to be the party's secretary-general.

OZAWA'S LIBERAL PARTY

When the Shinshinto broke up in January 1998, Ozawa took his faction and established the Liberal Party, which held its first meeting on January 6, 1998, and promptly elected Ozawa as its president. The Liberals, which began and finished the year with 42 HR and 12 HC members, surprised some political observers by surviving 1998 as a separate political party. Not only did the Ozawa party survive the year, but in December 1998 it engaged in a series of discussions with the LDP to establish a coalition government of the two parties, which would lead to the Liberals having at least one seat in the 1999 Obuchi cabinet. The coalition discussions struck many Japanese observers as being hard to understand from the perspective of the LDP, since the Liberals brought nothing to the LDP in terms of the HR—the LDP already had a majority in that chamber. Where it needed help was in the HC, where the LDP was 22 seats short of a majority and the 12 Liberal HC members did not help the LDP a great deal. The reduction of the number of cabinet ministers by two to a new total of eighteen was one of the administrative reforms adopted prior to the January 1999 Obuchi cabinet reshuffle. The reform meant that there were two fewer cabinet positions to reward senior members in the LDP's growing number of factions. To give one to the Ozawa party made no sense unless it was done as a ploy to lure the Ozawa group back into the LDP. The LDP had played such a game successfully in the mid-1980s by including the NLC of Kono Yohei in two successive cabinets and then accepting the NLC's members back into the LDP.

ORGANIZED LABOR, THE DSP, AND THE SECOND PARTY SYSTEM

Actually, the Shinshinto split into six small groups in the weeks following its collapse. Among the groups was one formed by former members of the DSP, which had been disbanded when they merged to form the Shinshinto in 1994. Since each of the major parties of the First Party System have been discussed elsewhere in this book, let us take the opportunity to discuss the DSP, organized labor, and their roles in both party systems.

The DSP has never been able to establish itself as a reasonable alternative to the conservative rule of the LDP. Many reasons could be advanced to explain the failure of the DSP to legitimize social democracy in Japan, but the most fundamental was the party's inability to convince the Japanese voters that, amid the growing prosperity they enjoyed under LDP rule since 1955, they should abandon the existing system and turn to some vague alternative. The concept of social democracy simply has not been considered a viable economic and political system for the postwar Japanese society.

Like the NLC and the SDF, the DSP was a splinter from one of the two largest parties operating in post-1945 Japan. Its "mother party," then the Japanese Socialist Party (now SDPJ), has been torn by internal conflict over ideological orientations throughout its long history. During the prewar years, the Right tended to dominate the organization of the socialist movement, but after the war the Left gradually established its domination. After the Katayama coalition cabinet fell in March 1948, the JSP continued its pattern of intraparty ideological struggles. It split and merged several times during the 1950s. The first Left-Right split occurred in January 1950, but the party reunited after seventy-five days. A more serious split over the party's position on the San Francisco Peace Treaty and the Japan-U.S. Security Treaty began in October 1951. The two wings of the Socialist Party ran separate slates of candidates during the next three general elections. The right wing came to victory over the left in the October 1952 election by securing 57 seats. Yet this election was actually a leftist victory because the Left increased its seat totals from the midteens to over 50. In the April 1953 elections the Right increased its seat totals to 66, but the Left won 72. Finally, in February 1955, the Right won 67 seats, whereas the Left captured 89 seats. Soon after the last election in this series, the two wings merged into a reunited Socialist Party. The reunification was initiated by the moderate Right.

The differences between the two wings came to a head over the renewal of the U.S.-Japan security treaty in 1960. The left wing would settle for nothing less than the termination of the treaty. The right wing, representing the JSP faction that had come from the moderate right wing of the prewar socialist movement (the Shamin, or Socialist People's Party), bolted the party. Later that year, part of the old Nichiro faction (from the Japan Labor Peasant Party, a more middle-of-the-road Socialist party of the prewar period) also split with the JSP and joined Nishio. In January 1960 the two groups established the Democratic Socialist Party (Minshu Shakaito). Nishio Suehiro was elected chairman of the new party, which initially had a total of 40 Diet members. However, the next election was a disaster, inasmuch as only 17 seats were captured, and since then the party has not won even 40 seats in the HR. The DSP won 32 seats in 1980 HR elections, 38 in 1983, and only 26 in 1986. It plummeted to a mere 14 seats in 1990 and won only 15 in its last election as an independent party in 1993.

The reason for existence for the DSP largely disappeared when Japanese labor reorganized under the new umbrella organization called Rengo in the late 1980s. The DSP was viewed by many Japanese as the political arm of Domei, the All Japan Labor Federation (Zen Nihon Rodo Sodomei). For the most part, organized labor in Japan formed around four central organizations, or national centers, that are the most influential among the 308 nationwide joint labor organizations. These were Sohyo, Domei, Shinsanbetsu (National Federation of Industrial Organizations), and Churitsuroren (Federation of Independent Unions). Sohyo was the largest, and Domei the second largest of these national centers. Sohyo, a confederation of fifty national organizations—including national unions, industrial federations, and joint councils—is leftist in its political orientation and has been a strong supporter of the JSP since the 1950s. Churitsuroren and Shinsanbetsu were much smaller, with ten and four affiliated organizations, respectively.

At the beginning of the 1990s, there were approximately 45 million workers in Japan. Slightly over 12 million were labor union members, with 78 percent of that number belonging to private-sector unions and 22 percent to public-sector unions. Only 25.2 percent of Japanese workers are unionized. This percentage has been constantly declining and represents a record low percentage since labor union membership surveys began in 1953. The 12 million unionized Japanese workers belonged to over 30,000 individual labor unions organized on a company-by-company basis.[18] By 1997, the size of the Japanese workforce had shrunk for the third straight year. The number of unionized workers stood at 12.29 million in June 1997, representing a decline of 166,000 from the previous year. Union members now accounted for only 22.6 percent of the workforce. At its peak in 1949, organized labor accounted for over 55 percent of the work-force.[19]

Prior to 1989, private-sector unions were represented primarily by the Domei labor confederation. Until 1989 Domei was a confederation of Japanese trade unions that principally represents the private sector. As of 1981, it included a total of thirty-one unions and federations representing a membership of 2.1 million workers.[20] The largest constituent Domei-affiliated trade unions were Zensen Domei (494,896 members: textiles), Zenkin Domei (313,612: metalworkers), and Zosenjuki Roren (220,697: shipbuilding and heavy machinery workers). The geographic distribution of Domei membership was heavily concentrated in the urban industrial prefectures. Tokyo (231,885 Domei members), Kanagawa (169,212), Osaka (238,013), Hyogo (141,169), and Aichi (148,450) prefectures represented the real Domei strongholds.[21]

Just as the right wing of the Sohyo was eventually forced out of that labor confederation to form Domei, the right wing of the JSP was forced out during the 1959–1960 period and formed the DSP. This split in the JSP in 1960 was accomplished with a great deal of encouragement by the Sohyo defectors. Very quickly after its formation, the DSP established firm ties with Domei, and the two were political partners until 1993.

The Domei led the movement in the 1980s to reunify the organized labor world. In September 1980 Domei and Sohyo, along with Churitsuroren and Shinsanbetsu, agreed that "our basic stance will be the attempt to unify all labor organizations beginning with those representing workers in the private sector and progressing to include those in the public sector. In 1988 and 1989 the pieces were put together for the establishment of Rengo (Nihon Rodo Kumiai Sorengokai) under the leadership of Yamagishi Akira. Rengo was formed by merging seventeen unions from Sohyo and twenty-one unions from Domei, for a combined total membership of over 7.6 million. As of 1990, the Japanese labor world consisted of the new Rengo; the Zenroren (Zenkoku Rodo Kumiai Sorengo), with 835,000 members and politically supporting the JCP; and the Zenrokyo (Zenkoku Rodo Kumiai Renraku Kyogikai), with 290,000 members primarily from the Tokyo Metropolitan Government Workers Union and close to the left wing of the JSP.

A revolution has occurred in the Japanese world of organized labor with the merger of Sohyo and Domei into Rengo. Initially, Rengo operated to undercut the labor support for the JSP (later SDPJ) and the DSP. Rengo fielded its own slate of candidates for the 1989 HC elections, and 11 of them were elected. This was a great labor victory that actually set the stage for the demise of both the DSP and the JSP in the mid-1990s.

The merger of these two longtime labor rivals caused some confusion regarding the nature of the appropriate campaign support for the two Socialist parties. Rengo decided to run its own candidates in the 1989 upper house elections and postpone the tough political decisions on which of the two Socialist parties it would choose. Of the 12 Rengo candidates who ran in the HC prefectural districts in the July 1989 elections, 11 were successful and largely contributed to inflicting the first national-level election defeat on the LDP in those elections. Following this unexpected victory, Rengo talked about running candidates in as many as 47 districts in the 1990 HR elections. However, only 4 Rengo candidates ran in Osaka, Hyogo, and Gunma prefectures. The two Osaka candidates were also supported by the JSP, DSP, and SDF, but they fell an average of 3,500 votes short of winning seats. In contrast with the 1989 HC results, only one of the Rengo candidates (in Hyogo's 5th District) was successful in 1990. In the 1992 HC elections, Rengo was completely unable to repeat its previous victory of 1989. Not a single Rengo candidate was elected to the HC in 1992. By the time of the 1993 HR elections, Rengo had completely changed its electoral strategy. It no longer sought to elect its own labeled candidates to the Diet but instead sought to work with candidates from various parties, including the JSP and DSP, plus the new parties that had emerged from the splits in the LDP. The Rengo leader, Yamanashi, was one of the primary forces behind the establishment of the Hosokawa cabinet in 1993. It facilitated the formation of the Hosokawa government by constraining the left wing of the JSP, which opposed the idea of a coalition with former LDP Diet members; by preventing the DSP from entering into a coalition with the LDP; and by encouraging the Japan New Party and Sakigake into entering the coalition.[22] Rengo was the single largest group supporting the Hosokawa government.[23] Finally, the moderate Japanese labor movement had access to the prime minister and cabinet, and in October 1993 the first Japanese prime minister since 1947 gave the keynote speech at a national labor organization.[24]

After the Hosokawa government fell in the spring of 1994, Rengo searched for other ways to seek influence in the Diet and Japanese government. It continued to support the fatally weak Hata government in 1994.

However, when the three-party LDP-DSPJ-Sakigake government emerged in the summer of 1994, Rengo moved to facilitate a reorganization of the opposition parties by supporting the foundation of Shinshinto.

In the 1996 HR elections, Rengo was strongly pressured by the LDP's supporting corporations to vote for LDP candidates. Many Rengo unions moved closer to the LDP in that election, and the old labor supported parties (DSP and SDPJ) performed badly in the October 1996 election. Actually, the labor movement toward the LDP had begun in the 1970s and 1980s as the Labor Party realized it had been excluded from Japan's decision-making process and needed to create access with the ruling LDP.[25]

One of the reasons Rengo had so much trouble delivering its vote in the 1996 election was the lack of commitment of many of its union members to the organization's political agenda of supporting anti-LDP parties. A Rengo survey in June 1996 disclosed that almost 59 percent of polled members supported no political party, nearly 15 percent supported Shinshinto, 14 percent supported the SDPJ, 7.2 percent supported the LDP, and 2 percent supported the Sakigake or the JCP.[26]

Rengo not only was unable to elect its own candidates to the HR but also was unable to support many of the DSP candidates the Domei had helped to elect in so many previous elections. The LDP reacted to its 1989 HC loss by pressuring Japanese businesses into forcing their labor unions to support LDP candidates in the 1990 elections. This was a successful strategy, for two major Rengo unions—JR Soren (General Federation of Japan Railroad Unions) and Shogyo Roren (Federation of Commercial Labor Unions)—openly supported the LDP.[27] The automobile workers' unions, which had been strong DSP supporters since the 1960s, were placed under impressive pressure by Japan's automobile companies to support individual LDP candidates. DSP candidates from various parts of Japan reported that they were not receiving the same support from automobile unions and companies that they had enjoyed in previous elections. Both Nissan and Toyota, along with several hundred other corporations, were strongly asked to support the LDP, and they issued appeals to their branches, plants, and sales networks throughout the nation to support LDP candidates. As a result of this successful LDP strategy and the Rengo confusion, 18 of the DSP's candidates finished as runners-up in their districts. Twenty-one DSP candidates lost by an average of over 18,000 votes behind the final seat winners. Only 6 DSP candidates lost by 5,000 votes or less. Only 14 DSP HR candidates won in 1990.

The DSP's main role has always been that of a moderate alternative to voters who may favor either the LDP or the SDPJ. For decades the DSP was the most logical coalition partner for the LDP if the latter lost its majorities in the HC. Such an event happened in the 1979 HR elections, and the DSP began to formulate a list of its demands to be presented to the LDP if the latter party was in need of a coalition partner. The DSP demands read much like the reforms of the 1990s: a reform of the electoral laws, especially in the area of political finance; a freedom-of-information act and changes in the election laws to allow increased media advertising in election campaigns; administrative reforms on the local-government level, as well as a reduction in the number of public officials, including public corporations; and reforms in the Japanese welfare system. The LDP got enough independents to switch to the party to avoid the necessity of such a coalition, and then in the 1980s it formed a minor coalition with the NLC instead of the DSP. The DSP also engaged in planning for a possible coalition with the LDP in 1990.

Clearly, the DSP was a party seeking power in a supporting position with an LDP government. It had largely given up on trying to bring about a non-LDP coalition government.[28] Ironically, it became a governmental party in the 1990s, not with the LDP but with the other long-suffering opposition parties, the SDPJ and Komeito in the Hosokawa and Hata cabinets. The DSP had won 15 seats in the 1993 HR elections and became one of the nine parties to form the Hosokawa cabinet in the summer of 1993 and the subsequent minority Hata cabinet a year later. The DSP secured its first ever cabinet ministry in the Hosokawa government when the DSP chairman Ouchi Keigo served as the health and welfare minister.

When the Shinshinto was formed in late 1994, the DSP merged its members into the new party and remained there until the party collapsed in January 1998. For a time after the collapse, former DSP members formed a new group, but eventually they moved into the newly rebuilt Democratic Party. As the 1990s come to an end, Rengo has become a major supporter of the Democratic Party, and the quest since the 1960s by moderate organized labor for a moderate political party able to effectively contest elections with the LDP seems to be successful.

CONCLUSIONS

The First Party System and its division of political power between the LDP and the JSP died in the spring of 1993 and was replaced by a new configuration of parties largely dominated by splinters from the LDP. By 1999, the three dominant parties of the Second Party System were the revived LDP and its two largely conservative rivals, the Democratic Party and the Liberal Party. The other significant party is the resurrected

Komeito, which emerged in 1998 from the wreckage of the Shinshinto. The irony of this new system is that all three of these major parties are now led by LDP or former LDP leaders. From the Right-Left divisions of the First Party System, the Second Party System now has a decidedly Right-Right axis that has changed the nature of Japanese political debate as the new century dawns.

NOTES

1. *Asahi Shimbun,* January 12, 1996.
2. *Asahi Shimbun* polls, "Live by the Numbers: Die by the Numbers," *By the Way,* September-October 1994.
3. *Japan Times Weekly,* November 28, 1994.
4. *Japan Times,* December 19, 1994.
5. *Nihon Kaizai Weekly,* December 19, 1994.
6. *Yomiuri Shimbun,* June 24, 1995.
7. *Yomiuri Shimbun,* June 26, 1995.
8. *Nikkei Shimbun Weekly,* August 12, 1996.
9. *Japan Times,* December 19, 1994.
10. *Yomiuri Shimbun,* June 1, 1996.
11. *Economist,* EIU Country Report, 4th Qt. 1995. November 11, 19997.
12. *Japan Times,* November 10, 1997.
13. *Japan Times Weekly,* December 12, 1997.
14. *Nihon Keizai Shimbun,* September 2, 1996.
15. *Japan Times,* February 2, 1998.
16. *Asahi Shimbun,* July 15, 1998.
17. *New York Times,* December 12, 1998.
18. *Asahi Shimbun,* November 21 and 27, 1989.
19. *Japan Times,* January 19, 1998.
20. Ministry of Labor, "Labor Union Survey," June 30, 1981.
21. "This Is Domei." (Tokyo: Domei, December 1979)
22. Lonny E. Carlile, "Party Politics and the Japanese Labor Movement: Rengo's New Political Force," *Asia Survey* 34 (July 1994): 606–620.
23. *Rengo,* vol. 6 (July 1993).
24. Carlile, "Party Politics and the Japanese Labor Movement," pp. 618–619.
25. Ibid., p. 611.
26. *Japan Times Weekly,* September 9, 1996.
27. *Sankei Shimbun,* April 12, 1990.
28. Gerald Curtis claims the DSP was formed too early to obtain broad support from the Japanese electorate. In 1960, when the DSP began, Japan was still divided between conservative and progressive camps, and the DSP did not fit well into either. The DSP, continues Curtis, was too weak and was captured by the Domei to exploit new opportunities in the 1970s and 1980s. Gerald Curtis, *The Japanese Way of Politics* (New York: Columbia University Press, 1988), pp. 23–24.

six

The Komeito Returns:
The Party of "Buddhist Democracy"

Ronald J. Hrebenar

In many respects the Komeito, or Clean Government Party (CGP), is the anomaly within the Japanese political party system. It is the only religious party in modern Japanese history, and it is the most disciplined party organization in Japanese politics. Feelings toward the Komeito among the Japanese people are seldom neutral. They range from intense support to intense dislike. The reason for this intensity lies in the Komeito's relationship with the giant Buddhist lay organization, the Soka Gakkai. To understand the position of the Komeito in Japanese society and politics, one must have an understanding of its parent, the Soka Gakkai.

But before I explore the background of the Komeito, I should provide an explanation for the title of this chapter: "The Komeito Returns." This refers to the fact that between 1994 and 1998, the Komeito as a political party had disappeared, having merged into the New Frontier Party (NFP, or Shinshinto). However, as the punchline of the old joke notes, "The reports of its demise were exaggerated." Parts of the Komeito still lived, and when the NFP collapsed in late 1997, the Komeito leaders began planning for the reappearance of their once again unified party in the late fall of 1998. The Komeito lives, but for what purpose? The answer to that question forms the core of this chapter.

THE SOKA GAKKAI-KOMEITO CONNECTION

At the Komeito's eighteenth national convention held in early December 1970, party chairman Takeiri Yoshikatsu spoke to the party activists and stressed the separation of the Komeito from its founding organization, the Soka Gakkai. Subsequently, during the 1970s, the Komeito leadership went to great lengths to establish an image of the separateness of the two powerful organizations. Because the Soka Gakkai and the Komeito were and are so totally intertwined, an awareness of the nature of the parent organization is crucial to an understanding of its creation.

THE RISE OF THE SOKA GAKKAI

The Soka Gakkai is clearly the largest and most successful of all the "new religions" *(shinko shukyo)* that came to prominence in the post–World War II years. By the time its third president, Ikeda Daisaku, had resigned in April 1979, the Buddhist lay organization claimed to have grown to a membership of 10 million. The Soka Gakkai, whose name literally means "value-creating academic society," is a religious movement of lay believers who are attached to a traditionally nationalistic Buddhist sect, the Nichiren Shoshu (Orthodox Nichiren Sect).[1] The Nichiren Shoshu is a very popular sect in Japan that traces its beliefs back to the Buddhist monk Nichiren (1222–1282), who sought to establish what he believed was the one correct sect of Buddhism in Japan (and whose teachings reflected this belief). Nichiren condemned all other religions for heresy and taught that all its precepts are absolute.[2] The Nichiren Shoshu is just one of the many sects within the Nichiren school of Japanese Buddhism, and the Soka Gakkai is a lay organization charged with the "world-wide propagation of Nichiren Shoshu's doctrines and the creation of social programs which will enable the sect's religious ideals to be transferred into social reality."[3] By the mid-1990s, the Soka Gakkai was just one of thirty-eight organizations that claim to represent the teachings of Nichren.[4]

The Soka Gakkai was created on November 18, 1930, by Makiguchi Tsunesaburo, a schoolteacher in Tokyo, who sought to reform the nature of Japanese society by restructuring the nation's education system. After seven years of failure, Makiguchi switched to advocating a religious revival based on a belief in Nichiren Shoshu to set the stage for his goal of educational reform. Both Makiguchi and his successor, Toda Josei, were imprisoned by the Japanese military during World War II for failure to support the war effort. Makiguchi died in prison, but Toda survived and immediately after the war began to transform the organization into a "religious movement dedicated to the creation of a Buddhist society in Japan."[5]

At the core of this reconstructed religious movement, the Soka Gakkai's central objective is the improvement of Japanese society in particular and the world in general through the reformation of human character. The movement continues to uphold Nichiren's intolerance of other "false sects," and its adherents still believe that Nichiren is the true

Buddha and that Shakyamunu was a transitory Buddha. The truth of this true Buddha and his religion is to be communicated to all so that humankind can become enlightened and thus construct a far better life and society. Consequently, each member of the Soka Gakkai must actively participate in proselytizing the unconverted into the organization. This aggressive conversion process (called *shakubuku*, meaning literally "to break and subdue" or "to vanish evil aggressively") occasionally involved continual pressure on a prospective convert until the Soka Gakkai members had achieved their purpose—one aspect of the organization that contributes to the group's strongly negative image among many Japanese.[6]

More than any of the other postwar "new religions," the Soka Gakkai melds the religious and secular worlds into a single world. Political ideas are a natural product of this religion. The "Buddhist democracy" *(Obutsu Myogo)* sought by the Soka Gakkai is defined as a combination of "social welfare and individual happiness."[7] Such a democracy would occur when all realize the truth of Nichiren Buddhism and are thus converted to the true faith.

Hence the Soka Gakkai conceives of this democracy as a form of socialism or neosocialism that anticipates an important role for governmental institutions. Accordingly, it was quite logical for the Soka Gakkai to branch out into politics during the 1950s and to form its own political party in 1964. In an unprecedented action (within the context of modern Japanese history), the Komeito was invented with a view toward using politics to convert the nation.[8] Or, as one political scientist has put it, "It was the transition from Soka Gakkai religious politicking to Komeito political religioneering." In short, the party was formed to mold the environment toward acceptance of its religious objectives.[9]

In defense of their creation of the Komeito, Soka Gakkai leaders point to the Christian Democratic parties of Western Europe as being analogous to their Buddhist party in Japan. In addition, they have repeatedly tried to reassure the Japanese public that they have no intention of forcing Nichiren Shoshu on an unwilling nation. Statements to support this position include a promise not to make Nichiren Shoshu the state religion in defiance of the constitution. Former president Ikeda has commented on this problem by saying: "A religion which tries to impose itself on people by the use of state power proves by that it is impotent."[10] Despite such statements, however, many knowledgeable Japanese fear that the promises of the Komeito and the Japan Communist Party (JCP) to protect freedom of religion, freedom of speech, and democracy may not be kept if total power is won by those parties.

Generally speaking, the Japanese have not been considered a very religious people. Many of them profess to support one or more religions, but few seem to take these religions seriously except as institutions within which special ceremonies (e.g., weddings, funerals) are performed. In this nation of approximately 125 million people, about 98 million profess to be followers of Shinto, another 88 million follow Buddhism, and still another million are Christians. Of course, these figures imply almost two religions per person—quite a feat in a nation that is not very religious! Such a situation can exist only in a society where such affiliations are lightly held.

James White has noted that the Soka Gakkai differs in some important respects from the rest of the new religions of postwar Japan. Whereas the new religions, in general, were considered tolerant, eclectic, and attentive to everyday life, and were characterized by a belief in faith cures, the Soka Gakkai was considered intolerant, exclusive, and characterized by a strong group orientation.[11]

As noted earlier, the Soka Gakkai and the Komeito generate strong negative feelings among many Japanese. In a Nippon Television (NTV) survey conducted in the spring of 1964, 42 percent of the 1,500 respondents chose the word *fanatical* to describe the Soka Gakkai.[12] James Dator's poll of non–Soka Gakkai respondents discovered that 4 percent liked the Gakkai, 57 percent disliked it, 16 percent were neutral, and 23 percent had no answer.[13] Other students of the Gakkai noted that it was described by many Japanese as "militaristic," "fascistic," "sacrilegious," "dangerous," and "ultranationalistic."[14] The U.S. magazine *Newsweek* noted that "the Soka Gakkai looks like an Oriental blend of Christian Science and the John Birch Society."[15] Although these negative feelings toward the Soka Gakkai have also been attached to the Komeito to a certain degree, the Komeito has gradually managed to earn a certain respect after being seen as extremist in its early years. Clearly, its professionalism and zeal are respected by many Japanese.[16]

The main characteristics of the Soka Gakkai include a complex organizational structure, an intensity of commitment on the part of its members, and a vigorous and wide range of activities. Its organization comprises two hierarchies. The first is a religious guidance and membership indoctrination structure based on the religious conversion process, in which a new member becomes a disciple of the member who converted him. The basic unit (or cell) is composed of approximately 10 families, who meet daily for discussion meetings. Still larger units are made up of groups (50–100 families) and districts (500–1,000 families).[17] Districts are combined to form chapters, general chapters, local headquarters, and general headquarters. In all, the Soka Gakkai encompasses tens of thousands of cells.

The second hierarchy, also geographically based, utilizes the *buroku* (block) system, which was developed to facilitate the entry of the Soka Gakkai into the world of politics. The blocks are carefully combined and directed to concentrate the organization's political power within the appropriate political subdivisions being contested. Prior to 1983, the system was apparently flexible enough to concentrate a combination of blocks for a town- or village-level election and to combine membership in several prefectures for a House of Councillors (HC) national constituency election.[19]

On April 24, 1979, Soka Gakkai president Ikeda Daisaku unexpectedly resigned, sending a shock wave through both the parent and the offspring organizations. Ikeda, without doubt, had been the most influential and charismatic of the four Soka Gakkai leaders. Under his leadership the organization grew tremendously, from approximately 1 million families in 1959—the year prior to Ikeda's rise to the presidency—to 7 million families only a decade later.[20] By the time of Ikeda's resignation, 7,880,000 families were claimed by the Soka Gakkai. By the mid-1990s, the organization claimed slightly over 8.1 million families, a number that has held steady in recent years. Ikeda's personality, intensity, and commitment to the Soka Gakkai combined to give him an unprecedented amount of power in an organization structured on authoritarian principles. His abrupt resignation was viewed by many as having been forced by unhappy leadership in the Nichiren Shoshu sect, which objected to the worship of Ikeda as a godlike figure by many members of the Soka Gakkai. Some of the members even considered Ikeda the "true Buddha."

What further increased tensions was Ikeda's policy of constructing Soka Gakkai assembly halls, which tended to separate the lay organization even more from the Nichiren Shoshu. Despite a series of apologies directed to the Nichiren Shoshu, tensions rose to the point that Ikeda was forced to tender his resignation not only as president of the Soka Gakkai but also as worldwide leader of all the Nichiren Shoshu lay associations. As has often happened in Japan, Ikeda was given the position of honorary president and remained president of Soka Gakkai International. Moreover, many speculated that he would remain firmly in control of the apparatus of the Soka Gakkai despite his resignation. That seems to have been the case.

Ikeda twice demonstrated the enormous financial potential of his organization. In 1965, approximately 35.5 billion yen was raised in only four days to construct a hall of worship. According to Harashima Takashi, the former chief of the Doctrine Study Department of the Soka Gakkai, many members gave all the money they had saved for marriages, canceled their insurance policies, and took out personal loans. A second sum of 67 billion yen was collected between 1964 and 1977 for assembly hall construction.[21]

Such sums seem enormous, given the basic nature of the Soka Gakkai's membership. Many members are recruited from the underclass of Japanese society—those who were affected by Japan's demoralizing in World War II and by the alienating aspects of the rapid urbanization and increased complexity of modern life. As Arvin Palmer has argued, the most important reason behind the tremendous growth in the Soka Gakkai has been the basic breakdown of the traditional social structure and value system, which has forced many Japanese to seek purpose, identity, and a sense of belonging.[22] The organization responds to these needs and offers relief from misery, as well as a sense of belonging and a hope of economic prosperity. In short, Soka Gakkai propaganda is clearly "an appeal to the down and out, the economically deprived and the socially disoriented."[23]

Several surveys of Soka Gakkai members were conducted in the early and mid-1960s. James Dator summarized the findings of these Japanese research projects by noting that Soka Gakkai members are below average in income and have a lower-than-average standard of living. They also exhibit less formal education than the average Japanese. It should be emphasized, however, that although many Soka Gakkai members are below average in income, they do not represent the lowest rung in the national income ladder.[24] The surveys indicate that many join because of problems they were having prior to their affiliation. One survey, for instance, found nearly 60 percent gave negative reasons for joining the Soka Gakkai, including poor health (26 percent), economic distress (3 percent), poor human relations (7 percent), and other troubles (23 percent).[25] Azumi Koya, in his study of 386 members, found that 97 joined for reasons of ill health, 38 because of loss of success in work, 27 because of family frictions, and 34 because of "undisciplined lives."[26] And a Tokyo University study in 1962 discovered that 81 percent of the Soka Gakkai members surveyed related some problem as the reason they joined.[27] Dator saw members of the Soka Gakkai as a somewhat less satisfied and more friendless group whose members generally had no religious affiliation before joining.[28] Finally, Azumi concluded that these members tend to be no more or less apathetic politically than the general Japanese population but also that their turnout at elections is nearly 100 percent once they have joined the Soka Gakkai.[29]

Daniel Metraux, writing in the 1990s, suggests that impressionistic observations of contemporary Soka Gakkai members indicate that the new type of member is better educated and more professional in occupations than the older types of members. One piece of evidence to support this observation comes from the more professional nature of Komeito's new generation of Diet members.[30]

Soka Gakkai members were seen as consistent, but critical, supporters of the Liberal Democratic Party (LDP) during the years prior to the formation of Komeito.[31] One study of Gakkai members' voting habits during this period indicated that 51 percent supported the Right (LDP) and 37 percent supported the Left, with 31 percent supporting the Japan Socialist Party (JSP) and 3 percent the JCP. The remaining 12 percent supported one side or the other depending on the situation.[32] Many political commentators have noted the close relationship between top Komeito leaders and members of the Tanaka-Takeshita-Obuchi faction in the LDP. After Ozawa left the faction and then the LDP in 1993, the close relationship between him and Komeito leader Ishida allowed them to work together to form the Shinshinto.[33] In fact, one of the reasons for the breakup of the Shinshinto in 1997 was the frequent complaint that the Komeito members held too much power in the Ozawa-led organization.

Voters' surveys, as expected, show very similar demographic patterns for Komeito supporters. Generally, they are more likely to be women than men (59 percent versus 41 percent, respectively), younger more likely than older, workers in small or medium-sized business, or manual laborers, and less educated. In short, Komeito supporters come from the Japanese lower middle class and middle class. This generalization is supported by the voting pattern for the Komeito in that the party performs best in districts characterized by low income and low levels of education.[34]

Recognizing these membership characteristics and the psychological attitudes associated with them, the Soka Gakkai has structured itself to appeal to the needs of the people involved. It has constructed an entire educational system, including its own university, Soka Daigaku. Several million young men and women are organized by men's, women's, and student departments. Other major departments emphasize athletic, musical, dance, and drama skill development.

Accurate numbers regarding Soka Gakkai membership are difficult to obtain. One set of figures suggests the presence of about 2,000 members in 1943, when Makiguchi Tsunesaburo was imprisoned. After the war, Toda Josei built the organization from about 5,000 families to 750,000 during his lifetime. By 1982, the Soka Gakkai claimed a membership of about 4 million, whereas 7,910,000 had embraced the Nichiren Shoshu faith.[35] Another source states that when Ikeda became president in 1960, the organization consisted of 172,000 families. This total grew to 500,000 families five years later and totaled 800,000 families in 1981. In the first six months of 1981, the Soka Gakkai claimed an increase of 100,000 members, mostly from the Tokyo and Osaka areas.[36]

In recent years, then, the Soka Gakkai's rate of growth has dramatically slowed, a decline that has obviously hurt the Komeito. Various explanations have been advanced to explain this decline. Perhaps the continued prosperity of postwar Japan was responsible; or the recruiting efforts of the Soka Gakkai may have been undermined by the constant scandals of the late 1970s. In any case, Akiya Einosuke, now president of Soka Gakkai, said in a 1980 newspaper interview: "We are now in a period of stabilization after an era of very rapid growth. Our organization has become so huge and has problems that need adjustment."[37] It remains to be seen if the recession of the 1990s has any impact on the Komeito's numbers.

THE SOKA GAKKAI CREATES A POLITICAL PARTY

The history of the Soka Gakkai's direct involvement in electoral politics dates back to November 1954—a full decade prior to the founding of the Komeito. In that month a department of cultural affairs was established within the Soka Gakkai organization to promote a variety of activities in political, economic, cultural, and educational fields. Such a department was based on the organization's belief in the necessity of creating a cultural state founded on Buddhism. In the April 1955 local elections, 51 Soka Gakkai members running as independents were elected to mark the first Gakkai effort in the world of politics. The following year, 3 out of 6 Gakkai candidates won election to the HC.

A primary reason underlying the desire of this religious group to embark upon a course of political activities was the avowed goal to establish a national ordination hall *(kokuritsu kaidan)*. Such a hall would be a state-sponsored temple for the ordination and confirmation of the followers of Nichiren Shoshu. An editorial in the Soka Gakkai's official newspaper, *Seikyo Shimbun,* in 1954 indicated the high priority of the project: "We must work to have this message [a Diet order for the construction of a national ordination hall] issued. Because a majority of the members of the House of Representatives (HR) will have to agree to its issue, our activities to propagate the true faith must acquire a new dimension."[38]

In August 1957 Soka Gakkai president Toda wrote a series of articles on the theory of Obutsu Myogo, which postulated the combination of secular government and Buddhism into a single entity of "Buddhist Democracy." At the annual meeting of Soka Gakkai leadership in 1959, the new president, Ikeda Daisaku, stated that "the Soka Gakkai is participating in elections because it must overcome the obstacles to the construction of a national ordination hall, obeying the supreme order of our great Saint Nichiren."[39]

By late 1959, Ikeda had concluded that it was time to upgrade the organization of the Soka Gakkei's political arm. In May 1961 the Cultural Affairs Department was upgraded to a bureau, and a separate Political Affairs Department was established. A new organization of the religion's politicians, the Komei Political League (Komei Seiji Renmei), was created in November 1961. At its founding, it had 9 HC members; 7 prefectural assembly members; and 268 municipal and ward assembly members.[40] The league's charter and platform indicated the reliance of the group on the "Great Saint," and among the four points in the platform was a strong opposition to nuclear weapons. In fact, this antinuclear stance has long been a policy of the Soka Gakkai. In 1982 Ikeda led a Soka Gakkai delegation to the United Nations to give a speech opposing nuclear weapons.

Following the successes scored in the 1962 HC elections (15 seats won by Gakkai members), the organization decided to create a regular political party to facilitate the Gakkai's advance into the HR. Thus, on November 17, 1964, the Komeito was formed by the Soka Gakkai. The party platform indicated that the goals of the Komeito were to be as follows: world peace, humanitarian socialism, a mass party based on Buddhist democracy, and the eradication of corrupt politics.[41] Immediately following the party's victory in the next general elections in 1967 (25 new seats in the HR), Takeiri Yoshikatsu and Yano Jun'ya were named chairman and secretary-general, respectively, of the new party. They remained in these offices from 1967 until the late 1980s, thus giving the Komeito extraordinary stability in terms of the party's leadership. No other party in Japan has been so stable in terms of its leadership.

In those early days, it was clear that the Komeito was merely a political arm of the Soka Gakkai. Ikeda has been quoted as saying that the "Komeito cannot exist without the Soka Gakkai," and that these two organizations are "one and indivisible."[42] All of the Komeito leaders and Diet members held highly visible leadership positions in the parent Soka Gakkai. Komeito chairman Takeiri Yoshikatsu was an executive director of the Soka Gakkai; Yano Jun'ya, the secretary-general, was also a vice chairman of the Soka Gakkai national board of directors.[43] In addition, all of the party's candidates for public office were drawn from the ranks of the parent body. This pattern continued through the rest of the 1960s until the so-called Fujiwara affair, which occurred in late 1969 and early 1970.

Fujiwara Hirotatsu is a political scientist whose book *I Denounce Soka Gakkai* (Soka Gakkai O Kiru) criticized the Komeito for its attempts to make Nichiren Shoshu the Japanese state religion.[44] The Soka Gakkai exerted considerable pressure in order to suppress criticism of the organization during this period. It urged journalists not to write articles unfriendly to the religion and threatened to boycott newspapers that planned to carry any such articles. Initially, the Soka Gakkai tried to prevent Fujiwara's book from being published; failing that, it then sought to halt the book's distribution and subsequent sale. Apparently, the services of then LDP secretary-general and, later, Prime Minister Tanaka Kakuei were requested by the Komeito chairman to try to halt publication of Fujiwara's book. Fujiwara fought back, and, with the assistance of *Mainichi Shimbun* reporter Naito Kunio (who later lost his job at the newspaper), the book became a best-seller and the center of political debate during early 1970. Later, during the Diet debate on this issue, the JCP, JSP, and Democratic Socialist Party (DSP) tried unsuccessfully to exploit the "suppression of free speech" issue but were blocked in these attempts by the LDP leadership. Ultimately, the criticism of the Soka Gakkai's actions became so loud that the organization was forced to withdraw formally from politics. On May 3, 1970, it officially separated from the Komeito, and all party references to the goal of establishing a national ordination hall were dropped. All Komeito leaders and office-holders had to give up their leadership posts in the Soka Gakkai, and the Komeito made a considerable effort to recruit non–Soka Gakkai members and candidates. At the 1970 annual meeting of the Soka Gakkai, President Ikeda announced that the planned ordination hall need not be maintained by the state; that it would no longer be referred to as a "national hall"; and that "no Diet resolution would be sought for such a hall." Finally, he announced that a new set of rules and policies would be established for the Komeito in 1970 (to be examined later in this chapter).[45]

One result of this scandal and others that rocked the Soka Gakkai during the 1970s has been a decrease in the number of new conversions to the religion and a small exodus of former believers. Moreover, because the media seem to be less intimidated by the religion issue, the scandals that came to light in the late 1970s were well covered in the national press and newsmagazines.[46]

Nevertheless, in everything the Komeito does, it must be aware of its subordinate position vis-à-vis the Soka Gakkai. As Akiya Einosuke, then a vice president of the Soka Gakkai, warned in 1980: "If the Komeito goes beyond the limit of acceptability from our point of view, we will indicate our concern to the party."[47] Such a concern might revolve around the question of state recognition of the Yasukuni Shrine or around the defense issue in general.

THE SOKA GAKKAI SCANDALS

The Soka Gakkai suffered through a period of particular strain at the end of the 1970s and the beginning of the 1980s as a series of scandals rocked the Komeito's parent organization. These scandals may have contributed to the party's terrible showing in the 1980 HR elections; they certainly received a great deal of public attention and were gleefully reported and commented upon by nearly every facet of the nation's mass media.

The Yamazaki affair centered on the person of Yamazaki Masatomo, a lawyer and adviser to the Soka Gakkai. Yamazaki apparently participated in many of the organization's most secret and sensitive activities during the 1970s. When he allegedly threatened to divulge these secrets to the media, the Soka Gakkai paid him 300 million yen to keep quiet. It was only after Yamazaki allegedly demanded an additional 500 million yen that the Soka Gakkai turned the case over to the police. The organization's leadership defended the initial payoff by arguing that Yamazaki was intimately involved in the negotiations between the Nichiren Shoshu and the Soka Gakkai, claiming that if those sensitive talks failed, the possibility existed for "10 million members of the Soka Gakkai being excommunicated." As Miyakawa Kiyohiko, chief of the Youth Department of the Soka Gakkai, has noted, "The fact that we paid it shows the importance of ties with the sect for us."[48]

In a different but related case, Yamazaki was charged with the wiretapping of JCP chairman Miyamoto's home from June to July 1975. Yamazaki, in Tokyo District Court hearings, said that he and others committed this act on orders from Hojo Hiroshi, then vice president and later president of the Soka Gakkai.[49]

When he resigned, Harashima Takashi was the chief of the Soka Gakkai's doctrinal study office late in 1979; in the spring of 1980 he began to criticize his old employers, for which he was subsequently expelled in August 1980. Harashima's central attack was directed against the role played by former president Ikeda. He charged Ikeda with reigning over the Soka Gakkai "as an absolute dictator and behaving toward the members as if he were the reincarnation of Nichiren." Harashima blamed Ikeda for many of the problems the organization has had with the leadership of the Nichiren Shoshu sect, noting that the "antagonism grew strong among the Nichiren Shoshu priests, particularly the younger ones. As a result, the Soka Gakkai has repeatedly had to beg the sect's pardon. Eventually, Mr. Ikeda found it necessary to resign as president of the organization."[50]

Finally, Ikeda was involved in a well-publicized libel suit against an editor of a monthly magazine. The magazine published a pair of stories in 1976 alleging that Ikeda had had extramarital affairs with two female Soka Gakkai members who later became Komeito Diet members.[51] This case also received a great deal of attention from the media during 1982 and 1983. Such negative press attention cannot help but have a weakening effect on the Soka Gakkai and, of course, on its offspring, the Komeito.

October 1982 was an especially bad month for Soka Gakkai leader Ikeda Daisaku, who appeared in court three times to deny having affairs with Komeito Diet members, to testify in the Yamazaki blackmail case, and to acknowledge that Soka Gakkai members had wiretapped the house of JCP leader Miyamoto Kenji.

THE SOKA GAKKAI–JCP ACCORD

On July 27, 1975, an Agreement of Reconciliation was announced by the leadership of the Soka Gakkai and the JCP. It provided for the coexistence of the two organizations aiming at the common goal of world peace. Both parties recognized the need for noninterference between them in their respective political stands, as well as for the JCP's acceptance of the freedom of religious propaganda and the espousal of faith. In return, the Soka Gakkai promised not to view communism with hostility. It was also agreed that both sides would take action to help prevent nuclear war and to banish nuclear weapons. Finally, both the JCP and the Soka Gakkai promised to refrain from name-calling and to settle disputes by mutual negotiation.[52]

Later in 1975, the *Mainichi Shimbun* brought together Ikeda and JCP chairman Miyamoto for a series of dialogues, which were given extensive publicity.[53] Meanwhile, Ikeda argued in a journal article that the agreement could be the basis of coexistence with the Communists in order to secure fundamental stability in Japan during the next twenty to thirty years.[54]

Many political analysts in Japan have speculated on the actual motivations behind this agreement. Some believe that Ikeda sought an understanding with the JCP in order to facilitate the Soka Gakkai's future expansion into Communist countries. Indeed, it could be argued that given President Ikeda's visits to the People's Republic of China and the Soviet Union, he may have wanted to establish the idea that Soka Gakkai and socialism have doctrines in common.

The Komeito's leadership and general membership reacted with shock to the announcement of the accord. Takeiri and Yano had apparently fought against the agreement prior to its announcement, but they lost that battle. The July announcement precipitated a series of meetings by the top leaders of the Komeito as they tried to devise a plan to react to this bombshell from their parent organization. Ever since its founding in 1964, the Komeito has taken a firm anti-Communist line as one of its fundamental principles, and this stance can be found in nearly every part of its activities. It takes every opportunity to highlight any JCP missteps in its publications, and its campaigners have frequently clashed in the streets during election campaigns with those workers of the JCP.[55] Its antagonism toward the JCP seems to be based on two factors: a conflict between the philosophies of Marxist-Leninism and Nichiren Buddhism, and a national competition between the two organizations for membership, with both drawing their support largely from the same lower-class urban voters (especially in the large cities of Tokyo, Osaka, and Nagoya).

The Komeito's reaction was to reject the implications of the accord and to continue the same anti-Communist line it had taken previously. Takeiri stated that the basic policies of his party would not be affected by the agreement, which definitely did not imply any type of "joint struggle" or "united front" with the JCP. Ikeda later restated his adherence to this position and also reaffirmed that the support relationship between the Soka Gakkai and the Komeito had not changed in the slightest.[56]

Komeito officials frequently voiced their suspicions concerning the motives of the JCP. Secretary-General Yano was noted in the press as maintaining that the JCP had three basic political objectives to be achieved by the agreement—namely, that it sought to change the Komeito's course in the JCP's direction, to alienate the Soka Gakkai from the Komeito while drawing Soka Gakkai members toward the JCP, and to have Komeito Chairman Takeiri replaced.[57] In short, the Komeito's leaders saw the accord as nothing less than a full-scale attack on the party's very existence. They could not help but notice that Miyamoto had called for "a people's unified opposition front without the participation of political parties."[58]

Continuing its strongly anti-Communist posture, Takeiri warned of the JCP's objectives of violent revolution. On the other hand, the JCP and its daily newspaper, *Akahata*, escalated the party's attacks on the Komeito as an ally of the LDP and as being unworthy of the name of a "progressive political party."[59] By the end of the decade, the JCP was repeatedly attacking the Soka Gakkai for killing the accords. The December 29, 1979, issue of *Akahata* carried a two-page special supplement that proclaimed the death of the accords, and the Soka Gakkai was severely criticized for reverting to its original hostile stance toward "scientific socialism" and communism.[60] It is interesting to note that the JCP seemed to refrain from directly attacking the Soka Gakkai until Ikeda had resigned as its leader in April 1979.[61] Finally, in an *Akahata* editorial in February 1980, the Soka Gakkai's endorsement of a coalition of the Komeito, the DSP, and the JSP was described as an act of treachery.[62]

The Komeito survived the "accord crisis" largely because it was able to ignore the implications of the parent body's agreement with its arch-opponent and to successfully argue that such an intellectual agreement had little relevance to the world of politics. When the Komeito put together its coalition agreements for the 1980 elections, the one issue it would not compromise on was its demand for the exclusion of the JCP from any future coalition government. The two bitterest enemies in Japanese politics are still the JCP and the Komeito. The "accords" also provide some evidence regarding the types of situations in which the Komeito can pursue a line independent from the Soka Gakkai.

THE ORGANIZATIONAL STRENGTH
OF THE KOMEITO

Of all the political parties currently operating in Japan, the Komeito probably has the strongest organizational structure. Its only close competitor in this connection would be its arch-rival, the JCP. The Komeito's strength is almost totally dependent on the extensive organization of the Soka Gakkai. Each Soka Gakkai member is expected, at the very least, to support Komeito-recommended candidates at the polls. In addition, the Komeito has a larger army of volunteer workers than any other Japanese political party, providing it with a great advantage in elections. Jooinn Lee noted the case during the 1965 Fukuoka prefectural elections in which a large group of Soka Gakkai members, estimated at between 10,000 to 20,000, moved from the neighboring prefectures of Kumamoto and Saga to help elect Komeito candidates. Many of these Soka Gakkai members who had made this move were day workers with few ties to any given area, but the discipline and obedience they displayed were indeed impressive.[63]

Because the Komeito is based on the multimillion-member organization of the Soka Gakkai, it is somewhat surprising that it claimed a party membership of only 157,000 as of mid-1981. The Komeito has never released any details regarding the geographic distribution of this membership base, nor has the Soka Gakkai released any numbers regarding its membership other than gross totals of the estimated number of families enrolled in the organization. Still, the Komeito membership total easily makes the party the third largest in Japan. Most experts estimate that about 10 percent of the membership is composed of non–Soka Gakkai individuals.[64]

This Komeito membership base is a dedicated, hardworking core of party activists. By relying on such a base, the Komeito does not have to pay campaigners to distribute literature and to perform other campaign activities (as other parties, except the JCP, must do). As mentioned earlier, the Komeito keeps the details of its membership an internal secret. When Azumi submitted a survey questionnaire to the Tokyo Komeito leadership in 1966, a question concerning whether or not Soka Gakkai members always voted for a Komeito candidate was deleted as "quite unnecessary since they were absolutely certain that 100 percent of the members would answer in the affirmative."[65] However, when an *Asahi Shimbun* poll asked Komeito supporters in 1979 if they always voted for the candidates of the same party in general elections, the supporters replied in the affirmative 76 percent of the time. This was the highest such support rate in Japan.[66] The gap between the Komeito estimate of 100 percent support rate and the 76 percent discovered by the *Asahi Shimbun* may be partly explained by the fact that many Komeito supporters may not have Komeito candidates to vote for in their home districts; in addition, they may have been urged by the party to vote for other party candidates in recent elections in which the Komeito has cooperated with other parties.

The structure of the Komeito party organization appears to be very similar to that of the LDP and the Socialist parties. Its central party headquarters in Tokyo is situated in Minamoto-cho, Shinjuku—a location somewhat removed from most of the other party headquarters, which are clustered around the Diet building near the Nagatocho area. (The JCP is another exception, given that its national headquarters are located in a working-class section of Tokyo in Yoyogi.) Komeito's offices are situated in a modern building that communicates a sense of professionalism and organizational competence to visitors. The national headquarters had a staff of some 300 persons in 1981. Approximately half of these employees perform party work for the general affairs bureau; the others work for the publications bureau, which turns out the many polished publications of the party.[67]

Imazu has argued that the Komeito organization is basically a copy of the Soka Gakkai organization, which on every level of Japanese politics serves as a base for Komeito activities. He has also noted that the *shakubuku* (evangelical conversion campaign) of the Soka Gakkai is a form of election campaigning for the Komeito.[68] Others have indicated that Komeito campaigns serve as a proselytizing effort to bring new converts to the Soka Gakkai. Whichever way it may be, and it certainly could be either or both, the two organizations are very closely linked in almost all respects. As Arvin Palmer concluded, the "Komeito is a subsystem of the Soka Gakkai and integrated at every level with the main organization." He also noted that for the Komeito, "any but the most limited autonomy is prevented."[69]

The resignation of Ikeda from the presidency of the Soka Gakkai inevitably affected the operations of the Komeito. Initially, the event shocked many Komeito members. As Chairman Takeiri said at a press conference on April 24, 1979, "I believe that the announcement was a big shock to most of the party members, Komeito Diet members, and the personnel of the party headquarters."[70]

The new Soka Gakkai president, Hojo Hiroshi, was quick to declare that "Soka Gakkai's attitude toward the Komeito will not change." The JCP immediately observed that Ikeda's resignation would result in the Komeito's movement toward the LDP and, more generally, in the adoption of a more conservative posture—a conclusion derived from the transfer of power from Ikeda, who approved the accord with the JCP, to Hojo, who seemed less interested in such ties during his tenure. However, after only a short time in office, Hojo died and was replaced by the then vice president, Akiya Einosuke.

Komeito leadership during the early 1990s was reelected at the party's national convention in November 1990. CGP chairman Ishida Koshiro and the party's secretary-general Ichikawa Yuichi represented second-generation leadership; founders Takeiri Yoshikatsu and Yano Jun'ya ran the party from 1967 to the late 1980s.[71] Initially, Takeiri and Yano were handpicked by Soka Gakkai president Ikeda, as were all the other top-level Komeito executives and candidates. Of the two leaders, Yano was perhaps the more interesting to study. He was a registered Communist during his years as a student at the elite Kyoto University, and his political debut as a Komeito man in the Osaka Prefectural Assembly reportedly astonished many of his former classmates.[72] Takeiri, on the other hand, came from Nagano prefecture, became a Japanese National Railway employee in 1948, and then won a seat in one of the Tokyo ward assemblies in 1949. In 1963 he was elected to the Tokyo Assembly, and in 1967 he was elected for the first time to the national HR, along with Yano.

Relatively little is known about the nature of the subnational units of the Komeito's organization. Following the formal separation from the Soka Gakkai in 1970, an effort was made to create a distinctly separate party organization. However, as with some of the other parties in Japan, most of the Komeito organization seems to be operating out of the offices of Diet members and prefectural or local-level assembly mem-

Komeito's public support levels. Why, then, they ask, does the party get voting percentages of 10 percent or more in recent elections? Clearly, some Japanese may be reluctant to say to pollsters that they support the Komeito, but it is also true that the Komeito's supporters vote at very high turnout levels, and that the party seems to attract some protest votes as well.

It is worth noting that the Komeito's public opinion support is relatively intense when compared with the other parties. As one would expect from its largely Soka Gakkai base, Komeito supporters strongly identify with and support their party. On the other hand, the party receives very little support from the 35 percent of the population that does not support a given political party. Although 22.1 percent of this latter group is favorably inclined toward the LDP, only 1.4 percent is inclined toward the Komeito.[86]

With respect to the personal characteristics of Komeito supporters, an *Asahi Shimbun* poll uncovered the following pattern:

Occupation

Industrial workers	25.4
Small-business employees	21.4
Clerical workers	17.4
Self-employed people	15.8
Administrative employees	7.1
Agricultural workers	6.3

Education

Junior high school or less	62.7
High school–educated	31.7
College-educated	5.5

Imazu Hiroshi concluded, after analyzing these numbers, that the average Komeito supporter runs a small business, is an employee of a very small union enterprise, or is an industrial worker.[87] Perhaps the most distinctive characteristic of the typical Komeito supporter is a low level of formal education.

Candidates for the HR, whether officially supported or recommended by the Komeito, are more likely to come from professional backgrounds than are candidates from other parties. Yet, as is appropriate for a party with its particular support base, among the major parties the Komeito tends to have the lowest percentage of candidates who are university graduates. If a party is known by its candidates, then the Komeito is characterized by a strong local flavor because it has the largest number

bers. Perhaps the best description of local-level party organizations in Japan can be found in the research performed by James J. Foster in Hyogo prefecture. Foster found that the Komeito, like all the other major parties, maintained a full-time office in the prefectural capital of Kobe. The party also established a set of intermediary organizational units called *so-shibu*. Each of the five Komeito *so-shibu* was located in cities in which the party had a large local assembly delegation; however, in late 1979, none of these units had offices or staff members. The lowest level of organization in Hyogo is the *shibu*, and all 63 Komeito *shibu* were connected with the Soka Gakkai organization. As Foster has noted, prior to 1970 the Komeito operated only through the existing Soka Gakkai organization, and only after 1970 did it open up its prefectural-level office in Kobe. Komeito campaigns in Hyogo are run by Soka Gakkai members who belong to personal support groups (*koenkai*) organized by Komeito candidates; for the most part the official party offices seem to be left out of this important activity. The Komeito Hyogo chapter has claimed about 7,000 members throughout the 1970s, and this membership base is composed almost entirely of Soka Gakkai members. Foster discovered that the Komeito had the smallest income and weakest party organization among the major parties in Hyogo. Komeito, he concluded, simply relied on the activities of its elected officeholders and the Soka Gakkai organization to turn out its large vote in elections.[73]

Although some parties are most active on the national level (e.g., the DSP), the Komeito is extremely active on all levels of Japanese politics. It is known among Japanese experts of politics as a party that works hard on the local and prefectural levels on so-called bread-and-butter issues. Cecil Brett gives a different picture from that of Foster of the Komeito organization in Okayama. In particular, Brett discovered that the party had a prefectural office in Okayama, four or five regional offices in smaller cities, and more than fifty branch offices scattered around the prefecture.[74] He did not, however, note how active these offices were, or if they were separate from the Soka Gakkai offices.

The range of Komeito activities is nearly impossible to fathom. In October 1982, for example, Chairman Takeiri journeyed to a suburb of Peking, the capital of the People's Republic of China, to help open a chicken farm at the Sino-Japanese Friendship People's Commune. This modern farm, capable of raising 120,000 chickens at a time, was built with technical and financial assistance from the Komeito and Japanese private companies.[75]

Takahashi Harashima, the former head of the Doctrine Study Department of the Soka Gakkai, commented in 1980 that the financial burden on Gakkai members of supporting the Komeito is considerable: "In every election, they are asked to make more contributions to the

Komeito."[76] Dues-paying members of the Komeito pay a minimum of 1,000 yen per year, but they are asked for much more during campaigns.

A significant number of the Komeito's activities revolve around the party's string of "consulting centers," which constitute part of the organization's strategy of "working for the people." These centers numbered around 7,300 in 1969 and recorded hundreds of thousands of consultations per year in the late 1960s. By 1980, the number of "people's consultations" had risen to 1.3 million per year. Over 10 million cases were accepted between 1964 and 1980.[77] About half of the cases deal with citizen complaints concerning housing, welfare, education, and sanitation. In other words, for a long time the Komeito has been operating a private "ombudsman" system to help citizens deal with the Japanese governmental bureaucracy. (Incidentally, the JCP offers very similar services in competition with the Komeito.) The casework tends to revolve around local-level Komeito assembly members and is available to all constituents. The image of the Komeito as a party of action, protecting the common people from harmful governmental intrusions, has been a crucial element of the party's attempt to earn respect in Japan. In a 1976 *Asahi Shimbun* poll, Japanese respondents were asked whether a political party existed that one could consult. Affirmative answers were very low among supporters of the JSP (14 percent), the LDP (18 percent), the DSP (19 percent), and even the JCP (23 percent). Only a large percentage of Komeito supporters (60 percent) answered in the affirmative.[78]

The Soka Gakkai offers an extensive internal program of self-improvement, education, and entertainment; the Komeito does not. Perhaps the Komeito feels that such a party education program would be redundant given the Soka Gakkai's youth, athletic, music, drama, and a complete school system (including Soka Daigaku, the organization's own university).

The Komeito makes extensive use of the various media to communicate with its supporters and to reach potential supporters. Its daily mass circulation newspaper, the *Komei Shimbun,* has one of the largest circulations in Japan, with weekday sales of 860,000 copies and sales of the Sunday edition at the 1.4 million level.[79] Of the major parties, only the Komeito and the JCP (*Akahata*) publish their own daily newspapers. The Komeito also publishes a wide range of magazines. To these must be added the various publications of the Soka Gakkai, including its daily newspaper, the *Seikyo Shimbun,* which reportedly is the third most widely read daily newspaper in Japan; the theoretical journal, *Dai Byaku Renge;* and a picture magazine, *Seikyo Graphic.*[80]

Japanese labor unions have not been a fruitful recruiting area for the Komeito. Most labor federations (e.g., Sohyo and Domei) have been hostile and difficult to move toward support of the Komeito.[81] When the

Komeito and the Social Democratic Federation (SDF) cooperated in the 1979 elections, the Komeito opened communication channels with several labor unions, including Zentai (Japan Postal Workers Union), Zendentsu (All Japan Telecommunication Workers Union), and Kokuro (National Railway Workers Union).[82]

Finally, in contrast to most of the other Japanese parties, there is no strong pattern of factional politics inside the Komeito organization. Some indications of internal conflict within the Soka Gakkai do exist, however, and this conflict could adversely affect the loyalty of Gakkai members toward the Komeito. As Lee has noted, there may be at least four factions in the Soka Gakkai, and some of the organization's youth groups, such as the 120,000-member Shingakudo (Student League), have adopted some very militant, leftist policy positions.[83] However, these factions are neither obvious to the outsider nor an identifiable part of Komeito politics. In the early 1990s it appeared that the major factional divisions within the CGP revolved around whether the party should move closer to the LDP during the 1990s or maintain the 1980s strategy of cooperating with the JSP and DSP in overthrowing LDP rule on the national level.

KOMEITO SUPPORT AS MEASURED IN ELECTIONS AND PUBLIC OPINION POLLS

There are many ways to measure the popular support of a political party such as the Komeito. The most obvious procedure would be a close examination of the vote totals of the party in the various constituencies within which it operates. A second would involve an examination of the public opinion support patterns. It is this latter method that I will turn to initially; then I will conclude with a look at voting patterns.

Public opinion polls conducted by Japan's major newspapers have discovered that Komeito support has remained remarkably stable for the last decade. The *Mainichi Shimbun* polls observed a 6 percent support level in 1969 and a 5 percent level a decade later.[84] In recent years the party has ranged between 4 and 5 percent in popular support according to the *Asahi Shimbun*'s polls. In one such poll conducted in March 1982, the Komeito secured the support of 4 percent of the population and had no "leaners" at all. This is an interesting characteristic of the Komeito polling pattern: It has almost no visible support from those citizens who call themselves "nonparty supporters" and then later "lean toward one party or another." The JSP, for example, in 1982 received the support of 12 percent of the population plus an additional 5 percent from "leaners."[85] There is a strong feeling among some Japanese political experts that the newspaper polls consistently underestimate the

of candidates who can claim local government experience.[88] These candidates also tend to be younger than those of the other parties. Prior to 1972, Komeito candidates were selected by the national-level Soka Gakkai leadership, although there is now some reason to believe that more local decision-making is involved in the candidate selection process.[89] Only in the late 1970s did the party try to run non–Soka Gakkai candidates in order to broaden the party's image and appeal. In the 1980 double elections in Aichi prefecture, two non–Soka Gakkai Komeito candidates won seats—one in each of the twin chambers of the Diet. In the 1983 HC national constituency, the top five Komeito candidates in the proportional representation (PR) contest were not members of the party. All were elected on the Komeito ticket.

Since the Komeito entered the HR arena in 1967, it has managed to stabilize its seat totals near 50 in recent elections. Its seat totals since winning 25 seats in 1967 have been in the high 40s or 50s in every election since 1976 except for the double elections of 1980. The only party to be badly hurt by the double elections in 1980 was the Komeito. Its HR seats fell from 58 to 33, whereas its vote increased over 1979 totals by 47,000 votes. The large increase in total voter turnout in 1980 had the effect of raising the minimum number of votes needed to win an HR seat above the vote-gathering capacity of many of the previously successful Komeito Diet members. The average vote total per Komeito candidate actually increased in 1980 over 1979 from 82,542 to 83,280 votes. But the increase of 47,000 votes for all of the Komeito candidates was the smallest increase in votes of any major Japanese party in 1980. The DSP, in contrast, increased its average vote per candidate in 1980 by almost 9,000.

Because of the inelasticity of the Komeito vote (i.e., the failure to capture a significant portion of the so-called floating vote), high turnouts have reduced the Komeito's chances of winning marginal seats. The *Mainichi Shumbun* estimated that the high turnout recorded in 1980 cost the Komeito 16 seats (and the JCP 5 seats), which would have been captured if the cutoff line had been the same as in the 1979 elections.[90] Equally significant, Komeito's record high number of seats won in the 1981 Tokyo Metropolitan Assembly elections were won in the election marked by the lowest voter turnout (54.2 percent) in the history of the assembly.

Some Komeito leaders viewed the 1980 electoral disaster as an opportunity to rebuild the party during the following decade. The chairman of the Komeito Diet Policy Committee, Okubo Naohiko, commented that 27 Komeito house candidates finished as runners-up in their districts in 1980. Included in the total were many of the most promising young

Komeito Diet members. Okubo noted that after the party's defeat in the 1972 elections, it modernized and became a truly national political party.[91] In 1990 the Komeito won 8 seats in Tokyo, 7 in Osaka (1 in every district), 4 in Fukuoka, and 4 in Kanagawa. Thus, although 21 percent of the nation's HR seats are in these four metropolitan prefectures, the Komeito won 42 percent of its seats there in 1990.

After running candidates (either official or recommended) in 64 of the nation's 130 HR districts in 1979, the Komeito decided to run the same number in the 1980 elections. Between 1976 and 1979, 42 Komeito candidates experienced vote declines, including the party's secretary-general. Some political analysts have attributed these declines to the series of crises besetting the Soka Gakkai. However, the Komeito leadership has argued that the reduction of candidates and the cooperation strategy with the other centrist parties, especially the DSP, resulted in just such a decline in the party's vote total in 1979. Actually, they have claimed that it was not so much a decline as a shift in strategy resulting in a transfer of Komeito voters to DSP candidates as part of the "joint efforts" of the 1980 campaigns.[92]

Because the Komeito and the JCP seem to be battling for the same general constituency, one might guess that if the Komeito decided to run fewer candidates in HR elections, the JCP might significantly increase its vote. However, the statistics show that the LDP and DSP gained 5 percent and 4 percent, respectively, in these constituencies. With respect to seat transfers between the Komeito and other Japanese parties, it is notable that almost none of the 24 seats the Komeito lost in 1980 went to its arch-rival, the JCP. Although the Komeito won 1 seat from the LDP, it lost 14 to that party, 5 to the JSP, 4 to the New Liberal Club (NLC), and 1 each to an independent and the JCP.[93]

Komeito's policy of cooperation with other centrist parties produced a mixed bag of results in 1980. All 4 of the CGP-JSP candidates won, but of the 34 joint CGP-DSP and other party candidates, only 14 won. This poor performance compared very unfavorably with the results in 1979, when the CGP-DSP cooperation was successful in 17 of 24 districts. Of the 21 "joint effort" winners in 1980, only 7 were Komeito members. In terms of the HC local constituencies, the Komeito cooperated on 25 candidates in 22 constituencies; 10 won in this case, but only one was a Komeito candidate. There was a strong feeling among many Komeito members that these "joint efforts" produced an overly one-sided result.[94]

In the 1983 HR elections, the Komeito cooperated with the DSP in 28 constituencies, electing 14 out of 15 CGP candidates and 11 of 13 DSP candidates. In the Komeito cooperations with the JSP, 5 out of 6 candidates were elected (3 JSP members and 2 CGP members). Thus, of the 34 candidates the Komeito ran or supported in other parties, 30 won. Cooperation was a great success in 1983.

However, cooperation agreements in 1990 proved to be difficult to establish with both the JSP and the DSP. Few joint efforts were made, and one outcome was the large number of Komeito (11) and DSP (18) candidates who finished as runners-up in their districts. The CGP runners-up needed only an average of 9,500 additional votes to have won seats in the HR. By running only 61 candidates in 1986 and 59 in 1990, the CGP continued its election strategy of putting its resources into sure and almost-sure winning situations. It had 46 winners and 12 runners-up in 1990; only one CGP candidate failed to finish as a runner-up, and that candidate lost by only 8,000 votes.[95]

Because the Komeito (like the DSP) ran in fewer than half of the nation's 130 house constituencies, the best way to ascertain its national vote is to examine the party's vote in the HC national constituency. In recent elections it has ranged between 6.0 and 7.4 million votes. In this measurement the Komeito often is nearly the equal of the number two party of Japan's First Party System, the SDPJ, which in 1983 captured only 275,000 more votes than the Komeito. It is interesting to note how the Komeito collects its votes across Japan's 47 prefectures. Its lowest prefectural percentage in 1989 was 5.3 percent in rural Toyama, and its highest was 16.8 percent in Osaka. These were also the low and high percentages in the 1986 HC elections. In the most congested prefectures (Tokyo, Osaka, and Nagoya) and their "bedroom" prefectures, the CGP scored its highest vote percentages: in Tokyo, 13.0 percent; Kanagawa, 11.0 percent; and Saitama and Chiba, 11.4 percent. The only exception to this pattern was the CGP's strength on the rural island of Shikoku, where it also won vote percentages in double digits. The CGP has been unable to convert this voting support into a comparable number of seats either in the HR or in prefectural assemblies. On Shikoku Island, for example, Komeito members in 1990 held only a handful of prefectural assembly seats and only 2 of the 25 HR seats in the Diet.

Another way to measure a party's real strength is by looking at its seat-winning success at the grassroots levels of politics. In the 1983 unified local-level elections, Komeito candidates won 182 seats in the 44 prefectures holding elections that year—an increase of 16 seats over its previous peak in 1975. With approximately 200 seats in prefectural assemblies (about 7 percent of the total number of seats), the Komeito showed a significant improvement over its 1971 figure of 4.4 percent of the seats. And since Japanese voters tend to select area representation over ideological representation on the local levels of politics, the tendency toward rejection of ideological representation would work in favor of the conservatives, who win the vast majority of local- and pre-fectural-level seats. As of 1990, the CGP held 5 percent of Japan's 67,278 prefectural, city, and village council seats. Included in this total are 217 prefectural assembly seats, 1,924 city council seats, 1,132 village council seats, and 203 of the 1,051 council seats found within the political sub-units of Tokyo. At the various levels of local government, the Komeito is strongest in Tokyo city government, with almost 20 percent of the seats, but wins only about 7.5 percent of the prefectural assemblies. Traditionally, it has been strongest in the urban prefectural assemblies of Tokyo and Osaka and relatively well represented in others, such as Hyogo, Kanagawa, and Fukuoka. Many rural prefectures, on the other hand, have only one or two Komeito members, and frequently there are none.

Until the 1983 elections, zone voting was one of the distinctive charac-teristics of the Komeito organization, especially in the national con-stituency of the HC. The phenomenon of zone voting illustrates both the strong discipline imposed by the Komeito leadership on its supporters and the total electoral strength of the party. In 1980 the Komeito ran 9 candidates in the national constituency, and all 9 were elected. Their vote totals ranged from 689,042 to 814,950, and they ranked between 27 and 45 out of the 50 winners that year. Since the bottom-ranked winner needed over 627,272 votes, even the last-place Komeito candidate seemed safe. It was the zone voting that made such an impressive show-ing. Each of the 9 CGP candidates was assigned a geographic group of CGP supporters. Outside of each candidate's zone, these candidates col-lected few votes, but they received massive vote totals in their respective zones.

KOMEITO'S POLICY POSITIONS

As one might expect, the policy positions of the Komeito have been well grounded in the philosophies of the Soka Gakkai and the Nichiren Shoshu. When the Komeito's predecessor, the Komei Political League, was created in 1962, its charter and platform stated that "our political ideal is the spirit of the Great Saint Nichiren's teaching that national security be realized through true Buddhism; on the basis of the supreme philosophy and compassion of the Great Saint, we will conduct activities as a modern and most democratic organization."[96]

The original declaration of the founding of the Komeito issued in November 1964 was characterized by frequent Buddhist references to Nichiren (i.e., to the ideal of *Obutsu Myogo*). Yet, from the beginning, the Komeito emphasized the goals of world peace, humanitarian socialism,

Buddhist democracy, and the eradication of corrupt politics. The 1964 action policy of the party included specific opposition to harmful amendments to the constitution, support for global disarmament, an independent foreign policy, and a strong commitment to the welfare of the masses. As Matsumoto Shiro has noted, an action policy based on the establishment of a Buddhist orientation hall and the concept of *Obutsu Myogo* was not a sufficient policy foundation for a modern political party: "The party began with a clean policy slate . . . and gradually the Komeito's policies on welfare, national security, Japan-China relations, and other issues took shape."[97] Again, according to Matsumoto, Komeito chairman Takeiri reportedly followed newspaper reporters' advice to adopt a reformist line in opposition to the LDP and to continue its successful tactic of pressing for reform of the corrupt style of politics that has tended to characterize the image of the LDP. Yet, beyond the long-term goal of "clean government," the Komeito followed an ad hoc approach to practical policymaking and thus tended to switch policy positions on given issues repeatedly throughout its history.

After 1970, the Komeito officially dropped its goal of a national ordination hall and began to concentrate on more mundane policy areas such as pollution and defense. At its Eighth Annual Convention, held in 1970, the Komeito dropped its references to *Obutsu Myogo* and Buddhist democracy, and began to use such contemporary Komeito policy terms as *humanitarian socialism* and *middle-of-the-road reformism*.

In addition, the party runs on a pacifist and democratic platform. The four basic principles of the 1982 Komeito platform are presented, as follows, in the party's own words:

1. The Party shall maintain its stand as a political party based on middle-of-the-road reformism, whose purpose is to promote the welfare of all people in this nation. Holding highest respect for human dignity, it shall pursue its goals together with the people, with zeal for reform and sincere practice of its principles.
2. Founded on a new concept of "humanitarian socialism," the party values the dignity of human life above all else, and it aims to establish an economic system that will guarantee free and responsible economic activity with fair distribution of the fruits thereof, and to construct a welfare society that will permit the realization of social prosperity and individual happiness.
3. Firm in the belief that all peoples of all races and nationalities are equal citizens of one world, the party shall endeavor to bring about permanent peace and prosperity for all people through independent and peaceful diplomacy formulated on the principles of

equality, reciprocity, and noninterference in the internal affairs of other peoples or nations.

4. Upholding the constitution of Japan and respecting the dignity of human life, liberty, and equality, the party shall protect the fundamental rights of freedom of religion, assembly, and expression, and shall endeavor to establish fundamental social rights and create a firmer foundation for parliamentary democracy, eliminating all forms of violence.[98]

MIDDLE-OF-THE-ROAD REFORMISM

"Middle-of-the-road reformism" is generally discussed by the Komeito within the context of the crisis that engulfs current politics in Japan. The world is described as being affected by an extreme form of social anomie and a change in basic values. The only way to alleviate the crisis is to reestablish the primacy of values over politics. The Komeito believes it offers a special type of reformism, one that differs greatly from that practiced in Western democracies. As Chairman Takeiri has stated: "The essence of reformism lies in the will and practice to pursue reform in every reality around you without being submerged in and complacent with daily life."[99] This concept is then coupled with "images of moderation, steadiness, and harmony," as well as with the image of constant struggle for change. The sense of militancy derived from the parent Soka Gakkai is evident in the party statement: "A political philosophy without a fighting spirit is only a degraded slogan."[100] And the "fighting spirit" of the party is best articulated in the official party slogan: "Talk with the people, fight with the people, and die among the people." To many Westerners, such a slogan may seem more appropriate to the more radical Socialist or Communist parties than to the pacifist Buddhist party of Japan.

The Komeito characterizes its middle-of-the-road reformism in terms of humanism, holism, gradualism, and pacifism. Humanism places "ultimate value on man as he exists" and argues that "everything exists in order for man to be able to lead a better life." Within this context, people must strive for freedom and equality. Holism is a method of seeing the individual and the totality of society. Consequently, politics must be viewed as an integral part of the larger Japanese society and treated accordingly. All reforms must be accomplished gradually and peacefully: "Komeito clearly rejects any kind of violence, and it supports the establishment of parliamentary democracy." Not only physical violence but also "mental violence" and the "violence of numbers, speech, and negligence" are opposed as well. Gradual changes in the Japanese democracy, such as the correction of the Diet malapportionment and the liberalizing of election campaign laws, must be pursued. "Pacifism," as one Komeito leader has claimed, "is definitely the most outstanding feature of our party platform. There are no good or bad wars"; hence the Komeito claims to be the first party to make the peace constitution a part of its platform.

HUMANITARIAN SOCIALISM

Many who have come into casual contact with the Komeito since its founding in 1964 are surprised to discover that it considers itself a Socialist party. The Komeito rejects both the Marxist and the Fabian Socialist paths: "As long as private interest remains the dehumanizing principle of the economy, it will be impossible to overcome the short-comings of any kind of capitalist system."[101] Human rights and dignity would be damaged, and the "dehumanizing evils of capitalism— pollution, inflation, and the growth of the industrial-military complex— would remain to proliferate." Indeed, Socialist systems suffer from hardened institutions and disregard for the human rights of freedom of religion, assembly, and speech: "Komeito's political and economic beliefs are socialist, but with a major difference: they are based on respect for human dignity. Our socialism is, therefore, progressive and democratic, totally pacifist; it is rooted in Japan's economic and political realities, and at the same time universal in its outlook on the world and the future."[102]

Such a Socialist world as envisaged by the Komeito's leadership would be achieved very gradually and very incrementally:

> We are rejecting radicalism as a means of achieving our goals. We shall instead attempt to carry through reform step-by-step in vigorous daily efforts, in a spurt of innovation and hope. We are convinced that if we keep up our fight against the daily worries, taxes, housing shortages, traffic accidents, and the long-term problems of inflation and pollution, among others, and if we press relentlessly to ease the problems of the rural poor and the struggling small businesses, we will have opened up the way for effective and permanent economic reforms.[103]

In keeping with this spirit of gradual socialism, the Komeito calls for the gradual nationalization of key manufacturing and energy industries, the utilization of progressive real estate and inheritance taxes, and a reduction of inequalities in the distribution of wealth.

The Komeito's domestic policy, developed in the 1960s—fighting inflation, housing shortages, traffic congestion, pollution, and public hazards, as well as seeking lower taxes—continued to be central to the party's public image in the 1980s. An examination of Komeito news releases and news films will disclose not only a survey of the nuclear power issue in Japan but also a summary of the activities of Komeito women in local assemblies "striving to solve the various problems of city suburbs"; there are stories detailing, for instance, the struggle of a female Komeito municipal assembly member to establish a welfare center for old people, and of Komeito members "going all out to aid the victims of a typhoon."[104]

TOWARD A COALITION GOVERNMENT

In its 1982 brochure, the Komeito gave top priority to an explanation of its coalition policies:

> On December 6, 1979, Komeito and the Democratic Socialist Party (DSP) agreed on a plan for a middle-of-the-road coalition government. Our party also reached a similar agreement with the JSP on January 10, 1980. The common features of the two coalition plans are, first, that they spell out realistic, political principles and goals that can be applied to international and domestic situations expected to emerge in the first half of the new decade. Second, the three parties have agreed that the JCP will be excluded from the projected coalition. Although there may be some fine differences in nuance between the two plans, they are nevertheless identical in substance, especially as they concern actions for the first half of the 1980s.
>
> The LDP won by a substantial margin in the June 1980 elections for both houses of the Diet, but as far as we are concerned, it was only a temporary aberration. We still believe that our concept of coalition government is basically sound and provides a valid formula for the age of transformation. We must renew our determination to unite and advance forward to seize a golden opportunity for the opposition parties to form a coalition government for the first time in threedecades.[105]

Asserting that the opposition parties can only grow from the experience of the 1980 electoral defeats, Komeito leaders have argued that the "concept of coalition government will regain strength ... and the 1980s will indeed emerge as an era of coalition government."[106] One of the key aspects of the 1980 coalition agreements for the Komeito was the exclusion of the JCP from any future coalition government. The Komeito's reasons were that the JCP cannot guarantee freedom and democracy, that its policies were too far from the other parties to form a partnership, and that "anticommunism" has been an important part of Komeito's policy orientation.[107] A glance at the Komeito's list of Japanese-language publications, for instance, would reveal the following titles translated into English: *Criticism of the JCP; Dictatorship Problems of the JCP and Its Declaration of Freedom; An Exposé of the Deception of the JCP in Its Proletarian Dictatorship Problem and Freedom Declaration;* and *The JCP's Inability to Reply on the Issue of the Constitution and Its Contradictory Principles.*

In the party's draft action program for 1983, special emphasis was placed on the recouping of its Diet strength in elections anticipated in 1983 to pre-1980 levels—*prior* to any full-scale continuation of electoral cooperation with other centrist parties. It thus established a two-step process toward an eventual coalition government: First, each party's seat totals in the Diet would be built up; then, a plan of full-scale cooperation would be created to form a limited front for a coalition government. The Komeito reaffirmed its desire to seek such a coalition government with the JSP, the DSP, and the NLC-SDF.[108] By winning 58 seats in the December 1983 HR elections, it raised its seat totals to the highest level in the Diet.

KOMEITO SHIFTS ON SECURITY
AND DEFENSE QUESTIONS (1978–1989)

Komeito's security and defense positions appear to have undergone considerable change since the founding of the party in the early 1960s. The early Komeito positions were ones of strong opposition to the Japan-U.S. security treaty and the Japanese Self-Defense Forces (Jietai). By the mid-1970s, however, it had become clear to the Komeito leadership that some modification of the party's security policies would be necessary if political power was to be attained on the national level in coalition with either the LDP or the centrist parties.

At the Fifteenth Annual Komeito Convention (January 1978), the party officially shifted its security policies. Chairman Takeiri stated: "Our party recognizes the 'right of self defense. . . .' [The existence of the Self-Defense Forces] is an established fact. Therefore, I believe that we should no longer relegate them to an ambiguous status."[109] Still, the Komeito's official position regarding the SDF held that the Self-Defense Forces had to be reorganized into a "National Guard . . . equipped with the minimum arms necessary to protect our territory from invasion and maintain neutrality."[110]

With regard to the Japan-U.S. Security Treaty, the early position of the Komeito called for an "abrogation of the Japan-U.S. security setup by gradual stages." In 1973 it called for "immediate abrogation" of the treaty; by the early 1980s, the Komeito, as a result of the coalition agreements it had concluded with the DSP, had adopted a very moderate stand on the treaty: "Since immediate abolition of the Japan-U.S. Security Treaty would bring about rapid change in the international situation and might intensify tension in Japan and Asia, we therefore support the continuation of the Japan-U.S. Security Treaty for the time being, while endeavoring to create an international environment conducive to the discontinuation of the Japan-U.S. arrangement."[111]

This new Komeito security position was justified and approved at the December 1981 convention after being drafted by the party's enlarged Central Executive Committee meeting held in October 1981. Fundamental to this revised position was a set of new perceptions of a series of international events. The end of the Vietnam War, the Soviet invasion of Afghanistan, the Polish situation, and the Soviet military buildup in the formerly Japanese, now Soviet-occupied Northern Islands were all influential in setting the mood for a policy shift by the Komeito. Yano and Takeiri had led delegations to Europe, the United States, and South Korea, and the resulting discussions had helped to broaden the perspectives of the leadership. Clearly, Takeiri and other leaders had concluded that the party needed to adopt defense and security policies closer to those of the LDP in order to be perceived by the electorate as a reasonable alternative governing party.[112]

KOMEITO POLICY DEBATES IN THE 1990s

Increasingly in 1990, Komeito leaders debated the wisdom of continuing the policies and strategies of the 1980s. Prior to the November 1990 Komeito national convention, party leaders called for a reexamination of the party platform, which had been adopted in 1970. At the convention, Chairman Ishida indicated that the Komeito had decided to abandon its long-term strategy of being a part of a JSP-based coalition government and to begin a study of the prospects of joining the LDP in a coalition government during the 1990s.[113]

Komeito leaders had lost patience with the JSP's inability to convert the Socialists' 1989 HC victory into a lower house victory in 1990. Komeito criticized the JSP for its inability to develop realistic policies in the defense and security sectors, as well as in a number of foreign policy areas such as Korea.[114] The last part of 1990 was dominated by the policy debate in the Diet and the country over the Kaifu government's request for permission to send members of the Self-Defense Forces to support the U.S. military coalition in Saudi Arabia. The DSP and CGP agreed to support the LDP-backed bill, but JSP and JCP opposition managed to kill it. Thus, the continuing inability of the opposition parties to agree on a joint policy position on military security threatened to split the five parties further and reduce their chances of securing control of the Japanese Diet without the participation of the LDP.

CGP leadership has also called for the careful review of central parts of the party platform, such as "humanistic socialism" and "centrism." With the destruction of socialism in Eastern Europe in 1990, the utility of the concept of socialism is being questioned by some, and others are demanding that the party sharpen some of its other symbols and concepts to make it more attractive to voters. Clearly, the Komeito appears to be on the verge of a long-delayed self-evaluation that may perhaps set it on a new political course.

KOMEITO IN THE SECOND PARTY SYSTEM

Komeito joined the Hosokawa cabinet in the summer of 1993, receiving four cabinet ministries and for the first time in its history becoming part of the ruling coalition of Japanese national government. Komeito's ministries were relatively minor ones: Post and Telecommunications (Kanzaki Takenori), Labor, Management and Coordination Agency, and Environmental Agency. Its 50-some seats in the HR were crucial to the survival of the Hosokawa government. The JCP could be and was excluded from the first non-LDP government since 1948, but the government could not be formed without the participation of the Komeito. It also supported the Shinseito minority government of Prime Minister Hata in the summer of 1994 for the two months it existed until it collapsed. Hata awarded Komeito with six ministries in his minority coalition, which tried to survive without the support of the SDPJ. Again, the ministries given to Komeito were minor ones: Transport, Post and Telecommunications, Construction, Management and Coordination, Science and Technology, and Environmental.[115] After only two months, the Hata coalition collapsed, and the LDP-dominated Murayama (SDPJ) government pushed the Komeito into the opposition's ranks once again.

The Komeito did well in the last HR election (1993) of the First Party System. It went into the election with 45 members of the HR and won 51 seats. Then, in the 1996 HR elections, while running its candidates under the label of the New Frontier Party (Shinshinto), a total of at least 40 former Komeito candidates succeeded in winning seats in the new slightly smaller 500-seat HR.

When Ozawa and Hata continued to push for a new, unified (except the JCP) opposition party, Komeito leadership strongly supported the concept. Some commentators noted a long-term close relationship between the then Komeito chairman Ichikawa Yuichi and Ozawa.[116] The Komeito disappeared from the Japanese Diet in December 1994, when it merged with several other parties to form the Shinshinto, or New Frontier Party. Strangely enough, the Komeito disappeared, but still survived. Komieto's 50-some members in the HR merged into the Shinshinto, as did the Komeito HC members who ran for reelection in the 1995 HC elections. The Komeito members of the HC who were not up for reelection in 1995 and Komieto local assembly members were organized under the title of the Komei Party. The party's leader was Hamayotsu Toshiko, a four-term female member of the HC representing the Tokyo prefectural district. Hamayotsu represents the new generation of Komeito Diet members—well educated and attractive to non–Soka Gakkai voters. She is a lawyer who was elected to the Diet in 1992 at the age of forty-seven. She was famous for her legal activities involving children and the aged. Metraux argues that there is a second generation of Komeito Diet members such as Hamayotsu who typically have a university education and a record of professional accomplishments before getting involved in politics.[117]

Komeito continues to be an independent power on the local and prefectural level of Japanese politics. In the most important of the local-level assemblies, Komeito has been the second most powerful party in the Tokyo Metropolitan Assembly for most of the past thirty years. It still maintained that position after the 1997 elections, when all 24 of the Komeito candidates won seats to finish behind the LDP (54 seats) and JCP (26 seats).[118] Across the nation, the Komeito managed to win over 1,900 seats in prefectural and local government assemblies as of 1997. On the prefectural level, its total of seats was second only to that of the powerful LDP.[119]

The Shinshinto was led by Ozawa and Hata, but its organizational and vote-gathering power core was the Komeito and its Soka Gakkai voter base. Shinshinto leaders acknowledged that in the 1995 HC elections, the Komeito organization was responsible for about half of the Shinshinto's 12.5 million votes. In fact, the powerful position held by Komeito within the largest opposition party was one of the reasons for its demise at the end of 1997. Strong opposition to the growing power of the former Komeito members developed among the various other factions, which represented former LDP defectors and other parties such as the DSP.[120]

When the Shinshinto collapsed in late 1997, the former Komeito members in the HR emerged from the wreckage and formed a new party called Shinto Heiwa (New Peace Party) as a transitional organization until the Komeito could be reorganized in 1998. The other major parties that emerged from the Shinshinto collapse were the Jiyuto, or Liberal Party, which gave Ozawa a platform to continue in national-level politics, and several of the other parties joined with the Democratic Party (Minshuto). Following these parties into the Minshuto was not a viable option for the Komeito members, since one of the reasons these groups left the Shinshinto was to avoid continued relationships with both Ozawa and the Komeito.

So, for most of 1998, two organizations represented former Komeito Diet and local government assembly members. In July 1998 Shinto Heiwa leader Kanzaki Takenori, a four-term member of the HR, and Komei leader Hamayotsu reached a merger agreement for the reestablishment of the Komeito in the fall of 1998. The leadership of the re-created Komeito was Kanzaki, taking the top post in the new party, and Hamayotsu as the Komeito's secretary-general. The Soka Gakkai leadership has also apparently blessed this merger and the establishment of a new Komeito.[121]

Thus, in late 1998, the Komeito is just about where it was in the early 1990s. It still controls about 10 percent of the seats (50 of 500) in the HR and almost the same percentage in the HC (24 out of 252). In terms of its power in contemporary Japanese politics, the Komeito has returned to where it was at the end of the First Party System in early 1993, when it had maneuvered itself into a position to become a potential coalition partner for the LDP if the latter party loses its majority in the HR. Following the LDP losses in the 1998 HC elections, the LDP still had its restored majority in the HR and was looking for support in the HC to make governing easier. The Komeito seemed willing to be considered a possible informal partner of the LDP. This is a return to the role it had considered prior to the 1993 political earthquake. After considering various options, the LDP rejected a possible coalition with the Komeito and instead selected the somewhat curious coalition with Ozawa's Liberal Party. It was curious because it failed to give the LDP enough seats in the HC to control that chamber.

By the time the Komeito had merged into the Shinshinto, many Japanese were questioning just where Komeito fit into the Japanese ideological spectrum. Some pointed to a series of conservative positions the Komeito had taken during the 1990s. The highest priority of the Komeito during the Murayama administration and those that followed it in the mid-1990s was the killing of the revisions in the 1951 Religious Corporations Law, which provided for grants of very broad freedoms from official regulation for the 183,970 registered religious organizations in Japan. The LDP-led move to revise the law came after the Aum

Shinrikyo sect used poison gas on Tokyo subways in March 1995. The Soka Gakkai and its allies threw their resources into a fight to kill any such increased regulations on religions, their fund-raising, their educational activities, and the business-related incomes. One of the key provisions of this bill was to give supervision of religious groups to the Ministry of Education.[122] Earlier, in 1992, the Komeito joined with the LDP to support the law that authorized Japanese Peace Keeping Operations (PKO) under United Nations control in such countries as Cambodia. Both of these policy positions were on the conservative, or status quo, side of the political spectrum. Some argued that as the Soka Gakkai membership has become more prosperous and well educated in recent decades, the policy positions of the Komeito have also become more conservative.

By the time of the 1998 HC campaign, the election platform of the Komeito was typical of this "centrist-progressive-conservative" party. It called for a 10-trillion-yen tax cut; further deregulation; various welfare reforms, including expanded assistance for child rearing and care for the aged; and several environmental policies relating to the regulation of hormone-disruptive chemicals and global warming.[123]

THE ROLE OF THE KOMEITO IN JAPANESE POLITICS

The Komeito occupies a sensitive and significant role in contemporary Japanese politics. As the number three party in a six-party First Party System, the Komeito, along with the DSP, anchored the moderate position within the five-member opposition camp. Without the Komeito, the moderate opposition (DSP, SDF, and right-wing JSP) would have had no chance of creating the viable moderate alternative necessary to break the LDP-JSP dominance. The problem was that many members of these other opposition parties were very suspicious of the Komeito and the sometimes "authoritarian" nature of the Buddhist party. Overall, in fact, the main dilemma of Japanese politics was (and continues to be) that, without the Komeito, the Japanese party system would have only a small prospect for a power pattern reversal; still, it seems difficult for the Komeito to become an acceptable part of the new coalition. The key to ending the LDP's position of sole power holder on the national level was a two-part change in the informal rules of politics: The LDP had to have a serious split, and the Komeito had to be accepted as a legitimate coalition partner in a non-LDP government. Both of these changes occurred in 1993, and the First Party System died.

Although the Komeito has been welcomed into Japanese politics as "a worthy opposition party with a moderately reformist platform" and as a "political party with a solid support basis . . . [and] an asset to our democracy," there is still a great deal of concern about its authoritarian tendencies and the policies it would enact if it gained national political power.[124]

Despite the efforts of the Komeito leadership, there is little indication that the party has broadened its appeal significantly beyond its Soka Gakkai base. Because only 10 percent of its members are unaffiliated with the Soka Gakkai and are apparently unable to consistently capture more than a small share of the floating vote, the prospects of significant growth appear to be relatively small in the foreseeable future. The party is still able to win about 10 percent of both the national vote and seats in the Diet. As such, it cannot be ignored unless the LDP is able to win pure majorities in both chambers.

One can say that the Komeito has drastically changed the nature of Japanese politics. Its formation in 1964 siphoned off an important part of the LDP religious constituency and changed a two-party system into the multiparty system currently in existence. By cutting into LDP support, it hastened the decline of that party during the 1960s and 1970s. In addition, the Komeito functioned as the bridge between the two Socialist parties (the JSP and DSP), which, although they did not get along very well together, often cooperated when they came together with the Komeito in "joint struggles"—hence Palmer's reference to the Komeito as the "equilibrator for the Japanese political system."[125] If we analyze the Komeito using some of the functional labels applied to parties and groups in other political systems, additional functions become obvious. The party serves both as an articulator and as a broker in representing the 10 to 15 million people who are Soka Gakkai members. The party's natural constituency is one that does not automatically obtain representation elsewhere in society. Moreover, these people are socialized into the larger political system and encouraged to participate politically as voters and candidates of the Komeito. Innovative ideas have been advanced by the Komeito in its role as part of the governing coalition in many of Japan's larger cities. The Komeito, as the Clean Government Party, continues to function as a "watchdog" that focuses on excesses committed by Japanese politicians, especially those of the LDP and JCP.[126] In particular, the Komeito has been a leader in exposing LDP corruption (though relatively silent on the Tanaka scandals—Tanaka being an old ally of the party) and has supported its conservative version of the welfare state on all levels of Japanese politics. The Komeito is also the key party in the formation of any coalitions if the LDP falls short of a majority in the lower house. It stands ready to join either the LDP or opposition parties such as the Democratic Party to form a coalition government. It is the invaluable missing link of Japanese politics. However, for any party joining the Komeito in such a coalition government, there will be significant costs.

It is very difficult, however, to place the Komeito on a Left-Right scale of Japanese politics. It claims to be a militant Socialist party, but many argue that its constituency is basically conservative and that its rhetoric is not matched by its day-to-day deeds.[127] As Lee has suggested, the Komeito takes a slightly leftist policy position in the Diet, but on the local level it has often adopted right-of center positions.[128] In addition, the Komeito leaders themselves have argued that the party is outside the Left-Right continuum altogether in that the party represents all the people inasmuch as it rises above class and other social cleavages.[129]

From the perspective of the Soka Gakkai leadership, the original objectives behind the creation of the Komeito have been more than fulfilled. As Imazu has noted, the pressure from the LDP and other religious groups on Soka Gakkai members has been relieved, and the values of the Soka Gakkai have been projected into Japanese politics.[130] Perhaps more significantly, the Komeito has helped to legitimize and moderate the image of the Soka Gakkai for the general Japanese public. But the most significant aspect of the Komeito lies in its role as a continuing, stable force in national and local politics.[131] At the same time, it is feared by many—both conservative and leftist—as a possible force in support of an authoritarian type of government if it ever has the opportunity to control the national government. However dangerous it may seem to many in Japan, it does not seem likely that the Komeito will have the opportunity to acquire such power in the foreseeable future and test the proposition that Buddhist democracy is a threat to Japanese democracy. On the other hand, with 7.5 million votes gathered for Komei candidates in the 1998 HC elections and a total of Diet members making it the third-largest party in the national legislature and thousands of elected officials across the nation, the Komeito is a powerful force in Japanese politics.

In October 1999, the New Komeito joined with their old opponents, the LDP, to form a three party coalition government. The new cabinet, Prime Minister Obuchi's third, had Tsuzuki Kunihiro included as Management and Coordination Agency Director General. The inclusion of New Komeito in the government offered the LDP majority control of both the HR (with the Liberal Party votes) and the HC with both Liberal and New Komeito support. Just a year earlier, the New Komeito leadership said it could never support the LDP, but the LDP's agreement with the Liberal Party to try to cut some 50 seats in the proportional representation constituency of the HR forced the New Komeito to offer their votes in the HC in exchange for reducing the seats reduction to just 20 seats. The New Komeito is especially good at winning seats in the PR constituency. Practical politics seems to have defeated the politics of idealism once again.

NOTES

1. J. W. White, *The Soka Gakkai and Mass Society* (Palo Alto, Calif.: Stanford University Press, 1970), p. 1.

2. Arvin Palmer, *Buddhist Politics: Japan's Clean Government Party* (The Hague: Nijhoff, 1971), p. 54.

3. Daniel A. Metraux, "The Last Word: Japan's Soka Gakkai," *Asian Mail*, November 1977, p. 23.

4. "The Power of Soka Gakkai," *Time* (Asian edition), November 20, 1995.

5. Ibid.

6. *Japan Times*, May 8, 1979.

7. Palmer, *Buddhist Politics*, p. 58.

8. Kiyoaki Murata, *Japan's New Buddhism* (New York: Walker-Weatherhill, 1969). The critical works in Japanese on both organizations include Naito Kunio, *Komeito No Sugata* (Tokyo: Ierv, 1969); Murakami, *Sokagakkai-Komeito* (Tokyo: Aoki, 1967); and Sawaki Toshio and Nakagawa, eds., *Komeito Soka Gakkai Hihan* (Tokyo: Shin Nippon Shuppan, 1970).

9. Jooinn Lee, "Komeito: Soka Gakkai-ism in Japanese Politics," *Asian Survey* 10, no. 6 (June 1970), 501–518.

10. *Japan Times*, January 15, 1967, p. 8.

11. White, *The Soka Gakkai*, pp. 21–22.

12. James A. Dator, *Soka Gakkai: Builders of the Third Civilization* (Seattle: University of Washington Press, 1969), pp. 79–80.

13. Ibid., p. 81.

14. Lee, "Komeito," p. 502.

15. *Newsweek*, March 7, 1966, p. 86.

16. See generally Palmer's *Buddhist Politics* for a positive treatment of this group.

17. Ibid., p. 39. In 1969 there were 57 general headquarters; 195 local headquarters; 718 general chapters; 3,818 chapters; 17,453 districts; tens of thousands of groups; and hundreds of thousands of cells in Japan.

18. Nishijima Hisashi, *Komeito* (Tokyo: Sekkasha, 1968), p. 65.

19. See White, *The Soka Gakkai*, pp. 310–311.

20. Ibid., p. 303. (It should be noted that units other than families are referred to in some sources, so that organization numbers may seem to vary.)

21. *Mainichi Daily News*, December 15, 1980.

22. Palmer, *Buddhist Politics*, pp. 34–35.

23. Ibid., p. 32.

24. Dator, *Soka Gakkai*, pp. 63–70.

25. Ibid., p. 79.

26. Azumi Koya, "Political Functions of Soka Gakkai Membership," *Asian Survey* 11 (September 1971): 929.

27. Dator, *Soka Gakkai*, p. 79.

28. Ibid., p. 93.

29. Azumi, "Political Functions," p. 928.

30. Daniel Metraux, *The Soka Gakkai Revolution* (New York: University Press of America, 1994), p. 60.

31. Nishijima, *Komeito*, pp. 128–134.

32. Azumi, "Political Functions," p. 928.

33. Metraux, *The Soka Gakkai Revolution*, chap. 3.

34. Roger Benjamin and Kan Ori, *Tradition and Change in Post-industrial Japan: The Role of the Political Parties* (New York: Praeger, 1981), p. 45. The control the Gakkai exerts over its members is the greatest advantage of the Komeito in terms of facilitating the formation of the party's electoral strategies. Apparently, when the Soka Gakkai leaders speak to their followers on political matters, such pronouncements are considered to be religious commandments that must be followed. See Kashimoto Koichi, *Politics in Japan* (Tokyo: Japan Echo, 1982), pp. 44–45.

35. Kiyohiko Miyakawa, chief of the Soka Gakkai Youth Department, *Mainichi Daily News*, December 12, 1980.

36. *Japan Quarterly* 28, no. 2 (April-June 1981).<AU: Supply page numbers.>

37. *Japan Times*, November 29, 1980.

38. *Seikyo Shimbun*, January 1, 1954.

39. Quoted in Shiro Matsumoto, "Twists and Turns of Komeito," *Japan Echo* 9, no. 1 (1982): 61; originally published in *Sekai*, December 1981, pp. 36–44.

40. Ibid.

41. Ibid., p. 62.

42. Ibid., p. 43.

43. Benjamin and Ori, *Tradition and Change*, pp. 146–150.

44. Fujiwara Hirotatsu, *Soka Gakkai O Kiru* (Tokyo: Nisshin Hodo, 1970).

45. Azumi, "Political Functions," p. 921.

46. *Japan Echo* 9, no. 1 (1982): 107.

47. *Japan Times*, November 29, 1980.

48. "Soka Gakkai Controversy: Part 5," *Mainichi Daily News*, December 13, 1980.

49. "Soka Gakkai Vice President Speaks Out," *Japan Times*, November 29, 1980.

50. Interview with Harashima Takashi, *Mainichi Daily News*, December 4, 1980.

51. *Japan Times*, October 16, 1982.

52. *Japan Times*, July 28, 1975.

53. Miyamoto Kenji and Ikeda Daisaku, "In Quest of Civilized Coexistence," *Bengei Shunju*, October 1975.

54. Miyamoto Kenji, "At a Historical Turning Point," *Bungei Shunju*, October 1975.

55. See Naito Kunio, "History of Antagonism Between the JCP and the Soka Gakkai," *Gakkai Shokan*, October 1975. See also *Mainichi Daily News*, December 26, 1975.

56. "Ikeda Speech," *Asahi Evening News,* August 2, 1975.

57. "Nagatacho Doings," *Mainichi Daily News,* September 10, 1975.

58. *Mainichi Daily News,* July 17, 1975.

59. *Japan Times,* October 2, 1975.

60. *Akahata,* December 29, 1979.

61. *Asahi Evening News,* December 31, 1979.

62. *Akahata,* February 8, 1980.

63. Lee, "Komeito," p. 513.

64. *Japan Quarterly* 20 (April-June 1981): 155.

65. Azumi, "Political Functions," p. 924.

66. *Asahi Shimbun* poll, September 10, 1979.

67. Letter from Komeito headquarters to author dated August 29, 1981.

68. Hiroshi Imazu, "The Opposition Parties: Organization and Policies," *Japan Quarterly* 24 (April-June 1977), 148–180.

69. Palmer, *Buddhist Politics,* p. 67.

70. "Nagatacho Doings," *Mainichi Daily News,* May 2, 1979.

71. Yano was forced to resign from the party leadership because of his involvement in the Recruit Cosmos stock scandal of 1989–1990. Yano rose to the chairman position when Takeiri resigned in December 1986.

72. *Mainichi Daily News,* September 26, 1975.

73. James J. Foster, "Ghost Hunting: Local Party Organization in Japan," *Asian Survey* 22 (September 1982): 846–847.

74. Cecil C. Brett, "The Komeito and Local Japanese Politics," *Asian Survey* 19, no. 4 (April 1979): 373.

75. *Daily Yomiuri,* August 25, 1982.

76. *Mainichi Daily News,* December 5, 1980.

77. Komeito press release, September 18, 1980.

78. *Asahi Evening News,* April 5, 1976.

79. See the party publication entitled *Komeito* (Tokyo: Komeito, 1980).

80. *Time* (Asian edition), November 20, 1995.

81. Lee, "Komeito," p. 512.

82. "Nagatacho Doings," *Mainichi Daily News,* October 13, 1979.

83. Lee, "Komeito," pp. 503, 514.

84. *Mainichi Shimbun,* October 3, 1979.

85. *Asahi Shimbun,* March 17, 1982.

86. *Yomiuri Shimbun,* November 3, 1982.

87. Imazu, "The Opposition Parties," pp. 166–169.

88. Jung-suk Youn, "Candidates and Party Images: Recruitment to the Japanese House of Representatives," in *Parties, Candidates and Voters in Japan,* ed. John Campbell (Ann Arbor: Center for Japanese Studies, University of Michigan, 1980), pp. 106–109. Komeito lower house members were better educated in 1990 than were their CGP predecessors in previous decades. Of the 45 CGP candidates elected to the HR in February 1990, 32 had college degrees and another 7 had some college education. In terms of identifiable occupations prior to being elected to the Diet, 13 were prefectural or local assembly members; 19 were Komeito party workers; 7 were lawyers; and 4 came from educational positions.

89. Ibid., p. 113.

90. *Mainichi Shimbun,* June 24, 1980.

91. *Asahi Evening News,* October 4, 1980.

92. Tawara Kotaro, *Look Japan,* March 10, 1980, p. 3.

93. *Asahi Shimbun,* June 24, 1980.

94. *Tokyo Shimbun,* June 24, 1980.

95. Komeito was forced to fight the 1990 HR elections from a weakened position after its long-term party leader Yano was implicated in the Recruit Cosmos stock market scandal and a top aide of Ikeda Daisaku was also involved in a money scandal.

96. Matsumoto, "Twists and Turns," pp. 61–62.

97. Ibid., p. 63.

98. *Komeito* (Tokyo: Komeito International Bureau, 1982).

99. *Komeito Shimbun,* September 30, 1969.

100. *Komeito,* p. 12. (The remaining quotations in this section are also attributed to this party publication.)

101. Ibid., p. 16.

102. Ibid.

103. Ibid., pp. 16–17.

104. Komeito press release, no. 42, November 21, 1978.

105. *Komeito,* p. 3.

106. Ibid., p. 7.

107. Ibid., p. 37.

108. *Japan Times,* October 19, 1982.

109. "Komeito's 15th Annual Convention Summary," January 1978.

110. Komeito press release, no. 58, November 30, 1981.

111. *Komeito,* p. 29.

112. "Tilting Toward the Right: Sweeping Changes in Komeito Defense Policy," *Japan Quarterly* 29, no. 1 (January-March 1982): 1–5.

113. At the convention the CGP formally decided to establish a panel to discuss cooperation with the LDP after the CGP breaks with the JSP and DSP. The CGP justified this shift by arguing it would give ordinary citizens a better chance of voicing their views in politics. Komeito secretary-general Ichikawa gave three criteria for cooperation with the LDP: that both parties observe the constitution, seek clean politics, and champion ordinary citizens. *Yomiuri Shimbun,* November 29, 1990.

114. "Komeito Action Plan Draft," *Asahi Shimbun,* March 31, 1990.

115. *The Soka Gakkai Revolution,* Metraux, pp. 64–65.

116. *Mainichi Daily News,* September 29, 1993.

117. *The Soka Gakkai Revolution,* Metraux, p. 116.

118. *Japan Times Weekly,* August 11, 1997.

119. Home Affairs Ministry, "Elections Report" (December 1997).

120. *Time* (Asian edition), November 20, 1995.

121. *Mainichi Shimbun,* August 18, 1998.

122. *Time* (Asian edition), November 20, 1995.

123. *Daily Yomiuri,* June 18, 1998.

124. *Japan Times*, Editorial, May 8, 1979.

125. Palmer, *Buddhist Politics*, p. 78.

126. Ibid., p. 2.

127. Some have suggested that the Komeito is really a conservative party. See, for example, Murokami Shigeyoshi, *Komeito* (Tokyo: Shin Nippon Shuppan, 1969), pp. 174–182.

128. Lee, "Komeito," p. 512.

129. Azumi, "Political Functions," p. 918.

130. Imazu, "The Opposition Parties."

131. For more information on the Soka Gakkai and the Komeito, see Noah S. Brannen, *Soka Gakkai: Japan's Militant Buddhists* (Richmond, Va.: John Knox Press, 1964); James Allen Dator, "The Soka Gakka: A Socio-Political Interpretation," *Contemporary Religion in Japan* 6 (1965): 205–292; Dator, "The Soka Gakkai in Japanese Politics," *Journal of Church and State* 9 (Spring 1967): 223; H. Neill McFarland, *The Rush House of the Gods* (New York: Macmillan, 1967); Felix Moos, "Religion and Politics in Japan: The Case of the Soka Gakkai," *Asian Survey* 3 (March 1963): 36–42; Robert Ramseyer, "The Soka Gakkai and the Japanese Local Election of 1963," *Contemporary Religions in Japan* 4 (December 1963): 287–303; Charles Seldon, "Religion and Politics in Japan: The Soka Gakkai," *Pacific Affairs* 33 (December 1960): 382–386; and James White, "Mass Movements and Democracy: The Soka Gakkai in Japanese Politics," *American Political Science Review* 61 (September 1967): 744–750.

seven

The Social Democratic Party (Formerly Japan Socialist Party): A Turbulent Odyssey

J.A.A. Stockwin

The Japan Socialist Party (JSP), now the Social Democratic Party (SDP), has walked from hell to heaven and back again more than once in the decade from 1986 to 1996.[1] Reduced to a mere 15 seats in the October 1996 elections for the House of Representatives (HR), the party may not quite be ready to have its obituary written. But neither is its long-term, or even medium-term, survival guaranteed. Even though it, in effect, won the 1989 upper house elections, depriving the Liberal Democratic Party (LDP) of its majority, and although it provided a prime minister between June 1994 and January 1996, it has now ceased even to be the largest party on the Left, and Japan's political left wing is itself much reduced.

We should remember that the JSP has been written off, or regarded as politically inconsequential, many times in the past, and it has done much to deserve such opinions. The party's present condition may indeed prove terminal, but some of the things it has stood for have been influential causes over Japan's last half century, and its presence has exercised a powerful brake on the ambitions for change manifest among members of the political Right. Where it has had most influence is where its policies have overlapped or coincided with those of moderates within the LDP and other parties. The severe defeat of its forces in 1996 following a party split, and in the context of a changing political scene, suggests that right-wing forces may become harder to keep in check.

The JSP was out of power at the national level between the fall of the Ashida coalition cabinet in October 1948 and the formation of the Hosokawa coalition cabinet in August 1993. There was no Socialist prime minister between the resignation of Katayama Tetsu in February 1948 and the appointment of Murayama Tomiichi in June 1994. For most of the intervening period, the reins of government were held by the LDP, long the JSP's principal rival. It thus seemed an extraordinary change of fortune when, in August 1993, the JSP entered government as the largest party in an eight-party coalition that excluded the LDP from power for the first time in a generation, and then an even more astonishing reversal when less than a year later a coalition government was formed uniting the old ideological rivals, the LDP and the JSP (together with a minor party, the *Sakigake*). The electorate could be pardoned for wondering what on earth was going on.

When we look back over the history of the JSP/SDP, it quickly becomes evident that the party's problems go back a long way. Moreover, its decline was not of recent origin. Although the party enjoyed the support of about one-third of the voting public in the late 1950s, this proportion had apparently declined to about one-fifth by the early 1980s. Its image was generally lackluster and even old-fashioned, so that many Japanese regarded it as poorly organized, indifferently led, narrowly based, doctrinaire and irresponsible in policy, lacking in autonomy, poor in human talent, and overly prone to ideological and factional division.

There was always, however, a more positive side to the JSP—a side that, although it should not be exaggerated, may serve to modify slightly the bleak picture of chronic decline. From the 1950s until the early 1990s, the JSP always remained the largest of the various parties of opposition, regularly managing to win more than twice as many HR seats as those obtained by any other opposition party. It maintained a nationwide organization of reasonable (though hardly impressive) effectiveness based largely on what used to be Japan's largest labor federation, Sohyo, now dissolved into the Rengo labor federation.

Unlike the Komeito (Clean Government Party [CGP]) and the Japan Communist Party (JCP), the JSP's support since the 1960s has not been heavily concentrated in metropolitan areas. Perhaps the main reason for this was that the public service unions forming the core membership of Sohyo had enough members spread throughout the country to give the party a chance of parliamentary representation in many rural and semi-rural constituencies.[2] It also differs from the Komeito and the JCP in its form of organization. Whereas the latter parties have centralized authority, the JSP has had an organizational structure that militates against the imposition of strong central authority and thus permits formally subordinate groups of various kinds to function with considerable freedom.

In some ways, however, this loose structure was disastrous for the JSP, as factional disputation could not be curbed and the party leaders often appeared to preside but not to rule. These difficulties, in turn, had a conservative effect on the making of public policy, inasmuch as the compromises once hammered out between factious groups were too delicate to risk amending and updating. The party frequently appeared on the brink of splitting asunder, and indeed it has done so on a number of occasions in its turbulent history. On the other hand, there may also be some advantage to the organization of the JSP as compared with the authoritarian approach of its smaller rivals. Whereas the JCP and the Komeito impose a uniformity of approach on a highly committed membership, therefore tending to restrict their appeal to the alienated and suggestible, the JSP has presented a more "comfortable" and familiar image, which, though not enormously attractive, has also not been particularly demanding for the individual supporter.

In the Japanese political context, the Socialist Party has been recognized as indigenous, even traditional, despite its leftist rhetoric. Indeed, strange as it may seem, the party that has most resembled the JSP in structure is not the JCP (with which it might seem to have the most in common ideologically) but the LDP, which is likewise loosely organized and gives much leeway to the maneuverings of interest groups and factions. In a curious and suggestive way, moreover, the linkages that prevail between the LDP and the public sector have had a parallel in the linkages between the JSP and the public-sector unions.

In the past, the JSP has been of further significance because it has been a genuine party of opposition. Felicitously (or notoriously, depending on one's point of view), government policymaking has for the most part been controlled since the end of the Allied Occupation by a broad combination of public servants, conservative politicians, and representatives of powerful private-interest groups. Single-party dominance by the LDP between 1955 and 1993 resulted in a widespread analytical neglect of the JSP, on the grounds that as a party of "permanent opposition," it did not control policymaking and had no apparent prospect of doing so.

Nevertheless, the JSP articulated important alternative perspectives on policy and represented interests that, until the 1990s, were normally excluded from representation in government. There is, however, a strong tendency in an opposition long excluded from power (as well as in interest groups similarly excluded) to seek accommodations with those normally in control of the mechanisms of policymaking. In a situation of apparently permanent exclusion from office, such accommodation may seem preferable to permanent exclusion from any influence whatever on policy decisions. The JSP, unlike the centrist parties in the 1980s, was heir to a tradition of confronting government rather than compromising with it. Indeed, it was often pilloried as the party of "opposition to anything" (*nandemo hantai*). In practice, however, and particularly in respect of its role in the management of parliamentary business, the JSP was often much more prepared to compromise with government and the LDP than was commonly understood.[3] The jettisoning of much of its traditional platform by a Socialist prime minister in 1994 amazed observers and alienated much of the JSP's traditional base of support, but it is less difficult to understand once one realizes the extent of de facto accommodation that had taken place over many years.

The ideological distinctness of the JSP proceeds in part from the Marxist framework and language in which many of its pronouncements have been couched. Unlike the West German Social Democratic Party, the JSP in the late 1950s failed to shake off the major Marxist elements in its heritage—hence the defection of its right wing, which formed the Democratic Socialist Party (DSP) in 1959–1960. Even so, much of its Marxist orientation remained at the level of rhetoric, and other elements vied with it for attention within the party. In any case, it seems unlikely that the majority of those who voted for the JSP in the 1950s and 1960s did so out of sympathy with the Marxism contained in its message. More important was the image that the party was able to cultivate as champion of the democratic and pacifist reforms of the Allied Occupation, particularly of the earlier stages of the Occupation before a conservative reaction had set in.

Many of the JSP's policies were conceived in reaction against the conservative governments of the 1950s, particularly against the power of what the JSP chose to call "monopoly capital." It repeatedly inveighed against rearmament, which (in its view) defied the "Peace Constitution," Japanese membership in an anti-Communist alliance of nations led by the United States, erosion of the powers of the National Diet, antilabor legislation (including withholding the right to strike from public-sector workers), exclusion of labor unions in general from central decision-making, attempts by the Ministry of Education to increase its control over the teaching profession and the curriculum, and so on. Its general strategy was to paint the LDP government as reactionary and strongly antidemocratic as well as potentially militaristic. The argument that successive conservative governments were engaged in a conspiracy to subvert the postwar democratic reforms had a certain appeal, particularly among urban intellectuals and workers in the period before rapid economic growth had added so conspicuously to general prosperity.

The choices confronting policymakers in Japan of the 1990s are far more complex than those in the 1950s and 1960s. In essence, Japan and the world have changed enormously, and although the JSP/SDP made efforts to modernize to fit contemporary realities, it ultimately proved unable to maintain the electoral popularity that it experienced in 1989 and 1990, or to capitalize on its prime minister from June 1994 to January

1996, piloted Japan (shakily, it is true) through the difficult period of the great Hanshin earthquake and the release of poison gas by a religious sect on the Tokyo subway; as prime ministers go, he was not unpopular, but his party conspicuously failed to maintain either its unity or its electoral support.

In the rest of this chapter I will seek to describe and analyze the turbulent odyssey of this extraordinary party.

PARTY HISTORY

History has weighed heavily on the JSP and at crucial points in its development inhibited certain necessary changes. The party was founded in November 1945, but its founders came bearing miscellaneous intellectual baggage from the prewar period—notably from the initial period of left-wing party building in the latter half of the 1920s. That period saw the emergence of a three-way split in the Socialist movement, thus also reflecting labor union divisions. The reasons for this split, and even some of the leading personnel involved, were carried over into the postwar JSP and formed the background of persistent factional conflict within that party. Indeed, much of the factional division in the JSP during the first two postwar decades becomes comprehensible when one realizes that the party as formed in 1945 was a loose amalgam of the Shamin-kei on the Right, the Nichiro-kei in the center, and the Rodo-kei on the Left.[4] Each of these groups derived from separate small parties that had briefly come into existence in the late 1920s. The ideological differences among the three are too complicated to describe in detail, but the strands of thinking about labor unionism differed radically between the right-wing and left-wing groups. The Shamin-kei represented a form of thinking about the role of unions that assumed that workers' interests could best be secured through cooperation between labor and management on the basis of an enterprise, union structure. The Rono-kei, on the other hand, took a far more confrontational stand, seeking to foster industrial unionism and to "take on" government and management across a range of policy issues. In the postwar period the differences between the two extended to fundamentally contrasting views about foreign and defense policy, particularly about the peace settlement that ended the Allied Occupation in 1952. The Rono-kei was deeply opposed to the pro-U.S., anti-Communist foreign policy line of post-Occupation governments, and it advocated a nonaligned or neutralist foreign policy, to be guaranteed by the major powers.[5] It was also strongly opposed to any rearmament by Japan, however disguised by euphemistic language. On all these issues the Shamin-kei was the most muted in its criticism of the government, and both its domestic and foreign policy attitudes were influenced by an acute suspicion of and hostility toward anything that smacked of communism.

On most of these issues, the Nichiro-kei supported policies that fell somewhere between the policy lines espoused by the other two parties, such that its attitudes were less clearly defined. In any case, because it had provided much of the leadership of the 1930s Shakai Minshuto (Social Masses Party), which had developed close links with various ultranationalist groups, its influence was greatly weakened in the democratic atmosphere of the late 1940s and 1950s.

In great contrast to its impotence in later years, the JSP in the first few years after its foundation was generally recognized as a realistic contender for political power. In the first postwar general election for the HR, that of April 1946, the JSP won 92 seats (with 17.8 percent of the vote) to become the third-largest party; in the second election, just a year later, it actually turned out to be the largest party, with 143 seats (on 26.2 percent of the votes cast). The reason it could reasonably expect to participate in government at this stage was that the conservative camp was highly fragmented. With conservative unity established after 1955, even considerably better results (as in 1958) left power a long way from its grasp.

In the fluid political situation of the immediate postwar years, virtually any coalition arrangement that could guarantee a majority in Parliament seemed possible, although this is not to say that any coalition would prove able to provide effective government. In June 1947 a coalition government consisting of the JSP, the Japan Democratic Party, and the People's Cooperative Party was launched under the prime ministership of Katayama Tetsu, a Socialist. This government was a chaotic affair, faced by a tumultuous political situation in the country at large, as well as by severe internal strains that quickly tore it apart. An attempt by the Socialist element within the coalition to nationalize the coal mines did much to threaten the coalition's unity, and attempts to control galloping inflation failed. At the same time, a number of the most significant reforms of the Occupation were implemented during the coalition's tenure of office.

The worst result of its period in government was the escalation of already serious policy and personality differences between its left and right wings. The balance of intraparty power in the Katayama government was heavily in favor of the Right (particularly the Shamin-kei), but by the time of the cabinet's collapse in February 1948, the Left (mainly Rono-kei) was substantially in revolt against the right-of-center leadership. Indeed, the government's fall was precipitated by the decision of the Left to vote against the budget.

The Katayama cabinet was succeeded by another coalition in which the same parties participated, but the leader this time was a prime minister, Ashida Hitoshi, from the Japan Democratic Party. This administration struggled on, through a series of crises, until its resignation in October 1948. Thus ended the JSP's one and only positive experience of participation in office, which it enjoyed up to the beginning of the 1993–1996 coalition governments of Hosokawa, Murayama, and Hashimoto.

Some idea of the turbulence of the JSP during the Occupation years is suggested by the number of splits and defections it suffered during that period—a period that, in a sense, replicated the troubled history of Japanese socialism in 1926–1932.[6] The first defection took place in January 1948 when a right-wing group led by Hirano Rikizo, previously dismissed as minister of agriculture, broke away. This was followed by a left-wing splinter in September 1948, when Kuroda Hisao and his faction left the JSP (some were dismissed from it) after voting against the Ashida government's budget. This, in turn, led to the formation of a left wing mini-party, the Rodosha Nominto (Labor-Farmer Party), which rejoined the (by then) reunited JSP in 1957 (Figure 7.1).

In January 1950 the JSP briefly split into three fragments roughly corresponding to the Shamin-kei, Nichiro-kei, and Rono-kei divisions previously mentioned, but they came together again in April of the same year. A far more serious and durable split occurred in October 1951, when the party divided into two over the San Francisco peace settlement, with the Left strongly opposing it and rejecting any form of rearmament, whereas the center and Right were prepared to give it qualified approval.[7] Two separate parties, both calling themselves Nihon Shakaito (Japan Socialist Party) but generally known as the Left Socialist Party and the Right Socialist Party, were in existence for four years between October 1951 and a painfully effected reconciliation in October 1955.[8]

Underlying the numerous splits and defections in the first postwar decade was a steady shift in the balance of power from the Right, which was initially dominant, toward the Left. This was partly a reaction against the chaotic experience of the Katayama and Ashida governments, in which the JSP had participated under a right-wing leadership. The party was drastically repudiated by the electorate in the aftermath of the Ashida government's collapse, and it recorded by far its worst electoral result up to the present time in the lower house general elections of January 1949.

A further and more significant reason for the rise of the Left in this period relates to the struggle for control over the labor union movement, which was going on at the time between the Communists and various kinds of Socialists. During the early part of the Occupation, the JCP made a strong bid for control over the newly formed unions, but by 1949–1950 control of many unions and union federations had been wrested from the hands of the Communists by union leaders closely aligned with the Rono-kei, or left-wing, faction of the JSP. The formation of the Sohyo federation of labor unions in 1950—ironically, with strong support from the Occupation authorities—was a high point in the establishment of left-wing Socialist control. As can readily be seen from Table A.1, during the period of two Socialist parties (1951–1955), the electoral strength of the Left Socialists increased more rapidly than that of the Right Socialists, so that at the time of reunification in October 1955, the Left was in a substantially more dominant position than it had been at the time of the 1951 split. The organizational advantages accruing to the Left from increasing close links with Sohyo-affiliated unions, in competition with the Right, whose base of support was more heterogeneous and whose links with the union movement were weaker, were clearly reflected in the patterns of Left Socialist electoral advance. Over the long term, however, the advantages were less sure. By the 1960s the Sohyo unions had become the established base of support for the JSP to the extent that the organizational structure of the party itself was allowed to atrophy, and the party became identified in the public mind with a restricted set of union interests. The bulk of the unions affiliated with Sohyo were based on workers in the public sector, who had sectional grievances against the government because of the restrictions on the right to strike and organize introduced in 1948. The leftist radicalism of the Sohyo unions was much stimulated by these grievances, which were of limited interest to those not directly concerned.

The ideological divide between the right and left wings of the JSP ran very deep and has continued to bedevil the party to the present day. The parameters of the argument were quite clearly set out in the Inamuraura-Morito debate, which took place in 1949. Essentially, the debate was about whether the JSP should be a "class party," as argued by the Left, or a "mass party," as the Right believed it should be. Connected with this issue were arguments about revolutionary versus evolutionary approaches to political change and disagreements about whether the party should concentrate on parliamentary or "extraparliamentary" activities. The intellectual origins of the respective ideas of the two sides were, of course, quite diverse. Morito Tatsuo, the right-wing spokesman in 1949, derived many of his ideas from the British Labor Party, the Fabians, and Christian humanitarianism; hence, he was committed to gradual reform, parliamentary democracy, and the creation of a base of support that would extend well beyond the working class, strictly defined.

The intellectual antecedents of the Japanese Left, on the other hand, could be traced back to the German Marxism of the 1920s, although the Left had many quarrels with Marxism-Leninism, at least as interpreted by the JCP. Its differences with the Communist Party, which were genuine, were sharpened during the struggle for control of the union movement during the late 1940s. The Left consisted, however, of "Socialists first and Democrats second," whereas many on the Right were inclined to place their priorities the other way around. The leftists were also broadly within the lines of the Rono school of Japanese Marxism of the prewar period, which held that a single-stage revolution was possible in Japanese circumstances, as opposed to the two-stage revolution advocated by the Communists.[9] Perhaps even more significant than the actual arguments used was the fact that the Rono school had long ago rejected any kind of international Communist control of their activities and therefore constituted a distinctly national Marxist tradition.

This tradition proved crucial in guiding the dominant political perceptions of the JSP over the succeeding two or three decades. As a mode of thinking it was not entirely inflexible, nor did it remain unmodified by pragmatic considerations of political competition and the pursuit of power. It did, however, mold political perceptions in significant ways. Although it is difficult to disentangle rhetoric from practice, the Rono tradition tended to narrow the target of the party's appeal to those definable as "working-class." This tradition also resulted in a confrontational approach to "monopoly capital" and to the government-business establishment in general. Faced by an apparently permanent conservative majority in Parliament, during the 1950s and 1960s the party and associated groups, including labor unions, were quick to take to the streets in massive demonstrations rather than confine themselves to parliamentary debate. Moreover, in foreign policy an ostensibly neutralist program was repeatedly pulled in the direction of sympathy toward Peking and, to a slightly lesser extent, Moscow, and in the direction of hostility (at times extreme) toward the United States.

Foreign and defense policy was indeed a most crucial source of JSP concern, to the extent that the party was almost constantly at loggerheads with the ruling establishment. It remains the policy area in which the JSP image is most clearly established and best known. The party's longstanding position as champion of the "Peace Constitution," as well as advocate of the notion that Japan should repudiate the Security Treaty with the United States and phase out the Self-Defense Forces in order to become both unarmed and nonaligned, serves as a mark of identification.

Over the years, the security policy has also been the source of much dis-agreement within the party itself.

The origins of this policy can be traced at least as far back as the "three peace principles" accepted by the JSP in December 1949 during the national debate over the prospective peace settlement. The peace principles were as follows: "a peace treaty with all the belligerent pow-ers" (as distinct from a treaty signed only by the anti-Communist nations that had fought against Japan), "permanent neutrality," and "no military bases to be given to a foreign power." The outbreak of the Korean War and the authorization by General Douglas MacArthur of a quasi-military "Police Reserve" made the issue of rearmament a focus of intense political controversy. In January 1951 a fourth principle was therefore added to the three peace principles already endorsed by the JSP: "opposition to rearmament." The principles, however, were rejected by the Shamin-kei, and this rejection became the basis for the four-year Right-Left split in the JSP that began in October 1951. This scenario, then, was the background to the endorsement of "positive neutrality" as an alternative to the government's pro-U.S. foreign policy in the late 1950s.

The political compromise hammered out in 1954 and 1955 between the Left Socialist Party and the Right Socialist Party was achieved in an atmosphere of optimism occasioned by the rapidly improving electoral fortunes of the two parties in the first half of the decade. It was also facil-itated by the fact that both parties were led by their moderate wings and that political tensions were relatively relaxed at the time of the negotia-tions. The appearance of unity, however, was to prove relatively short-lived. The Sohyo labor federation itself had split in 1954, after a substantial section of its private industry union membership had revolted against what it saw as the unduly confrontational policies of the then current Sohyo leaders. The formation of the Liberal Democratic Party shortly following the Socialist reunification was demoralizing to the Socialists, because it meant that governmental office was removed much further from their grasp. The policies of the Kishi Nobusuke gov-ernment, which emerged in 1957, were also particularly provocative to the JSP across a range of issues, both domestic and foreign, while inter-national tensions also increased to some extent after the relatively relaxed period of the mid-1950s.

From the time of Kishi's abortive attempt to revise the Police Duties Law in 1958, massive demonstrations against the government became the order of the day for the Socialists. These demonstrations culminated in mass protests against revision of the Japan-U.S. Security Treaty in May and June 1960, thus forcing the prime minister to cancel President

Eisenhower's visit and leading indirectly to Kishi's resignation. The events of 1960 were in a real sense a turning point in Japan's postwar politics, marking both a watershed between the politics of Left-Right confrontation on highly charged political and foreign policy issues and a more incrementalist politics based on rapid economic growth and expanding shares.

It was becoming clear even before 1960 that the expansion of JSP electoral support that had been taking place throughout the 1950s was tapering off. Moreover, the party was conspicuously weak at the grassroots level, having become heavily reliant on the surrogate organization provided by Sohyo-affiliated unions. Its performance in elections for local government assemblies and local chief executive positions was proportionally much weaker than its performance in elections for the National Diet. But even at the national parliamentary level, the party appeared unable to jump the barrier of just over one-third of the lower house seats. Evidence was accumulating that younger voters were less enthusiastic about the party than they had been a few years earlier.

The late 1950s also saw a gradual drift to more extreme left-wing positions by the carefully chosen "moderate" leaders of the reunited party. Secretary-general Asanuma Inejiro created a furor in Japan when, in the course of a JSP mission to China in March 1959, he remarked that "American imperialism is the common enemy of the peoples of Japan and China." The fact that Asanuma was a veteran leader of Nichiro-kei (i.e., centrist faction) origin clearly indicated how polarized Japanese politics had become by the late 1950s, as the Kishi government proceeded with its revisionist program. The JSP was coming increasingly under the influence of an intellectual pressure group called the Shakaishugi Kyokai (Socialism Association), led by Professor Sakisaka Itsuro of Kyushu University. Sakisaka's group espoused an extreme version of the Rono school of Marxist analysis referred to earlier, while, although it was critical of the Japan Communist Party on many points of doctrine, had also completely rejected the possibility of achieving socialism through democratic parliamentary methods.

The influence of the Shakaishugi Kyokai and the leftward drift of the JSP leadership was too much for the right-wing Shamin-kei group led by the former union boss Nishio Suehiro, who was uncompromisingly anti-Communist. In October 1959 Nishio pulled his faction out of the party and was followed by some members of the Nichiro-kei. The next year they founded the Democratic Socialist Party (DSP).[10] The background to this split was related in part to the defections of right-wing unions in 1954 from the Sohyo federation. During the late 1950s a number of long-drawn-out strikes by left-wing unions had resulted in the creation of "second unions," which sought to negotiate compromise agreements with management. Relations between first and second unions were naturally extremely strained, and these tensions were reflected in the divisions both at the union federation level and within the JSP. Sakisaka's organization had been particularly active in promoting union intransigence in the strike at the Miike coalfields in Kyushu, where relations between first and second unions became violent at times. By 1959, therefore, the task of holding together a party composed of such diverse and mutually antagonistic elements had become impossible.

Even though the DSP did not prove as electorally successful as some had predicted, the loss of its right wing seriously depleted the parliamentary ranks of the JSP. Moreover, the traumatic experiences of the May–June crisis of 1960 over revision of the Japan-U.S. Security Treaty, and the November 1960 assassination of JSP chairman Asanuma Ineiiro by an ultranationalist forced the party to reassess many of its basic policies. Under a new leader, Eda Saburo, the party was introduced to a new doctrine of gradualism (though still with Marxist overtones) known as "structural reform." The emergence of this doctrine, with its nonrevolutionary emphasis on slowly altering the balance of power between labor and capital, was also closely connected with factional realignments and struggles for leadership.

Eda's grip on the sources of power in the JSP proved temporary and fragile.[11] By the end of 1962 he was already being eased out of the leadership; and by May 1965, with the election of Sasaki Kozo as chairman, the Left was once more firmly in control. The early 1960s, however, saw a remarkable substitution of moderate for extreme policies on the part of the government (under Ikeda Hayata) and the principal party of opposition, the JSP, under its moderate chairman, Kawakami Jotaro.

The second half of the 1960s was a different story. The Vietnam War and associated issues re-created tensions between the government and opposition over policy toward the United States. Fears that Japan was increasingly being used by U.S. forces as a staging post for its operations in Vietnam, and that Japan's security was therefore being jeopardized rather than enhanced by the Japan-U.S. Security Treaty, prompted an extremely confrontational stance by the JSP leaders against the Sato government. The questions of continued U.S. occupation of Okinawa, bad relations between Japan and China, the prospect of a further renewal of the Security Treaty in 1970, and the eruption of student radicalism on campuses throughout the nation in 1968–1970 added to the political turmoil, as well as to the extremism of the JSP leadership.

For the party also, the 1960s were a period of electoral decline, particularly toward the end of the decade (see Table 7.1). In the lower house general elections of December 1969, the JSP lost 50 seats, and its total fell from 140 to 90 as a result of the decline in its proportion of the total vote by 6.5 percent. Admittedly, the working of the multimember constituency system produced a greater loss of seats than was really warranted by the loss of votes. Nevertheless, this event was recognized within the JSP as a disastrous defeat, and once again the party was forced to take stock.

As with the scenario in 1960, when the JSP was weakened by the formation of the DSP, the electoral decline of the late 1960s must be analyzed not only in terms of popular reaction against the party's policies (a factor that was demonstrably involved) but also in terms of the undermining of JSP support by the emergence of new political forces. Not only the formation of the DSP in 1960 but also the emergence of the Komeito in the late 1960s and the electoral resurgence of the JCP a little later made inroads into the electoral support of the JSP as well as of the LDP. A particularly striking fact is that erosion of JSP support occurred most heavily in those metropolitan areas along the Pacific coast that had been the Socialist heartland in the 1950s. According to one study, just 50 percent of the seats classifiable as "metropolitan" went to the JSP in the lower house elections held in 1958; the figures were 24.7 percent for the 1967 elections and a mere 19.7 percent for the elections of 1972. The corresponding figures for "urban" seats were 34.0 percent (1958), 28.1 percent (1967), and 23.5 percent (1972); for "semiurban" seats, 34.2 percent (1958), 30.8 percent (1967), and 28.3 percent (1972); and for seats classified as "rural," 31.8 percent (1958), 30.3 percent (1967), and 23.3 percent (1972).[12] In other words, although the number of JSP seats had decreased in all categories, the party lost ground more heavily in Japan's biggest cities, particularly Tokyo, Osaka, and Yokohama, than in other parts of the country. Indeed, by 1972 the party was doing marginally better in

TABLE 7.1   JSP Multiple Candidatures, 1958, 1979, 1990, and 1993 HR elections

	1958			1979			1990			1993	
A	B	Total	A	B	Total	A	B	Total	A	B	Total
46	91	115	9	27	130	15	23	130	2	20	129
(40%)	(79%)		(7%)	(21%)		(11%)	(18%)		(2%)	(16%)	

NOTE: A = constituencies in which the JSP won two or more seats; B = constituencies in which the JSP put up two or more candidates; Total = total number of lower house constituencies.

SOURCES: Data calculated from Asahi Nenkan, 1959, 1980, and 1994; Mainichi Shinbunsha, '90 Sosenkyo ['90 election] (Tokyo, 1990), pp. 14–19.

rural and smalltown Japan than in the larger cities and towns. These latter were precisely the areas in which the Komeito, the JCP, and, to a
lesser extent, the DSP were picking up support.

Komeito and Communist successes were premised on a vigorous and
precise approach to organization in which the membership of large
numbers of committed individuals was a major factor. The JSP, with its
continued reliance on surrogate organization by Sohyo-affiliated labor
unions, could not match. Although it could maintain a good part of the
support of those who had been attracted to its cause in the late 1940s
and the 1950s, it had difficulty persuading new voters to rally to its
side, particularly those who might have been expected to grant their
support on the basis of their residence in singularly alienating conditions in large metropolitan apartment blocs or other, often low-quality,
housing.

The JSP was also ill equipped to take advantage of the new style of progressive politics that was emerging in the early 1970s, centering on issues
of environmental pollution and related questions and involving the emergence of citizens' movements as a vital and to some extent unpredictable
political force at the grassroots level. Nevertheless, Socialist backing was
an important element in most of the newly emerging "progressive local
authorities" that made their appearance around this time in the larger
cities and urban prefectures. Sometimes, as in Kyoto during the campaign
prior to the 1974 elections for governor, the Socialists found themselves
outclassed organizationally by the Communists, such that participation in
progressive coalitional arrangements at the local level was not always a
comfortable experience for them.

If the 1960s were a period of rapid and disturbing decline for the JSP,
the 1970s saw a certain consolidation of its electoral strength, even
though the overall trend still appeared to be one of gradual diminution.
It was difficult to find a commentator prepared to argue that the JSP had
come close to sorting out its problems or turning itself into a vital and
dynamic party of opposition. Indeed, the prevailing image was one of
stagnation and conservation of outdated policies and attitudes, although
fundamental intraparty ideological divisions remained. To some extent,
however, it was true that things were not as bad as they had been in the
1960s. For one thing, after the turbulent leadership politics of the 1960s,
greater stability of leadership was achieved in the 1970s. Between 1970
and 1977 the top two party posts of chairman and secretary-general
were in the hands, respectively, of Narita Tomorni and Ishibashi
Masashi, neither of whom had strong factional connections. In other
words, they were free to exercise the arts of compromise and conciliation
between the Left and the Right.

The stability, however, was only relative. During the early and middle 1970s, Eda Saburo was actively exploring the possibility of creating a new left-of-center coalition (or even a single party) combining the DSP, the Komeito, and sympathetic sections of the JSP. The problem with this approach was that it could succeed only at the cost of splitting the JSP once again, since the left wing of the JSP was most unlikely to accept such an arrangement. The official JSP policy, which reflected the need felt by the Narita-Ishibashi leadership to conciliate the Left as well as the Right, was that the party should work for an alliance of all opposition parties, including the JCP. However unrealizable such a program might have appeared, it at least had the merit of not provoking internecine strife among the various factions of the JSP.

While Eda and his supporters were exploring an alternative "opening to the center," Sakisaka's extreme left-wing organization, the Shakaishugi Kyokai, was revealing substantially increased strength at party congresses. Although it remained weak among JSP Diet members, by the mid-1970s the Shakaishugi Kyokai commanded impressive support among rank-and-file activists.

The year 1977 was a time of crisis for the JSP, torn as it was between the fissiparous tendencies of the Eda group on the Right and the Shakaishugi Kyokai on the Left. An ironic result of the latter's emergence as a major force within the party was that Sasaki and Eda, rivals for leadership in the 1960s, found themselves working together to prevent its takeover of the JSP. The Atarashii Nagare no Kai (New Current Society), a grouping of various anti-Kyokai elements, had been formed essentially for this purpose, but in early 1977 it appeared to have its back against the wall in the face of ample evidence of Kyokai resurgence. In the spring of 1977 Eda finally defected from the party, to be joined later in the year by Den Hideo and a few others. The defections that occurred during the year were not large in number, but they resulted in the formation of a new mini-party, the Shakai Minshu Rengo (Shaminren), or Social Democratic League. Eda, however, died shortly after leaving the JSP and did not live to see the formation of the new party.

Narita and Ishibashi resigned from the two top JSP posts in the summer, and the new chairman was Asukata Ichio, the progressive mayor of Yokohama. He believed in decentralizing administration and encouraging local initiative, which contrasted with JSP tradition. At one time, however, he had been a Socialist Diet member (on the Left of the party) and retained important elements of Marxist thinking.[13] He was able to have his own conditions for nomination accepted.[14] Asukata sought to increase party membership and instituted a system whereby the party chairman was elected by the total membership of the party instead of by delegates to the party congress—a system that paralleled one newly introduced into the LDP.

Asukata's reforms did not, however, effect a radical breakthrough in the chronic structural and ideological problems of the JSP, which by the end of his term in 1983 seemed marginally less demoralized than it had been when he assumed office. The party fared poorly in the lower house elections of 1979 and 1980, as well as in the upper house elections of 1980 and 1983. Many of the progressive local administrations (*kakushin jichitai*), which had dominated the big-city scene in the early and middle 1970s and had formed an important bulwark of Asukata's political philosophy, had been replaced by administrations of a conservative coloring by the early 1980s. Plainly, there was a conservative mood in the country that was not especially receptive to the messages the JSP had to offer, even if the JSP had been able to overcome the structural problems that had weakened its impact over the years. Moreover, Asukata himself was widely criticized both within and outside the party for his indecisiveness and lack of an appealing image. Several political decisions between 1980 and 1983 harmed his reputation, and in the summer of 1983 he announced his resignation. Ishibashi Masashi was elected, unopposed, as his successor.

Ishibashi proved to be a vigorous and reformist leader. Determined—as he reiterated at every opportunity—to transform the JSP from a party of perpetual opposition into a party ready to participate in power, he set out to galvanize the JSP into modernizing itself, which meant relinquishing many of its ancient shibboleths. The road to reform was not easy, however, and like other chairmen before him, he faced strong resistance from the left wing. Sometimes the result was an uneasy compromise. For instance, the party congress of February 1984 came up with a policy position regarding the Self-Defense Forces, which held that they were unconstitutional but also, because their existence was based on parliamentary approval, that they should be considered "legal." The party also softened somewhat its previous hostility to nuclear power stations.

The most important change promoted by Ishibashi was the rewriting of the party's 1964 platform, "The Road to Socialism in Japan," a document heavily infused with Marxist concepts and rhetoric. After much difficult debate, a modernized platform replacing the 1964 document was approved by the party congress in January 1986.

In July 1986 simultaneous elections were held for the upper and lower houses of the National Diet. The elections produced a sweeping victory for the LDP under Nakasone Yasuhiro, and the JSP was crushingly defeated, seeing its lower house seat total reduced to 86. Ishibashi accepted responsibility for the defeat and resigned the party chairmanship. In his stead the party chose Doi Takako, a JSP lower house Diet member since 1969.

The choice of a woman as leader of a political party for the first time in Japanese history caused an immediate sensation in the mass media, which thrives on political sensations. Doi's election, however, was no nine-day wonder. Over time, she developed a strong profile as a political leader skilled in communication, with a gift for presenting political issues to ordinary people in ways that could be readily understood. Even though her capacity to reform the party has arguably proved limited, there seems little doubt that the upsurge in support for the JSP apparent in 1989–1990 owed much to the charisma that she has been able to establish.

Doi Takako was born in 1928 as the second daughter of a medical doctor working in Kobe. Before entering Parliament in 1969, she taught constitutional law at Doshisha University in Kyoto and spoke frequently on constitutional issues as party leader. Her intellectual background should hardly be seen as radically reformist in terms of the party's history, and her style was to speak out trenchantly in defense of the Peace Constitution, against government proposals for taxation reform, and against the lifting of agricultural protection, particularly of rice. She turned out to be an impressive campaigner, and her cultivation of the women's vote paid off well. Government proposals for tax reform helped the JSP electorally in the second half of the 1980s. Both Prime Minister Nakasone's abortive attempt in early 1987 to introduce a type of value-added tax, and his successor Takeshita's successful introduction of "consumption tax" *(shohizei)*—announced March 1988, effective April 1989—enabled the JSP to reap electoral rewards.

Beginning in the summer of 1988, Japanese politics in general and the Takeshita administration in particular were increasingly traumatized by what became known as the "Recruit scandal." The ambitious head of a company specializing in employment information saturated the political world with unlisted shares in a subsidiary company, Recruit Cosmos. The shares could be sold at a profit once the company was listed on the stock exchange, but the whole operation was highly questionable under Japanese law. Revelations concerning the Recruit scandal came cumulatively, and politicians of almost all persuasions were found to be implicated. In November a JSP Diet member, Ueda Takumi, admitted that his secretary had accepted Recruit Cosmos shares, and Ueda promptly relinquished his seat in the Diet to accept responsibility. This prompt action by one of its parliamentarians enabled the party to escape the opprobrium that came to attach more and more to other parties, and in particular to leading members of almost every faction in the LDP. Public opinion polls revealed rapidly declining support for the Takeshita cabinet, and in April Takeshita announced his resignation, being succeeded in June by Uno Sosuke.

Uno had scarcely taken up the reins of prime ministerial office when allegations began to be made about inappropriate activity in his private life. It is hardly surprising, therefore, that when the House of Councillors (HC) elections were held in July, the LDP found itself at the nadir of its support.

When the election results were announced, the JSP was for the first time the largest party by numbers of seats, having won 35.1 percent of the vote in the national (proportional representation) constituency and 31.6 percent in the prefectural constituencies. For the first time in its history, the LDP was forced into a minority position of 109 seats out of 252. The effective total of JSP seats was further augmented by the success of several candidates standing under the label of the recently formed Rengo (Alliance) labor union federation. Doi Takako, quoting a poem by the turn-of-the-century feminist poet Yosano Akiko, announced: "The mountains have moved."[15]

Apart from the Recruit scandal, the issue of consumption tax, and the prime minister's private life, another issue that undoubtedly swung many votes from the LDP to the JSP (and Rengo) in agricultural areas was the earlier decision to lift protection on some agricultural products, notably beef and citrus fruits. Thus in the 26 single-member constituencies, which were mostly rural/agricultural prefectures away from the big cities, an LDP majority of 25 out of 26 was converted to a JSP/Rengo majority of 23. Another feature of the election was the unprecedented number of women candidates standing for the JSP, of whom 12 were elected. This was known in the press as the "Madonna strategy" and gained the party a great deal of (mostly favorable) publicity.

With the substitution of Kaifu Toshiki for the hapless Uno as prime minister following the elections, the LDP gradually managed to restore a degree of normality to its affairs, and little by little the steam went out of the various issues that had lost the party the upper house elections. Thus, although it lost seats in the HR elections of February 1990, it emerged with a healthy majority. The JSP did not fulfill its promise of winning the elections (which was in any case unlikely), but it succeeded in increasing its seat total from the abysmal 86 lower house seats it had been reduced to in 1986, up to 136 seats in 1990.

The elections of 1989 and 1990 thus ushered in a period in which the JSP, though it had failed to convince the electorate that it was capable of governing the country, had asserted convincingly its primacy among the opposition parties—a position that it had once occupied but that over many years had appeared to be slipping away. The long years in the remote political wilderness had bred low morale and a certain complacency within the party's ranks. The task facing the Doi leadership as a result of its political resurgence was to convert the JSP from a "party out of power" *(yato)* to one capable of mounting effective opposition and, ultimately, of achieving power.[16]

One manifestation of the changes being wrought in the party by its electoral successes was the formation of a body called the New Wave Society (Nyu Uebu no Kai), consisting of 28 out of the 50 lower house Diet members newly elected in the February 1990 elections. Nine of the 28 were lawyers, and others followed a variety of occupations, but the labor union representation was minimal. The New Wave Society, which maintained close links with the Shaminren (Social Democratic Federation) was actively exploring ways of reforming the party structure and policies in such a way as to make it a party of true opposition and potentially of government.

Unfortunately for the party, the successes of 1989 and 1990 could not be sustained. In part, this was because these successes were brought about by factors that proved to be temporary. Once the Kaifu government had consolidated its position in the lower house elections of February 1990, things more or less returned to normal. It was, however, in the foreign policy area that the JSP was to face its biggest test, and to be found wanting in the eyes of the electorate. The Gulf crisis, which began in August 1990 and culminated in the brief war of January-February 1991, not only created intense pressure on the Kaifu government to contribute to the multinational force but also placed the foreign policy positions of the JSP under intense scrutiny. Ironically, this scrutiny was the more intense because the LDP no longer enjoyed a majority in the HC since the JSP victory of July 1989. This meant that in order to pass legislation through Parliament enabling Japan to contribute to the multinational force, the LDP needed to gain the cooperation of other parties in the upper house. The JSP, however, adopted an uncompromising stance, based on its traditional support of the Peace Constitution, and the government's proposals for the establishment of a United Nations Cooperation Force foundered in the Diet in November 1990. No doubt because of the bad publicity given to Japan abroad by its failure to provide a physical (as distinct from a financial) contribution to the task of forcing Iraq to withdraw from Kuwait, the JSP lost much of its electoral support over the period of the Gulf crisis and war.

In April 1991 the party suffered a humiliating defeat in local elections, and especially in the contest to elect the governor of Tokyo prefecture, where the party leaders spent several weeks in a futile but well-publicized attempt to find a credible candidate. The little-known academic chosen late in the day could barely scrape together 7 percent of the vote and was even behind the candidate promoted by the Communists. In the wake of this fiasco, Doi Takako, at the nadir of her popularity, stepped down as party chairperson and was succeeded in July by Tanabe Makoto, an experienced but less charismatic leader who had built up significant links with certain LDP politicians.

In 1992, while momentous events were developing on the conservative side of politics, the JSP and its ally, the Shaminren (Social Democratic Federation), mounted a determined but unsuccessful campaign to defeat the second attempt by the government (now led by Miyazawa Kiichii) at a Peace Keeping Operations (PKO) Co-operation Bill. The campaign encompassed "cow-walking" (moving very slowly through the voting lobbies) and a threat that JSP and Sharninren Diet members would resign their seats en masse. The bill, however, passed both houses with the support of most other parties, and the unpopularity of its tactics was indicated by the JSP's poor results in the HC elections held in July, when it won 24 fewer seats than in 1989.

These election results weakened the grip of the party chairman, Tanabe Makoto, whose long-standing connections with the disgraced LDP politician Kanemaru Shin brought suggestions of corruption onto his head. Tanabe stepped down in December in favor of a leading politician on the Right of the party, Yamahana Sadao.

During the early months of 1993, events were unfolding that were to bring the long years of uninterrupted LDP rule to an end. The failure of the Miyazawa government's attempt to reform the lower house electoral system led to the defection from the LDP of two separate groups, led, respectively, by Takemura Masayoshi and Hata Tsutomu (the key figure in the second group was Ozawa Ichiro). The government was defeated in a no-confidence motion on June 18, 1993, and dissolved Parliament. In the subsequent general elections, held on July 22, the LDP lost its parliamentary majority for the first time in the party's history. Newly formed parties, including the Shinseito (Hata and Ozawa), the Nihon Shinto (formed in 1992 by Hosokawa Morihiro), and the Shinto Sakigake (Takemura) did well.

For the JSP, the elections were rich in irony. On the one hand, the party lost nearly half its seats in the HR, ending up with a mere 70 seats. This was its worst electoral result since 1949. On the other hand, it took office as the largest party in a new coalition government, led by Hosokawa Morihiro, a former LDP prefectural governor, consisting of seven parties and one upper house grouping. The new government took office on August 9 with massive public support and a mandate for wide-ranging reforms, particularly in the areas of deregulation, decentralization, reform of the electoral system, and measures against political

corruption. Yamahana proved to be a skillful negotiator in the talks leading to the formation of the new government. The new Speaker of the HR
was Doi Takako.

For the JSP, its first taste of government in over four decades was an
opportunity, but also a painful experience. Divisions between the left
and right wings of the party remained intense, and in September 1993
the Left forced the resignation of Yamahana, to take responsibility for the
electoral defeat in July. He was replaced by Murayama Tomiichi, a leading member of the party's left wing.

Toward the end of 1993 and into January 1994, intense negotiations
were conducted, both among the coalition parties and between the government and the LDP, on the content of an electoral reform package,
including measures to combat corruption. On January 20, 1994, 17 JSP
members of the HC voted against the package that had been hammered
out, ensuring its parliamentary defeat. One of the main issues for the rebels
was that, in their view, too many lower house seats were to be contested in
single-member constituencies, and not enough by proportional representation. As a result of their rebellion, however, a government-LDP compromise, brokered by Doi Takako as lower house Speaker, created a further
shift toward single-member constituencies (300, as against 200 to be
elected by proportional representation).

For reasons that need not concern us here, Hosokawa unexpectedly
resigned as prime minister in April 1994. A minority government, led by
Hata Tsutomu, was formed in its stead. The new government was to
consist of the same elements as the old one, but the JSP pulled out in
protest against an abortive scheme by Ozawa to unite all the coalition
components except the Socialists into a single party. The Hata government lasted nine weeks and resigned in June 1994.

Negotiations were held between the coalition partners and the
Socialists to come back into the coalition and form a majority government once again, but the talks failed. Instead, an entirely new coalition,
enjoying a comfortable majority, was formed between the LDP, the JSP,
and the Shinto Sakigake. The new prime minister was the JSP chairman—a post to which he had acceded the previous September—the sev-
enty-year-old Murayama Tomiichi.

In the eyes of many observers, this was an astonishing development.
The two principal parties of the coalition government had been ideologically polarized for so long that a coalition arrangement between them
had appeared unthinkable. In fact, however, as indicated earlier, personal
linkages between certain of their leaders went back a long way. Moreover, since the adoption of its new platform in 1986, the party's Marxist
heritage had declined in importance, and most Socialist members of

Parliament were essentially practical politicians, representing their constituents. The JSP was still concerned to defend the Constitution and oppose any moves toward serious projection of military force, but here again, the party had not been entirely united in its opposition to the various PKO bills earlier in the decade. Even though its stance on constitutional and defense matters put it at loggerheads with the right wing of the LDP, its views were not so distant from those of LDP moderates. In any case, since the ending of the cold war at the beginning of the decade, inhibitions about having in government a party with a Marxist past had receded, and the uniting of the union movement into the Rengo federation had given labor (the JSP's principal backer) greater access to government than it had enjoyed in the past. Protection of strategic interest groups against "excess competition" was a feature of both the JSP and the LDP.

Within two months of becoming prime minister, Murayama dropped the time-honored JSP policies of opposing the existence of the Self-Defense Forces and the Japan-U.S. Security Treaty, and the use of the national flag and national anthem in schools. These changes were narrowly endorsed at a subsequent party congress but risked alienating much of the core support that the party had relied on in the past. Murayama argued that he had no choice, as prime minister of a coalition government with the LDP, other than to change tack on these issues.

In December 1994 most of those parties that had formed the earlier coalition government under Hosokawa, and now remained in opposition, amalgamated into a single large party, the Shinshinto (New Frontier Party). Around the same period, parallel moves were taking place within the JSP to form a new party on "democratic liberal" principles. Yamahana was the key figure in this movement. On January 17, 1995, however, the Great Hanshin earthquake occurred in and around Kobe, and the movement was placed on hold, thus inevitably losing momentum.

Murayama was widely criticized for the government's slow response to the earthquake disaster, in which many people probably died unnecessarily. It was followed in March by the release of sarin gas at stations in the Tokyo subway, a crime of which the Aum Shinrikyo, a religious cult with political ambitions, was accused. Nineteen ninety-five turned into a year of reflection on natural and man-made disasters. Even though the JSP managed to avoid a split, it lost a further 25 seats in the 1995 July HC elections.

In January 1996 Murayama resigned as prime minister in favor of the LDP leader, Hashimoto Ryutaro, although the coalition government continued. Negotiations for amalgamation between the JSP and the Shinto

Sakigake began in the autumn of 1995 but collapsed in April 1996. With a lower house general election anticipated in the latter half of the year, an intense process of maneuvering took place for party realignment. After some months of complex negotiations, a new centrist party, the Minshuto (Democratic Party), was formed late in September 1996. This party recruited members from several existing parties, including the JSP, which had recently renamed itself (Social Democratic Party, or SDP). By the time of parliamentary dissolution for the general elections to be held on September 20, so many defections had taken place (principally, though not entirely, to the Minshuto), that the SDP was reduced to 30 members of the HR. Soon before the elections Murayama stepped down as chairman, and Doi Takako returned to the post she had relinquished in 1991. This did not prevent electoral disaster, and the party could win only 15 out of the 500 seats, of which no more than 4 were from single-member constituencies. (At least 20 of those elected under the Democratic Party label were former Socialists.) For the first time, the party had fewer seats in the lower house than the Communists (with 26). The party appeared to have reached the nadir of its influence, and its survival is far from certain.

PARTY STRUCTURE AND ORGANIZATION

The formal organizational structure of the JSP incorporates substantial elements of democracy. The most important of these elements is the congress, which must be held at least once per year (although provision is also made for extraordinary congresses). The congress acts as more than a sounding board for rank-and-file opinion, given that major party posts are determined by congress votes, and congressional resolutions are expected to be taken seriously by the leadership. The role of the party congress in the JSP is much greater than the role of the equivalent body in the LDP, partly, no doubt, because the JSP is out of office. The main organs whose members are chosen by the congress are the Central Executive Committee (CEC), the Control Commission, and the Central Committee. Of these, the CEC is by far the most important; in effect, it constitutes the party's central governing body. The Control Commission is supposed to deal with matters of party discipline, and the Central Committee, which is supposed to take over from the congress when it is not in session, in fact plays a minimal role.[17]

In one respect, the character of the party congress has been subject to crucial fluctuations. Delegates to the congress include officials of central party headquarters and representatives of local branches. Until 1962 it was normal for Diet members to qualify automatically as delegates to the national congress in Tokyo. From 1962, however, they could become delegates only if elected from local branches. This change took on considerable importance in view of the general tendency for Diet members to be relatively conservative and pragmatic in contrast to rank-and-file branch activists, who have tended to be more militant and concerned with ideological purity. This exclusion of JSP Diet members became a particular problem in the mid-1970s, when a large number of Shakaishugi Kyokai members and sympathizers were being elected to the Congress, whereas the Kyokai enjoyed the support of only a tiny minority of Diet members. In 1977, as a result of the serious intraparty crisis of that year, the situation more or less returned to that existing before 1962, and the influence of the Shakaishugi Kyokai in the party congress subsequently declined.

As is common in Japanese political organizations generally, strenuous efforts are made to avoid open contests in the election to party posts at each Congress. In the JSP these efforts are a reflection less of the cultural norm of consensus than of the crucial necessity of prearranging selection to posts if damaging factional and Left-Right wrangles are to be avoided on the floor of the Congress. The party's worst crises (e.g., those in 1949–1951, 1959–1960, at various times during the 1960s, in 1977, 1982, and 1994–1996) tend to occur when either the Left or the Right is seen by the other to be seeking to monopolize executive positions. A balanced ticket has therefore been a practical necessity if damaging conflict and, ultimately, the splitting of the party are to be avoided. Unfortunately, however, a balanced ticket is not always the best way of producing innovative, appealing, or even clear and comprehensible policies given the gulf that, for much of its history, has divided the JSP between Marxists and Democratic Socialists. This, in a sense, has been the party's ultimate dilemma.

The CEC, as the party's chief executive body, is responsible for general policy formulation and oversight of party organization. As the party rules describe it: "The Central Executive Committee represents the party as its highest executive organ, and is responsible to the National Congress and the Central Committee."[18] It meets frequently, and much of its work is done in functional branches *(kyoku)* and committees. The role of the chairman of the Executive Committee (often simply referred to as "party chairman") in relation to the committee itself is controversial. The determination to maintain intraparty democracy and rank-and-file influence has often meant a relatively weak role for the chairman.

In the early 1990s the JSP experimented with a "shadow cabinet" system on the British model, but it never seems to have amounted to much more than window dressing. In any case, when the party found itself in office as part of a coalition government between August 1993 and April 1994, and then again between June 1994 and October 1996, the strains set up between ministers (including especially Murayama as prime minister) who had to follow agreed coalition government policy, and the party organization, were at times intense. Such strains were most conspicuous over reforming the electoral system in 1993–1994 and in relation to Murayama's decision to throw over certain traditional Socialist policies shortly after he became prime minister.

The leaders of the party at the national level include the chairman of the CEC (the party chairman), a small but variable number of vice chairmen (usually between two and four), the secretary-general, the chairman of the Control Commission, chairmen of the branches and committees of the CEC, and a number of party advisers, or elders *(komon)*. Throughout most of the party's history, the national congress elected the chairman, but Asukata instituted a process of election among the party membership at large. Leadership selection in the JSP has been a question to which enormous attention is paid within the party; indeed, the choice of chairman and secretary-general, as well as the distribution of top posts generally, has often been obsessively contested among various factions and other intraparty groups. Even though the number of posts and the degree of power, opportunity, and prestige they carry are less than those associated with the LDP, there are marked similarities between the scramble for position in the JSP and that in the LDP. Despite the difference between the two parties in the greater role accorded by the JSP to the National Congress, they are very much alike in adhering to the practice of rotating positions so as to satisfy the aspirations for office of the different intraparty groups. Moreover, although this rotation occurs as a result of regular contests, maneuvers, and calculations about a shifting balance of power, there is an unwritten expectation that ultimately all interested groups will be given some share in the power available. In the JSP the failure, even over a relatively short term, to fulfill such expectations creates disruptive friction and stress, as we have seen. It may also be noted that this system of leadership selection differs only in practice from that employed by either the Komeito or the JCP— especially in the case of the former, in which the tenure of top positions by the same individuals has been of much greater duration.

The party chairman plainly occupies a key position in the party, even though the chairman commands far less power and fewer resources than the president of the LDP. It is difficult to generalize about the fourteen chairmen and one acting chairman experienced by the party between 1945 and 1996.[19] Nearly all these individuals came to the chairmanship after long experience in the party or, in the case of the earlier postwar incumbents, in the prewar Socialist movement, which would include left-wing parties and labor and tenant organizations. Asukata was an exception: Although he had been a Socialist Diet member until the early 1960s, he was fully occupied in his post as mayor of Yokohama between 1963 and 1978. He was therefore the only chairman who could be said to have been brought into the party from the outside. Eda Saburo, acting chairman for a few months following the assassination of Asanuma in October 1960 and a key contender for the chairmanship throughout the early 1960s, was somewhat exceptional in having been very little known outside the party until 1960, and then for having bought the wholesale reform of the party's policies and image without first serving a long leadership "apprenticeship." It should be noted, however, that this experiment was ultimately not successful.

The chairmen up to the late 1960s—namely, Katayama Tetsu, Suzuki Mosaburo, Kawakami Jotaro, Sasaki Kozo, and Katsumata Seiichi—were all faction leaders of long standing, and Asanuma Inejiro, though not technically leading a faction (he belonged to the Kawakami faction), had essentially come from the same mold as other faction leaders (Katayama's case is also perhaps a little doubtful). Narita Tomomi (the chairman from 1969 to 1977), like Ishibashi Masashi, his long-standing deputy in the position of secretary-general, had always avoided strong factional identity, and this was also the case with his successor, Asukata Ichio. Ishibashi Masashi and Doi Takako were also closely identified with established factions, so that the party may be said to have established a definite pattern in this regard, whereby chairmen derive their acceptability from their believed neutrality, or at least nonpartisanship, in factional contests. Such neutrality has not precluded chairmen from vigorously pursuing fundamental reforms to policy and organization.

In the case of Doi Takako, a new element entered into the situation, namely, that her national popularity in the scandal-ridden late 1980s was a major (though not the only) element leading to improved election results. Being the first woman to lead a political party in Japanese history and her ability to use the media to communicate with ordinary people gave her, for a while at least, some degree of independence of party institutions. As her charisma faded, of course, so did this independence decline. Doi's successors, Tanabe, Yamahana, and Murayama, have all been clearly aligned with either the right or left wings of the party (right, in the cases of Tanabe and Yamahana, left in the case of Murayama). In the unstable political conditions of the 1990s, and with the party taking part in coalition governments over a three-year period, the dire effects of strong partisanship for internal party cohesion became plain for all to see.

Factionalism

As should now be abundantly clear, factionalism has been a pervasive feature of the JSP since its inception. Much has been written about factionalism in Japanese political parties, and it is easy to regard JSP factionalism simply as a further example of a common phenomenon.[20] In some ways, of course, one may reasonably regard JSP factions merely from the standpoint of the nation's political culture and refrain from much further exploration. Factions in the JSP exhibit symptoms of traditional *oyabun-kobun* (surrogate parent–surrogate child, or "boss-henchmen") relationships, compete for intraparty posts for their members, serve as channels for funding to help members fight elections, and seek to influence the party leadership and party policies in various ways. Hence they resemble the factions in the LDP, except that their contests are political sideshows, whereas those in the LDP occupy center stage.

Important and interesting differences do exist, however. First, conflicts of policy and ideology appear to assume a greater importance for the JSP factions. Parallels may be found in other countries, where the parties of the Left appear to be more prone to factional division based on ideological difference than do the parties of the Right. Second (and equally obvious), the discipline of power, which is present in the LDP, is absent in the case of the JSP. This is not to say that factionalism is absent in the first and present in the second, but rather, that for the JSP there is no restraint on factional disruption imposed (as for the LDP) by the desire to retain power. A comparison of the history of splits and defections in the two parties is at least suggested in this regard.[21]

The third difference concerns the significant change that occurred in the character of factionalism in the JSP from the 1940s and 1950s to the 1970s and 1980s. JSP factions in the later period appear to be more amorphous and fluid than they had been in the earlier period. One possible reason for this stems from the former election system. It has long been recognized that in the larger parties the multimember constituency system tends to create or at least exacerbate factional divisions by forcing candidates of the same party to stand against each other in the same constituency. Clearly, the larger the party is, the more likely this factor will operate—and the LDP is the example usually given. The JSP's Diet representation has declined over the period in question (i.e., 1955–1994). Thus, it is at least possible that the apparent change in the character of factionalism might be casually connected with a decline in the number of constituencies in which more than one JSP candidate is running.

From Table 7.1, it can readily be seen that multiple candidates on the part of the JSP drastically declined between the 1958 elections (when the

JSP was at its height) and those of 1979. Whereas in 1958 the party put forward more than one candidate in almost four-fifths of all lower house constituencies, the proportion fell to just over one-fifth in the 1979 elections. Constituencies in which more than two Socialists were successful amounted in 1958 to two-fifths of the total, but in 1979 to less than one-tenth and in 1993 only 2 percent. Moreover (although this is not shown in the table), eight constituencies in 1958 elected three Socialists, but in 1979 only one, and in 1990 and 1993, none. Interestingly enough, by 1990, despite the JSP resurgence, the proportion of multiple candidates and seats did not greatly differ from 1979. This shows that by comparison with the late 1950s, JSP electoral support remained widely spread rather than concentrated in urban areas. Whereas in the late 1950s the JSP was similar to the LDP in presenting several candidates in many constituencies, in more recent times, it elected one candidate in nearly all constituencies (93 percent in the 1990 elections), but more than one in rather few (11 percent in 1990). We are unable to establish with complete certainty a connection between this and a change in the character of JSP factions. We suggest, however, that a connection does exist, and that it can be described in the following way.

Factionalism exists to some extent in all Japanese political parties, although in one or two instances it is actively suppressed. In the smaller parties factions are somewhat amorphous groupings around particular leaders, but in the LDP up to 1994, they constitute highly organized machines designed for the pursuit of political power. Among the reasons for which LDP factions need to be organized as sophisticated political machines was the necessity to run competitive political campaigns against the campaigns of other candidates from the same party. Because elections are extremely expensive, factions, rather than the party itself, served as the main channels of funding to candidates. Factions in the JSP were never organized with the degree of sophistication attained by LDP factions, but up to the 1970s they were cohesive and had a strong sense of identity and separateness. It was unusual to find two members of the same faction fighting the same constituency, and factions not only took on electoral tasks for their members but also competed in struggles for party leadership.

As can be seen from Figure 7.1, at its inception in 1945 the party consisted essentially of four factions, three of which were previously identified as Rono-kei, Nichiro-kei, and Shamin-kei. (The agriculturally based Hirano faction left the party in January 1948 and was henceforth of no significance.) By the time of JSP reunification in 1955, the party contained five factions, three of which (those let by Suzuki, Kawakami, and Nishio) were lineal descendants of the three just mentioned. Apart from these, the left-wing Wada faction was the following of Wata Hiroo, a former official of the Ministry of Agriculture and Forestry and, later, minister of agriculture. Because of the bureaucratic origin of its leader and some of his closest associates, this faction was known in the press as a "bureaucrat's" faction. On the extreme Left there was also a small grouping called the Heiwa Doshikai (Peace Comrades Association), headed at that time by the leader of a repressed minority caste, Matsumoto Jiiichiro. Apart, perhaps, from the Heiwa Doshikai Heiwa Doshikai, these factions had strong leader-follower characteristics, much like the factions in the LDP.

In 1959–1960 the Nishio faction and part of the Kawakami faction defected and formed the DSP. Within the JSP, the emergence of "structural reform" as a new doctrine promoted by Eta Saburo and others was the focus for major factional realignment. Following Suzuki's retirement, his faction split between the followers of Sasaki Kozo, who opposed it. The remnants of the Kawakami faction and the Wada faction (which became the Katsumata faction after Wada's death in 1967) largely supported structural reform, whereas the Heiwa Dshikai split between supporters and opponents, and the Shakaishugi Kyokai, which was becoming a force in the party from the early 1960s, saw it as ideologically revisionist and strongly opposed it. During the 1970s, the main political alignments related to a division between a broadly leftist alliance backing the chairman, Narita Tomomi, and the Atarashii Nagare no Kai, which sought to combat the increasing influence of the Shakaishugi Kyokai.

The factional situation did not fundamentally change under Doi Takako, except that the far Left rapidly declined, especially after the death of its principal mentor, Sakisaka Itsuro, in 1985. Doi, like Ishibashi, was largely nonfactional but appeared to move from center Right toward the Left during her period of leadership.[22] The party under Tanabe and Yamahana was clearly led from the Right, so that the displacement of Yamahana (at the time a minister in the Hosokawa government) as party chairman in September 1993 and his replacement by the left-wing leader Murayama constituted a major factional shift. Given that Yamahana was a crucial figure in the formation of the Hosokawa coalition government that excluded the LDP, whereas less than a year later Murayama engineered the party's entry into an alternative coalition centered on the LDP, with himself as prime minister, the danger of the party's falling apart was all too evident.

In Table 7.2 is a compilation of skeleton information, largely serving an illustrative purpose, on the various groups and factions that existed in the JSP in the late 1980s and early 1990s. JSP factions are much more

FIGURE 7.1 **Factional history of the Japan Socialist Party**

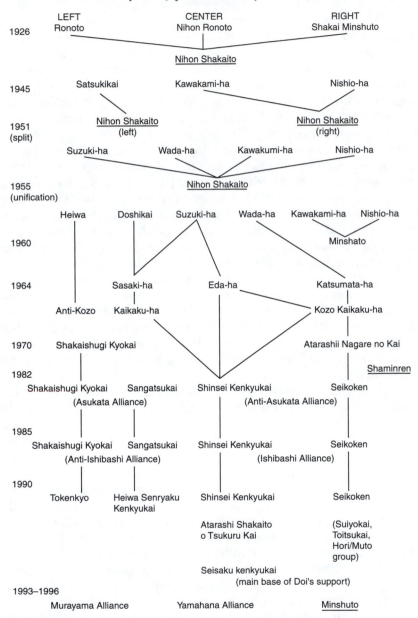

NOTE: Parties underlined.
SOURCE: Compiled by author.

shadowy organizations than those in the LDP, and far less information is available about them in the press. Their comparatively amorphous nature is illustrated by the fact that different JSP Diet members will provide intraparty factions lists that are somewhat different than each other. Factions are normally designated as study groups rather than leader-follower groups, but leadership is not unimportant. It should be clear from Figure 7.1 and Table 7.2 that the relatively firm factional and ideological divisions of twenty-five and thirty years earlier have become jumbled and confused, and the remnant of the far Left is perhaps the only group attempting to maintain much continuity with the past.

Interest Group Ties, Party Finances and Membership

For many years the principal organization and financial backing for the JSP were provided by the Sohyo Federation of labor unions. The amalgamation of the various labor union federations into a single organization, Rengo, was one of the factors prompting the JSP to seek to broaden its base of support.[23] Although Sohyo, as Japan's largest union federation, with over 4 million members, was in some ways a powerful and effective backer, the dominant influence within Sohyo of public-sector unions severely limited the JSP's appeal, given the parochial nature of the interests and grievances of those unions. In any case, several of the enterprises whose workers were powerful within Sohyo were privatized during the 1980s, thus reducing the size and effectiveness of public-sector unions as a whole. Indeed, this was one factor in the dissolution of Sohyo and formation of a single major union center.

Despite the dissolution of Sohyo, union support for JSP Diet candidates remained important, essentially for three reasons. One was that many JSP candidates received their principal organizational support from unions that were strong in their constituency. Often it was a case of the union giving support for a candidate who has emerged from the ranks of its own officials, which leads to the second reason that unions are influential. Many JSP Diet members are former union officials (in the past, at times over half of them). This has had the effect of restricting the opportunities for talented people not of union background to be chosen as Diet candidates.

The third reason concerns funding. Although the actual amount of money received by the party is impossible to estimate with any accuracy (as in the case of the LDP), membership dues have clearly made up only a relatively small part of total funding. Much of the supplement has come from the union movement, but the party has received money from a variety of sources as well, including a certain amount from business firms.

TABLE 7.2   JSP Factional Composition, Late 1980s and Early 1990s

A.   *"Right-wing"* factions

Suiyokai [Wednesday Society] (former Eda faction). 28. Tanabe Makoto, Yamaguchi Tsuruo.

Toitsukai [Unity Society] (former Kawakami faction). 9. Kawakami Tamio, Kawamata Kenjiro.

Hori/Muto Group. 5. Hori Masao, Muto Sanji.

These three were also grouped together as *Seiken Koso Kenkyukai (Seikoken)* [Political Power Structure Study Group]. 55.

These groups are ideologically most in sympathy with European social democratic and labor parties and worked assiduously for revision of the party platform, finally achieved in 1986, along social democratic lines. Apart from the three groups listed above, some members of the former *Atarashii Nagare no Kai* [New Current Society] also belong to *Seikoken*. These groups have constituted the core backing for the successive chairmanships of Ishibashi and Doi.

B.   *"Centrist"* factions

Seisaku Kenkyukai [Policy Research Group] (former Katsumata faction). 9. Ishibashi Masashi, Ito Shigeru, Kadoya Kenjiro.

This group can trace its history back to the faction led by Wada Hiroo, a former civil servant and early postwar minister of agriculture, and later by Katsumata Seiichi, who was party chairman briefly in the late 1960s. Ideologically it was formerly regarded as "moderate left" within the party but is now generally seen as "centrist."

Shakaishugi Kenkyukai (Shaken) [Socialism Research Group] (former Sasaki faction). 10. Hirose Hideyoshi (retired before 1990 lower house elections).

This group inherited a pro-China position from its former chairman, Sasaki Kozo, in the late 1960s, when it was regarded as extremely radical. Not much of this still remains. It has expended much energy combating the far Left. A once-powerful faction, but now in decline.

Atarashii Shakaito o Tsukuru Kai [Society to Create a New Socialist Party]. 20. Yamamoto Masahiro, Ogawa Jinichi, Ohara Toru.

Shinsei Kenkyukai (Shinseiken) [New Life Research Group]. A rather heterogeneous and amorphous centrist grouping, with some tendency to lean to the left. 14. Shimazaki Yuzuru.

C. *"Left-wing"* factions

Heiwa Senryaku Kenkyukai [Peace Strategy Research Group]. 32 (but some overlapping membership with other groups). Shitoma Hiroshi, Yadabe Osamu.

This is the former Sangatsukai [March Society], which was in essence the representatives in the National Diet of the former Shakaishugi Kyokai [Socialism Association], the latter being strong in some constituency parties but weak in the National Diet.

To Kensetsu Kenkyu Zenkoku Renraku Kyogikai (Tokenkyo) [National Liaison Council for Party Construction Research]. 4. Takazawa Torao, Shibutani Sumio.

This is the remnant of the former Shakaishugi Kyokai, originally founded by the late Professor Sakisaka as a Marxist-Leninist, strongly pro-Soviet ideological organization, quite distinct, nevertheless, from the Japan Communist Party. It was strong in constituency branches in the 1970s but has since declined, particularly since the death of its founder in 1985. It still has a following in some party constituency branches.

D. *"Nonfactional"* grouping

Nyu Uebu no Kai [New Wave Society]

This group, founded by 28 JSP Diet members newly elected in the lower house elections of February 1990, is dedicated to preparing the party as a genuine alternative government. Several of its members are lawyers, and the feature that most sharply distinguishes it from the rest of the party is the almost total absence of former labor union officials in its ranks. It has established close links with the Shaminren, led by Eda Satsuki, son of the late Eda Saburo.

NOTE:　L to R: *name of faction* [translation] (former name). Approximate number of JSP Diet members affiliated. Leading member(s).

SOURCES:　Information given by persons connected with the JSP during several visits by the writer to Japan. *Asahi Shinbun*, September 19, 1989. *Asahi Janaru*, August 11, 1989, pp. 14–18. Uezumi Mitsuharu, Nihon Shakaito Kobo shi [A history of the rise and fall of the JSP] (Tokyo: Jiyusha, 1992), p. 37.

It would be incorrect to suggest that the JSP is completely dominated by labor unions, since a variety of other interests in small business, the professions, the intellectual community, and even the farming sector have given it a certain amount of support.[24] Although it is almost always politically useful for interest groups to make contacts with the LDP and the government bureaucracy, the JSP role in Diet committees and elsewhere has always meant that some interest groups consider it worthwhile to cultivate the JSP to some extent.

One issue that much exercised the JSP over the years has been the question of individual membership. During the early 1970s party membership, never high, had fallen to perhaps as low as 30,000. Successive party chairmen sought to increase membership, and Asukata talked of eventually having a million members in the JSP. Even though much of the effective organizational support for the party came from union members who were party backers and, on occasion, from workers but who were not formerly enrolled as workers, it was embarrassing to have a far lower level of membership than parties electorally much weaker, such as the Komeito and the JCP. During the 1980s the number of members began to creep upward, and this process was much accelerated in 1988 when Doi Takako announced a scheme for "cooperative party members" *(kyoryoku toin)*, who for a membership fee of 500 yen per month were given a vote in JSP chairmanship elections. According to one report, membership numbers had advanced to an unprecedented 125,000 by the summer of 1989.[25] With the party's decline in the 1990s, membership has also dropped.

Until the upper and lower house elections of 1989 and 1990, JSP organizational ability was conspicuously lacking by comparison with that of several other parties. The typical campaign by a JSP candidate was based, not unlike the campaigns of LDP candidates, upon *koenkai* (personal support groups) composed of individuals who were influential locally and thought able to deliver a certain number of votes. These individuals were predominantly labor unionists, but some Diet members had *kownkai* with quite diverse memberships. Of course, as the JSP for many years polled more than 10 million votes in general elections, those who vote for it extend well beyond the ranks of unionists and their families. Indeed, studies have found that those who vote for the JSP were particularly hard to categorize beyond the fact that they tended to be concentrated in the middle-age groups and the less well off sections of the community.[26]

The campaigns of 1989 and 1990 contained much the same elements as previous campaigns but with the additional factors of a popular and forceful leader, a considerable number of women candidates, and burning issues (such as the Recruit scandal, agricultural protection, and consumption tax), adding emotional heat to the campaign. It was worth noting that in preparing for the lower house elections of February 1990, the party found it difficult to decide how many candidates to put forward. In the end it advanced 149 candidates (of whom 136 were elected). This was rather more than in previous elections but still far short of half the total seats in the house (256, or one-half of 512 at that time). With previous experience in mind, party leaders were fearful of fielding too many candidates in the multimember constituencies, in case they would split the party vote and many of them fail to be elected.

A further reason seems to have been that the JSP had real difficulty in finding suitable candidates. In any event, the party still relied heavily on its traditional sources of recruitment for Diet candidates: former labor unionists and local party officials. Of the 55 newly elected JSP Diet members in February 1990, no fewer than 19 (34.5 percent) came from labor unions and 7 (12.7 percent) from the ranks of local party officials. Of the rest, a quite impressive 9 (16.4 percent) were lawyers, 5 (9 percent) were from the mass media, 4 (7.3 percent) were from agriculture, with the remaining 11 (20 percent) being miscellaneous others. Unprecedentedly, 6 (10.9 percent) of the 55 were women.[27] An increasing number of candidates had participated in citizens' movements of various kinds. The kind of appeal made by JSP candidates in elections was traditionally very confrontational. This was particularly marked during the 1950s and 1960s, when the JSP lost no opportunity to attack the government for its defense and foreign policies, for its alleged attempts to subvert the constitution, for the influence of "monopoly capital," and for its antilabor policies in general. In the early 1960s Eda Saburo attempted to develop a less rhetorical and more down-to-earth campaigning style, discussing issues that touched people's everyday lives as he aimed to appeal to the concerns of a rapidly emerging consumer society. Such an approach was only fitfully followed by his successors, but the issues of the late 1980s and early 1990s lent themselves much more to the kind of approach that Eda pioneered a quarter of a century earlier. Doi Takako followed this line, but she continued to press home the party's traditional message in defense of the constitution and against what were considered to be the narrow interests of big business (as on the tax issue, or on the lifting of agricultural protection).

For the most part, therefore, JSP parliamentary candidates now sought to appeal to the voters on the basis of issues that concerned their real interests. They also, of course, resorted to the time-honored technique of using local connections and the organizational backing of sympathetic unions. The attempt to turn the JSP from a union party to a "citizens party" moved a certain distance, but conservative forces within it remained strong.

Parliamentary Behavior

Much as in the case of electoral campaigns, the parliamentary behavior of the JSP has undergone some modification since the 1950s and 1960s. (It must be noted, however, that fluctuations have also resulted from the changing balance of forces within the National Diet.) Throughout much of the 1950s and 1960s, the party engaged from time to time in disruptive tactics in the Diet with the view toward preventing the passage of controversial legislation. These tactics included boycotts (whether of particular Diet committees or of the plenary session), various methods of filibuster such as "cow-walking," and, as in the famous episode in May 1960 when the party was seeking to prevent passage of the revised Mutual Security Treaty, physically preventing the Speaker from putting the motion to the vote.

There were several reasons for resorting to such methods. First, from the party's point of view, the Liberal Democrats were engaged in a dangerous program of reactionary change with regard to the constitution, foreign and defense policy, union legislation, education, the economy, and so on. It was crucial that the government be frustrated in its endeavors, however unorthodox the methods. Second, as noted earlier, the left-wing factions of the JSP were by no means wholeheartedly committed to parliamentary methods, which some Socialists saw through Marxist eyes as institutional devices designed to further the interests of the capitalist class. Some also believed in "parliamentarism plus"—that is, the use of the National Diet backed up by the use of extraparliamentary demonstrations. A third reason (though it may have been as much an excuse as a genuine reason) was that the party, especially during the Security Treaty revision crisis, was prepared to criticize the principle of majoritarianism as constituting a "tyranny of the majority." Such a resort to the traditional Japanese principles of decision-making by general consensus rather than by the view of the majority prevailing suited the JSP's interests during the period of long-term LDP majority rule. Fourth, because the government, according to the rules of the National Diet, did not have complete control over the parliamentary timetable, there were occasions on which actions by the JSP resulting in delay of the passage of legislation could actually result in the failure of such legislation.[28]

During the period from 1976 to 1980 in the HR and from 1974 to 1980 in the HC, the LDP majority was reduced to the point where it lost its control of a number of parliamentary committees. As a result, the opposition parties were, to some extent, given the capacity to influence policy by working within the parliamentary system. Since by this time the JSP was merely primus inter pares among the opposition parties themselves, it was motivated both to work within the system and to operate in coordination with the other opposition parties. Although the difficulties of coordinating strategy with the other parties of opposition were considerable, inasmuch as policy could be effected only if all the opposition parties acted together in a given committee, occasional successes were achieved.

Following the LDP victory in the 1980 double elections, this situation no longer applied. The LDP, however, lost control of upper house committees following the 1989 elections. In the 1990s the JSP for the most part followed normal parliamentary procedures, but its resort to "cow walking" against the PKO bill in 1992 brought much criticism. Being in the government from 1993 to 1996 (except for the nine weeks of the Hata government) removed the need for obstructive tactics, but party discipline and unity proved increasingly difficult to maintain.

The position of the JSP in local politics has in the past generally been weak, and even in the period during the 1970s when "progressive local administrations" were common in large cities and elsewhere, the JSP had to share participation with other opposition parties. At that time the party faced the dilemma that when the opposition as a whole appeared to be capable of using local politics as a springboard for power at the national level, the JSP was conspicuously giving ground to the other opposition parties in the larger cities, where the new developments were taking place.

From the late 1970s, most of the "progressive local authorities" (meaning chief executives—governors of prefectures and mayors of cities, towns, and villages) were defeated, as a new conservative trend manifested itself in local politics. Since then a common pattern throughout the country has emerged, whereby chief executives are elected with the backing of all or nearly all the major and minor parties. This puts the LDP and the JSP (as well as other parties) on the same side in joint sponsorship of a single candidate. Although JSP support in local elections rose to some extent in the late 1980s, it fell away badly in the 1990s.

CONCLUSIONS

The year 1996 was catastrophic for the JSP/SDP. It is ironic that fate should have been so unkind precisely when the party finally decided to call itself in Japanese "Social Democratic Party" rather than "Japan Socialist Party." The theme of conflicting emphasis between "democratic" and "socialist" ran like a twisted skein through the party's turbulent history. Its resolution at the annual congress held in January 1996 came too late to save the party from near destruction. Factional and ideological conflicts that had simmered on over the years without usually boiling over (though there had been such episodes in the past), in the unstable politics of the 1990s split the party asunder. The Socialists were the principal victims, as it turned out, of a general process of political realignment. If the 1955 political system ended in 1993 with the LDP removed from office for the first time in thirty-seven years, 1996 saw the LDP almost regain its absolute majority but also saw the party's principal rival since the 1950s practically annihilated. The problems this will pose for the maintenance of political balance need careful monitoring.

The problems facing the JSP/SDP have been canvassed extensively in this chapter. Many arguably date to the time of the Katayama and Ashida coalition governments of 1947–1948, to the failures of those governments, and to the leftist reaction within the JSP that they provoked. The dominance of the left wing of the party from the early 1950s relegated it to a prolonged stay in the political wilderness in conditions of rapidly increasing prosperity. There is a parallel with the party's experience of entering coalition governments between 1993 and 1996. Once again it was unable to maintain unity and purpose in the face of the compromises that had to be made as one of several government parties, and the electoral consequences were adverse. The ability of several social democratic and labor parties in Europe and Australasia to become parties of government managing a market economy, and retaining credibility with the electorate, somehow eluded the JSP. There were times when it seemed to be moving along a more promising track, such as with the Structural Reform movement of the early 1960s, the period of "progressive local authorities" in the 1970s, the Doi ascendancy of the late 1980s and early 1990s, or at times in the coalition governments of the mid-1990s, but it could not consolidate its successes. Indeed, at times the party gave the impression of fearing success, and the responsibility that success would bring.

The contrast with the LDP over the period of its ascendancy could not be more striking. The conservatives succeeded in forging an alliance that remained sufficiently popular with the electorate to ensure its continued tenure. The collapse of that ascendancy in 1993 gave to the JSP a golden opportunity, but it did not prove capable of rising to the occasion. The question is "Why?" The answer to this crucial question will be divided into three parts: policy, organization, and environment, and then the connections between them will be shown.

The most common accusation directed against the JSP is that its policies have been "extreme" or "unrealistic." The party's vigorous defense of the peace clause of the Constitution, its opposition to both the Self-Defense Forces and the Mutual Security Treaty, its policy of unarmed neutralism in relation to cold war rivalries, its links with North Korea, and its tendency to show sympathy with Communist states against the United States have often been cited as proof of both extremism and unrealism. In fact, however, most of these policies had become much attenuated in the 1980s and 1990s, although defense of the Constitution remained strong. Shortly after the Murayama government was formed in June 1994, Japan's Socialist prime minister proceeded to jettison much of the traditional platform, as we have seen. Even so, the Socialists in the Murayama government worked for restraint in defense spending and humane policies in various fields. Murayama's promotion of a Diet resolution of apology for Japanese actions in the war, on the fiftieth anniversary of its conclusion, was fiercely opposed by the right wing of the LDP, but a watered-down version passed the Diet by a majority vote.

Rather than extremism, the problem with JSP policy has been its tendency to incoherence. The party platform of 1955 and the basic statement of 1964 were a compromise between Left and Right, and as such proved difficult to revise. Ishibashi's great achievement as JSP chairman was to promote acceptance of a revised statement of fundamental policy. Another example of incoherence has been the party's tendency to promise high levels of agricultural protection in the countryside and cheaper food in the cities.[29]

At the deepest level, policy incoherence has stemmed from the division with the party between Marxist and non-Marxist thinking. The JSP always found it difficult to convince the electorate about the effectiveness of its policies when it was unsure whether its policies were based on the principles of Marxism or of social democracy. With the collapse of the Soviet Union, Marxism lost much of its appeal. This was reflected in the decline of the Marxist Left within the JSP, and should have made it easier for the party to restore its policy coherence. Factional rivalries from the past, however, continued to place obstacles in the path of this endeavor.

Organization, too, has long been a problem, in part because of the party's need to rely so heavily on labor union support for funding and in election campaigns. The privatization drive by government in the 1980s shook up the union movement and was the crucial factor leading to the formation of a single major union federation. It also created at least the opportunity for the party to broaden its base beyond the ranks of a narrow segment of union activists. In 1989–1990, under Doi Takako, the party was indeed recruiting substantial numbers of middle-class candidates (including lawyers in particular) and activists in citizens' movements. The novelty of choosing significant numbers of women candidates was popular.[30] Unfortunately for the party, however, it was the new candidates elected in 1989 and 1990 who were disproportionately defeated when the electoral tide turned against the JSP/SDP in the 1990s.

Thus, we are led to the question of environment, which has two aspects. First of all, working-class consciousness, which has sustained a number of social democratic and labor parties in Western Europe and elsewhere, is weak in Japan, partly because of increased prosperity and partly because of the deliberately inculcated Japanese style of "cooperative" labor-management relations. Between the 1960s and the 1980s, the JSP, because of the narrowness of its organizational base and of its appeal, allowed other parties such as the Komeito, the JCP, the DSP, and the LDP itself to pick up votes of less prosperous sections of the workforce, particularly those in small and medium firms. The brief period of JSP resurgence in 1989 and 1990 suggested that with a new agenda the JSP had the opportunity to reinvent itself. The emergence, however, of a number of new parties from 1992 meant that protest votes moved elsewhere. The bold move in 1994 of entering a coalition government with the LDP made sense in terms of parliamentary arithmetic and even of policy, but it created a severe backlash among an electorate disillusioned with what looked like an abandonment by the party of its long-standing principles.

Second, the political environment was radically changed by the formation of the LDP out of previously warring conservative factions in 1955. The coalition governments of 1947–1948 and of 1993–1996, in which the Socialists participated, were possible only because of the failure of the conservatives to unite, or remain united, as a single party in those disparate periods. Socialist participation in a coalition government was always eminently possible in conditions of conservative disunity. On both occasions, however, the opportunity was to prove a poisoned chalice. Habits of complacency and internal bickering born of long years in the political wilderness were to prove too much for Japan's Socialists once they found themselves participating in government in the challenging conditions of the 1990s.

NOTES

1. Until January 1996 the party was called Nihon Shakaito in Japanese, which translates as Japan Socialist Party (JSP), but thereafter it became the Shakai Minshuto, or Social Democratic Party (SDP). I shall use these translations for the periods to which they applied, even though from early 1991 (and also for part of the early postwar period) the official English title of the party was Social

Democratic Party of Japan. Where a period on both sides of the change of name is referred to, I shall use JSP/SDP.

2. Under the former electoral system for the HR (superseded in 1994), candidates were commonly elected with less than 20 percent of the vote in a given constituency. Under the new (post-1994) system, a candidate needs to win a plurality to be elected in any of the 300 single-member constituencies, which meant that minority parties had a serious chance only in the remaining 200 constituencies elected by proportional representation.

3. Ishikawa Masumi and Hirose Michisada, *Jiminto—Choki shihai no kozo* (Tokyo: Iwanami Shoten, 1989), chaps. 1, 3.

4. A fourth element, the Nichiro-kai, an agriculture faction led by Hirano Rikizo, left the party in 1947 and may be disregarded for the present purposes.

5. See J.A.A. Stochwin, *The Japanese Socialist Party and Neutralism* (Melbourne: Melbourne University Press, 1968).

6. The standard works in English on the prewar and early postwar Socialist movements are George O. Totten, *The Social Democratic Movement in Prewar Japan* (New Haven: Yale University Press, 1966); and Allan B. Cole, George O. Totten, and Cecil H. Uyehara, with a contributed chapter by Ronald P. Dore, *Socialist Parties in Postwar Japan* (New Haven: Yale University Press, 1966).

7. For details, see Stockwin, *The Japanese Socialist Party*, chap. 4; Cole et al., *Socialist Parties*, chap. 3.

8. For details, see Stockwin, *The Japanese Socialist Party*, chap. 7; Cole et al., *Socialist Parties*, chap. 3.

9. Deriving from the writings of Yamakawa Hitoshi and others in the prewar period, the Rozo school had taken issue with the two-stage revolution theories of the Koza school. The two were essentially schools of Japanese historiography, whereas the Rono-kei, although sharing the same kind of ideas, was a factional grouping within the JSP.

10. The best source in English on the 1959–1960 split is D.C.S. Sissons, "Recent Developments in Japan's Socialist Movement," *Far East Survey* (March 1960): 40–47; *Far Eastern Survey* (June 1960): 89–92.

11. That is, Eda was temporary chairman, from November 1960 to March 1961, following the killing of Asanuma. He subsequently occupied the position of secretary-general for a period.

12. J.A.A. Stockwin, *Japan: Divided Politics in a Growth Economy* (New York: W. W. Norton, 1975), p. 167.

13. Terry E. MacDougall, "Asukata Ichio and Some Dilemmas of Socialist Leadership in Japan," in *Political Leadership in Contemporary Japan*, ed. Terry E. MacDougall (Ann Arbor: University of Michigan Press, 1982), pp. 51–92.

14. Ibid., p. 64. The conditions were as follows: (1) direct election of the party chairman by the entire party membership; (2) giving top leadership the authority to break deadlocks in the CEC, and the chairman authority to break deadlocks among the top three leaders; (3) opening the party to advisers and specialists from outside its ranks, by creating advisory panels.

15. For the text of the poem and a view of its use by the JSP chairperson, see Kukushima Horomi, "Yama no ugoku hi wa kuru ka" [Will the day come when

the mountains move?], *Keizai Hyoron,* special issue on the JSP, October 1989, pp. 112–113.

16. See Nakamura Kenichi, "Teiko seito kara taiko seito e no shohosen" [From a party of resistance to a party of opposition: A prescription], *Asahi Janaru,* July 20, 1990, pp. 22–24. Yamaguchi Jiro, "Shakaito wa 'taiko seito' ni dappi subeshi" [The JSP must turn into an opposition], *Ekomomisuto,* October 9, 1990.

17. Cole et al., *Socialist Parties,* p. 247.

18. "Nihon Shakaito ketto 20 shumen kinen jigyo hakko iinkai," in Nihon Shakaito 20 nen no kiroku [The twenty years' record of the Japan Socialist Party] (Tokyo: Nihon Shakaito, 1965), p. 247.

19. A useful table, giving the dates and backgrounds of most of the earlier JSP chairmen, can be found in MacDougall, "Asukata Ichiro," p. 92.

20. See, for instance, J.A.A. Stockwin, "Factionalism in Japanese Politics," *Japan Forum* 1 no. 2 (October 1989): 161–171.

21. Pressure from industry upon the IDP to remain as one party may also have significantly helped that party stay together. Similar union pressure on the JSP has also been observed but evidently is less effective.

22. J.A.A. Stockwin, "On Trying to Move Mountains: The Political Career of Doi Takako," *Japan Forum* 6 (April 1994): 21–34.

23. See Fujii Shozo, *Rengo no tanjo* [The birth of Rengo] (Tokyo: Rodo Junposha, 1989).

24. For instance, the member for Yamagata No. 1 constituency, Endo Norburu, initially elected in February 1990, was first and foremost a representative of the local agricultural interests. Interview, July 29, 1990.

25. Nishii Yasuyuki and Nishimae Teruo, "Shaikaito kenkyu: sono jinmyaku, soshiki, seisaku" [A study of the Socialist Party: Personnel relations, organization, policy], *Asahi Janaru,* August 11, 1989, p. 15.

26. According to one 1970s study: "Among JSP voters there are many who are of an 'indeterminate' (chukanteki) type, and indeed they include not one type in particular but all types of people. There are many manual workers (though not as many as among Komeito voters), but manual workers are a minority. JSP voters include the largest proportion of labor unionists of the voters for any party, but even so unionists are quite a small proportion of JSP voters, and even among unionists less than half actually vote. In their demographic characteristics, such as education, age, degree of satisfaction, housing and class consciousness, they are 'indeterminate.' They have no particularly outstanding characteristics. The fact that there are so many JSP voters among middle-aged people shows that it is becoming a party of 'nostalgia.'" Ogawa Koichi, Hasuike Minoru, Araki Toshio, and Abe Shiro, *Daitoshi no kakushin hyo: To Sapporo to Sendai mo baai* (Tokyo: Bokutakusha, 1975), p. 356.

27. Calculated from data in Mainichi Shinbunsha, *'90 Sosenkyo* ['90 general election] (Tokyo: Mainichi Shinbunsha, 1990), pp. 19–48.

28. See Hans Baerwald, *Japan's Parliament: An Introduction* (Cambridge: Cambridge University Press, 1974).

29. For the text of this policy, see Nihon Shakaito, *Detabukku Shakaito* [Socialist party data book] (Tokyo: Nihon Shakaito, 1990), pp. 288–297.

30. For instance, Ito Hideko (Hokkaido No. 1) won the largest number of votes (261,170) gained by a single candidate in the lower house elections of February 1990. Doi Takako (Hyogo No. 2) came in third, with 225,540 votes. *Detabukku Shkaito,* p. 39.

eight

Japanese Communist Party: The "Lovable" Party

Peter Berton

The Japanese Communist Party (JCP, or Nihon Kyosan To) has not played a decisive role in the political life of Japan, nor is it likely to do so in the foreseeable future, barring catastrophic economic and social collapse. The party currently captures about 15 percent of the popular vote in national elections, but because the electoral system favors the incumbent Liberal Democratic Party (LDP), the JCP ends up with proportionately fewer seats in the two houses of the National Diet than it deserves on the basis of the popular vote. The party has never held political power in Japan, not even as a junior coalition member. And yet we would do well to remember how few members the Bolsheviks had on the eve of the October Revolution.

The JCP also has more active members, more affiliate groups and front organizations, a larger budget, many more subscribers to its party publications, and better organization than most other parties in Japan. Thus, the JCP perhaps deserves closer scrutiny than other Japanese opposition parties of its size.[1]

HISTORICAL BACKGROUND

The Japanese Communist movement is part of a larger social movement that has developed since the end of the nineteenth century. Its influence represents an amalgam of Marxism, Christian humanism, socialism, and anarcho-syndicalism. Some of the early Communists were also influenced by Russian social thought and, in particular, Tolstoyan humanism.[2] More directly, however, the Communist Party came into being as a result of the Russian Revolution and the subsequent establishment of the Third Communist International, widely known as the Comintern. Meetings between Japanese revolutionaries and Comintern functionaries in Bolshevik Russia as well as in Shanghai led to the formation of the Japanese Communist Party.

The JCP was formally organized on July 15, 1922, at the home of one of its founders in the middle-class district of Shibuya in Tokyo. But nine months earlier, a manifesto and regulations of the JCP had been published in a Soviet journal in Irkutsk in Siberia.[3] This event has symbolic implications given that the most important documents of the Japanese party during the prewar period were, in fact, "made in the USSR." The JCP was also known as the Japanese Branch of the Communist International, and was in reality directed and manipulated by Moscow.

From the beginning, the JCP was a small, conspiratorial group bent on abolishing the emperor system, militarism, and capitalism. But the match was very uneven. The powerful, centralized Japanese state, which operated in a small territory and a closely knit society, had at its disposal a vast apparatus of law enforcement and efficient civil and military intelligence services. The prewar history of the party is thus a sad story of organization, repression, restarts, mass arrests and imprisonment, new instructions from the Comintern, arrival and prompt arrest of the replacements trained in Moscow,[4] recantation by prominent leaders, and long prison terms for unrepentant Communists.

POSTWAR DEVELOPMENTS TO 1955

In early October 1945 I happened to be in front of Tokyo station, near my office in the Civil Intelligence section of the Allied Occupation Headquarters, when I saw truckloads of emaciated Japanese waving red flags and shouting as if in intoxicated delirium. They were Communist political prisoners released from jails by order of General MacArthur—the hard-core survivors of Imperial Japan's thoroughly efficient repression by the thought police and the army gendarmerie. For many of them, freedom came after long periods (in several instances, as many as eighteen years) of detention.[5] A few weeks later, on December 1, 1945, the Japanese Communist Party was officially revived at its Fourth Party Congress. In February 1946, following the return to Japan from Yenan of Nosaka Sanzo (the Japanese delegate at the Comintern headquarters in Moscow during the 1930s),[6] the Fifth Party Congress was convened. The party leadership claimed that in the intervening three months, membership rose from an estimated 1,000 members to 7,000. In April, during the first postwar election, the party managed to elect 6 members to the 464-seat HRC and began to participate in electoral politics. Nosaka's idea was to create a "lovable" Communist party and to proceed along a parliamentary road to power—not an unreasonable position given the reality of U.S. military occupation.[7]

In the 1949 national elections the party received 3 million votes, or almost 10 percent of the total vote (up from 2.1 million, or 3.8 percent, and 1.0 million, or 3.7 percent, in the 1946 and 1947 elections, respectively), and elected 35 of the party's candidates. This increase in the number of seats came entirely at the expense of the Socialists, whose popularity plummeted following the failure of their coalition government. (As it happened, it would be twenty years before the JCP would again receive 3 million votes, which by then represented only 6.8 percent of the total vote.)

In January 1950, shortly after the JCP achieved its greatest electoral success, the Communist Information Bureau (Cominform) issued a blistering attack against Nosaka's peaceful parliamentary tactics, urging the party to adopt a militant line. Stalin had his own reasons for insisting on this policy change, which went against the best interests of the JCP.[8] The party mainstream under Secretary-General Tokuda Kyuichi hesitated,[9] but an "Internationalist" faction, which ironically included Miyamoto Kenji (the future supreme leader and later an advocate of a soft parliamentary line), urged the adoption of the Cominform instructions to pursue a violent leftist course. The party leadership eventually succumbed to pressure from Moscow and Peking and, especially after the outbreak of the Korean War some six months later, took a direct turn toward the Left.[10] General MacArthur ordered the Japanese government to purge the entire Central Committee of the party, which then set up an underground organization, with the top leaders and a number of middle cadres going illegally to Peking.

The underground party tried to stage some acts of terrorism and industrial sabotage to help the Communist Korean War effort, but these were sporadic and ineffectual. This suicidal policy had immediate results at the polls. There were no JCP members in the Diet after the next election to the HRC in October 1952.

In 1953 Stalin died, the Korean War came to an end, and Soviet and Chinese policy gradually became more moderate. The JCP followed suit.

THE MIYAMOTO LINE: A PARTY DICTATOR SELLING PARLIAMENTARY DEMOCRACY

Since the mid-1950s the JCP's development and policies have borne the imprint of one man, Miyamoto Kenji, who only a few years ago reluctantly relinquished power in his mid-eighties.[11] The Miyamoto period, from the mid-1950s to the mid-1990s, represents roughly half of the party's almost eighty-year history. Born in 1908, Miyamoto graduated from Tokyo Imperial University, the most prestigious institution of higher learning in Japan. He was a prominent literary critic in his twenties, and his late wife, Yuriko, was a noted member of the Proletarian School of literature. Miyamoto joined the JCP in May 1931, was arrested in December 1933, and spent twelve years in prison. An unusual aspect of his case was that he was accused of "lynching" a suspected police infiltrator. Upon release from prison in October 1945, Miyamoto returned to active party work; he was one of seven Central Committee members at the first postwar party congress. But he was not a member of the "Mainstream" Tokuda faction, and it was not until the mid-1950s that Miyamoto maneuvered himself onto center stage in the aftermath of the militant-line debacle. He steered party fortunes through consolidation and the establishment of "a new people's democratic revolutionary policy," which led to rapid growth in JCP membership, electoral successes, attempts to form united fronts with other opposition parties, and an independent stance in the international Communist movement.

Since 1970, Miyamoto's closest associates have been the Ueda brothers: Ueda Koichiro (born in 1927) and his younger brother Fuwa Tetsuzo (born Ueda Kenjiro in 1930), who joined the JCP while still students at the prestigious First Higher School.[12] Both brothers moved on to the elitist Tokyo University, the elder majoring in economics (Miyamoto had graduated from the same department a generation earlier) and the younger brother in physics. Upon graduation, Fuwa became an official of the iron and steelworkers union, where he stayed on for eleven years, at the same time helping his brother with theoretical assignments at the JCP headquarters. In May 1964 Fuwa quit his union post and became a full-time staff member at the party headquarters, working under his brother. Fuwa's career in the JCP was phenomenal: In six years he rose from candidate member of the Central Committee to become the director of the Secretariat and member of the Presidium in 1970. While heading the Secretariat for a dozen years, he became a member of the Standing Committee, then its acting chairman, and, in 1982, its chairman, at which point Miyamoto moved to the post of chairman of the Central Committee. A bright organizer with a theoretical bent, Fuwa is the author of many JCP documents that have tried to refurbish Marxist-Leninist theory by making it palatable to the Japanese electorate. In the 1970s he turned his attention to relations with the Eurocommunist parties, in the 1980s to Mikhail Gorbachev's perestroika and "new thinking," and in the 1990s to a critique of Stalin's "great-power chauvinist" policy of interference in the affairs of the JCP. In 1990 Fuwa selected thirty-five-year-old Shii Kazuo, a graduate not only of his alma mater Tokyo University but also of his own department of physics, to become director of the Secretariat. With Fuwa now in full control (and Shii as heir apparent), the JCP is certain to continue its soft line in the post-Miyamoto period. (At the Party's Twenty-first Congress in September 1997, Miyamoto, in failing health at age eighty-nine, was officially kicked upstairs as chairman emeritus.)[13]

EVOLUTION OF POLICY

How does one characterize Miyamoto's policies in the postmilitant period, 1955 to the present (1999)? Were they influenced by the Soviet, Chinese, Eurocommunist, or other models? Have they changed over time? And, if so, what factors were responsible—domestic, external, or intra-Communist?

Overall, Miyamoto's policies can be characterized as a continuous soft line when compared with the hard, militant line of the prewar and 1950–1955 periods. But during the past four decades or so, one notices an evolution from an almost grudging acceptance of parliamentary tactics to an appreciation of the transformation of postwar (especially post-Occupation) Japan into an advanced industrial (in many respects even postindustrial) democratic society, in which neither the Soviet nor the Chinese—only the Eurocommunist model—had any relevance.

For convenience, let us consider the evolution of the Miyamoto line over three periods: (1) 1955–1961: consolidation of power and rejection of Togliatti's structural reform theories; (2) 1961–1968: growth, rejection of the Soviet and Chinese models, and declaration of independence; and (3) 1968 to the present (1999): growing convergence with Eurocommunism and nationalism.

Consolidation, 1955–1961

This was a complex and controversial period in JCP history. A number of young cadres returned from their refuge in Peking, and the party emerged from its militant episode with two competing factions. Eventually Miyamoto switched from the "Internationalist" to the "Mainstream" faction in a successful bid to become secretary-general. But the JCP was not the only party in turmoil. The international Communist movement itself was undergoing a metamorphosis that began with Nikita Khrushchev's de-Stalinization speech at the Twentieth Congress of the Communist Party of the Soviet Union (CPSU) in early 1956. This was followed by Palmiro Togliatti's "polycentrism" and structural reform theories,[14] the Polish and Hungarian revolts, and further Yugoslav shifts to the right—all leading to the break between Moscow and Peking that shook up the entire movement.

The JCP was much affected by the epochal changes in international Communism. Many Japanese Communists and socialists alike were attracted to Togliatti's position. Others saw the principal enemy to be "U.S. imperialism"; they believed in a kind of "national liberation" along the lines of the Chinese model, with at least the option of violent action, although most agreed that under prevailing Japanese circumstances a militant, violent line was counterproductive. These personal rivalries, factional struggles, and foreign influences were resolved after a fashion at the Eighth JCP Congress in July 1961 with the expulsion of the advocates of structural reform and the victory of Miyamoto and his allies. West European ideas were thus rebuffed, and "U.S. imperialism" (along with Japanese monopoly capitalism) was proclaimed as the principal enemy (clearly a Chinese position in opposition to Soviet "peaceful coexistence" and détente). At the same time, the JCP cautiously returned to the peaceful parliamentary tactics of Nosaka's "lovable" party, advocating a "united national democratic front" in a National Diet considered to be an important "tool" of the people. In the international Communist arena, the JCP, although clearly sympathetic with the Chinese position, was hewing cautiously to a neutral line and endorsing the ambiguous 1960 Moscow Statement, all the while enshrining in the party program "the camp of socialism headed by the USSR."

Rejection of the Soviet and Chinese Models, 1961–1968

This was a traumatic period for the JCP leadership, which first had to take sides and then had to break umbilical ties to both Moscow and Peking. It was also a period of mass expulsions and of threats to the party posed by splinter groups favoring the CPSU or the Chinese Communist Party (CCP). It is a measure of Miyamoto's political talent that he kept the party together while presiding over the period of its greatest growth in membership, which, in turn, toward the end of these years, was translated into dramatic gains at the polls. Two JCP congresses, in 1964 and 1966, consolidated Miyamoto's power, reiterated the policy of pursuing peaceful parliamentary tactics, and proclaimed the party's independence from outside influence and control. At the same time, *Akahata*, the party organ, reprinted Chinese articles on the People's War and violent revolution, including Lin Piao's famous 1965 manifesto—a violent revolutionary formula that was considered unacceptable only "under present circumstances." The JCP's relations during this period were heavily tilted toward Asian Communist parties, with very few personal ties to the parties of Western Europe.

Most important, this period saw the severance of the JCP's ties with the two fraternal Communist superparties: first with the CPSU in 1964 over the Partial Nuclear Test Ban Treaty, which the Soviet Union had initiated and which the JCP repudiated in support of the Chinese position, and then with the CCP in 1966–1967 over Mao Zedong's insistence that the JCP join an anti-U.S. and anti-Soviet united front. The Japanese party was now essentially on its own.

The Eurocommunist Model and Nationalism, 1968 to the Present (1999)

The Soviet invasion of Czechoslovakia graphically demonstrated to the JCP leadership the need to emulate the Italian Communist Party (PCI)—that is, to draw away from the Soviet Union and pursue a more peaceful, parliamentary road to power.

In July 1969 a member of the Standing Committee of the JCP Presidium declared that if the party came to power, it would permit the free functioning of opposition parties, unless they resorted to unlawful means. This statement, made in an election year, may have been intended simply to improve the party image, but the same criticism of one-party dictatorship showed up the following year in an official party program submitted to the Eleventh JCP Congress. (To create an image of an "open" party, the congress for the first time was thrown open to the public and the press.) In its next two congresses, in 1973 and 1976, the JCP continued to advance its autonomy and independence, on the one hand, and its commitment to peaceful change, on the other.

To stress the relevance for Japan of the West European model (and thus the irrelevance of the Soviet and Chinese models), the JCP, in commemoration of its fiftieth anniversary in July 1972, staged an International Conference on Theory devoted to the problems encountered by Communist parties in advanced capitalist countries. The Italian, French, Spanish, British, West German, and Australian parties sent delegates. The topics discussed included parliamentary and constitutional experiences; united front tactics; methods for making the transition from capitalism to socialism in a democratic setting, including structural reforms; and the question of terminology, such as the proper rendering of the phrase "dictatorship of the proletariat" in various languages. In fact, at the Twelfth JCP Congress the following year, the JCP dropped the word *dokusai* (dictatorship) in favor of *shikken* (regency or exercise of power) in translating "dictatorship of the proletariat," and at the Thirteenth JCP Congress in July 1976 that phrase was dropped altogether in favor of "working-class power." Marxism-Leninism itself suffered the fate of dictatorship of the proletariat. At the 1970 Eleventh JCP Congress, rules were amended to make Marxism-Leninism only a "theoretical basis" and not a "guide to action."[15] The term was given the coup de grace six years later, at the Thirteenth JCP Congress, when references to Marxism-Leninism were either eliminated completely or replaced by "scientific socialism" in the party's program and constitution. The Central Committee tried to explain that, whereas the terms were essentially synonymous, it had been almost a century since Marx and Engels were active and more than half a century since the death of Lenin, and therefore scientific socialism constituted more than just the theories of Marx, Engels, and Lenin. Furthermore, aware that in Japan, Marx and Engels were less controversial than Lenin, the party cleverly dissociated itself from the latter (and in the process from Russia and, by implication, also from China), at the same time stressing Japan's position as an advanced industrial country.[16]

Repeated declarations of independence by the JCP were officially formalized in 1973 at the Twelfth JCP Congress through an amendment to the basic party program of 1961 designed to eliminate the reference to the USSR in the phrase "the camp of socialism headed by the USSR." The JCP also tried to dissociate itself from student violence by branding such activities as Trotskyist. Miyamoto even declared that "violence, along with sex, drugs, and gambling, was one of the four sins."[17]

Along with eliminating this or that offending term, the JCP sought to promote the image of a party devoted to the preservation and expansion of freedoms in Japan. This was necessary partly to erase the totalitarian image of Communism and partly to counteract the LDP slogan "Defend the Free Society." In the spring of 1976, Fuwa published a nine-part essay entitled "Scientific Socialism and the Question of Dictatura—A Study of Marx and Engels," in which he stressed "the institutions of a democratic state, with the Diet as an organ of supreme authority of the country in name and reality" (previously, the Diet had been termed only a "tool" of the people).[18]

Fuwa's essay was followed by a draft of the far-reaching "Manifesto of Freedom and Democracy," which was officially adopted on July 30, 1976, at the Thirteenth Extraordinary Party Congress. The manifesto mentions approvingly the American Declaration of Independence and the French Declaration of the Rights of Man. The third section ends with this eloquent declaration of JCP independence:

> The Communist Party of Japan reiterates that it will make no model of the experiences of any foreign countries, such as the Soviet Union and the People's Republic of China. As a consistent defender of free-

dom and democracy of the people, it will correctly inherit the original stand of scientific socialism; it will seek a creative development of socialism under the condition of a highly developed capitalist country, Japan; and it will continue to pursue a unique way to an independent democratic Japan and a socialist Japan, hand in hand with the people.[19]

The JCP was dealt a great blow in the press and in the Diet by the official reopening of the "lynching case"—the accusation that back in the 1930s Miyamoto had taken part in the murder of a JCP member who was thought to be a police spy. If Miyamoto was guilty of murder, he was serving time before and during World War II as an ordinary criminal and not as a political prisoner eligible to be released by order of the U.S. Occupation authorities.

Another factor in the party's weakness was its inability to promote and become a member of a united front of all so-called progressive opposition parties. Its failure did not come about for lack of trying, however. Indeed, at party congresses held during the 1970s, considerable attention had been paid to the concept of a "progressive united front," especially with the Socialist Party (JSP) and some future "democratic coalition government."

Yet another important factor in the JCP's electoral reverses has been the move of the Democratic Socialist Party (DSP) and the Komeito (Clean Government Party, or CGP) to the center, accompanied by a similar trend on the part of the Japanese voting public. (Public opinion polls for the past quarter century have consistently shown that larger and larger segments of the Japanese people consider themselves part of the middle class, with the figure falling around 90 percent.) This trend erodes the traditional support of the "progressive" parties, especially those—as with the JCP—perceived to be on the extreme Left.

Although the JCP's strident defense of democracy and freedom was largely a reaction to domestic developments and the growing "Communist allergy" of the Japanese public, it has fed suspicions about the party's motives. This "allergy," coupled with attacks by the mass media, has forced the JCP to the defensive. In fact, its Fourteenth Congress in October 1977 concerned itself with the "anti-Communist counteroffensive,"[20] and subsequently the JCP characterized the domestic situation as being the second worst for the party since the end of World War II.

It is probable that media attacks on the JCP have been effective in moving the Japanese electorate further away from the party. In 1976, attention centered on the validity of the party's commitment to democracy and on Miyamoto personally.[21] These points were underscored by potentially the most damaging party purge—the expulsion of Hakamada Satomi, vice chairman of the Standing Committee of the Presidium, as well as Miyamoto's prison mate and erstwhile right-hand man. Hakamada openly characterized Miyamoto's rule in the JCP as "despotic" and directly linked him to the "lynching" case, to which he was a witness.[22] Furthermore, even the JCP membership does not evaluate the leadership of the party very highly.[23]

Aside from launching a counteroffensive against anti-Communist forces, how did the party react to these electoral setbacks? One measure was the revamping of study texts for all levels of membership. For several years the party de-emphasized the writings of Marx, Engels, and other Communist classics and stressed indigenous JCP documents. The Fourteenth Congress went even further. Since then, the list for new members contains predominantly JCP documents, and only the highest level contains a substantial number (about one-half) of non-Japanese materials.[24] Significantly, these materials omit the writings of Mao Zedong, Stalin, Tito, Castro, and even Togliatti. Curiously, *The Communist Manifesto* of Marx and Engels was added to the list in May 1962; taken off the list in July 1974, a couple of years before the promulgation of the "Manifesto of Freedom and Democracy"; reintroduced in December 1977; and again taken off the list in December 1995. The JCP is stressing its Japanese heritage, but its borrowings betray its real policy of favoring Lenin over Togliatti. Two comments, one from a Japanese and the other from a U.S. analyst of the JCP, sum up the matter: The JCP under Miyamoto can be characterized as following a "structural reform line without structural reform theory" and as pursuing "iron discipline" with a "smiling image."[25]

JCP POLICIES AND PROBLEMS AS EXPRESSED IN PARTY CONGRESSES

In the past two decades (1980–1999), the JCP held seven congresses. A brief comparison of the circumstances, policies, and resolutions of these congresses will illuminate the concerns and future direction of the party.

The Fifteenth Party Congress was held in February 1980, after the October 1979 HRC election in which the JCP recouped its losses from 1976 and immediately after Miyamoto's trip to Moscow and the normalization of relations with the CPSU after fifteen years. The atmosphere at the congress was upbeat and, because of peace with the Soviets, was well attended by thirty foreign Communist Party delegations.[26] Ironically, as the JCP broke out of isolation in the international

Communist movement, it became more and more isolated on the Japanese political scene.

The Sixteenth Party Congress, which was held in July 1982, coincided with the celebration of the party's sixtieth anniversary;[27] it also followed the disastrous 1980 double election to both houses of the National Diet (in which the party lost heavily) and occurred in the midst of strained relations with the CPSU because of the events in Afghanistan and Poland and other matters. Yet, in spite of these problems and the worsening domestic isolation of the JCP, the party staged elaborate celebrations, including an International Symposium on Theory.

The Seventeenth Congress was held in November 1985 following the Miyamoto-Chernenko summit of December 1984 (devoted exclusively to the "abolition of nuclear weapons"—a public relations event) and elections to the Tokyo Metropolitan Assembly, where the party registered some gains (as will be discussed later).[28]

The Eighteenth Party Congress was held in November 1987, over a year after the double election to the National Diet in which the JCP generally held its seats in spite of an LDP landslide. The Nineteenth Congress in July 1990 came four months after a disastrous election to the HRC in which the party lost almost half of its parliamentary delegation in spite of only one percentage point drop in the popular vote. Of course, the election was held right after the collapse of communism in Eastern Europe, the disintegration of the external Soviet empire, and the retreat of ideology and centrally planned economy in favor of market reform in the Soviet Union.

Two congresses were held in the 1990s: the Twentieth in July 1994 and the Twenty-first in September 1997. The circumstances surrounding these two congresses were quite different: The Twentieth Congress was held while the party fortunes were stagnant in terms of electoral results following the July 1993 HRC elections, whereas the Twenty-first Congress was held in September 1997, following a significant upturn in terms of votes and seats in both the October 1996 HRC and the July 1997 Tokyo Metropolitan Assembly elections. Both congresses were held amid economic recession and political instability and fluidity.

Let us now look at the drafts, reports, discussions, and resolutions of these crucial party meetings. The leadership reports generally deal with the international situation, the domestic scene, and the party work at hand.

On the international level, at the Fifteenth Congress, Fuwa stressed the need to dissolve all military blocs including, of course, "the struggle to abolish the Japan-U.S. military alliance." At the Sixteenth Congress, the draft resolution stated that the plans for limited nuclear war are "threats to the peoples of the world" and spoke of the "harm done by Big Powerism" (code words for Soviet interventions in Afghanistan, Poland, and elsewhere, and especially the Soviets' meddling in the affairs of the JCP itself), whereas the Seventeenth Congress addressed itself to the elimination of nuclear weapons, the defense of Nicaragua, and, more broadly, the right of nations to self-determination. The resolutions of the Eighteenth Congress stressed contradictions in the capitalist world and the importance of the antinuclear peace movement, although attendees hardly realized that two years later the contradictions in the Socialist world would lead to the collapse of communism in all of Eastern Europe. The Nineteenth Congress took up not only this unhappy development for Communists everywhere but also the demise of the world Communist movement. The JCP lashed out against Gorbachev's "new thinking" and stressed the correctness of Japanese "scientific socialism" and the need to continue the struggle against nuclear weapons, military blocs, and hegemonism and "Big Powerism."[29] The resolution of the Twentieth Congress went even further by blaming all Soviet postwar leaders, declaring that "scientific socialism had nothing to do with Stalin's social imperialist deviation, Khrushchev's 'peaceful coexistence' theory subservient to the United States, Brezhnev's theory of 'equilibrium of military strength' with the United States, and particularly the 'new thinking' advocated by Gorbachev."[30] Three years later, at the Twenty-first Congress, the emphasis was on the "outrageous behavior and contradictions of U.S. hegemonism" and on the fact that the world capitalist economy faced new increasing contradictions.[31]

On the domestic front, at the Fifteenth Congress, Miyamoto described the situation as "Amidst Tense Counteroffensive JSP's Rightward Degeneration" and called for a Progressive United Front through the expansion of "Progressive Unity Forums." At the Sixteenth Congress, Fuwa predicted "the bankruptcy for the JSP-CGP agreement," while the Seventeenth Congress assailed the Nakasone cabinet and warned of the danger of revival of the "Imperial Rule Assistance Politics" (a reference to the prewar merger of all political parties except for the illegal JCP) and of "opening the way to Japanese-style fascism."[32] The resolutions of the Eighteenth Congress condemned the policies of the new Takeshita government as a continuation of the bad policies of its predecessor and deplored the ongoing "rightward fall" of the Socialists. The party also expressed concern over the rightward realignment of the Japanese labor movement and skyrocketing land prices. At the Nineteenth Congress, the party called for the breakup of the old political order, dominated by big capital and the LDP, and the Japan-U.S. military alliance. On the defensive because of the developments in Eastern Europe, the party resorted to platitudes: "The Japanese people should truly share in the benefits of the world's second largest economy, democracy should flower, and the people should be masters of their own destiny."[33] The resolution at the Twentieth Congress had practically nothing to say about domestic politics, other than to note "the impasse of LDP and its successors' politics" and again bring out the bogey of "increased danger toward Japanese-style fascism."[34] At the Twenty-first Congress, the party touted "JCP's Historic Advance" and called the present era "LDP-JCP" confrontation, because all the other parties "just mimic the LDP." "Capitalism without rules" should be remedied, and big business should "fulfill its social responsibility."[35]

Regarding party work in particular, the Fifteenth Congress stressed the "Four Pillars" of mass activities, election struggle, party building, and party defense. The Sixteenth Congress, held after serious setbacks, set "Two Pillar" goals: (1) strengthening of study and education and the establishment of disciplined party life, and (2) preparation for elections and creating bases for electoral support. The Seventeenth Congress called for "building a strong party in numbers and quality . . . with intellectual awareness and vitality . . . and . . . closely linked with the masses."[36] The four most recent congresses stressed revitalizing primary party units, achieving political and ideological "self-awakening," promoting mass activities and mass movements, and, especially, working toward increasing party membership and readership of party organs. It is significant that the party pledged to overcome the "vast vacuum" of young people and students (a topic that will be taken up later in this chapter).[37] The Twentieth Congress reduced the old "Four Pillars" to "Two Pillars for Expanding Party Strength: Increasing *Akahata* Readership and Increasing Party Membership," with the proviso that "the whole party should make special efforts to recruit new members among the youth and students."[38] The problem obviously remains, since the resolution of the Twenty-first Congress still includes "On Increasing *Akahata* Subscribers and Party Membership—Special Importance of Organizing Young Generation in Progressive Direction."[39]

Thus it would seem that in terms of membership and readership drives, the JCP, despite denials, is going after quantity instead of quality. The leaders probably feel that the policies that produced rapid growth in the 1960s might also to some extent work in the 1990s. Time will tell if they are right, but they are in total command, and there are no challengers.

Let us now examine just how the JCP is structured, led, and financed.

THE PARTY

Party Structure

The nerve center of the JCP is the national Party Headquarters in Tokyo. Like other Communist parties, the JCP is organized under the principle of "democratic centralism," maintaining the fiction that the party congress, consisting of "democratically" elected delegates from the party cells or branches (some 26,000 according to party figures), districts, and prefectures, is the party's highest authority. In practice, however, the JCP is run dictatorially, first by Miyamoto and later by his protégés, who freely co-opt members into the Presidium, the Secretariat, and the Central Committee and appoint the heads of all central party departments and national committees as well as prefectural and local party officials. Shown schematically in Figure 8.1 is the party organization, from the branches, through districts and prefectural committees, to the central party organization, with its governing Presidium and subordinate agencies.

Leadership

The present top personnel of the party, most of whom were carefully selected by Fuwa and his assistants and then "elected" at the Twenty-first Party Congress in September 1997, are grouped as follows:[40] Fuwa, chairman of the Presidium; three vice chairmen (his brother Ueda Koichiro is one of the three) of the 57-member Presidium, including 19 members of the Standing Presidium (average age sixty-one); Shii, director of the Secretariat;[41] 3 deputy directors of the 14-member Secretariat; the members of the Central Committee (CC) (158 full members and 29 candidate members); the members of the Control, Audit, and Petition Committees; and the Editorial Committee for Central Party Publications.

The present administrative structure of the party is as follows: Committee on International Affairs (includes the International Department); Committee on Policy (subcommittees on politics and diplomacy, economic policy, and social welfare policy); Propaganda Bureau; Press and Public Relations Department; Committee to Promote Peace and United Front; Labor Bureau; Women and Children Bureau; Farmers and Fishermen Bureau; Bureau on Citizens Movement and Middle and Small Enterprises; Youth and Students Bureau; Committee on Culture and Intellectuals (Culture Bureau, subcommittee on sports, bureau on intellectuals, subcommittee on religion); Education Committee; Electoral Policy Bureau; Local Government Bureau; Committee on National Diet Members' Regional Offices Policy (Office of HRC Members Group, and

FIGURE 8.1   JCP organizational chart (as of Twenty-first Party Congress, September 1997)

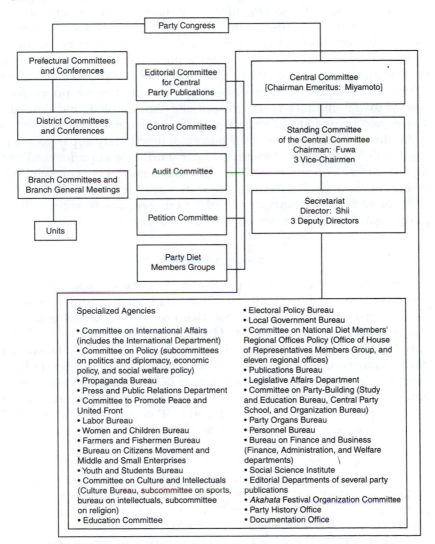

Specialized Agencies

• Committee on International Affairs (includes the International Department)
• Committee on Policy (subcommittees on politics and diplomacy, economic policy, and social welfare policy)
• Propaganda Bureau
• Press and Public Relations Department
• Committee to Promote Peace and United Front
• Labor Bureau
• Women and Children Bureau
• Farmers and Fishermen Bureau
• Bureau on Citizens Movement and Middle and Small Enterprises
• Youth and Students Bureau
• Committee on Culture and Intellectuals (Culture Bureau, subcommittee on sports, bureau on intellectuals, subcommittee on religion)
• Education Committee

• Electoral Policy Bureau
• Local Government Bureau
• Committee on National Diet Members' Regional Offices Policy (Office of House of Representatives Members Group, and eleven regional offices)
• Publications Bureau
• Legislative Affairs Department
• Committee on Party-Building (Study and Education Bureau, Central Party School, and Organization Bureau)
• Party Organs Bureau
• Personnel Bureau
• Bureau on Finance and Business (Finance, Administration, and Welfare departments)
• Social Science Institute
• Editorial Departments of several party publications
• *Akahata* Festival Organization Committee
• Party History Office
• Documentation Office

SOURCES: Nihon Kyosan To Chuo linkai no Kozo to Jinji, pp. 114–115; JCP 21st Congress, pp. 171–176.

eleven regional offices); Publications Bureau; Legislative Affairs Department; Committee on Party-Building (Study and Education Bureau, Central Party School, and Organization Bureau); Party Organs Bureau; Personnel Bureau; Bureau on Finance and Business (Finance, Administration, and Welfare Departments); Social Science Institute; Editorial Departments of several party publications; *Akahata* Festival Organization Committee; Party History Office; and Documen-tation Office.[42] In the past, there have been special agencies for policy with respect to U.S. military bases, the old and the disabled, and outcasts. These areas are undoubtedly handled through other relevant agencies.

In addition, there are about a thousand staunch party apparatchiks in the Tokyo headquarters, over 10,000 party officials in prefectural and district committees, and some 70,000 chiefs and members of branch leadership committees. The party headquarters regularly convenes conferences of prefectural chairmen, district chairmen, chiefs of prefectural party organ departments, and provincial activists.

The Gender Gap

Compared with other Japanese political parties, the JCP takes particular pride in the number of female candidates it officially endorses and the number of female members of the two houses of the National Diet elected under its auspices. In the HRC election of December 1983, the JCP elected 7 female parliamentarians, compared with 2 for all the other parties combined.[43] In later elections, the other parties began to field more female candidates. Nonetheless, as of December 1998, the JCP delegation of 26 included five women, a much higher percentage than an equal number of women in the LDP and CGP delegations of 263 and 52 members, respectively.[44] On the local level, the JCP claims that as of April 26, 1998, the number of Communist women in local assemblies was 992, whereas the other five parties combined had only 739.[45]

The number of women in the party hierarchy overall, however, is quite another story. Although women constitute almost 40 percent of the party membership, there are only 33 women (or 17.6 percent) in the 187-member Central Committee elected at the Twenty-first Party Congress in September 1997.[46] (There were 37 women, or 19.3 percent, elected at the Twentieth Party Congress in July 1994, so the trend is in the opposite direction to closing the gender gap.) As we go higher in the party hierarchy, women become even less visible. There are only 7 women (or 12 percent) in the 57-member Presidium, only 2 (or 10 percent) in the 19-member Standing Committee of the Presidium, and about a dozen women (or again 10 percent) in the top 100-plus positions in the party.

This compares very unfavorably with the reformed Italian Communists, who had guaranteed women members a 30 percent share of leadership positions, with a 50 percent goal for the future.[47]

Membership

As indicated in Figure 8.2, the growth of JCP membership following World War II has gone through five periods: (1) in 1945–1949 phenomenal growth occurred, from 1,000 to 84,000 members (an eightyfold increase); (2) in 1950–1958 the membership was reduced by half to 40,000, following the disastrous leftist course dictated by the Cominform and the CCP; (3) in 1958–1970 rapid growth occurred, amounting to a sevenfold increase in twelve years under Miyamoto's leadership, to roughly 300,000 members; (4) in 1970–1987 the growth was slow (65 percent in seventeen years), probably approaching the half-million mark; and (5) after 1987 came a slow decline. It was announced at the Twenty-first Congress in September 1997 that membership was down to 370,000 (or a loss of almost a hundred thousand members in ten years). Thus it seems that the JCP's goal of half a million members (and 4 million *Akahata* subscribers) will not be reached. Membership claims are party figures, and Japanese government analysts tend to dispute them, pointing out that the party typically sets membership goals for its congresses and during the preparatory periods carries a lot of "sleepers," that is, members who either have been delinquent in their payment of party dues or have not participated in party activities for a period of one year and can be subject to expulsion (Article XII of the JCP constitution). (Party dues are 1 percent of a member's salary.) Figure 8.2 also indicates party strength minus the "sleepers," whose number reached 100,000 in September 1990, and 115,000 seven years later, in September 1997 (reducing effective party membership to 255,000). Nevertheless, the JCP membership figure, however it is calculated, is greater than that of all other Japanese opposition parties combined and represents the largest nonruling Communist party in the world. This dramatic growth of party membership is one measure of Miyamoto's organizing skill.

Party Affiliate Organizations
and the Larger Network

An integral part of the Japanese Communist movement is its youth and women's affiliate organizations; its influence in certain labor unions, particularly those in which JCP members are in leadership positions and control the unions' affairs; and a whole range of front organizations

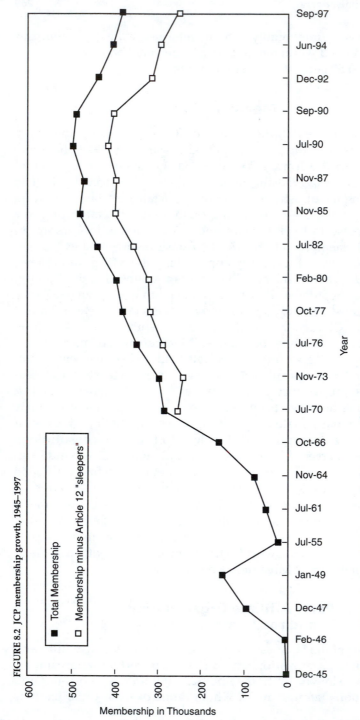

FIGURE 8.2 JCP membership growth, 1945–1997

Membership in Thousands

Year

■ Total Membership
□ Membership minus Article 12 "sleepers"

SOURCES: Secret document from JCP Organization Bureau reproduced in *Sekai Nippo*, Nov. 13, 1990; "Kyosanto 20-kai To Taikai Chokuzen Joho: Tonai Sotenken de wakatta kyogaku no jijitsu," *Zembo*, August 1994, pp. 4–7; *Sayoku Benran 1996*, p. 199; *JCP 21st Congress*, p. 119.

focusing on areas such as peace, international friendship, the antinuclear movement, welfare, and livelihood protection. Several of these organizations were constituent members of international Communist front organizations, even though their membership was by no means exclusively Communist. Many of the organizations were also part of larger federations of organizations on the Left, some of which, especially those originally cosponsored by the JCP and the JSP, have split into JCP and JSP groups. Most notable among these is the antinuclear movement of the early 1960s.

Some analysts have singled out the youth, women's, and small-business organizations as the party's "Three Great Families" (or Gosanke, an ironic reference to the three main branches of the Tokugawa family). More recently, three other organizations—namely, the associations of doctors, lawyers, and tax accountants—have been jokingly designated as the JCP's "New Three Great Families" in recognition not only of the importance the party attaches to these professions but also of the significant role these organizations have played in projecting an image of the JCP as a party that is helping people in their daily lives.[48]

Publications

The JCP recognizes the power of propaganda and at the same time, surprisingly, is able to make a nice living from it. It maintains a truly profitable big-business publishing empire, so that the party has been facetiously called "The Yoyogi Newspaper Publishing Company, Limited." This publishing business, as described in the next section, practically maintains the party by providing it with operating funds and makes it possible for the JCP to be independent of special interest groups. The most important party publication—its financial lifeline as well as a measure of its success in Japanese society—is the party organ *Akahata*, which comes out in a daily edition (and has since October 1945) and a weekly Sunday edition (since March 1959). Three times a month, the party organ also produces *Akahata Shashin Nyusu*, an illustrated wall newspaper for propaganda and advertising purposes, as well as a monthly reduced-size bound edition for libraries and a monthly in Braille. *Akahata* has maintained permanent correspondents in several major Communist capitals as well as in Washington, London, Paris, Rome, Berlin, Vienna, Mexico City, Manila, and New Delhi. As of 1999, there were correspondents in twelve countries, including China for the first time in thirty years. In Japan, *Akahata* has at its service some 13,000 correspondents, or stringers, as well as more than 50,000 unpaid delivery workers.

   Combined circulation figures of the daily and Sunday editions of
Akahata are used by the party as both a measure of its success and a
perennial target. For some years now, the party's goals were to achieve
an *Akahata* readership of 4 million. The figure reported by party leaders
at the Fifteenth Party Congress in 1980 was over 3.5 million, the highest
number ever claimed by party authorities. Since then, as seen in Figure
8.3, the circulation is down by more than one million (or a third) to just
over 2.3 million, although there are artificial increases before each party
congress when members try to sign up as many relatives, neighbors,
coworkers, and friends as they can. Nonetheless, *Akahata* easily surpasses the circulation of a party newspaper of any other nonruling
Communist party. In fact, Miyamoto bragged that his colleagues in the
French and Italian Communist parties were astounded when they
learned about *Akahata*'s readership of three million.[49] [*Zen'ei*, an authori-
tative theoretical monthly (since February 1946); magazines for women,
students, and elementary- and intermediate-level party members; an
illustrated semimonthly for potential party members; organs of the
party's youth, women's, and students' affiliates; a children's weekly;
monthlies for cadres in the labor union movement and for young workers; an economic theory monthly; and the organ of the Democratic
Literary League, *Minshu Bungaku.*] The circulation of these periodicals
ranges from 4,000 to 250,000, and total circulation figures, excluding the
Akahata, are about a million copies.[50] At the height of publishing activity
in the mid-1980s, the party also put out other journals, among them
Bunka Hyoron, a general cultural monthly; *Sekai Seiji*, a semimonthly on
international affairs; *Kurashi to Seiji*, a monthly report on parliamentary
affairs, which was revived in December 1998 after the party's electoral
successes under the title "Gikai to Jichitai" (The Diet and Local
Government). The Central Committee Publishing Bureau also puts out
millions of pamphlets, especially during elections, as well as a wide
range of books.[51] To publicize the work of the party abroad, the JCP
established a subsidiary company, the Japan Press Service, that since
November 1956 has continuously put out the *Japan Press Weekly*, a
twenty- to forty-page press release that routinely provides material in
English from *Akahata* and other party publications, and a number of
books (works by Miyamoto, Fuwa, and others; proceedings of party congresses; important party documents) in English and other European languages. Since 1993, the Japan Press Service has also published a monthly
four- to eight-page newsletter entitled *Dateline Tokyo:* for people-to-
people exchange, and since 1998, the JPS Daily News Service, also available in an e-mail version. In addition, the JCP headquarters issues from
time to time the *Bulletin: Information for Abroad* (in English, Spanish, and

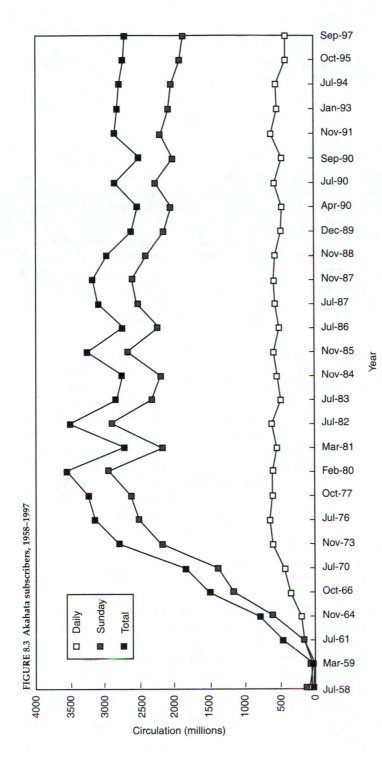

FIGURE 8.3 Akahata subscribers, 1958–1997

SOURCES: *Sayoku Benran 1989*, p. 217; *Sekai Nippo*, November 11, 1990; *Sayoku Benran 1996*, p. 199; *JCP 21st Congress*, p. 120.

other languages) that contains translations of important party documents, statements, editorials, speeches, and the like.

Party Finances

During the immediate postwar period, the JCP unquestionably benefited from the funds secretly provided by the Soviet mission accredited to the Headquarters of the Supreme Commander for the Allied Powers. Somewhat later, moneys earned by visiting Soviet performers were conveniently laundered and made their way into the party coffers. There were also some instances of unlawful importation of prescription medications and heroin.[52] In the 1950s and early 1960s, trade contacts with the Soviet Union, mainland China, and other Communist countries were deliberately structured in a way to benefit left-wing causes, including the JCP. Communist China, for example, moved most of its trade with Japan through the so-called friendly firms. But following the breaks with the CPSU and the CCP in the mid-1960s, the Japanese party was largely on its own, with the income from the sale of its publications constituting the predominant part of the budget, followed by "donations."

Although Japanese political parties have to report their income and expenditures to the government authorities, these figures must be handled with great caution, since they most probably reveal only a fraction of the actual income. Nonetheless, the figures are not without significance. For one thing, we can see the relative increases, as the reported party budget rose from $367,000 in 1958, to $1 million in 1961, $3.6 million in 1965, $11.4 million in 1970, and $40 million in 1975.[53] Since the yen fluctuates against the dollar, often quite substantially, more recent budget data are provided in the Japanese currency. From 1978 to 1989 the party's income almost doubled, from 16.7 billion yen to 29.9 billion yen. But because of the dramatic appreciation of the Japanese currency, the 1989 figure represents $260 million.[54] Unfortunately, the expenditure figures also rose correspondingly. During the next decade, party income went up about 10 percent, but as of 1997 it was back to the 1989 level (Table 8.1). About 90 percent of the income (but also 75 percent of the expenditures) is associated with party publications; dues constituted only about 4 percent.[55] In some years, party publications showed a healthy $50 million profit.

There are problems, however, in the distribution of the publications and the collection of subscription fees, and the party has a special committee for dealing with these problems. The party also experiences liquidity problems—especially in election years, when extra funds are needed. It has been estimated that the party spent around $3 million on

TABLE 8.1   JCP Income and Expenditure, 1997 (in millions of yen)

Income	Total	Percentage
Party dues	1,413	4.6
Donations	516	1.7
Party enterprises	27,313	88.4
Miscellaneous income	1,631	5.3
Total income	30,873	100.0
Carryover from the previous year	6,923	
Grand total	37,796	

Expenditure	Total	Percentage
Administrative expenses	5,051	17.1
Political activities		
Enterprise expenses	21,441	72.8
Other expenses	2,963	10.1
Total expeditures	29,455	100.0
Carryover to the next year	8,341	

NOTE: Not all subcategories are included in the table.

SOURCE: *Shiryo Tsushin,* Vol. 42, no. 19 (Oct. 15, 1998), p. 7.

each election campaign during 1969–1971, $5 million to $8 million in 1974–1977, and some $13 million in the four years between 1980 and 1983. In 1979 the combined cost of local and HRC elections (in the spring and fall, respectively) was as high as $18 million.[56] Since that time the cost of election has risen, and in some years expenditures exceed income, creating deficits for the party.

The Political Funds Control Law was amended to require all political parties, organizations, and groups to declare their total assets. As of December 31, 1993, the JCP declared assets totaling 9 billion yen (the largest items being 3.8 billion in bank deposits and 1.6 billion each for land and buildings). But confidential sources indicate that the party's training school campus near Atami in Shizuoka Prefecture, not far from Tokyo (where party congresses are held), alone is worth at least 15 billion yen (or about $130 million). This calculation is based on the fact that the land parcel measures 50,000 square meters, and the price for one *tsubo* (3.3 meters) in that vicinity is easily worth one million yen.[57] Clearly, the JCP has grossly underreported its assets.

An amazing fact is that according to official reporting, the JCP, since 1975, has been the richest political party in Japan, in spite of the fact that it refuses government funding. The LDP enjoys generous support of big business, and political donations are more easily concealable than the JCP income from its publishing empire.[58] Moreover, LDP supporters donate directly to the candidates rather than to the party. The reported JCP income for 1997 was 30.9 billion yen, followed by 24.5 billion for the LDP (14.9 billion of which was government funds), 13.3 billion for the Komeito, 10.9 billion for the New Frontier Party, 5.6 billion for the Democratic Party, and 4.5 billion for the Socialists.[59] These figures are even more remarkable if we recall that the other opposition parties enjoy the financial support of business, large labor union federations, or a religious organization. In other words, the JCP is not indebted to outside interest groups—an obvious advantage when one considers that the other parties get bad publicity because of "money politics" and conflicts of interest. Privately, LDP politicians have a grudging respect for the integrity of the JCP legislators, much as they despise the Socialists who were regularly being bought off by the government party.[60]

The Electoral Record

Since the establishment of democratic Japan by the U.S. Occupation, the JCP has participated fully in the electoral process at all levels: at the national level (for the HRC and the HC); at the prefectural level (governors and prefectural assemblies); and at the local level (mayors and assemblies of cities, towns, and villages). Of course, the JCP's electoral record can be measured in different ways: by the number of seats won in the national, prefectural, and local legislative bodies; in terms of party participation in prefectural and local governments; by the number of votes cast for party candidates; and by the percentage of votes and seats at all levels. The latter figure can be further broken down into percentages of all eligible voters, of the total election vote, of the total opposition parties vote, and of the total vote of the parties on the Left. But, broadly speaking, the party's performance in the postwar electoral politics of Japan has undergone five phases: (1) 1945–1949: a period of growth; (2) 1950s and early 1960: debacle and slow rebirth; (3) late 1960s to early 1970s: rapid growth; (4) mid-1970s to mid-1990s: stagnation, gain, and loss, or slow growth (depending on the electoral level or electoral indicator); and (5) since 1996: increased popular vote and representation in legislative bodies at both the national and the local level. Let us look first at the HRC , then the HC , then local elections, and finally the recent upward turn in JCP's electoral fortunes since the mid-1990s.

HRC

The most important elections in Japan are those for the 500 seats in the HRC , which is the lower but more powerful house of the National Diet. As can be seen in Table A.1, in 1946 and 1967 the party received a little more than 2 million votes, in 1949 and 1969 a little more than 3 million, between 1972 and 1993 around 5 million, and in 1996 over 7 million votes.

The postwar electoral system reflected the rural-urban distribution of population in occupied Japan, and in the absence of mandatory reapportionment to compensate for the massive urbanization that took place in the 1950s and in later years, rural and semirural districts were represented in the Diet entirely out of proportion to their population. Thus it would take 200,000 rural residents and over 600,000 urban dwellers to send one representative to the Diet. The system greatly favored the ruling conservative party, the LDP, because it received much support from rural and semirural districts. By contrast, the JCP suffered from the inequities of the system because its votes were concentrated in the large cities. Nonetheless, multiseat constituencies made it easier for smaller parties, like the JCP, to elect and send representatives to the lower house. Under the new system, it has become very difficult for the JCP to win in single-seat winner-take-all constituencies. On the other hand, the 200 seats reserved for proportional party representation guaranteed a more equitable distribution of seats for the JCP. But under both systems the JCP's percentage of the total vote was much higher than the percentage of party seats in the Diet (8 percent versus 3 percent in 1990; 13 versus 5 in 1996). In single-seat districts the inequity is even more telling: the JCP collected 12.6 percent of the votes but obtained only 0.7 percent of the seats, whereas the LDP, with 38.6 percent of the votes, got 56.3 percent of the seats. (If all 500 seats were allocated on a party proportional basis, the JCP would have had 60 seats and the LDP 160.)

In the 1972 elections the party's share of the total vote was almost 11 percent (5.7 million votes). During the next two decades, the total vote for the party fell to 4.8 million, which represented 7.7 percent.[61] (Of course, in some urban areas, such as Kyoto and Osaka, JCP candidates got around 20 percent of the vote, or more than double the national average.)[62]

Although from 1972 until 1996 the total vote for the Communist Party slowly declined, the number of Communist Diet members in the lower house has fluctuated wildly, especially between 1972 and 1980. The seat totals for the elections from 1976 to 1996 are as follows: 40, 19, 41, 29, 27, 27, 16, 15, and 26. How can one account for these variations, which occurred in spite of the relative steadiness of the total electoral vote?

One explanation is that in multiseat constituencies the difference between the last winner and the closest runner-up *(jiten)* is sometimes only a few thousand votes. Bad publicity can sway a number of votes and cost the party a few marginal seats. It can also be domestic, as in the Miyamoto "lynching" incident and the revelations of the purged vice chairman, Hakamada Satomi, or it can be international, as in the Soviet invasion of Afghanistan, the repression in Poland, the shooting down of a Korean airliner (with many Japanese passengers on board) by a Soviet fighter plane, the assassination of South Korean cabinet ministers by North Korean agents in Burma in 1983, and the Tienanmen Square massacre in June 1989. All such incidents create an *imeji daun* (image down)—that is, a worsening in the Japanese perception of Communist countries and of communism, which therefore affects the JCP. The disintegration of Communist regimes in Eastern Europe in late 1989 also must have had an impact on the Japanese electorate in the February 1990 and July 1993 elections.

A second, and more important, explanation is that the JCP could more easily win a seat in a multiseat constituency if all the other opposition parties fielded candidates and split the non-Communist vote. But the JCP electoral successes in 1972 and 1979 taught the CGP and the DSP to enter into election agreements, not to run against each other's candidates in certain constituencies. In fact, in the December 1983 election, 59 joint candidates were put up in 58 electoral districts, and 46 of them won, whereas in the February 1990 election 70 joint candidates were put up, and 48 of them were elected.

Finally, are fluctuations in the number of JCP seats correlated with the number of JSP seats, or the total number of Left or opposition seats? The only pattern of negative or positive correlation appears to be that associated with the JSP. It seems that in elections in which the JCP gained seats, the JSP lost them, and vice versa. This was certainly true in 1949, when the JCP's dramatic increase in seats occurred at the expense of the Socialists, again in 1990 when the Socialists gained seats at the expense of the JCP and other parties, and most recently and uncannily in 1996 when the JCP picked up 3.4 million votes and the JSP lost 3.3 million.[63]

HC

JCP fortunes in the upper house generally followed the trends in the HRC . As indicated in Table A.1, the party's popular vote in both the national and local constituencies grew from the 1959 election, when it was 1.6 million, until the 1974 election, when the JCP garnered 11.8 million votes (6.8 million, or 12.8 percent, in the local constituency and 4.9

million, or 9.4 percent, in the national) and had 20 members in the upper house. For the next two decades (except for 1986, when the party obtained 12 million votes), the total JCP vote went down by several million, reaching 8.2 million in 1995. Following electoral successes in the 1996 HRC election and the 1997 Tokyo Municipal Assembly elections, the JCP continued its forward march in the July 1998 election to the upper house when the vote for the party more than doubled, to 17 million. The number of JCP legislators in the upper house also went down from 20 in 1974 (the number fluctuated between 16 and 11) but reached a record 23 in 1998.

The JCP contingent in both houses of the National Diet topped off at 60 in 1977, only to go down to 26 in 1993. But even the dramatic advances in 1996 and 1998 raised the number to 49. Thus, to put it in historical perspective, only in the upper house is there a record number of JCP members (23).

As a group, at one point Communist parliamentarians in both houses of the National Diet were the youngest contingent of any party, and they are, after the LDP, the second most educated group.[64] They do their homework and, at least since the 1970s, have not engaged in opposition for opposition's sake.[65]

Local Elections

The JCP also vigorously contests elections at the subnational level—that is, elections of prefectural governors and mayors of major urban centers, cities, towns, wards, and villages, and elections to prefectural, municipal, town, ward, and village assemblies.

Party history was made in 1967 when a Communist was elected mayor of Shiojiri in Nagano Prefecture.[66] In general, however, the JCP has participated in broad left-wing coalitions to elect "progressives" as governors or as mayors of major cities (the election of Governor Minobe of Tokyo in 1967 being the most important). In subsequent years, all six of the largest cities came under nonconservative control. But as the "progressives" became entrenched in city government, the united front of the opposition parties collapsed; some elections became three-cornered affairs with one conservative and two "progressive" candidates. The JCP sometimes backed candidates in an election alliance with other opposition parties; at other times it ran its own candidates. In 1974 and 1975 the party succeeded in electing the governors of Kyoto and Osaka against two other candidates in each case. In April 1978, however, the party lost the Kyoto and Yokohama elections, and in April 1979 it lost Tokyo and Osaka. In the April 1983 local elections, the JCP ran its own candidate for the governorship of Osaka, a joint candidate with the JSP in Tokyo and Fukuoka, and it officially endorsed other candidates. Only in Fukuoka did the JCP-JSP candidate win the governorship; most other winners were candidates endorsed by the LDP, CGP, and DSP. Considering the fact that at one time the JCP participated in the election of governors in Tokyo, Osaka, Kyoto, Okinawa, Okayama, Kanagawa, Shiga, and Kagawa, the tide has clearly turned against the JCP and the JSP. In the mid-1990s, Japanese voters became disgusted with professional politicians of all stripes and elected personalities from the entertainment and other fields (the Japanese call them *tarento* [talent]), most visibly in the two most important cities—Tokyo and Osaka.[67]

While at the national level the JCP was losing votes and seats in the 1980s and early 1990s, the party's contingent in the prefectural and local assemblies oddly enough continued to grow: The total number of JCP-elected assembly members rose from 650 in 1958, to over 1,000 in 1964, to over 3,000 in 1977, and to over 4,000 in April 1997.[68] As of January 1999, there are 136 JCP members in prefectural assemblies, 105 in those of designated cities, 1,669 in assemblies of other cities, 159 in Tokyo ward assemblies, and 2,049 in town and village assemblies, for a total of 4,118 Communist assemblymen and women.[69] Party officials now brag that there are more JCP members in these assemblies than those who run under the LDP banner (3,657 in December 1996).[70] (The JCP overtook the CGP in 1979, the Socialist Party in 1981, and the LDP in 1995.)[71] But the truth is that there are almost 70,000 seats in these prefectural, municipal, and local assemblies, and most candidates are conservatives who run as independents.

In the June 1985 elections to the Tokyo Metropolitan Assembly, the JCP increased its delegation from 16 to 19 members (out of 127 seats). However, the number of votes and the percentage of the total vote declined compared with the previous election.[72] The picture was also mixed in the 1989 election: Although the total Communist vote slightly increased (from roughly 695,000 to 713,000 votes), the JCP percentage of the total vote declined (from 15.5 to 13.9 percent), and so did the number of JCP assembly members (from 19 to 14).[73] The JCP lost both votes and seats in 1993, only to recoup dramatically in 1997 (see later discussion).

Another measure of electoral success of the JCP below the national level is the number of local governments in which the JCP is the governing party or, more likely, a part of the governing coalition. The JCP's participation rose from 10 legislative bodies in 1960 to over 200 by the mid-1970s. Since that time, this number has declined to 113, with the present (1999) number being 122. To place these figures in perspective, it is necessary to consider that the total number of local self-governing bodies is 3,315. Moreover, according to Japanese law, a party must have one-eighth of the assembly seats to be able to introduce bills and have other privileges in the legislative body. In only 384 assemblies (or 10 percent) do the Communists have that right. But even the figure 122 (the number of assemblies where the JCP is not in opposition) is deceptive because it includes assemblies where the party is part of a coalition with other parties including the LDP. Only 79 assemblies are solely JCP-governed, and only 9 mayors are JCP members (2 city mayors, one Tokyo ward mayor, and six town mayors).[74] It is also significant that in 32 percent of all prefectural and local legislative bodies there are no Communist members at all.[75]

Upward Turn Since the Mid-1990s

In the July 1993 HRC elections, the JCP continued its gradual decline, dropping to 15 members, 4.8 million votes representing 7.7 percent of the electorate (all three figures being the lowest since 1972). But it was a disaster for the JSP and especially for the LDP, which lost power for the first time since its establishment almost four decades earlier, in 1955. Two years later, in the July 1995 House of Councillors election, the JCP went further down in the prefectural constituencies but improved in the proportional representation, gaining almost 35,000 votes and 9.5 percent of the vote (compared with 7.8 percent three years earlier). But the breakthrough began the following year, in the October 1996 HRC election that saw the JCP garner a record 7.23 million votes (up from 4.83 million), representing 13 percent of the electorate (up from 7.7 percent), also a record.[76] The following year, in the July 1997 Tokyo Metropolitan Assembly election, the JCP doubled its seats from 13 to 26, becoming the largest opposition party, outpolling the CGP.[77] The party gathered over 800,000 votes (180,000 votes more than in the previous election four years earlier), which represented 21.3 percent of the votes cast. The upward trend continued in the July 1998 HC elections, in which the JCP further advanced in all categories: the party obtained 8.2 million votes (or 14.6 percent) in the proportional representation (more than doubling its vote total of 3.9 million in 1995); voters cast 8.7 million votes (or 15.7 percent) for the JCP candidates in the prefectural constituencies (also more than doubling the previous vote); and it won 15 seats in both categories.[78] Adding the 8 uncontested seats, the JCP now has a record of 23 seats in the upper house. Is this upward trend likely to continue? Electoral prognoses will be taken up in the next section.

CONCLUSIONS

This chapter began with the observation that poor, repressive Imperial Japan was very inhospitable to the fledgling alien, radical Japanese Communist movement. Conditions in affluent and democratic postwar and post-Occupation Japan are, paradoxically, equally inhospitable to a "Eurocommunist"-type party, which strives to project an image of an indigenous Japanese party that was independent from both Moscow and Peking (the two poles of the now defunct world Communist movement) and a party that accepts parliamentary democracy and is prepared to play by the rules of a pluralist society in an open political system. Japan is, indeed, a postindustrial society with an ever-growing service sector of the economy.

One can argue, of course, that the ongoing shrinkage of the blue-collar working class will not affect the JCP much, since that class was never well represented in the party's membership and was virtually absent in the top leadership. Japan at the turn of the twenty-first century is on the road to being a welfare state with hardly any real proletariat, whose interests the JCP is supposed to uphold. Over 90 percent of the Japanese public consider themselves to be "middle class." Students and other young people in their twenties at one time voted Communist in great numbers, but this group is becoming, if anything, more conservative, as is the case in Western Europe and the United States.

This shift could mean a weakened JCP for the future. A few years ago, party leaders have admitted that over 60 percent of the party membership was in their thirties and forties and another 20 percent in their fifties, but only 10 percent were in their twenties. At every recent party congress this problem is being addressed again and again: "The percentage of party members in their teens and twenties is still low," "The whole party should make special efforts to recruit new members among the youth and students," "The whole party must welcome the younger generation into the party and warmly encourage their noble ideals," The whole party must place "special importance on organizing young generation in progressive direction."[79] These exhortations bring to mind a Russian proverb, "When something ails you, that's what you talk about." At the turn of the century, the party membership breakdown by age is even more discouraging. Only 5 percent of the party membership is in their teens and twenties, another 10 percent in their thirties, 60 percent in their forties and fifties, and 25 percent over sixty. Thus, the party baby boomers from the 1960s and 1970s are now middle-aged, and no young replacements seem to be in sight. This pessimistic prognosis is further strengthened if we look at the party's youth affiliate, the

Japanese Democratic Youth League (Minsei Domei). The organization peaked in 1974, with 231,000 members. The membership dropped somewhat to 209,000 in 1984, then fell further to 171,000 in 1989. In the next two years came a sharp decline in membership, with fewer than 120,000 members reported in October 1990. This decline continued precipitously during the 1990s to the point that at the organization's Twenty-sixth Congress membership was reported to be over 22,000 (that is, one-tenth of what it was a quarter century ago).[80] Because it is estimated that half of the organization's membership are also JCP members, it is clear that there will be no significant number of young people flowing into the JCP.

Then there are the intellectuals who over the decades have provided sympathetic support and leadership to the party. But they, too, reflect the growing conservatism of Japanese society. It would be hard to believe that many Japanese intellectuals are not disappointed, indeed dismayed, over the ideological bankruptcy of the former Soviet Union, with its repression of a humanist socialist regime in former Czechoslovakia and a truly working-class movement in Poland. And what should they make of the collapse of communism in Eastern Europe and the disintegration of the Union of Soviet Socialist Republics, invalidating seventy years of claims to build a new, progressive, just, and prosperous society?[81] Closer to Japan, there is the specter of China: It went through the horrors of the so-called Great Proletarian Cultural Revolution, only to begin, with the death of Mao Zedong, partially to dismantle socialism, to emulate certain key features of the capitalist system, and yet to engage in brutal repression in the Tienanmen Square massacre.

In spite of the JCP's protestations of commitment to nationalism, democracy, parliamentary pluralism, and independence from international centers of Communist power, the predominant image of the JCP among the Japanese public remains that of an alien political creature, espousing an ideology that is becoming less and less relevant to Japan and until recently run dictatorially by a radical prewar leader not quite cleared of homicide charges. The JCP occupies that awkward middle ground in which it is not revolutionary enough for the radical fringe and not trustworthy enough for the adherents of democratic socialism. Above all, the Japanese economic miracle was accomplished by aggressive free enterprise (albeit guided by a conservative government) in the free world markets. But reality is often ignored, especially by ivory-towered intellectuals. I remember, for example, hearing Japanese Marxist scholars talk about the pauperization of the Japanese farmer, at a time when a visit to the countryside just outside Tokyo would reveal a forest of television antennas and every conceivable type of electrical appliance and agricultural machinery. Perhaps there is a cumulative effect associated with Japan's economic growth and prosperity. It has become difficult to accept the fact that Chinese Communist leaders were not only speaking warmly about the U.S.-Japan security ties but also encouraging the growth of the Japanese military establishment. Then there was always the northern neighbor refusing to budge from four Japanese islands, turning them into military outposts directed against Japan and, until the breakup of the Soviet Union, relentlessly increasing its Pacific fleet, its nuclear-armed bomber force, and its strategic nuclear missiles. Seeing the leader of the JCP attending summit meetings in Moscow was not very reassuring, in spite of the party's rhetoric against Czechoslovakia, Afghanistan, Poland, or the shooting down of the Korean airliner.

Nonetheless, the party remains a formidable organization, at both national and urban levels. It claims the loyalty of close to 100,000 dedicated cadres and probably another 100,000 faithful adherents, if not all true believers. The JCP is also like an iceberg, with the party membership—the visible part—only a small fraction of the Communist potential in Japan. Beyond party rolls, there are the youth and women's affiliates and the dozens of front organizations either directly controlled by the party or partially manipulated by party members in critical positions of power. In addition, there are the party cells in labor unions, the government agencies, the private enterprises, the universities, and lower educational institutions. Japanese government analysts have been warning about the long-range effects on Japanese society of, for example, Communist teachers in elementary schools, labor union activists (particularly among governmental employees), and Communist lawyers who may advance in the judicial system perhaps all the way to the Supreme Court.

Finally, there are the millions of Japanese who vote Communist in general and local elections. It is significant that years after the tearing down of the Berlin Wall, accompanied by the disintegration of communism in Eastern Europe, and years after dissolution of the Soviet Union—the midwife who assisted the birth of the JCP—7 to 8 million Japanese voted for Communist candidates. Clearly, there remains a reservoir of commitment to the Communist cause in Japan, although there must be a good number of protest voters who are disgusted at the sight of conservatives squabbling among themselves and of all major parties (except the Communists) being sullied in the Recruit and other bribery scandals. The *Japan Times* called the JCP "a magnet for protest votes."[82] Goodwill is generated at the grassroots level, as the party tries to be attentive to the needs of local constituents, and its record in selected local areas is much better than at the national level, where many of the party's strongly held positions (e.g., against the U.S.-Japan Security Treaty or the Self-Defense Forces) run contrary to public opinion polls. At the same time, rapes and other crimes committed by U.S. servicemen reinforce the JCP's message, especially on Okinawa and near American military bases.

The JCP played a positive role when it helped defuse the violence of the far Left and neo-anarchist elements, violence that was particularly ominous in the late 1960s and early 1970s. Here the party came out strongly and forthrightly against what Lenin called left-wing infantilism, and the party's youth affiliates, along with other organizations, certainly provided a counterpoint to the very visible and vocal ultra-Left fringe. In the National Diet the party contingent in both houses can be counted on to be vigilant with respect to LDP corruption, to support welfare, environmental, and consumer legislation, and to oppose the imposition of or the increase in the national sales tax, as well as the use of public funds to bail out bankrupt housing-loan companies. JCP legislators often play a constructive role in local assemblies, emulating the example set by the PCI. The party has also been effective on the local level—especially in urban areas—in helping citizens to cope with the complexities of daily living and to deal with local authorities.[83] In contrast to the French and Italian Communist Parties, the JCP does not enjoy the support of organized labor federations. But that makes it the most independent of all Japanese political parties in the sense that it can pursue its policies without regard to special interest groups. And that might also pay dividends with the voting public, who perceive the Communists as honest, whatever else they might think of the party, its leadership, or its policies. Another factor in favor of the JCP is the general dissatisfaction of the Japanese public with the political process that is reflected in the dropping rate of electoral turnout, which went from 75 percent in 1980 to just under 60 percent in 1996. Local elections understandably attract fewer voters than national elections, a case in point being a 40 percent turnout in the Tokyo Metropolitan Assembly election in 1997.

Concluding a chapter on the JCP, it is useful to speculate on the status and future, indeed, the very survival, of communism in the world.[84] The Japanese Communists naturally reject the argument that "collapse of the Soviet Union equals the collapse of communism."[85] They argue that what took place in the Soviet Union was not the failure and bankruptcy of socialism and communism but "the collapse of the Stalin-Brezhnev type of regime."[86] First of all, a distinction should be made between ruling and nonruling Communist parties. At the turn of the century, Leninist parties held sway most prominently in China, Vietnam, North Korea, and Cuba. Marxist-Leninism, communism, and indeed socialism all seem not to be viable systems for economic development, and some of the Leninist regimes are busily dismantling command economies and state-owned enterprises, and promoting a variety of capitalist features without, of course, acknowledging so publicly. Others, like North Korea and Cuba, seem to be dragging their feet. The ruling Communist parties in Eastern Europe tried to survive by dropping the label Communist and masquerading as Socialists or social democrats. The voters' judgment in free elections was a massive rejection, even though some former Communist leaders have hung on in a few places by claiming to have been opponents of the ancient régime and promising to be reformers, and some former Communists even managed to get democratically elected after failures of inexperienced anti-Communists. The Communist Party of the Russian Federation is the largest party in the Russian Duma, and its leader will again be a serious contender for the presidency in the 2000 elections.

More relevant to the JCP is the position of nonruling Communist parties. Here the picture is complex. When the Berlin Wall came down and Communist regimes began to disintegrate in Eastern Europe, the Italian Communist Party moved from Eurocommunism to Euroleft, it sought to join the Socialist International, and as part of the process has dropped the word *Communist* from its name and become the Democratic Party of the Left.[87] Shortly thereafter the party abolished democratic centralism and in effect became a social democratic party. Even Gorbachev made some noises about the Soviet Communist party's affiliation with the Socialist International. But why should the democratic Socialists forgive and embrace their former bitterest enemies? Moreover, at the time, the Japanese Communists attacked perestroika, rejected Gorbachev's new political thinking, and accused him of betraying the most basic of Marxist dogmas by placing humanity's values over class values, clinging to the notion of the basic correctness of their "scientific socialism."[88] At present (1999), a Communist is the prime minister of Italy. The French Communist Party (PCF) repudiated democratic centralism only in 1994, and although it polled under 10 percent of the votes (down from over 20 percent at the height of its popularity in the 1970s), the PCF is a junior coalition member in a Socialist government, and three Communist members (two of them women) are ministers in the government. A comparison of foreign delegations at the recent PCF and JCP congresses is revealing: While the PCF Congress in 1994 attracted delegates from 125 countries, the JCP congresses in 1994 and 1997 could list delegates from only a dozen Communist parties (but did include delegates from Vietnam and Cuba).[89]

What were the reasons for the party's electoral successes in the late 1960s and early 1970s, and for the reverses in the mid-1970s and slow decline in the 1980s? The adoption of a Eurocommunist, independent, and nationalist line after 1968 has helped the party to grow and, more important, to capture a segment of the floating and protest votes. Paradoxically, these electoral successes had sown the seeds for subsequent failures. So long as the JCP was an insignificant political force, it attracted the floating and protest votes and competed with other opposition parties for votes on the Left. But as soon as it was perceived as a potential force (it emerged in 1972 as the second-largest opposition party in the lower house, and it is at present the largest opposition party in the Tokyo Municipal Assembly), uncommitted and protest voters become more careful about casting their votes. Only time will tell whether the electoral trends in the mid-1970s will be repeated at the turn of the century.

Will the JCP survive, whether under its present name or under a different name? The Japanese Communists are not ready to change the name of their party, even though they dropped Marxism-Leninism in favor of scientific socialism a quarter century ago. A Nihon Kagaku Shakaishugi To? A Japanese Scientific Socialist Party? In the short term this seems unlikely, since the JCP leaders contend that to change the name would imply that the party had made mistakes (which they deny). While in the past the Italian Communist Party has served as a model for the JCP (without the Japanese Communists ever acknowledging their debt), this time the Japanese are not likely to follow the Italians. Moreover, the benefits of a name change are also problematic. The Japanese Socialists first changed the English name of the party from Japan Socialist Party to Social Democratic Party of Japan, and only later did they formally change their name in Japanese to Shakai Minshu To (or Social Democratic Party; see also Chapter 4). The name change, however, did not help the catastrophic decline of the Socialists' fortune, and this may have added to the Communist leaders' reluctance to change the name of the party.

In politics, long-term predictions are very hazardous. Miyamoto's retirement was a blessing for the party because it removed one more reminder of the JCP's prewar alien and violent past, much as he must be credited with building up the party from the nadir brought about by misguided Soviet and Chinese policies.[90] The question remains whether his technocrat successors will be able to hold the party together, increase its strength quantitatively (and, more important, qualitatively), make inroads into the labor federations, reclaim the protest and the floating vote, and offer a program that is relevant to Japan at the turn of the century. Can they do this and also change the autocratic structure of the party to one of internal democracy to conform to the Japanese political environment?[91] Fuwa, the physics graduate, seems to have a talent for commenting on Marxist-Leninist-Stalinist classics and engaging in sterile debates. He has yet to come up with a creative look at the present political, economic, and social reality in Japan. His brother Ueda and Shii, another physicist (who is also said to have composed sonatas for the violin and piano),[92] are better known for their organizational talents than for their ideas. Thus, prospects are not good for the JCP to overcome its history and ideology and to be able to present new, relevant, and attractive ideas.

The party is very skillful in propaganda, however, and carefully stresses facts that are favorable and ignores or hides those that are not. For instance, as mentioned earlier, the party trumpets the fact that in prefectural, municipal, and local assemblies JCP members outnumber LDP members, not mentioning the fact that the vast majority of assembly members are conservatives who run as independents. The JCP proclaims with fanfare the increase in the party representation in the HRC from 15 to 26, but it fails to note the fact that two decades earlier there were 41. The leadership announces that 5,000 new members were recruited in recent months, but it does not refer to the time when some 40,000 to 50,000 new members joined the party in the same period of time.

The party also engages in hyperbole and sets unrealistic goals. After the 1996 HRC election, when the party amassed over 7 million votes, the leadership set a new membership goal of 726,000, or 10 percent of the JCP voters, and a new *Akahata* readership goal of 3,630,000, or 50 percent of the number of people who voted for the party[93]—totally unreachable goals given the current numbers and the steady downward trends. How could the party talk of capturing over 100 seats in the lower house and dozens of seats in the upper house "as the first stage toward a democratic government in the early twenty-first century,"[94] when in reality it only had 26 and 23, respectively? During the almost four decades of LDP dominance, the JCP could claim only a small fraction of the votes cast for the government party. But as conservatives split and established other conservative parties, the LDP share of the total vote naturally shrank. The party, however, used this occasion to proclaim that the JCP vote first equaled only 20 percent of the LDP vote in the 1993 HRC election, then went up to 40 percent in the 1996 general election, and finally up to 70 percent of the LDP vote in the Tokyo Municipal Assembly election in 1997.[95] All of this seems to be propaganda to boost party morale.

Public opinion polls underscore the low popularity of the JCP and the erosion of its support in the 1980s and the first half of the 1990s. One such monthly poll showed that support for the JCP fluctuated from just under 1 percent to a little over 3 percent; support for the JSP had varied from 8 to 12 percent, and for the LDP from 22 to 34 percent.[96] Nonetheless, according to an annual poll taken by the *Nihon Keizai Shimbun,* support for the JCP has risen dramatically from under 2 percent in mid-1994 to 5.5 percent in mid-1996.[97] The *Yomiuri Shimbun* poll showed a further increase to 6.5 percent in July 1998, whereas support for the Socialists and the new CGP was 4.2 percent each, and for the Liberal Party at 3.3 percent.[98]

How do Communist Party members feel about other countries? According to a monthly poll conducted for almost forty years for the Prime Minister's Office, surprisingly JCP members show the greatest admiration for Switzerland—that paragon of bourgeois values—58.8 percent (supporters of other parties range from 32 to 45), followed by Britain (44.1 percent), France (38.2 percent), the United States (23.5 percent), Germany (20.6 percent), China (11.8 percent), and South Korea (2.9 percent) (Russia, India, and North Korea are altogether off the screen). Of course, the figure for JCP members' admiration for the United States—23.5 percent—is much less than that of supporters of other parties, which ranges from 48 to 61.5 (LDP members—America's best friends). Understandably, the JCP figure for South Korea was also much lower (by a factor of two or three) than that for other political parties. The low figure for China—after all, it is a Marxist-Leninist-Maoist regime—is significant, especially since the Japanese and Chinese Communist parties have made up their differences after three decades of bitter estrangement, and Chairman Fuwa visited Peking in July 1998.

The second, reverse side of the poll is the question of which countries are held in low esteem (*kirai na kuni*—countries you hate). Japanese Communists seem to hate Communist North Korea the most (76.5 percent, higher than the LDP at 74.2), followed, surprisingly, by Russia (35.3 percent, but which is lower than the figure for members of other parties), the United States and South Korea (14.7 percent each), India (11.8 percent), China (8.8 percent), and Germany (4.2), with the other Western European countries off the screen, presumably not objects of JCP members' displeasure. Interestingly, the Japanese Socialists have expressed an even higher negative figure for the United States than the Communists (16.7 percent), whereas members of the other, conservative parties have much lower anti-American feelings, the LDP being the lowest at 2.4 percent.[99]

Will the JCP remain isolated on the Japanese political scene? What are the prospects for meaningful joint action with other opposition parties?

In the late 1960s and early 1970s, the idea was a "progressive" united front and, as mentioned earlier, Left coalitions were successful for a while in the big cities and metropolitan centers. But by the late 1970s and early 1980s the orthodox Japanese Socialists, the moderate Democratic Socialists and the CGP, had given up on any united front or joint action with the Communists. (See Chapter 6 for the Buddhist organization Soka Gakkai's 1975 agreement with the JCP, and later agreements with the DSP and the JSP.) Moreover, the right-leaning DSP and the CGP moved to the center, and distance from the Communist Party was helpful in promoting a centrist image. These two parties and the JSP eventually joined in an anti-LDP coalition led by breakaway LDP conservatives. In 1994 the JSP surprisingly forged a coalition with the LDP, and a socialist became prime minister. This, however, did not stop but rather accelerated the loss of electoral support for the JSP. In fact, in the 1996 HRC elections the JCP outpolled the JSP (or the Social Democratic Party of Japan), and a united front with a disintegrating party does not make much sense. Moreover, in the last decade of the twentieth century, the center of gravity of the Japanese political world has distinctly moved to the right. During the first four postwar decades, the combined forces of the Japanese Left captured roughly one-third of the electoral vote. At the turn of the century it is one-sixth. The orthodox Socialists lost two-thirds of their votes between 1993 and 1996: 9.7 million votes (15.4 percent) to 3.5 million (6.4 percent).

On the other hand, in the second half of the 1990s, the persistently pragmatic role of the JCP in the National Diet seems to have melted the isolation of the party. In June 1998 the JCP joined the Democratic and Liberal parties in submitting a nonconfidence vote in the lower house, the first such action in sixteen years.[100] A prominent conservative leader, and head of the Liberal Party, Ozawa Ichiro stated that he did not rule out a coalition with the Communists, if the JCP supports his party's positions and policies. The JCP achieved a great measure of legitimacy and credibility when in February 1998 Kato Koichi, secretary-general of the LDP, agreed to an exclusive one-to-one debate with Shii, the director of the JCP Secretariat, the first in Japan's television broadcasting.[101] This played into the hands of party propagandists, who have been describing the present era as "LDP-JCP" confrontation (Jikyo Tairitsu), with the JCP being the only true opposition party and the other parties simply "mimicking" the LDP. In December 1998 Fuwa lectured to chief executive officers and the heads of personnel departments of companies listed on the First Section of the Tokyo Stock Exchange (similar to the Fortune 500). Although the lecture was not particularly revealing—Fuwa said that the JCP aimed at gradual, step-by-step democratic reforms based on popular consensus, to be carried out within the framework of capitalism—the mere fact of such contacts reaffirmed the flexibility of the JCP and its growing political prestige.[102] Of course, flexibility comes at a price. The new conservatism and nationalism, the pretense of being "just like everyone else," must also disillusion and antagonize the more orthodox party members. And one should not forget that when the PCI embarked on a radical reform course, the hard core broke away to establish the Party of Communist Refoundation.[103]

On the international front, at the Twenty-first Congress invitations were sent out for the first time to South Korean and Chinese journalists, and, as mentioned previously, the JCP normalized relations with the CCP in 1998.[104] This also helps the JCP image, as representatives of the CCP are likely to attend the next congress of the Japanese Communist Party. The JCP plays the nationalist card in its insistence that Russia (and before that the Soviet Union) return all of the Kurile Islands seized by the Red Army in August and September 1945. This represents a maximum claim, since all the other parties claim to regain only four northern islands.[105]

Finally, we might speculate that, as in the case of German or Israeli politics, a relatively small party can play the role of kingmaker. It is not entirely out of the question that as the LDP and its main conservative opposition parties become roughly matched, neither party can obtain a majority in the lower house without Communist votes. Is this likely to happen? It seems unlikely in the short and long term but a possibility in the medium term. The LDP should not be counted out in the near term, and the country may not be ready yet for Communists in government (as is the case in Italy and France). At the other extreme of the time frame, the JCP's numerous but aging cohorts should pretty much disappear when the party "celebrates" its centennial in 2022. But in the medium term, say in the next five to ten years, the JCP might get a crack at direct involvement in a governing coalition. This just might be the only such opportunity. And so this chapter may end as it did in the last edition.

When monarchies were falling right and left after the end of World War I, it was said that if there would remain one king, it would be the king of England. Should we paraphrase this statement and say that if there will remain but one nonruling Communist party in the world, it will be the Japanese?

ACKNOWLEDGMENTS

The author wishes to thank Paul Langer of the Rand Corporation for his careful reading of an earlier draft of this chapter and his insightful suggestions. The staff of the Nihon Seiji Keizai Kenkyujo (Japan Politics and

Economics Institute, Director Katsumura Kazuo, Sato Yutaka, and Shimura Mitsuo) have graciously provided their invaluable research materials, as well as regularly exchanged opinions with the author on his numerous trips to Japan. Yakov Zinberg of Kokushikan University and Shigeyuki Iwaki of the National Diet Library gathered and made available very useful research materials on public opinion polls and related subjects. Final responsibility is, of course, the author's alone.

NOTES

1. There are several good English-language books on the Japanese Communist movement: Rodger Swearingen and Paul Langer, *Red Flag in Japan: International Communism in Action, 1919–1951* (Cambridge, MA: Harvard University Press, 1952); George M. Beckmann and Okubo Genji, *The Japanese Communist Party, 1922–1945* (Stanford: Stanford University Press, 1969); Robert A. Scalapino, *The Japanese Communist Movement, 1920–1966* (Berkeley: University of California Press, 1967); and Paul F. Langer, *Communism in Japan: A Case of Political Naturalization* (Stanford: Hoover Institution, 1972). Also very useful are the section on Japan in the annual *Yearbook on International Communist Affairs* (Stanford: Hoover Institution, 1967–1991); the monthly *Koan Joho*, no. 1-489 (1953–1994); handbooks periodically published by the Nihon Seiji Keizai Kenkyujo, especially in the 1983 edition entitled *Nikkyo, Minsei, Shakaishugi Kyokai, Shin Sayoku: Kenkyu, Chosa, Taisaku no Tebiki*, and the 1989 and 1996 editions, *Sayoku Benran: Kenkyu, Chosa, Taisaku no Tebiki* (hereinafter cited as *Sayoku Benran* 1989 and *Sayoku Benran* 1996), as well as the Institute's *Shiryo Tsushin—Research Bulletin* (hereinafter cited as *Shiryo Tsushin*), Kenkyu Tsushin, and Rosei Joho; and Shiso Undo Kenkyujo, *Nihon Kyosan To Jiten—Shiryo Hen* [An introduction to the Japanese Communist party] (Tokyo: Zembosha, 1978). Primary sources for the study of the JCP include its daily, *Akahata*, the monthly, *Zen'ei*, as well as other publications of the party and its affiliated organizations. English-language periodicals include the *Bulletin: Information for Abroad* (hereinafter cited as *Bulletin*), *Dateline Tokyo: for people-to-people exchange*, and *Japan Press Weekly*, put out by the Japan Press Service (JPS). Since 1998, the JPS has provided the *JPS Daily News Service*, also available in an e-mail version (e-mail: jpspress@twics.com). The JCP maintains a Web site that provides many documents, speeches, and other information in both Japanese and English: www.jcp.or.jp/English.

2. *The Russian Impact on Japan: Literature and Social Thought—Two Essays by Nobori Shomu and Akamatsu Katsumaro*, translated and edited and with an introduction by Peter Berton, Paul F. Langer, and George O. Totten (Los Angeles: University of Southern California Press, 1981).

3. "A Documentary History of the Japanese Communist Movement with Special Reference to Its Ties with Moscow and Peking" is under preparation by the author and his colleagues at the University of Southern California.

4. For a description of the prominent Japanese Communists, their role in the Party, the dates of Moscow links, and the fates of individual politicians, see Table 1 in Rodger Swearingen, *The Soviet Union and Postwar Japan: Escalating Challenge and Response* (Stanford: Hoover Institution Press, 1978), pp. 56–57.

5. *Tokuda Kyuichi and Shiga Yoshio, Gokuchu* Juhachi Nen (Tokyo: Jiji Tsushinsha, 1947).

6. A charter member of the British Communist Party, Nosaka spent many years in exile, first in Moscow and then, since 1940, in Yenan with Mao Zedong trying to indoctrinate Japanese prisoners of war. Nosaka Sanzo, *Bomei Juroku Nen* (Tokyo: Jiji Tsushinsha, 1946).

After serving many years as chairman emeritus, Nosaka was stripped of his title and expelled from the party in 1992, when secret documents from the Soviet archives revealed that in the late 1930s he had betrayed a JCP comrade to the Soviet secret police, who was subsequently executed. Nosaka died a year later at the age of 101. *Japan Times Weekly*, November 29, 1993.

7. See Omori Minoru, *Secret History of Postwar Japan*, vol. 4, *Akahata to GHQ* (Tokyo: Kodansha, 1975).

8. For Soviet views, see I. I. Tamginskii, "Iz istorii bor'by Kommunisticheskoi Partii Iaponii protiv pravogo opportunizma, 1945–1950," *Narody Azii i Afriki*, no. 3 (1980): 55–65; and I. I. Kovalenko, "Kommunisticheskaia Partiia Iaponii v bor'be protiv levogo ekstremizma, 1950–1955," *Narody Azii i Afriki*, no. 1 (1981): 40–52.

9. See the biographical sketch of Tokuda by Tomita Nobuo in Uchida Kenzo et al., *Nihon Seiji no Jitsuryokushatachi* [Significant figures in Japanese politics], vol. 3, *Postwar* (Tokyo: Yuhikaku, 1981), pp. 75–112.

10. The "1951 Program" was written by Stalin himself and imposed upon the JCP. See Peter Berton, "The Soviet and Japanese Communist Parties: Policies, Tactics, Negotiating Behavior," *Studies in Comparative Communism* 15 (Autumn 1982): 273–275. See also memoirs of the Soviet interpreter at the meeting, Nikolai Adykhayev, "Stalin's Meetings with Japanese Communists in the Summer of 1951," *Far Eastern Affairs*, no. 3 (1990): 124–134.

11. This section updates some of the material appearing in Peter Berton, "Japan: Euro-Nippo-Communism," in *Eurocommunism Between East and West*, ed. V. Aspaturian et al. (Bloomington: Indiana University Press, 1980), pp. 328–337.

12. For biographical sketches of approximately 160 JCP leaders, see Mizushima Tsuyoshi, *Shokugyo Kakumeika—Nikkyo Kambu 160 Mei no Rirekisho* (Tokyo: Zembosha, 1970).

13. *For a Democratic Government in Japan in the 21st Century: Japanese Communist Party 21st Congress*, September 22–26, 1997 (hereinafter cited as *JCP 21st Congress*) (Tokyo: Japan Press Service, January 1998), p. 171.

14. The polycentrism theory holds that the working class should move to accelerate capitalist reform, and the structural reform theory holds that quantitative reforms could lead to a qualitative change in the power structure.

15. *Asahi Shimbun*, July 7, 1970, p. 2.

16. *Akahata Extra*, June 7, 1976; *Bulletin*, no. 356 (July 1976): 31.

17. *Akahata,* January 8–9, 1976.

18. *Akahata,* April 27–May 8, 1976; *Bulletin,* no. 354, (July 1976): 74.

19. *Akahata,* July 31, 1976; *Bulletin,* no. 359 (October 1976): 17.

20. *Akahata,* October 18, 1977.

21. The alleged "lynching" incident must have hurt Miyamoto substantially at the polls: He ranked forty-first in the fifty-member national constituency of the HC in July 1977.

22. It is interesting to note that Hakamada also accused Nosaka of being a U.S. agent. See Hakamada's articles in the weekly *Shukan Shincho,* January 12 and February 2, 1978. See also Hakamada Satomi, *Kino no Doshi Miyamoto Kenji e* [Miyamoto Kenji: A comrade of yesterday], (Tokyo: Shinchosha, 1978). For official and unofficial JCP statements on the expulsion of Hakamada, and on Miyamoto's interview with a *Yomiuri* reporter, see *Akahata,* January 4 and 6, 1978; *Yomiuri Shimbun,* January 13, 1978; and *Bulletin,* no. 391 (January 1978); and no. 397 (May 1978).

23. In public opinion polls, when party supporters were asked why they supported the JCP, only 0.1 percent (the lowest category) said they did so because of party leadership, compared with almost nine times as many who listed ideology. Jiji Seron *Chosa Tokuho,* no. 863 (March 1, 1999): 4.

24. For a list of all three levels of the party's reading materials, see *Sayoku Benran 1996,* pp. 235–237. See also *Chi wo Chikara ni: Nihon Kyosan To no Kihon Bunken wo Manabu* (Tokyo: Shin Nihon Shuppansha, 1988), pp. 250–256.

25. Iizuka Shigetaro, *Miyamoto Kenji no Nihon Kyosan To* (Tokyo: Ikkosha, 1973), p. 312.

26. For documentation of the Fifteenth Party Congress, see *Akahata,* February 27–March 9, 1980; *Bulletin,* nos. 431–434 (April 1980).

27. *Akahata,* June 11 and July 28-August 5, 1982; *Bulletin,* nos. 488–492 (June–September 1982).

28. "Draft Resolution of the 17th Congress of the Japanese Communist Party," *Akahata,* September 9, 1985; *Bulletin,* no. 552 (October 1985): 2–9.

29. *Akahata,* November 26–28, 1987, and May 25, 1990. For a description and analysis of the JCP's reaction to Gorbachev's perestroika and new political thinking, see Peter Berton, "The Japanese Communist Party's View of Gorbachev's Perestroika," Acta Slavica Iaponica (Slavic Research Center, Hokkaido University, Sapporo, Japan), vol. 7 (1989), pp. 121–144.

30. *The 20th Congress of the Japanese Communist Party: July 19–23, 1994* (Tokyo: Japan Press Service, 1995) (hereinafter cited as *JCP 20th Congress*), p. 91.

31. *JCP 21st Congress,* pp. 42–51.

32. *Bulletin,* no. 552 (October 1985): 9–15.

33. *Akahata,* November 26–28, 1987, and May 25, 1990.

34. *JCP 20th Congress,* pp. 78–80.

35. *JCP 21st Congress,* pp. 7–9, 16.

36. *Bulletin,* no. 552 (October 1985): 23, 27, and 29.

37. *Akahata,* November 26–28, 1987, and May 25, 1990.

38. *JCP 20th Congress,* pp. 100–101.

39. *JCP 21st Congress,* p. 75; on the campaigns to increase JCP membership, see "Saikin ni okeru Nikkyo no Toin Kakudai Katsudo no Jittai," *Shiryo Tsushin* 41, no. 22 (November 30, 1997).

40. *JCP 21st Congress,* pp. 169–176.

41. For an analysis of the JCP leadership and the groupings of the Presidium members, see Haruhiro Fukui, "The Japanese Communist Party," in *The Many Faces of Communism,* ed. M. Kaplan (New York: Free Press, 1978), pp. 287–298.

42. *Nihon Kyosan To Chuo Iinkai no Kozo to Jinji,* pp. 114–115. For brief descriptions of the functions of party agencies, see *Shimpan: Nihon Kyosan To Shokai* (Tokyo: Nihon Kyosan To Chuo Iinkai Shuppan-kyoku, 1988), pp. 92–101.

43. *Asahi Shimbun,* December 20, 1983, p. 8. In subsequent elections, however, other opposition parties began to field more female candidates. In the 1986 election to the HRC , the JCP again elected seven female parliamentarians, but other parties elected nine women. In February 1990 the JCP elected only two female parliamentarians, compared with nine from the JSP and one from the CGP. See *Yomiuri Shimbun,* February 20, 1990, p. 1. This was primarily due to the popularity of Doi Takako, the female chair of the Socialist Party. In fact, the Japanese media called this phenomenon "the Madonna strategy." At the same time, it should be noted that it was the JCP that first championed female representation in the Japanese Diet.

44. Women Diet members represent 1.9 percent of the LDP delegation, 9.6 percent of the CGP representatives, and 19 percent of the Communist contingent. HRC Web site: www.shugiin.go.jp/, November 11, 1998.

45. "LDP-JCP Showdown: Local Politics at Crossroads?" *Dateline Tokyo,* no. 60 (June 1998): 4.

46. "Miyamoto Gicho ga Intai shita Nihon Kyosan To dai 21-kai Taikai no Zenyo," *Shiryo Tsushin* 41, no. 18.19 (October 15, 1997): 29.

47. Martin J. Bull and Philip Daniels, "The 'New Beginning': The Italian Communist Party Under the Leadership of Achille Occhetto," *Journal of Communist Studies* 6, no. 3 (September 1990).

48. Shiso Undo Kenkyujo, compiler, *1981—nemban Nihon Kyosan Tokei Dantai Yoran* (Tokyo: Zembosha, 1981), Preface, pp. 2–3.

49. *Shukan Asahi,* May 30, 1975, cited in the *Yearbook on International Communist Affairs* (1976), p. 304. The circulations of *L'Unita* and *L'Humanite* were about 1 million and 0.5 million, respectively.

50. Mizushima Tsuyoshi, *Kore ga Kyosan To* (Tokyo: Zembosha, 1977), pp. 94–105. See descriptions of party publications in *Shimpan: Nihon Kyosan To Shokai,* pp. 145–160. For a complete list of party-sponsored publications, see the table in Peter A. Berton, "Japanese Eurocommunists: Running in Place," *Problems of Communism* 35, no. 4 (July-August 1986): 10; and *Sayoku Benran 1996,* pp. 201–202.

51. Many books and journals are published under the imprint of Shin Nihon Shuppansha, a party affiliate organization.

52. J. P. Napier, *A Survey of the Japan Communist Party* (Tokyo: Nippon Times, 1952), p. 62.

53. Public Security Investigation Agency, *The Recent Aspects of the Japan Communist Party* (Tokyo, Home Affairs Ministry, 1959), pp. 10–11; and later editions in English and Japanese.

54. At the rate of 115 yen to the dollar in early 1999.

55. See also the official JCP discussion of its finances in *Shimpan: Nihon Kyosan To Shokai,* pp. 163–173. Reported party dues represent only 15 percent of the total dues allocated to the party headquarters. Of the remainder, 25 percent goes to the prefectural committee, 40 percent to the district committee, and 20 percent to the primary party unit.

56. See Mizushima Tsuyoshi, *Watakushi no Yoyogi Tokuhain: Nihon Kyosan To no Shindan* (Tokyo: Zembosha, 1981), pp. 189–191; see also the note on party election financing in *Zembo Tokubetsu Tsushin,* no. 788 (November 20, 1982): 1–3.

57. *Sayoku Benran 1996,* p. 241.

58. The LDP is, of course, structured in such a way that finances of the various factions and support groups need not be reported by central party headquarters.

59. *Asahi Shimbun,* September 11, 1998, p. 14.

60. Communist legislators even refuse to accept souvenirs that fellow Diet members customarily bring back from their travels in foreign countries and distribute to their neighbors in the Diet office buildings.

61. *Sayoku Benran 1996,* p. 207.

62. For a discussion of JCP policies and activities in the Kyoto area, see Ellis S. Krauss, "The Urban Strategy and Policy of the Japan Communist Party: Kyoto," *Studies in Comparative Communism* 12 (Winter 1979): 322–350. For a description of party activities in both urban and rural settings, see George O. Totten, "The People's Parliamentary Path of the Japanese Communist Party, Part I: Agrarian Policies," *Pacific Affairs* 46 (Summer 1973): 193–217, and "Part II: Local Level Tactics," *Pacific Affairs* 46 (Fall 1973): 384–406.

63. In the 1990 elections, the JCP lost 11 seats to the Socialists, 2 to the LDP, and 1 to the DSP. *Yomiuri Shimbun* (February 20, 1990), p. 1. The 1996 vote was compared to the proportional representation vote in the 1995 HC election. *Akahata,* October 22, 1996.

64. Taketsugu Tsurutani, *Political Change in Japan: Response to Postindustrial Challenge* (New York: Longman, 1980), pp. 143–144.

65. Hong N. Kim, "Deradicalization of the Japanese Communist Party Under Kenji Miyamoto," *World Politics* 28 (January 1976): 273–299, especially p. 299, Table V, entitled "Voting Records of JCP Diet Members, 1967–1971."

66. For a firsthand look at Shiojiri and its Communist mayor and his policies, see George O. Totten, "Progressive Administration in a Rural Japanese City: The Case of the First Communist Mayor, Takasuna of Shiojiri, Nagano, 1967–1971," in *Japan and Korea 2,* Proceedings of the 30th International Congress of Human Sciences in Asia and North Africa, ed. Graciela de la Lama (Mexico City: El Colegio de Mexico, 1982), pp. 141–181.

67. *Japan Times,* April 10, 1995.

While the Osaka governor "Knock" (Nokku) Yokoyama (real name Yamada Isamu) is running for reelection, the Tokyo "talent" governor comedian/writer

Aoshima is bowing out. The JCP is putting up its own candidate, an obscure former junior high school teacher, and as a result is not taking sides in the many-cornered race. The contest involves the former undersecretary of the United Nations as the official candidate of the LDP, a grandson of a former prime minister from the Democratic Party (endorsed by the outgoing "talent" governor), an LDP member who intends on running in spite of his party's objections, a novelist/politician, and a political commentator, among nineteen candidates.

68. *Sayoku Benran 1996*, p. 227. As of September 5, 1999, the total number of JCP local assembly members was 4,421. "What Is the JCP?" JCP web site: www.jcp.or.jp/English, December 14, 1999.

69. "Sen kyuhyaku kyujuhachi-kyujukyu nen: Nihon Kyosan To Katsudo no Kaiko to Tembo," *Kenkyu Tsushin* 52, no. 1 (January 15, 1999): 11.

70. "LDP-JCP Showdown: Local Politics at Crossroads?" *Dateline Tokyo*, no. 60 (June 1998): 4.

71. See note 69, p. 10.

72. *Yomiuri Shimbun*, July 8, 1985, evening edition, p. 1.

73. *Asahi Shimbun*, July 4, 1989, evening edition, p. 1.

74. See note 69.

75. *JCP 21st Congress*, p. 118.

76. *Yomiuri Shimbun*, October 22, 1996, Shoji Niihara, "JCP's Advance in the General Election and Its Historic Significance—Japanese People Have New Political Clout," *Dateline Tokyo*, no. 42 (November 1996).

77. *Japan Times*, July 14, 1997.

On the other hand, in the various assemblies in the Tokyo Metropolis there are 523 LDP members, 317 CGP members, and 282 Communists.

78. "Dai juhachi kai Saninsen ni tsuite," *Kenkyu Tsushin* 51, no. 14 (July 30, 1998); "On the Results of the House of Councillors Election—JCP Standing Presidium," JCP Web site, home page (English), November 27, 1998. See also *Zen'ei*, September 1998 issue.

79. *JCP 20th Congress*, pp. 101–102; *JCP 21st Congress*, p. 75.

80. Mizushima Tsuyoshi, "Choraku ichijirushii Minsei Domei," *Sekai Nippo* (November 16, 1990); "Minseido Dai Nijurokkai Zenkoku Taikai Tokushu," *Shiryo Tsushin* 42, no. 24 (December 30, 1998): 3.

81. On the other hand, books appear in Japan that expose the fallacies of socialism and communism. See, for example, Tanizawa Eiichi, *"Uso Bakkari" de Shichiju-nen* [Seventy Years of "Only Lies"] (Tokyo: Kodansha, 1994).

82. *Japan Times* editorial, *Japan Times Weekly International Edition*, July 21–27, 1997, p. 20.

83. In a traditional interview at the beginning of a new year, Miyamoto said that the party has assisted not only in solving tax problems, installment-sale fraud, and housing loan swindles but also in such personal matters as divorce and "finding a wife." *Akahata*, January 8, 1977; *Bulletin*, no. 367 (April 1977): 15.

84. Zbigniew Brzezinski had already pronounced the demise of communism a decade ago. See his latest book, *The Grand Failure: The Birth and Death of Communism in the Twentieth Century* (New York: Scribner, 1989).

85. Tadatoshi Tashiro, "The Japanese Communist Party's Revolutionary Course and the 'Manifesto of the Communist Party,'" JCP Web site: www.jcp. or.jp/ English, November 27, 1998, p. 7.

86. *JCP 20th Congress*, p. 156.

87. Joan Barth Urban, ed., *Moscow and the Global Left in the Gorbachev Era* (Ithaca: Cornell University Press, 1992).

88. Berton, "The Japanese Communist Party's View of Gorbachev's Perestroika," pp. 121–144.

89. "Saikin ni okeru Furansu Kyosan To no Doko to Mondai Ten," *Koan Joho*, no. 486 (March 1994): 110–114; *JCP 20th Congress*, pp. 234–238; *JCP 21st Congress*, pp. 177–179.

90. Miyamoto also rewrote JCP history to maximize his role. The official history of the party's first seventy years, published by the Central Committee in 1994, devoted just thirty-five pages to the first thirty-five years, 1922–1957 (or one page per year), and ninety-seven pages to the second thirty-five years, 1958–1992, under Miyamoto's rule (or almost three pages per year). *Nihon Kyosan To no Shichiju-nen* (Tokyo: Nihon Kyosan To Chuo Iinkai Shuppan-kyoku, 1994). One wonders what the seventy-five- or eighty-year party history will look like.

91. In a study of belief systems of leaders of the JCP and the Socialist Association, which was the JSP's left wing, the Communists as a group were shown to be more totalitarian and authoritarian. See Shigeko N. Fukai, "Beliefs and Attitudes of the Japanese Left During the Early 1970s," *Asian Survey* 20, 12 (December 1980): 1185–1209.

92. Sheryl WuDunn, "Free of Marx Communists' Stock Is Soaring in Japan," *New York Times*, October 19, 1996.

93. *JCP 21st Congress*, p. 76.

94. Minoru Seya, "Basic Change in Japan's Politics Called For," *Dateline Tokyo*, no. 57 (March 1998): 4.

95. "LDP-JCP Showdown: Local Politics at Crossroads?" *Dateline Tokyo*, no. 60 (June 1998): 4.

96. Calculated from the *Jiji Seron Chosa Tokuho* (Tokyo: Jiji Tsushinsha, 1975–1984).

97. *Nikkei Weekly*, July 15, 1996, p. 4.

98. *Daily Yomiuri*, July 24, 1998, p. 1.

99. *Jiji Seron Chosa Tokuho*, no. 863 (March 1, 1999): tables, pp. 29, 32.

100. "1998-nen 6-gatsu Nikkyo oyobi Sayoku Dantai no Shuyo Doko," *Shiryo Tsushin* 42, no. 13 (July 14, 1998): 6–7. It is also interesting to note that in a public opinion poll taken in August 1998 in response to the question "Which party would you like to win in the next general election?" only 41 percent of JCP members listed their own party, and a surprising 37 percent opted for the Democratic Party. Takafumi Yoshida, "Honsha Seron Chosa Shoho (Minshuto Shiji-ritsu): Seiji ni kanshin takai mutohaso ga ugoku," *Asahi Soken Ripooto*, no. 134 (October 1998): 112–137. (Tokyo: Asahi Shimbun Sogo Kenkyu Senta).

101. Seya, "Basic Change in Japan's Politics Called For," p. 3.

102. Yoshimichi Hironaka, "JCP's Star Is Ascendant, But Can It Keep Support?" *Daily Yomiuri, Daily Yomiuri* On-line News, February 1999.

103. It is this orthodox Italian Communist Party that dispatched a member of its Secretariat to the 21st JCP Congress.

104. Peter Berton, "The Japanese and Chinese Communist Parties: The End of Three Decades of Discord" (manuscript to be submitted for publication).

105. Berton, "Japanese Eurocommunists: Running in Place," pp. 1–30; Yakov Zinberg, "The Moscow Declaration, the Year 2000 and Russo-Japanese Deadlock over the 'Four Islands' Dispute," *Boundary and Security Bulletin* 6, no. 4 (Winter 1998–1999): 86–95. For the latest JCP statements, see Satoshi Morishita, "The Japan-Russia Territorial Issue: A Call for Meaningful Negotiations," *Dateline Tokyo*, no. 55 (January 1998): 1–4; and "JCP Chair Fuwa Comments on Japan-Russia Summit and Territorial Question," JCP Web site: www.jcp.or.jp/English, November 27, 1998.

In early 1999, some overtures were being made to Gennady Zyuganov, the leader of the Russian Communist Party.

nine

The Future of the Second Japanese Party System

Ronald J. Hrebenar

The Second Party System, which began in 1993 with the splits in the Liberal Democratic Party (LDP), the destruction of the Japan Socialist Party (JSP), and the subsequent establishment of a number of new political parties, represents a fundamental break with the politics of the First Party System (1955–1993). During the First Party System, party politics evolved from what was essentially a two-party system in 1955 to one characterized by fragmentation, with six parties on the national level. This situation has been called the *tatoka* (proliferation in minor parties) era by the Japanese. The opposition parties operated permanently out of power on the national level, and because of their fragmentation, they were unable to discover a political strategy that could be used to gain political power. It was a party system frozen in place—a permanent ruling party and a permanent opposition. The Japanese voters seeking to hold on to the prosperity of the postwar Japanese economic boom had nowhere to go except the LDP. The opposition, dominated by the JSP, could not be trusted to govern Japan, and the LDP, despite its corruption and arrogance, could not be seriously punished at the polls (Table 9.1).

THE CHARACTERISTICS OF THE SECOND PARTY SYSTEM

The Second Party System is in its early stages of development, and thus it is difficult to be certain about its enduring characteristics. As always, prediction by political scientists about the future course or direction of party and electoral politics is extremely difficult. Bearing these dangers in mind, let us review some of the early characteristics of the Second Party System and make some qualified predictions about where this system may be heading in the first decade of the new century.

TABLE 9.1   Comparing the Key Elements of the Japanese First and Second
             Party Systems

The First Party System: 1955–1993

One-party domination: LDP rules national level for entire period without need
    to resort to coalition governments.
Fragmented six-party system operates to keep LDP in power. Original two-party
    system (LDP + JSP) expands with vigorous JCP, splinters DSP and SDP, new
    Komeito plus NLC in 1976–1986 period.
Ideological cleavage is Conservative-Progressive centering around LDP and
    JSP/JCP.
Medium-sized constituency system operated to keep opposition fragmented,
    thus enhancing LDP rule. Operated as a de facto PR system.
Low levels of competition for HR/HC elections as well as prefectural governor-
    ships. Almost all governors are joint candidates of multiple parties. Many of
    the 130 HR districts had competition not between the LDP and opposition
    parties but among LDP candidates representing various factions within the
    party.
No major voting issue dominated the era. The old issue cleavages were on the
    Constitution and U.S.-Japan Security Treaty, but no new issue emerges to
    force Japanese voters to fundamentally rethink their political attitudes and
    behaviors.
Inept opposition fails to provide any serious challenge to LDP rule. Many voters
    feared voting for the JSP or JCP because such votes could destroy the politi-
    cal/economic system.
Nearly constant economic growth keeps voters happy with LDP rule.
Both LDP and JSP dominated by internal party factions. Intraparty conflict was
    more important than interparty competition.

The Second Party System: 1993–

Non-LDP governments for the first time since the 1940s. Prime ministers from
    New Japan Party, Shinseito, and SDPJ (Hosokawa, Hata, and Murayama) in
    1993–1996.
Divided party control in the Diet with non-LDP parties in control of the HC for
    the entire period of the Second Party System. LDP regains majority in HR in
    1997 due to defections from other parties.
Style of negotiation and compromise characterizes politics on national level
    between LDP and other parties.
Recession reduces voter satisfaction with LDP rule. Japan has been in period of
    economic decline since 1990.
New electoral system of single-seat districts and proportional representation
    seats does not produce a two-party system but tends to reduce number of
    significant parties to point where opposition is not so fragmented it cannot
    function as real balance to LDP. Second Party System parties are LDP,
    Democratic Party, Liberal Party, Communist Party, Komeito, and the dying
    SDPJ—a six-party system.

TABLE 9.1 (Continued)

Conservative-conservative conflict characterizes the Second Party System. The old Conservative-progressive split has disappeared with the Democratic Party's core being former members of the LDP and moderates from the DSP. The renewed Komeito, decaying SDPJ, and JCP form the largely isolated left wing of the opposition.

Reapportionment happens when new electoral system adopted in 1994 gives greater representation to urban and suburban areas and new support for opposition parties.

Still no new voting issues other than continuing concern about reform and economic recovery.

Voting turnout and voter intensity remain low. No real voting revolution has occurred except that the electorate now feels it can vote for non-LDP parties without destroying the nation.

Party factions have been greatly reduced in the SDPJ and are less important in the LDP.

Perhaps the most important new pattern of the early Second Party System was the change in government style from one-party governments of the LDP to a series of coalition governments. The first two of these coalition governments were led by former LDP politicians who emerged as heads of new conservative political parties, Hosokawa and Hata. The next two cabinets were led by a Socialist prime minister (Murayama), included a splinter party from the LDP (Sakigake), and had the LDP as the behind-the-scenes political string puller. By the October 1996 House of Representative (HR) elections (the last one covered in this book), the LDP felt confident enough to come to the front of the government and form two all-LDP cabinets under Prime Ministers Hashimoto and Obuchi. Even these two LDP cabinets had to rely on a noncabinet coalition of Social Democratic Party of Japan (SDPJ) and Sakigake votes in the HR for much of their time in office. The LDP regained its HR majority in late 1997 after opposition party defectors returned to the LDP. Finally, in early 1999, after another weak showing by the LDP in the 1998 HC (HC) elections, Obuchi moved to invite the Ozawa-led Liberal Party to join the cabinet in an effort to manage the HC and offer a path for the Ozawa group to return to the LDP.

Coalition governments seem to have become the norm in the early Second Party System. Of the eight cabinets organized since the end of the LDP monopoly of power in May 1993, seven have been coalition governments of one type or another. Two have been minority coalition governments (Hata and Hashimoto's second cabinet following the 1996 HR elections); four have been multiparty majority coalition governments (Hosokawa, both Murayama cabinets, and Hashimoto's first cabinet); and Obuchi's second cabinet featured a minor (and unnecessary) coalition with the Liberals. Only in Obuchi's first cabinet, from July 1998 to January 1999, did one party (LDP) have a majority in the HR and no coalition in the cabinet.

One outcome of all these coalition cabinets is a significant increase in governing experience among the senior members of nearly every party in the system, except the JCP. Each party has tasted power and enjoyed the status and prestige of having been part of the government. They tasted the power; they liked the taste; and they want to taste it again. The opposition parties in the post-1994 system are much more responsible than the First Party System's opposition of the JSP, Komeito, Democratic Socialist Party (DSP), Social Democratic Federation (SDF), and Japan Communist Party (JCP). None of that latter group had any experience in being in the government and having to come up with realistic policies for real problems. The new opposition has, and the party system should be more responsible because of it. Now everyone wants to be in the cabinet (except the JCP), and deals and compromises, which are the essence of politics, can be negotiated.

Another very significant change associated with the Second Party System has been the rise of the conservative alternative to the LDP. The largest opposition party to the LDP during the First Party System was the JSP. It usually had over 100 HR members and dominated the politics of the opposition from the end of World War II until 1993. The Second Party System has seen the elimination of Socialist power and political influence. All the old Socialist parties (DSP and SDF) have disappeared or, in the case of the JSP/SDPJ, have declined so far as to be functionally extinct. The old Right-Left axis of the post-1945 era has been replaced with a Right-Right or Right-center axis, and Japanese politics will never be the same. The leaders of the Democratic and Liberal Parties are the ex-LDP politicians who bolted for the opportunity to seek political power outside the sometimes rigid structures of the LDP. Many of them, such as Ozawa and his supporters, are as conservative, or maybe more so, as those who stayed in the LDP. If the complaint against the parties of the First Party System was that there was very little difference in the policy alternatives of the various parties, then that complaint may be more true of the new parties in the Second Party System.

With so little difference among the major parties of the new system, the new style of politics may be more personality or image oriented than ever before in modern Japanese political history. The "Kan Boom" in 1998 and the growth in popularity of his new Democratic Party provide evidence to support the subtle shift of focus from parties and issues to the "politics of personality and image." Another change in the style of Japanese election campaigns, noted in Chapter 2, is the somewhat greater use of mass media ads and television. Such a shift may also facilitate a more image-conscious style of politics. Of course, if this shift accelerates, one of the great ironies would be the fact that the LDP in its most recent presidential selection process, held in July 1998, elected one of the least charismatic party leaders in its history, Obuchi Keizo. When Obuchi was described as "a piece of cold pizza," he responded, "What's wrong with that?"

THE FUTURE OF JAPANESE PARTY POLITICS

There are a number of visions regarding the future of Japanese politics. Several astute political observers see the continuation of the current system of LDP domination with a weak conservative collection of opposition parties plus the JCP. Others look at the post-1993 party system as providing the central tendency to eventually produce a system with a central characteristic of two large political parties. Initially, it appeared that one of those parties would be the Ozawa-led New Frontier Party (Shinshinto), but that group collapsed, and currently the Kan Naoto–led Democratic Party (Minshuto) seems to be the possible core of that second major party. Survival is the key for these new consolidated opposition parties such as the Democratic Party. It survived its first HR election, which was held shortly after its establishment. As of this writing, it has not had to face an HR election as the largest opposition party. Shinshinto never even reached that point before it crashed.

Perhaps more interesting a vision is that provided by T. J. Pemple in recent years. Pemple suggests the Japanese party system is largely driven by the continuing problems of the Japanese economy as it has been battered by international pressures in recent years. Pemple argues that there has emerged in Japan a division between the winners and losers in the economic wars. The winners are the internationally competitive sectors, firms, workers, and consumers arrayed against those economic and bureaucratic organizations that need continuing protection and subsidies. He suggests that barring another split in the LDP or the merger of the anti-LDP forces into a strong (and lasting) formidable opponent, "bipolar contests are highly unlikely." More likely, suggests Pemple, is "the Italianization of Japan," in which Japan's economy and politics come to resemble those of Italy during the 1970s and 1980s. Characteristic of this scenario are highly fragmented and "inchoate" political parties, blurring policy divisions and working with bureaucrats to protect well-organized and inefficient constituencies such as farmers, noncompetitive businesses, and organized crime. Pemple uses the phrase "crony capitalism," from the collapsed East and Southeast Asian banking system, to describe the nature of Japan's protected economic and political system under this interpretation. His greatest worry regarding this future scenario is that it may produce a more dangerous style of politics than Japan currently experiences. It could produce a type of protest politics similar to the Le Pen movement in France, the Christian Right in the United States, the student movement in Japan in the 1960s, and Japan's rightist movement prior to World War II.

Pemple seems to despair that real reform may not occur in Japan in the near future. He sees the business world as being the crucial element to force real reform, as it did in 1955 to force the two conservative parties into the LDP. The business world is still fairly comfortable with the existing system. Most large Japanese companies still do "pretty well" despite a decade of economic stagnation. Pemple suggests that until Japan's internationalist businesses "put their money behind a group of internationalist politicians, the prospects for economic choice in Japan look quite bleak."[1] Coupled with that failure to make hard, often painful economic choices may be the continued stagnation of the political system and a party system marked by constant instability, an absence of policy alternatives and issues, and a lack of political vision and strong political leadership. These may be the characteristics of the Second Party System for the foreseeable future.

THE DEALIGNMENT FUTURE?

Another possibility is a continuing drift in the core essence of the Second Party System. This scenario suggests more of a dealignment of the Japanese party than a realignment. It would mean that the rapid establishment and subsequent collapse of one new party after another during the years that followed 1993 actually argue that the Japanese electorate is not looking for a new party or party system but is rejecting the choices being offered to them by Japan's political elite.

The concept of dealignment has been a frequent political science description of the American party system during the past forty years, as more and more American voters reject the Republican and Democratic Parties and claim to be independents.[2] The American party system has drifted on for more than sixty-five years, after the last realigning election in 1932. Given the fact that, since 1800, the average time from one realigning election to another has been thirty-two to thirty-six years, it seems clear that the American party system has largely dealigned.

The evidence that indicates the Japanese system may have dealigned can be found in several sites. First, the major parties have suffered significant declines in popular support as measured by the nearly monthly polls conducted by Japan's most important national newspapers. Iwami has reported the rise in the number of "no party" supporters in Japan in the 1990s. Between 1955 and 1992, the LDP and the JSP combined had the support of over 50 percent of the Japanese public in poll after poll conducted by the *Mainichi Shimbun*. However, in an October 1992 *Mainichi* poll, the LDP received only 29 percent support and the JSP only 11 percent, for a combined total of 40 percent. By April 1995 the LDP had dropped to only 20 percent support and the JSP (SDPJ) to 5 percent. Fifty-five percent of the respondents declared support for no political party. This is twice the level of no-party supporters compared with just four years earlier. In less than five years, the number of independents in the Japanese political system had doubled. Iwami points out that there have been four booms in the number of independents since the 1970s: the Kono boom for the NLC in the late 1970s; the Doi boom at the end of the 1980s for the JSP leader who led the opposition parties in defeating the LDP in the 1989 HC elections; the Hosokawa boom in 1992–1993, which lifted him to the prime ministership; and the Yokoyama/Aoshima boom in the 1995 Osaka and Tokyo governorship elections, where two "entertainers-independents" managed to defeat all the party candidates to win the leadership posts in Japan's two most populated city prefectures. It remains to be seen if the Kan Naoto "boomlet," which fueled the Democratic Party in 1998, will be sufficient to enable the party to survive the next general elections for the HRC.[3]

By late 1995 it seemed as though the system was dealigning. Further evidence to support this analysis came when the Shinshinto failed to capture the expected support it needed to survive. What was to be the party that would attract public support and make the Japanese system a real two-party system quietly disappeared in early 1998 after fighting only a single HR election. Its successor as the new alternative opposition party was the Democratic Party led by Kan Naoto, and for a time in early 1998 it seemed to be sufficiently popular to offer the prospect of reversing the public's unwillingness to support any of the non-LDP parties. The *Kyodo News* poll in mid-1998 had the Democratic Party at nearly 23 percent support level and the LDP at 26 percent. However, within a couple of months (and a sex scandal involving the DP leader Kan), the DP could claim the support of only 16.8 percent of the public, and the LDP had risen to 32.5 percent. It is interesting to note that the totals for these two parties have only again risen to nearly 50 percent combined total.[4] In terms of the two biggest parties' support, the Second Party System has replicated the old LDP-JSP pattern of the 1955–1993 era.

By late 1998 the Japanese economic crisis had become so serious that the Japanese public seemed to be returning to the LDP in hope that the old party of prosperity might be able to find the luck or policies capable of leading Japan out of its financial disaster. At least, the public's hope for a savior in the ranks of the opposition parties, and especially the DP, seems to have been reduced. Perhaps a realignment has been averted and the old pattern of a strong LDP and a quite weak alternative party— incapable of replacing the LDP—is reemerging and is largely sustained by an electorate unwilling to strongly commit to supporting any political party. This world of largely independent voters shifting back and forth among the various parties would be a classic version of a dealigned political system. Elections would have no clear-cut winners, and even the losers would be able to hold on and survive. The voters in such a system would give the LDP victories of a qualified nature in one set of elections and follow that up with taking away victory in the next elections and so on. Short-term forces would be the determining factors impacting the outcome of these elections. One election may be decided by sexual scandals; the next by financial scandals; and still another by a particularly unpopular policy such as raising the consumption tax. In short, elections would not be decided by parties and their loyal corps of followers but by the seasonal breezes that excite the media's and the public's attention for a short time.

A somewhat different perspective on contemporary Japanese voting behavior has generated much comment among Japanese scholars. Kabashima Ikuo, a professor at Tokyo University, has developed the concept of the "buffer voter" to explain some of the unusual election outcomes in the last decade.[5] Kabashima suggests that there is a group of voters who have party identities, but who frequently vote for candidates from other parties for strategic political reasons. These were the swing voters who tipped the balance against the LDP in the 1998 HC elections. These voters seek a more competitive political system and dislike the seemingly permanent rule of the LDP; consequently, they vote for opposition conservative parties in an effort to reduce the LDP's power and make politics a more even battle in the Diet.

Kabashima acknowledged that the LDP is still the biggest, most powerful party in Japan, and that it will tend to win most elections unless the divided opposition parties are able to recruit "great candidates" and find a way to cooperate. Kabashima also has forwarded the American concept of "retrospective voting" for explaining recent electoral patterns. Japanese voters in the era of no growth have decided to punish the LDP for the government's economic failures since the late 1980s. At the same time, the public opinion polls indicate very little confidence in any of the opposition parties. In fact, the comparative international polls indicate the Japanese electorate is much more cynical than those found in the United States and England. As the *Washington Post* summarized the

Harris polls: "The Japanese positively loath their elected leaders" and think their politicians are crooks.[6]

Be that as it may, we cannot predict the future with any certainty. The Second Party System is still in its infant years, and perhaps another decade may be required to see the long-term patterns that will characterize the system as it matures. One thing is certain: Few, if any, of us would have predicted the political party events of the past five years. Some of them, such as the LDP-SDPJ-Sakigake coalition governments, were simply too incredible for anyone to anticipate. Other such political surprises will happen in the coming years. We invite the reader to follow these twists and turns in Japanese party politics, and to sit back and enjoy the new politics and old patterns of Japanese politics.

One additional observation should be made. Japanese politics in the First Party System was often boring. It was highly predictable, with the LDP in complete control and the opposition parties in disarray. Very few Japanese political scientists devoted themselves to the study of Japanese politics—partly in reaction to its boring character. Over the past five years, Japanese politics has become very unpredictable and exciting, with new events seeming to happen all the time. As we began this book with an old Chinese saying, "May you live in interesting times," we end it the same way. These are more interesting times.

NOTES

1. T. J. Pemple, Toward the Italianization of Japan," *Japan Times,* July 22, 1998.

2. For an up-to-date discussion of the issue of realignment in the United States, see Ronald J. Hrebenar, Matthew Burbank, and Robert C. Benedict's *Parties, Interest Groups and Campaigns* (Boulder: Westview Press, 1999).

3. Iwami Takao, "Behind the Growth of the 'No Party' Camp," ("Aoshima-Yokoyama bumu no haikai") *Japan Echo,* Autumn 1995, pp. 10–14. Translated from *Chuo Koron,* June 1995, pp. 106–110.

4. *New York Times,* December 14, 1998.

5. Kabashima Ikuo, "98 nen San'in sen: Jimin Taihai no kozu," *Chuo Koron* (September 1998), pp. 34–46. An abridged version of this important article is found in the English-language journal *Japan Echo* no. 28 (October 1998): 6–8. Kabashima Ikuo is also the author of *Gendai Nihonjin no Ideoroji* [The ideology of the modern Japanese] and *Seiken kotai to yukensha no taido hen'yo* [Change of Governments and the Shift in Voters' Attitudes].

6. Richard Morin, "The Most Cynical Voters: We May Distrust Our Leaders, but the Japanese Hold Their Politicians in Even Greater Disdain," *Washington Post National Weekly* edition, January 25 1999, p. 34.

Appendixes

FIGURE A.1 Evolution of the Japanese pary system: Conservatives, 1945–1990

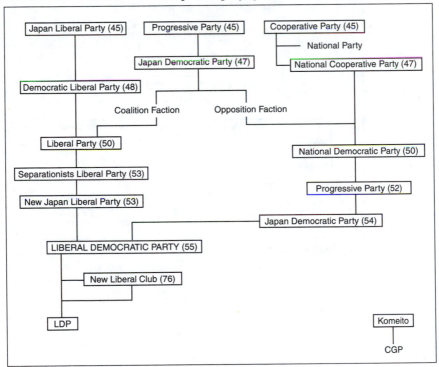

NOTE: Parentheses indicate year formed.
SOURCE: Compiled by authors.

FIGURE A.2   Evolution of the Japanese party system: Leftists, 1945–1990

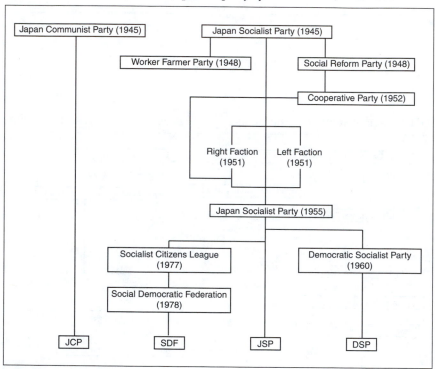

SOURCE: Compiled by authors.

FIGURE A.3   Major new parties of the Second Party System, 1992–1999

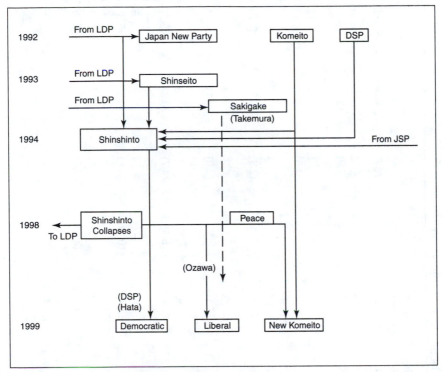

NOTE: LDP, JCP, and JSP continue on during this period. LDP suffers major defections, as does the Sakigake.

TABLE A.1 House of Representatives First Party System Election Results, 1955–1990

Election	Liberal Party	Democratic Party	Right-wing Socialist Party	Left-wing Socialist Party	Labor Peasant Party		JCP	Other	Independent	Total
Feb. 27, 1955	112 (26.6)	185 (36.5)	67 (13.8)	89 (15.3)	4 (0.9)		2 (1.9)	2 (1.3)	6 (3.3)	467 (100)
May 22, 1958	LDP 287 (57.8)		JSP 166 (32.9)				1 (2.5)	1 (0.7)	12 (5.9)	467 (100)
Nov. 20, 1960	296 (57.5)		145 (27.5)		DSP 17 (8.7)		3 (2.9)	1 (0.3)	5 (2.8)	467 (100)
Nov. 21, 1963	283 (54.6)		144 (29.0)		23 (7.3)		5 (4.0)	0 (0.1)	12 (4.7)	467 (100)
Jan. 29, 1967	277 (48.8)		140 (27.8)		30 (7.4)	25 (5.3)	Komeito 5 (4.7)	0 (0.2)	9 (5.5)	486 (100)
Dec. 27, 1969	288 (47.6)		90 (21.4)		31 (7.7)	47 (10.9)	14 (6.8)	0 (0.1)	16 (5.3)	486 (100)
Dec. 10, 1972	271 (46.8)		118 (21.9)		19 (6.9)	29 (8.4)	38 (10.4)	2 (0.2)	14 (5.0)	491 (100)

		NLC		SDF						
Dec. 5, 1976	249 (41.7)	17 (4.1)	123 (20.6)		29 (6.2)	55 (10.9)	17 (10.3)	0 (0.0)	21 (5.7)	511 (100)
Oct. 7, 1979	248 (44.5)	4 (3.0)	107 (19.7)	2 (0.6)	35 (6.7)	57 (9.7)	39 (10.4)	0 (0.1)	19 (4.8)	511 (100)
June 22, 1980	284 (47.9)	12 (3.0)	107 (19.3)	3 (0.7)	32 (6.6)	33 (9.0)	29 (9.8)	0 (0.2)	11 (3.5)	511 (100)
Dec. 12, 1983	250 (45.7)	8 (2.3)	112 (19.5)	3 (.6)	38 (7.2)	58 (10.1)	26 (9.3)	0 (0.1)	16 (4.8)	511 (100)
July 6, 1986	300 (49.4)	6 (1.8)	85 (17.2)	4 (.8)	26 (8.8)	56 (9.4)	26 (6.4)	0 (0.2)	9 (5.8)	512 (100)
Feb. 18, 1990	275 (46.1)		136 (24.4)	4 (0.8)	14 (4.8)	45 (8.0)	16 (8.0)	1 (0.4)	21 (7.3)	512 (100)

NOTE: Figures in parentheses represent the percentages of votes.

SOURCE: Ministry of Home Affairs.

TABLE A.2   1990 House of Representatives Election Results,
February 18, 1990

Party	Seats	Incumbents	Former	New	Seat Totals Prior to Election	Seat Totals after Independents Absorbed
LDP	275	228	4	43	295	285
JSP	136	64	16	56	83	139
CGP	45	34	0	11	54	46
DSP	14	8	3	3	25	16
JCP	16	10	2	4	26	14
SDF	4	4	0	0	4	4
Minor	1	1	0	0	1	1
Independent	21	4	1	16	7	7
Conservative	15	2	1	12	—	—
Leftist	5	1	0	4	—	—
Other	1	1	0	0	—	—

SOURCE: *Yomiuri Shimbun,* February 19, 1990.

TABLE A.3   1993 House of Representatives Election Results, Jul, 1993

Party	Seats	Incumbents	Former	New	Seat totals Prior to Election
LDP	223	179	18	26	227
JSP	70	64	1	5	134
CGP	51	24	1	26	45
New Japan	35	0	0	35	0
Renewal	55	34	2	19	36
DSP	15	10	4	1	13
JCP	15	8	4	3	16
Sakigake	13	9	0	4	10
SDF	4	4	0	0	4
Minor	0	0	0	0	2
Independent	30	11	4	15	15
Conservative	10	5	2	3	8
Leftist	20	6	2	12	7

SOURCE: *Asahi Shimbun,* July 19, 1993.

TABLE A.4   1996 House of Representatives Election Results, October 20, 1996

Party	Seats	Single Seat	PR	Seat Totals Prior to Election
LDP	239	169	70	211
NFP	156	96	60	160
DP	52	17	35	35
JCP	26	2	24	15
JSP	15	4	11	30
Sakigake	2	2	0	9
Minor	1	1	0	0
Independent	9	9	0	0
Totals	500	300	200	

SOURCE: *Yomiuri Shimbun,* October 22, 1996.

TABLE A.5   Public Opinion Support for Political Parties in the Second Party System (percents)

Party	March 1999	February 1999
LDP	28.3	25.1
DP	8.5	8.0
CGP	3.1	3.8
LP	3.2	3.6
JCP	3.6	3.5
SDPJ	2.5	2.4
No party	49.4	52.0

SOURCE: *Yomiuri Shimbun,* March 25, 1999.

Bibliography

The following is a selected bibliography of general books in English on postwar Japanese political parties. For additional sources, journal articles, and Japanese-language materials on the various parties and other aspects of the Japanese electoral system, see the notes at the ends of the appropriate chapters.

Abe, Hitoshi, Shindo Muneyuki, and Kawato Sadafumi *The Government and Politics of Japan*. Tokyo: University of Tokyo Press, 1994.

Allinson, Gary D., and Yasunori Sone, eds. *Political Dynamics in Contemporary Japan*. Ithaca: Cornell University Press, 1993.

Baerwald, Hans H. *Japan's Parliament: An Introduction* (London and Cambridge: Cambridge Uniiversity Press, 1974).

————. *Party Politics in Japan*. Boston: Allen and Unwin, 1986.

Benjamin, Roger, and Kan Ori. *Tradition and Change in Postindustrial Japan: The Role of the Political Parties*. New York: Praeger, 1981.

Berger, Gordon Mark. *Parties Out of Power in Japan: 1931–1941*. Princeton: Princeton University Press, 1977.

Blaker, Michael K., ed. *Japan at the Polls: The House of Councillors Election of 1974*. Washington, D.C.: American Enterprise Institute, 1976.

Campbell, John C., ed. *Parties, Candidates, and Voters in Japan: Six Quantitative Studies*. Michigan Papers in Japanese Studies, no. 1). Ann Arbor, Mich.: Center for Japanese Studies, 1981.

Cole, Allan B., George O. Totten, and Cecil H. Uyehara. *Socialist Parties in Postwar Japan*. New Haven: Yale University Press, 1966.

Curtis, Gerald L. *Election Campaigning Japanese Style*. New York: Columbia University Press, 1971.

————. *The Japanese Way of Politics*. New York: Columbia University Press, 1988.

————. *The Logic of Japanese Politics: Japan's Political Identity at the End of the Century*. New York: Columbia University Press, forthcoming.

Flanagan, Scott C. *The Japanese Voter*. New Haven: Yale University Press, 1991.

Flanagan, Scott C., and Bradley M. Richardson. *Japanese Electoral Behavior: Social Cleavages, Social Networks, and Partisanship*. Beverly Hills, Calif.: Sage, 1977.

Fukui, Haruhiro. *Party in Power: The Japanese Liberal Democrats and Policy Making*. Berkeley: University of California Press, 1970.

Ike, Nobutaka. *A Theory of Japanese Democracy*. Boulder: Westview Press, 1978.

————. *Japanese Politics: Patron-Client Democracy*. New York: Knopf, 1972.

Ishida, Takshi, and Ellis S. Krauss, eds. *Democracy in Japan*. Pittsburgh: University of Pittsburgh Press, 1989.

Jain, Purnendra, and Takashi Inoguchi, eds. *Japanese Politics Today: Beyond Karaoke Democracy?* New York: St. Martin's Press, 1997.

Johnson, Chalmers. *Japan: Who Governs? The Rise of the Developmental State.* New York: W. W. Norton, 1995.

Kohno, Masaru. *Japan's Postwar Party Politics.* Princeton: Princeton University Press, 1997.

MacDougall, Terry E. *Political Leadership in Contemporary Japan.* Michigan Papers in Japanese Studies, no. 1). Ann Arbor, Mich.: Center for Japanese Studies, 1980.

Murakami, Hyoe, and Johannes Hirschmeier, eds. *Politics and Economics in Contemporary Japan.* Tokyo: Japan Culture Institute, 1979.

Pempel, T. J., et al. *Uncommon Democracies: The One Party Dominant Regimes.* Ithaca: Cornell University Press, 1990.

————. *Regime Shift: Comparative Dynamics of the Japanese Political Economy.* Ithaca: Cornell University Press, 1999.

Pharr, Susan J., and Ellis S. Krauss, eds. *Media and Politics in Japan.* Honolulu: University of Hawaii Press, 1996.

Reed, Steven R. *Making Sense of Japan.* Pittsburgh: University of Pittsburgh Press, 1993.

Richardson, Bradley M. *Japanese Democracy: Power, Coordination and Performance.* New Haven: Yale University Press, 1997.

Richardson, Bradley M., and Scott C. Flanagan. *Politics in Japan.* Boston: Little, Brown, 1984.

————. *The Political Culture of Japan.* Berkeley: University of California Press, 1974.

Scalapino, Robert A. *The Japanese Communist Movement, 1920–1966.* Berkeley: University of California Press, 1967.

Scalapino, Robert A., and Junnosuke Masumi. *Parties and Politics in Contemporary Japan.* Berkeley: University of California Press, 1962.

Steiner, Kurt, Ellis Krauss, and Scott Flanagan, eds. *Political Opposition and Local Politics in Japan.* Princeton: Princeton University Press, 1980.

Stockwin, J.A.A. *The Japanese Socialist Party and Neutralism.* London: Cambridge University Press, 1968.

————, ed. *Dynamic and Immobilist Politics in Japan.* London: Macmillan, 1988.

Thayer, Nathaniel B. *How the Conservatives Rule Japan.* Princeton: Princeton University Press, 1969.

Tsurutani, Taketsugu. *Political Change in Japan: Response to Postindustrial Change.* New York: David McKay, 1977.

van Wolfren, Karl. *The Enigma of Japanese Power.* New York: Knopf, 1989.

Ward, Robert E. *Political Development in Modern Japan.* Princeton: Princeton University Press, 1968.

Watanuki, Joji. *Politics in Postwar Japanese Society.* Tokyo: University of Tokyo Press, 1977.

About the Author and Contributors

Peter Berton is distinguished professor emeritus of international relations at the School of International Relations at the University of Southern California. He received his Ph.D. in international relations from Columbia University and was editor of the journal *Studies of Comparative Communism* from 1970 to 1983. Dr. Berton has written numerous books and articles on Japanese, Chinese, and Soviet affairs and is one of the most respected experts on the Japanese Communist Party.

Ronald Hrebenar is professor of political science at the University of Utah in Salt Lake City. He received his Ph.D. from the University of Washington. He is the author, coauthor, or editor of a dozen books on parties and interest groups. He has also contributed articles to social science and political science journals in the United States and Japan. During 1982–1983, he was visiting Fulbright professor at the Faculty of Law and Political Science at Tohoku University in Sendai, Japan. He has also been a visiting professor at Meiji University and Daito Bunka University in Japan.

Akira Nakamura is professor of political science at Meiji University in Tokyo, Japan. He received his undergraduate education at Kwansei Gakuin University and the University of California, Berkeley. His graduate training was at the University of Southern California, where he attained a Ph.D. He has been a visiting professor at the University of Utah and a guest scholar at the Brookings Institution. He has published frequently on the topic of Japanese public administration, both in English and in Japanese. Among his recent publications in English are *Factions and Fragmentation: Party Politics in Japan; The Transformations of the Japanese Policy Making Process: The LDP Governance at the Crossroads;* and *Myth and Reality in Local Social Policy Implementation in Japan.*

J.A.A. Stockwin is Nissan Professor of Modern Japanese Studies and the director of the Nissan Institute of Japanese Studies at Oxford University in Great Britain. He performed his graduate work at Australia National University, where he wrote his Ph.D. thesis on the Japan Socialist Party. Between 1964 and 1981 he was successively lecturer, senior lecturer, and reader in the Department of Political Science at the Australian National University. His publications include *Japan: Divided Politics in a Growth Economy* and *Dynamic and Immobilist Politics in Japan and governing Japan*. He is considered one of the world's most knowledgeable scholars of the Socialist Party of Japan.

Index

electoral system
 impact of, 37–55
 reform of 1994, 49–50
elitist model, 132–33
Engels, Josef, 260
ERF. See Economic Reconstruction Forum
 (ERF, or Keizai Saiken Kondankai).
Erlander, Tage, Swedish prime minister, 13

Federation of Commercial Labor Unions,
 164
Federation of Economic Organizations
 (Keizai Dantai Rengokai), 99–100
Fifteenth Party Congress of 1980, 262
First Party System of 1955. See First
 Postwar Party System (FPWPS).
First Postwar Party System (FPWPS), 3–5,
 28, 30–31, 37–55
  development of, 101–02
  permanent opposition in, 10–17
Flanagan, Scott, 28
FPWPS. See First Postwar Party System
 (FPWPS).
French Declaration of the Rights of Man,
 260–61
Fukuda Takeo, prime minister, 109, 120–21
fund–raising in Japan, 69–70 problems of,
 81–82
Fuwa essay, 260

German Marxism of 1920s, 217
giri obligation, 19–20
Gorbachev, Mikhail, 264
grand coalitions, 86, 92
Great Saint Nichiren. See Nichiren,
 Buddhist monk.
Gulf War, 227

Hakamada Satomi expulsion, 262
Harbinger Party, 152–53
Hashimoto Ryutaro, Prime Minister of
 Japan, 28, 85–86, 110, 230–31
Hata Tsutomu, 153–57, 228
Hatoyama new party, 157
Haytoyama Yukio, prime minister, 157, 159
HC. See House of Councillors.
Heiwa Doshikai (Peace Comrades
 Association), 237
Herman, V.M., 11
Hirano Rikizo, 215
Hitachi, 73

Hosokawa Morihiko, 150–52, 228 resignation, 91 Japan New Party, 150–52
House of Councillors (HC), 1, 5, 7, 16,
 38–39, 66, 85–86, 151, 159
House of Representatives (HR), 1–2, 37–38,
 85–86, 151
HR. See House of Representatives (HR).
humanitarian socialism, 191, 193–94

Ichida Koshiro, 154
Ichikawa Yuichi, 182
Ike Nobutaka, 9
Ikeda Daisaku, Soka Gakkai president, 171,
 174–75, 178
Ikeda Hayato, 115, 220
Imazu Hiroshi, 186
Internet campaign ban, 51
Ishida Koshiro, 182
Italian politics, 30–31

Japan Communist Party (JCP), 8–9, 11,
 40–42
 Akahata, daily newspaper, 69,
  179–80 , 258, 265
 electoral record, 276
 finances, 274–76
 gender gap, 268–69
 House of Representatives, 277–78
 leadership, 266–68
 membership, 269
 party affiliate organizations, 269–71
 party structure, 266
 publications, 271–74
Japan Federation of Employers' Association
 (Nihon Keieisha Dantai Renmei), 99–100
Japan Labor Peasant Party, 161
Japan New Party (JNP), 149–52
Japan Socialist Party (JSP), 6, 8–9, 15–16,
 40–41, 53, 89, 92, 149–50, 185, 209–51
 factionalism, 235–39
 history of, 213–31
 interest group ties, 239–44
 parliamentary behavior, 244–45
 See also Social Democratic Party of
  Japan (SDPJ).
 structure and organization,
  231–35
Japan Steel Association, 75
Japan Times, 156–57, 284
Japanese Chamber of Commerce and
 Industry (Nihon Shoko Kaigisho), 100